An Enduring Love

Greta

FARAH PAHLAVI

An Enduring Love

TRANSLATED FROM THE FRENCH BY
PATRICIA CLANCY

miramax books
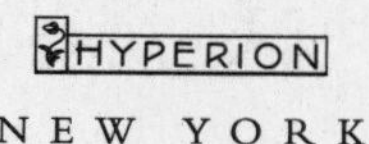
NEW YORK

PRINTED IN THE UNITED STATES OF AMERICA.

FOR INFORMATION ADDRESS:
Hyperion, 77 West 66th Street
New York, New York 10023-6298

ISBN 1-4013-5961-2

10 9 8 7 6 5 4 3 2 1

To the memory of those who have been
assassinated by obscurantism.

To the memory of those who gave their lives
for the integrity of Iran

To the Iranian people.

To my children.

For the love of my king.

“Remember its flight
The bird is mortal.”
—Forough Farrokhzad

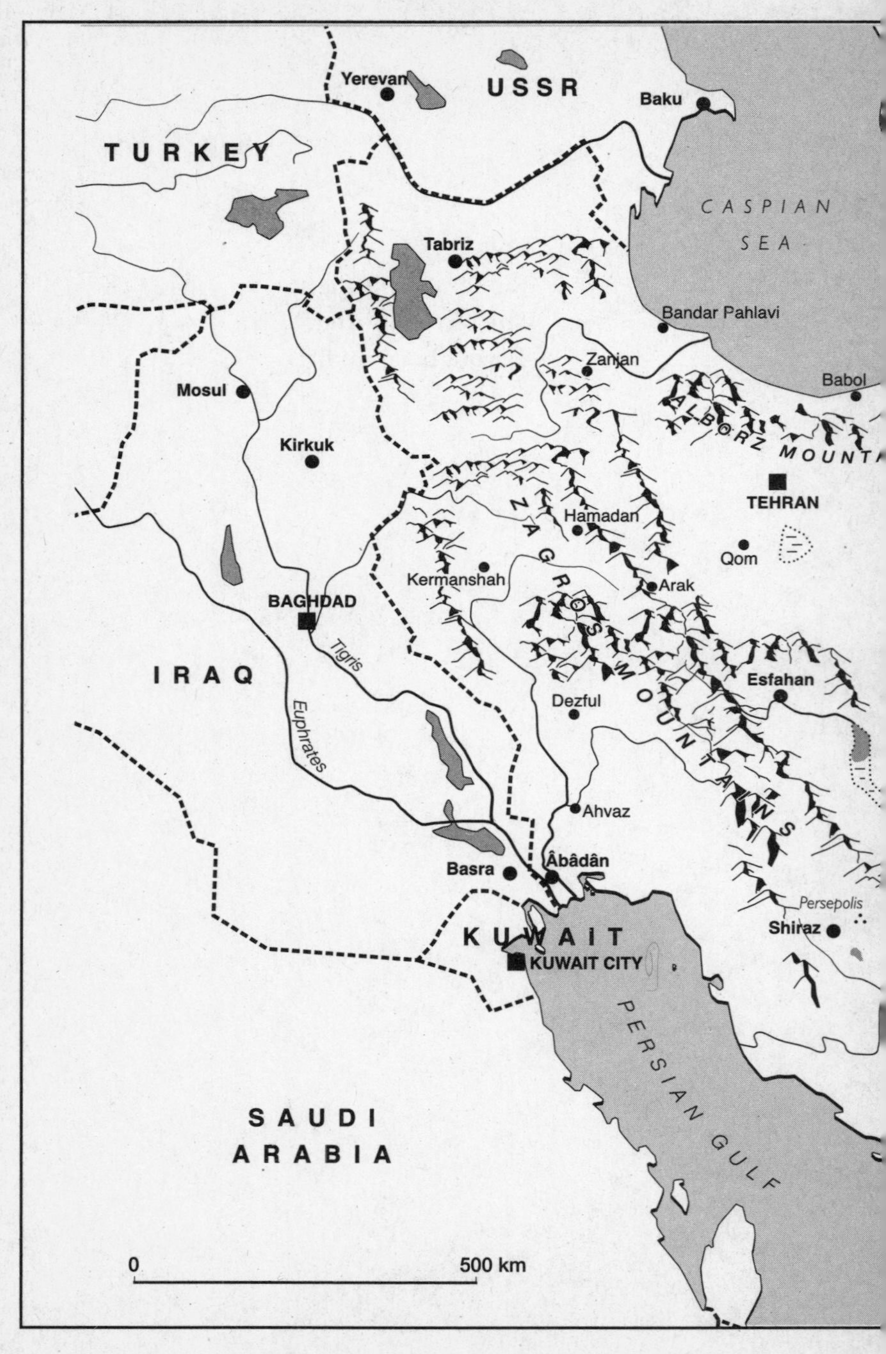

Yerevan
USSR
Baku
TURKEY
CASPIAN SEA
Tabriz
Bandar Pahlavi
Zanjan
Babol
Mosul
ALBORZ MOUNTA
Kirkuk
TEHRAN
ZAGROS MOUNTAINS
Hamadan
Qom
Kermanshah
Arak
BAGHDAD
Tigris
IRAQ
Esfahan
Euphrates
Dezful
Ahvaz
Âbâdân
Basra
Persepolis
Shiraz
KUWAIT
KUWAIT CITY
PERSIAN GULF
SAUDI ARABIA
0
500 km

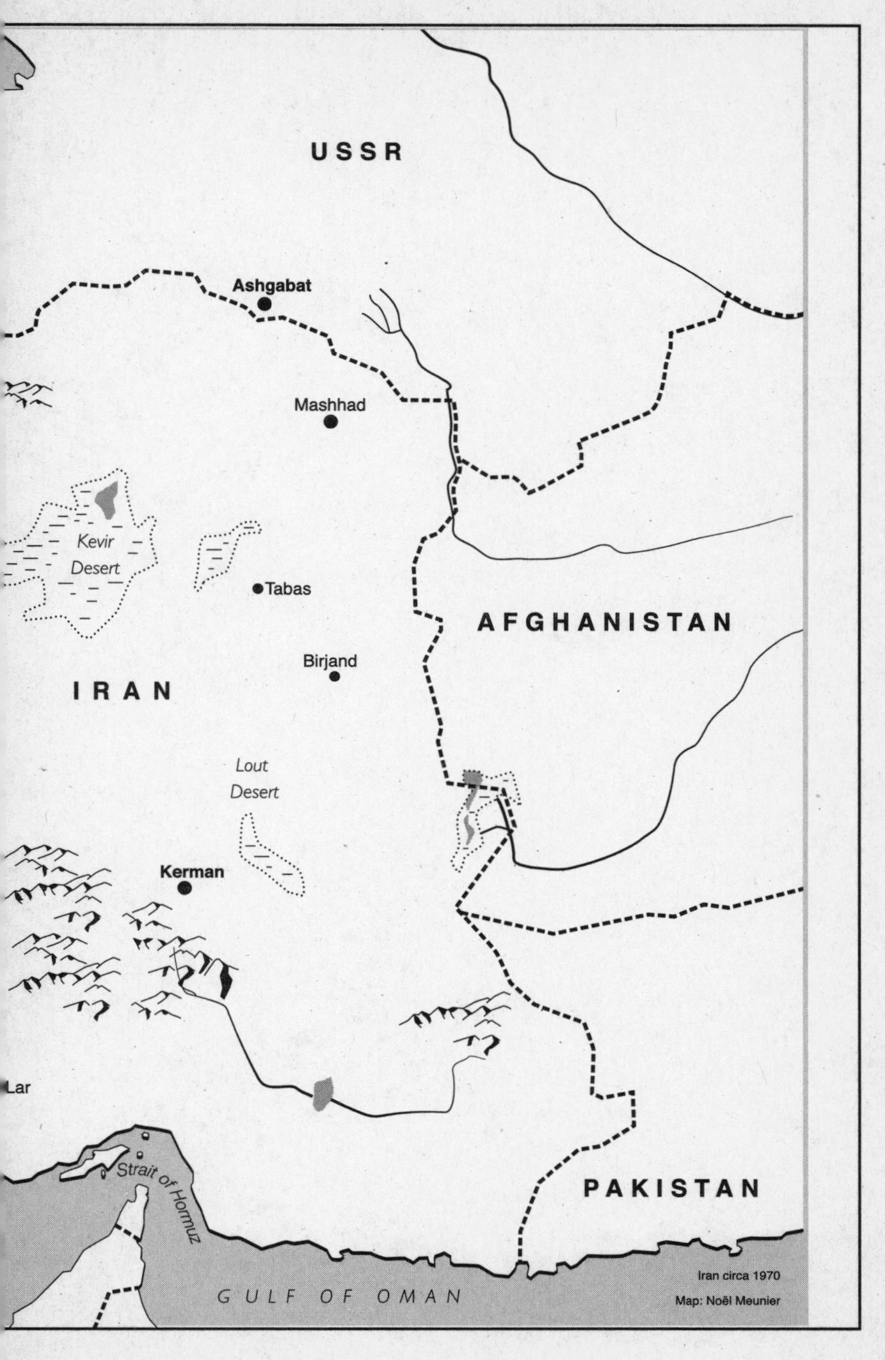
USSR
Ashgabat
Mashhad
Kevir
Desert
Tabas
AFGHANISTAN
Birjand
IRAN
Lout
Desert
Kerman
Lar
Strait of Hormuz
PAKISTAN
GULF OF OMAN
Iran circa 1970
Map: Noël Meunier

WHEN I THINK OF THAT MORNING IN JANUARY 1979, I feel that heart-wrenching grief again in all its intensity. Tehran had been under savage attack for months, but now a tense silence had fallen over the city, as if our capital were suddenly holding its breath. It was 16 January and we were about to leave the country, for we thought that the temporary withdrawal of the king would help calm the insurrection.

And so we left. The decision had been made about ten days earlier. Officially we were flying overseas for a few weeks' rest. That was the impression the king wished to convey. Did he really believe it himself? The deep distress I sometimes saw in his eyes makes me think that he did not. I fervently hoped that we were just going for a rest, but I was not entirely convinced of it either. Yet I could not believe that this man who had given thirty-seven years of service to his people would not regain their confidence someday soon. Under his reign Iran had made remarkable progress; once peace had been restored, everyone would surely acknowledge the fact. Yes, I was hopeful.

It had been snowing. The piercing wind sweeping down from the peaks of the Alborz made crystalline flakes swirl up in the dawn light. The night had been calm, strangely calm, and the king had been able to get a few hours' sleep. Weakened by illness and worn down by the situation, he had lost a lot of weight during the past year. In addition, despite the declaration of martial law, every night protesters had managed to defy the soldiers and climb onto the roofs. We could even hear their shouts of hate in the palace: *"Allahu akbar, marg bar Shah*—Allah is great, death to the Shah!" I would have given anything to protect the king from those insults.

From then on we were without the children. My little Leila's impromptu visits, the look in Farahnaz's eyes, timid but full of love for her father, Ali-Reza's unrestrained laughing and joking so affectionately tolerated by my husband, all that had now gone from the palace. I had put their departure off until the last minute, sensing that it would no doubt mean the end of a family life that had given us so much happiness for almost twenty years. Our elder son, Reza, was in the United States training as a fighter pilot. At that time he was seventeen, and he phoned us every day. The situation as it was reported on American TV worried him immensely. I tried to reassure him, to persuade him to stand firm and above all not to lose hope, even though I saw that the country was inevitably sinking into chaos. Work had stopped almost everywhere, the refineries had shut down, the state coffers were nearly empty. Every day brought its wave of demonstrations, hate, provocation, and misinformation. The king chatted briefly with his eldest son, making sure, as I did, that none of his own anxiety could be heard in his conversation on the telephone. And yet there were people fleeing all around us. Month after month, more and more business leaders, engineers, researchers, and managers were leaving the country. We would soon be the last "legitimate authorities" in this sinking ship that certain forces seemed determined to wreck.

Those last days before the children's departure had been terrible. At only eight years old, Leila did not seem to be aware of the dreadful tension we were experiencing, but Farahnaz and Ali-Reza, aged fifteen and twelve, did not hide their uneasiness. I saw our elder daughter stand for a long time behind the iron bars of the garden gate silently gazing at the empty streets, obviously surprised to no longer see the happy groups of children with whom she sometimes used to talk. Where had all the young people gone?

During this same period, there was an endless stream of generals, politicians, university professors, and a few clerics coming to the palace to offer their suggestions to my husband. Some advocated a peaceful, political solution. Others begged him to allow the army to open fire, to which the king invariably replied that a monarch cannot save his throne if the cost is the blood of his compatriots. "A dictator can, but not a monarch." And then he would firmly turn them away. When it seemed to the king that the wisest solution was to leave, we made up our minds to send away the children. Farahnaz had already left a month earlier, in mid-December 1978, to join her elder brother in the United States. Leila and Ali-Reza also went off to America in the care of my mother. I remember that Ali-Reza insisted on taking the imperial flag and a military uniform that we had specially made for him. When would we see the children again? After initially offering to receive us, the United States had begun to equivocate: it became obvious that we were no longer welcome. Egypt was to be our first destination, but it was far from the children.

We had breakfast separately that morning, as the king had risen very early and had gone to his office just as he would on any normal day. Did he have any idea that these were the last hours he would spend in the country he loved so much? Did he have any idea that he would never return there in his lifetime? Thinking about it today still breaks my heart.

I had the morning to put a few things together. I had been thinking during the night of the children's photos and the family albums and was dreadfully upset at the thought of leaving them behind. Quick! Get the albums! All the memories of our past happiness were contained in those pages. What else should I take? I was in such a state that I remember suddenly focusing my attention on a pair of boots that I liked wearing in the country. From now on we would have all the time in the world to walk, and walking was essential if we were to keep a balanced outlook and not lose heart. Yes, these boots were going to be my closest allies. In a strange way their presence calmed my mind. When I discovered them at the bottom of a suitcase a few days later, I gave a bitter laugh, "For heaven's sake! Why didn't it ever cross my mind that shoes like those can be found anywhere in the world?" What kind of cold, sparsely populated land of exile did I imagine was awaiting us?

Then, walking through the library, I selected some of my favorite books from the shelves. A member of the palace staff had come up to help me. We were in my office.

"These things are yours, Your Majesty. Take them."

I remember looking at the man very sadly.

"No. Of course not. Everything must stay here."

I was, of course, torn between the hope that perhaps we would come back and the horrifying, humiliating scene already forming in my mind of furious demonstrators entering the palace and opening our drawers and cupboards. I did not want to give them any reason to think that we had left taking our possessions with us. No, we were leaving with heads held high, sure of having worked ceaselessly for the benefit of the country. And if we had made mistakes, at least we had never thought of anything but the general good.

The previous day I had asked the curators of our museums to come and take some precious objects that had been given to us by various sovereigns and heads of state, as well as some personal possessions. They at least would never be stolen. I had no interest in keeping such valuable objects for myself. I wanted all the rest—pictures, personal belongings, carpets, everything—to stay where they were, even my Iranian clothes, which I deliberately left, as one leaves a part of one's soul behind. To forestall pillaging or malevolence, I had invited the television studio to come and film the interior of the palace. I had also invited Iranian and foreign journalists. At that time our lives were a part of Iran's destiny, and I feel proud that our personal possessions have never left our country.

The last hours went by quickly, too quickly, between periods of feverish activity and long moments when I just gazed at the trees in the garden, the harsh light of Tehran in winter, and those warm private places where we had lived so intensely. I remember having called Farahnaz in the United States while I was in this second mood, suddenly realizing that the poor child had left a month earlier in the belief that she would come back to her bedroom and all her teenage joys. How could she have suspected that she would not see Iran again, right up to the present day? What did she want me to take to her?

"Now think carefully, *Nanaz joune* (my life). Tell me, is there anything that you're particularly fond of?"

I was surprised to hear her ask for the poster of a singer, Sattar, already a great favorite in Iran, who had pride of place in her room. That was the only thing she really wanted. I think that, like me with my pair of boots, she was reassured by the promise this poster held for her. It hid the extent of the misfortune to come, which she no doubt suspected.

As for Reza, he had lived in a separate house on the palace grounds. The shutters had remained closed since his departure a few months earlier. The clothes he had worn as a child, which I had lovingly kept, the cassettes of his first words and first steps, his photo albums and all his memories were stored there. I didn't even have the presence of mind to call him. I left everything. How I would love so much to find these treasures again today.

The morning drew to a close. The king was still in his office, but now the atmosphere inside the palace was becoming more somber by the minute. I could feel the distress in the men and women of our staff. The older ones among them had served Reza Shah, my husband's father, and some had been present at our wedding twenty years before. Moving around the palace in unaccustomed silence, they all seemed stunned at the prospect of our departure. I realized that their wordlessness meant that they felt no hope. "We cannot go like this," I thought. "We must not lose faith."

They came in a group to bid us farewell. I explained to them that we were undoubtedly about to experience another of those sad times that have come and gone throughout the long history of Iran, but that spring would come again and we would meet again to rejoice in the king's return. Who could have imagined that our country would be engulfed in such a nightmare? We held back our tears, some even finding the strength to smile, and I then gave each of them a memento or some money, as one usually does before a long separation, to strengthen the bonds between us.

The king appeared at last. Everyone began to weep when they saw him. He was a man who normally had firm control over his emotions, but now he seemed to be struggling to hide his feelings. He had a word for each one of them. Many of them sobbed as they begged him to stay and not abandon them. When we were informed that the two helicopters which were to take us to Mehrabad airport were ready for takeoff, the palace staff spontaneously gathered on the palace steps. This time we were really leaving. Our bags had already been taken on board. Hands were stretched out to us and I still can see faces twisted with emotion. The king gave them all a last wave; I kissed the women who were closest to me. With the sound of the whirring rotors in my ears, I soon saw the palace disappear behind the buildings of Tehran.

The two helicopters set down near the imperial pavilion (we were in one and the security personnel in the other). A small group of people was waiting for us there: officers and a few civilians huddled together, battling the icy gusts of wind that swept across the tarmac. The king had asked people to stay at their posts in these difficult days rather than come to Mehrabad. We had known this thriving airport full of activity and the constant din of the jets; now it seemed as if it had suddenly been struck dead. The planes, grounded by the strike, presented a dismal sight, and the only sound in the empty sky was the whining of the wind coming down from the Alborz Mountains. Looking strained and standing very straight, my husband greeted these few friends and faithful followers. An officer of the Imperial Guard then threw himself at the king's feet, begging him to stay. The king leaned over to help him up and at that moment was overcome by emotion and the suffering he had been undergoing. I saw that his eyes were clouded with tears, he who always showed so much self-control. Several officers unable to hide their emotion also asked him not to leave, and he exchanged some words in particular with the army chief of staff.

There were a few Iranian journalists there, standing slightly apart, looking stunned. The foreign press had not been invited. After a while the king noticed them and walked toward them. He had just named Shapour Bakhtiar as head of the government, and at that very moment the new prime minister was waiting for his investiture by Parliament. The king did not want to leave the country before the Parliament had ratified his decision. "As I told you when the government was formed," he said to the journalists, "I am tired and need a rest. I also said that when things seemed to be going well and the government was in place, I would take a trip.

That trip starts now." He added that during its long history our country had been through times of crisis but that he remained confident: Iranian culture and identity would again prevail.

That was it. We were leaving on a "trip," disappearing for a while to allow people to come to their senses and their anger to calm down. After a few weeks, they would understand. Yes, we had to believe that and to believe in the future. I refused to give way to despair.

A few tense, painful minutes went by, then the king was informed that Mr. Shapour Bakhtiar had been invested by the *Majles* (the Parliament). He would arrive at the airport by helicopter at any moment. And indeed, there he was, coming out of the sky, getting out, bending down under the rotor blades, smoothing his clothes and his mustache before walking toward the pavilion. The president of the Parliament, Mr. Javad Saïd, was with him. The two men immediately came and paid their respects to us, greeting us with great feeling.

"Everything is now in your hands," my husband said quietly to Mr. Bakhtiar. "I hope you will succeed. I give Iran into your care, yours and God's." Thirty-seven days later, Mr. Bakhtiar had to flee for his life, his administration overturned by the Islamic government of Ayatollah Khomeini.

Now we could leave. Struggling against the wind, we reached the plane used for official journeys, a blue-and-white Boeing 707 called Falcon. When he reached the foot of the stairs, the king turned around and the little group accompanying us stood still. My memory of this last encounter is one of unbearable emotion. The men present were officers, pilots, members of the court, and the Imperial Guard who had all shown great courage, and yet on this occasion one could feel their extreme distress. One after the other, they kissed the king's hand, their faces bathed in tears. Even Mr. Bakhtiar who was in favor of our leaving had tears in his eyes.

"The demonstrations of trust they gave me when I was leaving moved me very deeply," the king wrote later in his memoirs. "Then there was a poignant silence, broken only by sobbing."

We entered the airplane at last, followed by a few people who had asked to accompany us. Amir Aslan Afshar, the chief protocol officer, was among them, as was Kambiz Atabaï, whose father, Abolfath Atabaï, had served Ahmad Shah and Reza Shah, plus Colonels Kioumars Jahanbini and Yazdan Nevissi who, with some non-commissioned officers of the guard, were in charge of our personal safety. A few people who had been in our service for a long time had joined them. At the last minute, I asked my four children's pediatrician, Dr. Lioussa Pirnia, if she would accompany us on this journey though its outcome was uncertain. She had immediately said yes and, leaving her family behind her, came on board with just one suitcase of clothes. Lastly there was our cook. Perhaps he had a premonition that it would be many months before he saw Iran and his kitchen again, for this extremely cautious man had brought with him his whole collection of huge copper pots and bags of chick peas, rice, lentils...in short, everyone clung to whatever they could.

Once on board, the king went and sat in the cockpit. Flying had always been one of his greatest pleasures. And so, in spite of the despondency he felt, or perhaps because of it, he wanted to be at the controls for this journey that was to take him far from Iran and his own people forever. Stunned by the extreme emotion we had just experienced, I cannot remember anything about the takeoff, but deep inside I was relieved and proud that I had not broken down.

My husband piloted the plane for the whole of the time we were flying over Iran. Once we had left our own airspace, he handed over the controls and joined us in the cabin. It was then that I became fully aware of the abyss that history was dragging us toward and, certain that I would go mad if I did not immediately resist in some way, I had the idea of appealing to the world to help our unhappy country. We were leaving behind several groups, opposed to the insurgents, who had no resources and would soon be tracked down. It was urgent that we get aid to them and alert the heads of state who were close to us. I immediately asked the king for permission to send messages to some of them. He looked at me inquiringly, then grudgingly agreed. And so, with Mr. Afshar's help, I undertook the task of composing these appeals.

On that day, as we were flying toward Aswan in southern Egypt, for the first time in our long exile I began frantically filling the first pages of a notebook that I kept until the king's death eighteen months later.

I have transcribed a few passages from it:

16 January 1979.

It was terrible in the palace, just terrible!...The final things to be done, the final telephone calls to make, so many people in tears.... Don't give in to despair, don't cry, give them hope....I'm leaving my whole life behind me, I hope to come back but at the same time my chest feels heavy with grief. All those people in the palace throwing themselves at our feet, their entreaties, their questions: "Where are you going? When will you be coming back? Why are you leaving us? We feel abandoned like orphans, orphans..." "No, please get up. Trust in God. We will be back." I was crying inside although they could not see it.

Smile as you get out of the helicopter, find the right words, stay strong. "I'm certain that national unity will prevail. I have confidence in the Iranian people," I told the journalists. One of them whispered, "May God go with you." Then everyone walked toward the plane. Once there, the men fell on their knees at the king's feet. My husband was overcome, his eyes were full of tears. The pilots, officers, journalists, guards, all of them were sobbing.

> We rise up into the wide expanse of empty sky. I have the dreadfully painful feeling of having lost everything: my children, my friends, my country. The feeling that my heart is broken, torn to pieces. I would rather have died in my own country than set out on this wandering life. Where will it take us? How can one go on living and breathing when one's heart is in pieces?

In my teens, when I wondered what my future life might be, I imagined myself living with an educated man I would be proud of. But I never thought of marrying before I had finished my studies. It was a time—the end of the fifties—when more and more women were rallying to take part in the development of Iran.

Nothing, however, could have led me to think that I would one day marry the most important man in our country.

"Why did you choose me?" I once asked the king.

He gave the slightest hint of a smile.

"Do you remember the afternoon, at one of our first meetings, when we'd been playing quoits? There were a lot of us, quite a crowd. Most of the quoits fell on the ground instead of the target, and you were kind enough to run and pick them up for everyone. You had already charmed me, but on that day I loved the way you were so natural."

PART ONE

Chapter 1

I STILL HAVE MY FATHER'S amazed and delighted account of my earliest days: a school exercise book he himself illustrated in which his love pours out of every line. Obviously delirious with joy, he noted down my weight, my smiles, my babbling, or what he thought I was saying. And then suddenly all this enchantment plunges into the worst nightmare. "This Friday," he writes on page five, "is one of the saddest of my life. Farah has caught a chill. The stupid nanny did not take proper care of her. I was in the center of Tehran when I heard the news and immediately hired a car to get back to Shemiran. My poor little girl was lying in bed; she looked terrible and her breathing was labored. Her mother was in tears. Dr. Towfigh arrived at last. She had acute tonsillitis! She has a high temperature. We applied compresses all through the night and didn't sleep until morning."

There is a big question mark and below it a sketch of me in bed with a large compress across my forehead. "Will she survive?" my father seems to be saying to himself. Mother is sobbing on my left and, on my right, Father has drawn himself with his head in his hands, clearly overcome by grief.

After a few days, however, my health improved. "Thanks be to God," my father wrote, "Farah has improved, but we were worried sick."

That was in 1939. At that time we were living to the north of Tehran in a house with an enclosed garden built at the beginning of the century. I grew up in that house, which we shared with my mother's brother, Uncle Mohammad-Ali, and his wife, Louise. The two couples had a large bedroom each on the first floor and shared a communal family living room. It is traditional in Iran to have reception rooms and the dining room on the second floor for the exclusive use of guests and entertaining. My father, however, had his study there also.

The Ghotbis had had a son six months before I was born, so my cousin Reza was no doubt the first child whose face I ever smiled at. We took our first steps together and Reza became the brother I never had. I found out much later, when I was grown up, that my parents had wanted to have another child but that the aftermath of the Second World War in Iran had made them decide against it. Once British and Russian troops occupied the country in August 1941, the future looked bleak for almost four years.

And so I stayed an only child, probably more precious than ever to my parents. I have been told how anxious my father was about me: he was haunted by the fear that I would suddenly catch some illness. As some inoculations were not yet available in our country, he thought it wisest to forbid people to touch me and especially to kiss me. That did not stop me from catching all the usual childhood diseases, and in any case, the older and more independent I became, the less he could prevent me from seeing people.

The closest to us, apart from the family, were those who worked for us in the house: my nanny, Monavar, a young woman with great charm and humor whom I loved dearly; the cook; the chambermaid; and also two men who did odd jobs around the house. Reza and I were fond of all of them, especially as they loved having us around them and spoiled us dreadfully. They lived in a recently constructed building at the other end of the courtyard. As soon as our parents had gone out, we would run over to them. Some of them would take us on their knees and sometimes tell us scary stories, which gave us an inkling that the world was much more frightening and mysterious than our mothers told us. In a storeroom attached to this building, we kept food to supply us for several months: dried beans and lentils, rice, sugar, almonds, cooking oil, and so forth. I can remember my mother shrieking when she entered the room one day and found mice running about. The cook ran to her aid, and Reza and I took advantage of all the confusion to creep behind him into this storehouse full of strong scents still unfamiliar to us.

We could hear the world of disease and danger, as my parents saw it, teeming outside the high, brick garden walls. We were, of course, forbidden to venture into the street, but as soon as my parents turned their backs, we settled ourselves on the smooth polished steps of the porch and watched people coming and going behind the iron gate. It was during the occupation and life certainly was not easy. As for the war, which was taking place far beyond the mountains in the USSR, our redoubtable neighbor to the north, we sometimes overheard the adults talking about it. And the jeeps of the British soldiers always fascinated us. There were many beggars who regularly came to us. We knew them by name, and my parents, in anticipation of their visits, never threw anything out. We gave them food, clothing, and even toys for their children. The streets were full of children when the weather was fine, and we chatted through the gate with those who were allowed to play outside. In those days people still traveled in horse-drawn cabs—very few had the means to buy a car—and I remember that one of the kids' favorite games was to grab on to the back of the carriage for a free ride. We were fascinated by that, especially as pedestrians would shout out to the coachman, "You've got someone on your back!" The coachman would then detach the young stowaway with a big circular crack of his whip. We were speechless.

But of all the sights in the street, the one that enchanted me most came from the hawkers. They brought seasonal fruits on hand-painted donkey carts or on big trays balanced on their heads. In winter it was mandarins, oranges, oven-cooked beets. Then we waited impatiently for spring when we could taste strawberries, green plums, fresh almonds, radishes, white onions and herbs: mint, tarragon, and basil, which the merchants watered constantly. And finally, in the first days of summer—always so hot in Tehran—cherries, rose-perfumed apples, and apricots arrived. Later there were rock melons and watermelons and, of course, the ice-cream sellers. We adored them, but naturally we were forbidden to approach them. Our parents took turns explaining to us what a danger these ices were to our health, full of the worst germs imaginable. And yet I can still see us scampering out of the porch to share some of that delicious poison between two wafers. Lollipops, which we called "sugar roosters," were also forbidden, as our parents suspected that the terrible dust from the street stuck to them.

But the real danger came from the water. It was a precious commodity in our country, and the water trade at that time was part of the rhythm of daily life. Drinking water was scarce, coming from only two springs that provided for the capital. It was delivered around the whole town by horses drawing water tanks. Like the vegetable sellers, the water bearer announced his presence with his own song. People came out with pitchers, which he filled for a few coins.

Water for washing and household use came from the Alborz Mountains overlooking Tehran through a system of open channels running down every street. Every district had its day for receiving this muddy running water. Directed by small dams, it flowed for a few hours into a tank under the house or a reservoir usually dug in the courtyard or the garden. We had both tank and reservoir, and I remember watching with great curiosity as all the water with rubbish collected further up the channel flowed into them: watermelon peel, dead leaves, cigarette butts, bits of wood. The water settled after a day or two and could be pumped up into a tank in the attic, which supplied the kitchen and the bathrooms. In spite of the quicklime added to the water in the tank, little worms proliferated there; our parents were forever telling us never to drink water from the faucet.

From time to time the toy seller would suddenly appear out of the fascinating swarm of people in the street, carrying his shop on his head. It was a jumbled collection of all the treasures children of the day dreamed about: wooden and terra-cotta flutes, multicolored paper windmills, balls, rackets, and castanets made of two terra-cotta disks held together with pleated paper. We were sometimes allowed a little something, but we mostly made toys ourselves or with the help of the men who worked in the household. I remember that we dragged our dolls about in shoe boxes, that the boys rolled old bicycle wheels for hoops, that our scooters were made of carefully salvaged bits and pieces. However, there are two marvelous things that I remember best: a doll that said "mama" and a real child's bicycle from the prestigious English firm BSA.

And sometimes behind the toy seller came the magician with his traveling picture show. He pushed a small cart with shining brass and four little windows a child could pay to look into. The man would then run through a series of pictures or drawings while telling us a magic story in a voice charged with emotion and amusement. Sometimes he would also sing. We could not bear to give up this enchantment, called *Shahr-e-Farang,* but it too, was forbidden. Our parents feared that we would catch trachoma, a terrible, extremely contagious bacterium that attacks the eyes and at that time made many children blind.

Reza and I luckily escaped trachoma, but I was not spared "the Oriental spot." Less serious than trachoma, this is a mosquito bite that leaves an indelible mark. Mine was on the top of my right hand. My father thought that as such things go, we had been lucky, since many are bitten on the face. He nonetheless asked the doctor to do the impossible, to limit the size of the scar. My mother told me he said, "You never know, Doctor, perhaps one day people will kiss my daughter's hand."

In spite of the many temptations offered in the street outside, my greatest pleasure as a child was to get out of Tehran in the summer and go to Shemiran on the slopes of the Alborz Mountains. We left the furnace-like heat and the dusty torpor of Tehran for the light air of the mountains and the surprising coolness of the evenings. Today Shemiran is a wealthy, much sought-after suburb to the north of Tehran. When I was a child, it was a delightful village about a dozen kilometers from the city center, high up at an altitude of 1,800 meters. Our parents rented a villa in this rustic paradise for two months in the summer. We squashed into my father's big Ford, with the rest of the household following in carriages. It was like a caravan, a veritable exodus. I adored that road as it wound between enormous plane trees and small bushes of yellow roses, from which our mothers picked buds to make candy.

At Shemiran we joined a whole string of little cousins and friends whose parents had properties there. I sometimes played with dolls, but never for very long. I was more of a tomboy, preferring dodge ball, hide-and-seek, donkey rides, or walking in the countryside and the mountains, anything that meant I could avoid a siesta. I loved making houses of earth with my hands in the mud or breaking fresh walnuts, which left black stains on my hands. I remember that we cleaned up by rubbing ourselves with mulberry leaves. I loved climbing trees. The trees were my friends. Pear trees, apple trees, walnuts, loquats, mulberries—I knew them individually, and once perched on a branch, I often forgot the game and had little desire to climb down again, especially when I made myself a comfortable nest with branches and a rug. I would gaze at the huge expanse of the sky and dream, sometimes until nightfall, or until the others began to worry that they would never find me.

Evenings at Shemiran were pure enchantment. We all gathered in the town square like one big family. Little stalls offered food on skewers, barbecued corn, fresh walnuts, all kinds of cakes and confectionary, not to mention ice cream, which for once we were allowed to eat. While our parents took a stroll or sat on a café terrace, we children chased each other around the stalls, wildly excited from the effects of so much laughter and sweets. When we went home we were often allowed to sleep all together in a large living room. Mattresses were put on the floor, and for Reza and me, who slept like good little children in our parents' rooms all winter, it was like another world, a wonderful party.

We were still at war when I first went to the Italian School in Tehran. My parents had chosen it because French was taught there. My father, Sohrab Diba, was a French speaker, very attached to France. He was from a prominent family in Azarbaijan that had served at court under the Qajars, then under Reza Shah. Son of a diplomat who spoke fluent French and Russian, Father was sent, with his young brother Bahram, to the St. Petersburg Cadet School at the age of twelve. They were caught by surprise by the Bolshevik Revolution of 1917—my father was sixteen at the time—but managed to get out with the aid of our ambassador. He then went to France, where he finished secondary school, studied law, and was accepted into the Military Academy of Saint-Cyr. After graduation he came back to Iran and soon began his service with the young army that Reza Shah, my future husband's father, was rallying to the flag. My mother Farideh, for her part, came from Gilan on the Caspian Sea and is a descendant of Ghotbeddin Mohammad Gilani, a revered Sufi. She went to school in Tehran at the École Jeanne d'Arc, run by French nuns, which I would also attend some years later.

I was six when I began at the Italian School. I remember that Mother had dressed me in a tartan skirt and white blouse. I was nervous. It had been explained to me that I should mix with the other children, but I stayed in my corner hugging my little schoolbag, in which my mother had put an exercise book, a pencil, and an apple for recess.

However, I took to school very quickly and to the freedom and access to the wider world that my new life brought with it. My father sometimes drove me in his old Ford, but he usually had a servant chaperone me both ways, giving her money for the cab fare. The young woman must have kept the money for herself, because I can remember walking long distances down the locust tree avenues of Tehran. I loved the acacias in bloom and, even today, their perfume pervades my yearning for Tehran.

At school one of the subjects we studied was the Koran. To be precise, we learned to read the sacred book without any explanation of what it meant. What surprised me most was not being able to follow the lines with my fingers: we were not allowed to touch the Koran and so we had to make a little pointer out of paper. Like most Iranians, my parents were Shiite Muslims, but my mother was more religious than my father. She took part in rituals in which religious men came and recounted the lives of the martyrs with great feeling. My mother and all the women present would weep copiously, sometimes in the presence of professional mourners. We children were too young to understand, but we liked these gatherings very much because at the end of the proceedings, the women comforted themselves with candy and invited us to share with them. My mother fasted for Ramadan, but she did not make us do the same. Reza and I simply ate a little less, practicing what Iranians call "the bird's Ramadan." But I did accompany my mother on visits to holy places. Those were times to reflect and make wishes. I remember going as a little girl to the holy city of Qom, where my grandfather is buried. Some time later, when I was about seven or eight and visiting a place of worship on the Caspian Sea, I became the victim of one of those apparently harmless scenes that nonetheless make a deep impression on a child's mind. Because my hair was not entirely covered, a mullah shouted at me angrily, "Hide your hair, or you will go to hell!" I've never been able to forget the fear that that man's intolerance made me feel, a fear that Ayatollah Khomeini would revive thirty years later.

I often found my father writing or reading in his study on the second floor. He liked listening to the radio broadcasts in Persian and foreign languages. I never knew him in uniform. He always wore very elegant suits, and even for tennis, his favorite sport, he would wear a white vest over immaculate trousers. He had been a legal advisor in the army, and during the war he worked in the Yugoslavian embassy. I can clearly remember that I was upset when he left the house. It was heart wrenching to see him go—I felt like he would never return. Did I have some intuition of the misfortune awaiting us? In any case, I cried so much that my mother requested that I not be told when he was leaving. But in the evening he would sit beside me while I did my homework and everything was forgotten. When he occasionally had to go out to dinner, he consoled me in his absence by leaving a little gift, which I found in the morning under my pillow.

The end of the world war brought the beginning of the Azarbaijan crisis in our country. If I experienced these events as a personal tragedy, it is because Azarbaijan was my father's province and my uncles and aunts who lived there were forced to leave at a moment's notice. Iran, occupied by British troops in the south and Soviet troops in the north, was to be liberated once peace had returned. Britain and the USSR had signed a treaty in January 1942 agreeing to withdraw their troops from our territory no later than six months after the end of World War II. Britain honored their undertaking, but the Soviets continued to occupy Azarbaijan. The Iranian Communist Party, Tudeh, created in 1941, had done particularly well in Azarbaijan, benefiting from the Soviet presence there. Its leader, Jafar Pishevari, now demanded autonomy for the province, and it was obvious that the USSR was just waiting for Azarbaijan to fall into its hands.

It would be something of an understatement to say that the Azarbaijan crisis was a tragic experience for my parents. Aunts and uncles in my mother's family were still traumatized by the forceful communist takeover between 1919 and 1920 that drove them from Gilan province, renamed for a time "the Soviet Socialist Republic of Gilan." It was because of that upheaval that my mother ended up in Tehran as a child. And now the same thing was happening, this time to Father's family in the nearby province.

The apprehension that I felt for a long time concerning the communists began in those years—1945 to '46—when I witnessed my parents' distress and the misfortunes of my uncles and aunts. I hated the communists because they were against the king. That was the only political thought I could have. My parents, who were deeply convinced royalists and believed in the rule of law, saw the

Tudeh as a party that had betrayed Iran and was therefore absolutely evil. It had served as the agent of a foreign power to separate a province from Iran.

My first picture of the young king, to whom I would join my life thirteen years later, also comes from the year 1946. Mohammad Reza Pahlavi had been on the throne since 16 September 1941. He had succeeded his father, Reza Shah the Great, taking up the reins of a nation that had been brought to its knees by the Occupation. The liberation of Azarbaijan was undoubtedly the first historic act to earn him the gratitude of the Iranian people. The government of Tehran, led by an able diplomat, our Prime Minister Ahmed Qavam-al-Saltaneh, and supported by the world community, the United Nations, the United States, and the steadfastness of the king, finally convinced Stalin to stand by his promise, and on 10 May 1946, Soviet troops were ordered to leave the Iranian province. But Azarbaijan, which had proclaimed itself an autonomous state, was still occupied by Tudeh insurgents. Consequently the army was sent to reestablish law and, on 12 December 1946, the capital, Tabriz, was liberated at last.

My parents were jubilant; it was a great day. When we learned that the king would be going through Tehran on his way back from Azarbaijan, people rushed into the streets to cheer him. The whole town came out. He was to go down the avenue at the corner of our street, where there was a garage. People climbed up on the roof and everyone jostled, shouted, and clapped when the king finally appeared. It was a dazzling sight for the eight-year-old child I was then.

That evening, or the next day, we celebrated at home with the family. As I did not know Azarbaijan, my father promised that we would go there together one day. He passed away the following year, before he could take me to see where his family had come from.

Chapter 2

MY FATHER'S ILLNESS struck just when there was finally light on the horizon for Iran and for the rest of the world, just when we could have begun to make plans for the future. He suddenly felt tired—he who had always led a healthy, well-ordered life. At the same time his eyes and his skin began to look yellow; the doctors thought it was hepatitis. What I remember most about those early weeks is his itching. He could not stop scratching his arms and legs, which made him very irritable, and nothing seemed to give him any lasting relief.

He was treated with the latest drugs for hepatitis, but he also took our traditional medicine. Our family had great faith in the gentle natural medicine that was widely used in Iran, and I have recourse to it even today in preference to manufactured laboratory products. And so he drank dandelion extracts and even ate tiny freshwater fish—all to no avail: neither his itching nor his complexion improved.

His illness preoccupied the whole household, but we nevertheless were managing to cope with it. Then one day it suddenly blocked out everything else and shattered our routine: my father went to the hospital. The doctors had arrived at an alarming new diagnosis. Having spent weeks treating him for hepatitis, they had just found out that he had cancer of the pancreas and needed an operation. I only learned of the diagnosis much later, but from that time on, I felt a silent, inexpressible anxiety. What was going to happen? I was taken to visit him, but the man I saw was unrecognizable—so thin, with the skin on his face tight, like parchment. He was too weak to speak to me. The thing that horrified me more than anything else was the tube—a drainage tube, Mother called it—through which a yellow liquid flowed from his abdomen. Why? What was wrong with him? When would he be coming home? Having retreated into silence and obviously depressed, my mother, my uncle, and my aunt all avoided my questions, replying with a strained smile, "Don't worry, darling, it'll be all right."

Suddenly there were no more visits to the hospital—for anyone—and when I expressed my surprise, I was told that Father had gone to Europe for treatment. It was a lie. He had died, but I clung to that lie with all my strength. I even managed to make it a subject of pride at school. In those days, very few Iranians were wealthy or important enough to go for medical treatment in Europe.

One day I came upon Mother and Aunt Louise in tears. They told me that an aunt of my mother's had died, which would explain why the household was in this state of mourning, especially my mother. I believed it. I think I would have swallowed anything rather than allow myself to admit the unbearable truth everyone was trying to hide from me.

However days, then weeks went by without any news from my father.

"Why doesn't Father write to us?"

"He's sick, Farah, and sick people can't write."

"That's not true. Aunt Effat is sick and she writes to her family."

This aunt really was in Europe, and her family regularly received long letters from her.

The realization came gradually, without ever being clearly mentioned, people stopped talking about my father, myself included. If I went into a room unexpectedly, everyone fell silent or quickly changed the subject. And my mother, her face pale and haggard, still wept, and much more than my aunt.

I cannot describe how it happened, but as the months went by, I gradually realized that I would never see Father again. Officially my father was not dead, since I had never been informed of his passing, since I had never gone to visit his grave. (I would go for the first time when I was seventeen. Father is buried south of Tehran, at Emam-Zadeh Abdollah.) So officially he was not dead, but I had lost him, in the literal sense of the word. A pall of melancholy, created by my feelings of emptiness and endless waiting, fell over my whole existence at that time. The unbearable had happened, without my being able to shed a tear. Today I know that people discreetly visit his grave, maintain it, and put flowers there. They were thoughtful enough to erase the name Diba so that it would not be desecrated.

Grief was to catch up with me forty years later in the course of a doctor's appointment. I had been widowed for a few years and we were talking about that loss, which was so painful for myself and the children, about the past and our family life after so many upheavals. There must have been something strange in the way I spoke about my father's "passing away," for the doctor suddenly asked me why I did not express it more explicitly.

"But your father is dead, isn't he? Why don't you say so?"

I thought I would never be able to do it, and when I finally managed to say those four words that were so difficult for me—"My father is dead"—I burst into tears.

A FEW MONTHS AFTER MY FATHER'S DEATH we had to leave the large house where I had spent my childhood: my mother and her brother no longer had the means to support the life we had had. We moved to an apartment at the top of a building, which I loved straight away for its big terrace with a fine view of a large part of Tehran and especially of the construction work going on at the university. It was the beginning of the fifties, when the university needed more space for the rising generations. I can't count the hours I spent on that terrace watching the cranes turning, and the trucks maneuvering and observing how a nineteenth-century town was being transformed into a large, modern capital city full of tall buildings and wide avenues to cater to the growing number of cars. A few years later I would choose architecture as a profession, and I think my interest in it comes from this time. My mother's brother, who shared the apartment with us, was himself an architect, and I loved to watch him in the evening as he made his sketches.

In summer we took our mattresses out onto the terrace to avoid the heat, all of us sleeping there together in the open air. I remember my favorite game before falling asleep was to reach out my arm and hook a star or the moon onto one of my fingers. I would close one eye to make the picture perfect and pretend I had a ring with a precious stone. On other evenings Reza and I would be fascinated by the giant screen of the open-air cinema, the Diana, as it sent reflections flickering across the sky like weird shadows.

The long summer holidays in Shemiran also disappeared from our lives, no doubt because my mother could no longer afford to rent a villa. Now I only went there for brief stays with one or another of my three uncles, who had properties there. My mother made up for this disappointment by deciding that we would henceforth spend our holidays with relatives in Gilan and

Azarbaijan, and we lost nothing by the exchange. In fact these holidays, especially the journeys north, are without doubt the happiest memories of my preadolescent years. We traveled by bus. In those days the roads were not paved, and dust, blown by the hot wind, whirled in through the wide-open windows. When we stopped to drink a glass of lemonade by the side of the road—we were not allowed to drink water—we children laughed uproariously. We were unrecognizable: our hair and eyebrows had turned white and we had changed into little old men and women.

In Azarbaijan we stayed with my father's brother, Manouchehr, who lived in Tabriz, in a large old family home. My uncle took us for picnics on his properties, which were full of fruit trees, and I stuffed myself with apricots and cherries. For all our cousins who lived on the land, drought was a constant, obsessive worry. They waited for rain, prayed to heaven, and I remember secretly thanking the Lord that I had no land, as this endless waiting for water slowly became an anxiety for me as well. I discovered the difficulties experienced by another world and saw the backwardness and injustice of country life. Agrarian reform had not yet taken place, and when a poor peasant stole a little wheat to feed his family or committed some other offense, the landowner beat him or punished him very harshly. I could not understand it, it revolted me, and I remember once or twice getting furious at the large property owners, to the point of crying with indignation. I had the same feeling of injustice when I saw them hunting gazelles at night in their big jeeps bristling with floodlights. Caught in their beams, the poor animals had no chance at all. Because my family was very fond of me, they took me seriously but without any real understanding of how such humiliating and cruel behavior could shock the little city girl that I was.

When we were with Father's sister, Aunt Aziz, who lived in Zandjan, we went visiting distant villages in a jeep, and my aunt took advantage of these expeditions to take medicine to some families in the area. These trips showed me the hinterland of Iran, and the dangers we encountered gave me a taste of the country's harshness. We had to cross rivers and the edges of ravines that took your breath away. The men were armed because we had to protect ourselves from animals—wolves in particular. On other days we simply rode horses through the countryside to talk with the peasants. At midday we sat on the grass, the men took out their knives, and we shared watermelons. People still spoke with dread of the time when Azarbaijan had almost fallen into the communist camp. One day when we were visiting an old stable, a man from the village stopped in front of a stall. "Look, Farah," he said to me, "this is the horse your uncle Mahmoud Khan rode when he fought the Tudehs (communists)." I saw a very old white horse, standing in a ray of sunlight. It was a beautiful, moving image, and I can still see it. Some large landowners had taken up arms against the communists.

To get to Gilan, where Mother's family lived, in particular her elder brother, my uncle Hossein, we had to cross the Alborz mountain chain that peaks north of Tehran at more than 4,500 meters. It's an amazing journey. You climb for hours over arid, rocky terrain, following a river bed, and suddenly the track descends into a green valley stretching as far as the eye can see, sloping down gently to the beaches of the Caspian Sea. Then come rice fields and tea plantations and weather that is suddenly damp under skies that are often low and heavy. In summer the smell of the rice and the orange blossom is quite heady. Unlike the land south of the Alborz, the Gilan plains receive a lot of rain. I can remember how delighted we were when we suddenly caught sight of the fig trees, the orange trees, the chestnuts, the mimosas, and the trees with pink flowers, the albizzia, which we call the "silk tree."

My uncle had tea plantations near Lahijan; tea had been imported from China for several centuries. I especially enjoyed joining in the harvest with my cousins. The women were paid every evening according to the weight of leaves they had picked, and we would help fill baskets of those who were the most tired. I still have memories of young mothers who were obliged to bring their babies with them. They used to give the infants a tiny dose of opium so that they would keep quiet and sleep. Once one of the babies went blue in the face, and we stood petrified, watching his young mother pour water on his head and pat his cheeks to bring him back to life.

Here, too, we were told about the fear and the exodus caused by the brief communist takeover of Gilan. It was clear as well, however, that peasants could not make a living under the present system, under which a privileged few owned most of the land while the majority had nothing but their labor for hire. Agrarian reform was urgently needed and they said that the young king was in favor of it. He had given an indication of his intention in the first months of his reign by handing over to the government a large part of his own land and requesting that it be distributed. Land Reform was regarded with apprehension by some and impatience by others. At the time I had no idea that it would be one of the major decisions taken by the king shortly after our marriage.

I was only eleven or twelve, but I understood that my country was much more than Tehran and its population and, like so many generations before me, I learned what it was to be Iranian. Schoolchildren in our country discover this feeling of belonging through the wonderful pages of the *Shahnameh—The Book of Kings*—by one of our greatest poets, Ferdowsi. For us children he was the incarnation of Iranian identity and pride. I had learned to love Ferdowsi at school and I used to read him with my cousin Reza. *The Book of Kings* relates the epic tales of the founders of Iran and the first four dynasties. After the passage of ten centuries the force and beauty of Ferdowsi's poetry brings to life the depiction of the struggle to retain the national identity of Iran. Ferdowsi is believed to have written his masterpiece around the year 1010 A.D. The *Book of Kings* relates in powerful poetry the epic tales of mythical heroes and the founders of the early Iranian kingdom.

Ferdowsi's stories fired our imagination both at school and at home, where I shared my feelings with Reza. In the course of a battle scene, sudden words of tenderness would fill us with emotion. "Can you justify having received life yourself and taking it away from someone else? Do not harm an ant dragging along a grain of wheat, for it has a life and life is sweet, even for an ant."

Through these epic tales, in which courage and strength vie with morality, *The Book of Kings* gives young Iranians respect for their 2,500-year-old identity. Such was one of the poet's intentions, and in the Iran of my childhood, storytellers still went around the country from village to village, as they had always done, reciting and singing Ferdowsi's work. The other purpose of *The Book of Kings* was to contribute to the political and moral education of monarchs themselves. "When you have written this book," writes Ferdowsi, "give it to the kings." For Ferdowsi believed that the greatness of Iran is closely linked to the permanence of the monarchy, and to the monarchy's renaissance should it decline or disappear.

This tradition inspired Joseph Santa Croce, a university lecturer in Tehran, to comment when I was first married that "the destiny of Iran seems strongly linked to *The Book of Kings*." "In the course of the centuries," he writes in one of his commentaries, "we have seen new dynasties appear. They restore the country's independence, its language, and once again enrich the civilization of the world. It would not seem rash or groundless to think that these successive renaissances have their origin in the work of Ferdowsi which enlightens great royal figures."

For Iranians of the fifties, the Pahlavi dynasty, which succeeded the Qajar dynasty in 1925, did indeed fit the logic of Ferdowsi's prophetic book. How could it be otherwise? When Reza Shah Pahlavi, my future husband's father, received the crown by act of Parliament, Iran was a medieval country without any leadership. Ahmad Shah, the last of the Qajars, then reigned over Tehran only. The country was in the hands of tribal chiefs and large landowners, and the only law was the law of the strongest. The main resources had been handed over to foreigners: the British operated our oil; our army, or what was left of it, took orders from Russian officers in the north and British officers in the south; Belgians ran our customs services, the Swedes our police, and so on. Iran was one of the most wretched countries on earth. Life expectancy was down to thirty years and infant mortality one of the highest in the world. Barely one man in a hundred was literate and women had no rights, not even to go to school. In short, unlike its great neighbors, India and Turkey, the country had few roads or railways and only one generator in Tehran.

A quarter of a century later, the Iran I knew had schools, universities, and hospitals; if the roads were not all paved yet, they did at least exist; finally, the Trans-Iranian Railway linked the Caspian Sea to the Persian Gulf. There was certainly a lot yet to be built, but for my parents' generation, who could see how much had been achieved, Reza Shah had given his country what Mustafa Kemal Ataturk had given Turkey: a bloodless industrial and cultural revolution. How could they not pay homage to him? And as for us children, who had learned from Ferdowsi to worship the enlightened monarch, how could we not see the renaissance predicted by the poet in this young Pahlavi dynasty?

We learned the work of Ferdowsi and other poets by heart. Iranians share a deeply ingrained passion for poetry; we have few prose writers and the school curriculum is essentially made up of classical poets. This interest in poetry was part of the rhythm of my daily life at school and at home. One of our favorite games with my mother, my cousin Reza, and his parents—one that many Iranian families play—consisted of linking verses, the last letter of one forming the beginning of the next, until one of us could not think of another verse. He or she was eliminated, and off we went again. The person who won was naturally the player who had the best memory and greatest knowledge.

My Uncle Ghotbi and my mother taught me to love Hafez in particular among all Persian poets. Later, when I had become queen, I visited his mausoleum at Shiraz to enjoy the calm of the evening and reflect on how good it is to be alive, as Hafez invites the pilgrim to his tomb: "Do not sit by my grave without wine and music, so that sensing the fragrance of your presence, I may rise dancing from my grave." Hafez is our most humane, noble, and most extraordinary poet. When one is in a state of utter confusion, not knowing what to do, one opens a volume of his poetry at a random page and the answer is invariably there, mysteriously whispered by the poet, rightly called "the voice of the Unseen."

Hafez is the one who is with you in difficult times, the one who gives you the strength to overcome sorrow and pain or to accept the course of destiny, if you cannot change it. He is also the one who writes, "If you have to cross the desert to reach your goal, go, pay no heed to the wounding thorns." Mother was steeped in poetry: for every event in her life a poem came to mind, which she recited, her face suddenly lighting up. My delight, when that happened, was to be able to reply with another poem. It was more than a game, it was a way of recognizing the fact that we were only visitors on this earth and of modestly joining in the wisdom of our thinkers. I also like Sa'adi, another poet from Shiraz; and Mowlana Jalal-al-din-Rumi; Omar Khayyam; and our contemporary poets, Forough Farrokhzad, Fereydoun Moshiri, Sohrab Sepehri, and many others.

With the passage of time, life in our household had become less melancholy, though the pain of Father's death still lay buried deep within each one of us. We lived very much within the family circle of cousins, aunts, and uncles; now I brought school friends home, which enriched our lives in general. I had a lot of girl friends and got on well with children and, what is more, I had the boundless love of the adults around me. After a while, I began to worry about that. Why was everyone so considerate toward me? I didn't think that I was more clever or more attractive than anyone else. It soon occurred to me that if the adults showed so much concern for my welfare, perhaps it was not for my looks or my personal charm, but because my father was no longer there and they simply pitied me. That worried me for months. I alternated constantly between the temptation of accepting these signs of affection and an inner voice that whispered to me that I should not believe all these things that were so nice to hear. Eventually I got over the anxiety. But I am still inclined to be suspicious of compliments paid to me, and for that reason, when I became queen, I always mistrusted flatterers and courtiers. I rarely took what they said literally, even if I was beguiled from time to time. I think that the habit of skepticism is what helped me to keep my feet on the ground. I find flattery and insincerity an insult to one's intelligence, a form of deceit. I don't contradict people who compliment me, as I don't wish to hurt their feelings, but it does offend me.

As if to show us that life must go on in spite of everything, the shared pleasure of Iranian holidays came around on fixed days that had been the same for thousands of years. The most important and the one that took the most preparation was without any doubt Now Ruz (literally, the New Day), the New Year, which falls on the first day of spring. This festival always increased family harmony, for, as children, we celebrated Now Ruz together as a family in the big house, and it was a time when parents and children made a point of showing their affection for each other in many different ways.

The holiday lasted a long time. The spring cleaning of the house from top to bottom began two weeks before, because Now Ruz is above all the symbol of renewal: you turn the page on the past, you wash, you put on new clothes and clean the house to usher in new times in a new frame of mind. All this housework was the first sign of excitement that would turn our little community upside down. Once the house was clean, the long preparation of the marvelous sweets could begin. For that we liked gathering at the house of my mother's sister, Amjad, who had an excellent cook. We all took up quarters in a big bedroom in the basement, so that we could lend him a hand. Cooking could last for days.

Finally, on the day before the festival, we set the table. All the symbols of earthly happiness are present for Now Ruz: eggs for birth, garlic for health, little dried fruits for love, apples for beauty, gold coins for prosperity, candles and a mirror for light, wheat that has been germinated in a nice pot for growth, a bitter orange in a bowl of water to signify the durability of the earth, as well as a hyacinth flower, symbol of our short time on this earth. Lastly, the holy book, according to the family's religion.

The exact time of the spring equinox varies from year to year, but when it comes, the members of the family gather around the table. They all kiss, compliment each other, give good wishes for the New Year, and the adults generally give children money in coins or new notes.

During the first day, the whole country is in a festive mood. It is traditional to visit the oldest member of the family first. Then come all the others—grandparents, uncles, aunts, and cousins—so that towns in Iran are soon in a flurry of activity, crisscrossed by joyful, brightly dressed family groups, their arms full of flowers, coming and going, laughing as they meet, and offering each other candy. This visiting goes on until sunset.

Thirteen days later is Sizdah be Dar, which must be spent out of the house, as staying inside is traditionally considered to bring bad luck. On this thirteenth day of the year, everyone goes out for a picnic. The wealthiest drive to the country in automobiles packed with food. The less well off set up in the street or by a stream. They roll out their carpet under a plane tree, set up the samovar, provide music, and cook vermicelli soup (*ashe reshte*) and kebabs over a charcoal fire in the first rays of spring sunshine. There are musicians everywhere playing the *tombak* (drum), the *tar* (our guitar), or the *sorna* (a kind of trumpet). Sizdah is the nicest time to eat outside in Tehran: it is not too hot and the peaks of the Alborz, which still have snow on them, bathe the town in soft, clear light. Before sunset, the germinated wheat has to be thrown in running water to bring us a good year. We used to perform the ritual with Mother, and even today, far from my country, my wheat sprouts are carried down other rivers. I remember once in the United States, already in exile, not knowing where to go, we had decided on the sea. But the beach was closed and my security people found themselves facing a guard. I had to explain to the man that it was an Iranian New Year tradition—Americans have great respect for traditions—and he allowed us to go on to the water's edge.

Before Now Ruz, we also celebrate the last Tuesday of the year, the *Chahar Shanbeh Souri.* On this occasion you have to jump over a fire. The act symbolizes shedding everything negative in one's body and soul into the flames and receiving warmth and light. We used to light fires for the occasion in the gardens of Tehran, in the country, or in the street if it was not possible to do it elsewhere. It's amusing in a way, because today, rather than give up these traditions that are so much a part of our identity, I simply light a candle and jump over it, as if this small gesture reaffirms my Iranian heritage and gives me the strength to cope with the pain of exile.

I WAS GROWING UP. Little by little I was leaving childhood, under Mother's watchful eye. Once a week, for as long as I can remember, she and I shared the ritual of the *hammam*. She packed a bag of clean clothes and we went hand in hand to the public baths. I dreaded this moment as a little girl because the woman who washed me held me tightly between her legs so that I could not escape; my skin prickled and the soap stung my eyes. Her name was Touba, and I remember that she used to sing to soothe me, "You won't be married to just anyone, and if the Shah comes with his army and his minister to ask for you, maybe you'll be given to him, maybe you won't."

As time went by I came to like the *hammam* and its ceremony. Each of us packed our bag, and we also had to take a round silver tray to sit on, as well as a copper bowl engraved with prayers, the *jame-doa*, to pour water over our heads at the end of our bath. The prayers were intended to protect us. For reasons of hygiene, we never sat directly on the tiles, and young girls were told that if they did, they might become pregnant. I can still remember being horrified by this silly belief. Now I liked Touba rubbing me vigorously with the horsehair washcloth. I liked these long sessions of body care and the feeling of starting afresh. In our country, the *hammam* is also one of the places where mothers pick out those who may have the honor of being introduced to their sons and, perhaps, the privilege of being chosen. One day a woman from Azarbaijan, thinking that I did not understand her language, said in front of me to a friend how charming she thought I was. *Bou guiz geuzal di.* “She’s a pretty girl,” in Turkish. It gave me a strange feeling of satisfaction and a new curiosity about the adolescent I was becoming.

Chapter 3

MY ADOLESCENCE BEGAN at the age of ten, when I entered the French École Jeanne d'Arc in Tehran. My mother had been a pupil there, and I am very grateful to her for choosing it: at that important transition period in life, I spent the most enriching years one could hope for there. This was thanks in part to my contact with a young nun, Sister Claire, whose initiatives were completely changing the old school. Among other things, Sister Claire had just formed a basketball team, which in the course of two or three years would transform the reserved child that I was into a confident, outgoing young girl.

I had only just arrived at Jeanne d'Arc when I decided to join the team and so found myself face to face with the dynamic French nun for the first time. I'll let her describe our encounter:

> I had decided to take girls only from the two grades above Farah. When children are too young, they are forever starting things and never finishing them. I don't know why, but it was love at first sight. I felt there was something special between us. We had a similar

> temperament, although she seemed more levelheaded. She was a neat and clean little girl with a very open expression. She wore a black apron with a collar edged in red. There was a hint of something very soldierly about her, together with a certain shyness and reserve. And yet she was very happy, a real bright spark. She never balked at doing anything. She was the first to go and fetch the ball I always kept in the convent wing. She was a happy child with no problems, in spite of losing her father when she was very young. As for her, I think she admired me more than the other sisters because I had initiative and a lot of energy.

After only one year I was chosen as captain of the basketball team. This was for my sporting ability no doubt but also, I think, because I was easygoing by nature. I was fairly straightforward and natural; I didn't like affectation or making a fuss; I didn't listen to malicious gossip, with the result that all the girls, or nearly all, were my friends. And if one of them was annoyed with me, I didn't mind, I just let her sulk until she got over it. Being the head of the basketball players at Jeanne d'Arc, I soon discovered that I had become a heroine, a kind of role model. Our team invariably won our matches against the other schools, and over the months we earned the title of champions of Tehran. Newspapers published photos of our group, and quite often I would hear children pointing me out to their parents: "Look, that's Farah!"

We were carried along by Sister Claire and, inspired by her example, I took up other competitions: the long jump, the high jump, and running. In those events I would be awarded the first national championships for women's athletics in 1954, receiving two medals and a small Iranian flag in the king's name from the hands of General Abbas Izad Panah, who was in charge of sport in Iran at that time. I can still see the medals. They had images of the king and Queen Soraya.

As for the rest, I went happily to school every day; I had lots of friends there, I liked most of my teachers, and I think they liked me. I also appreciated the spirit of self-discipline and camaraderie that typified Jeanne d'Arc. Housed in fine, L-shaped buildings a century old, the school immediately commanded respect and discipline. The sisters lived in one wing with a private garden; the classrooms were in the other, opening on to an asphalt courtyard shaded by tall pines. The church built within the school grounds lent a religious and sacred reference point. That didn't stop us from laughing, especially at lunchtime. There was no canteen in my day, so the girls had to bring their food in a metal container. We heated these meals on old coal-fired stoves in a basement room, which we found a bit scary and escaped as soon as we could.

What kind of child was I in these years of awakening both to myself and to others? Here I rely on Sister Claire's admittedly fond and rosy memory of me.

> She was no more brilliant than the other students, but she was intelligent, gifted, and conscientious. She took her classes in French, as the brightest students did, and was better in math and science than in literature. She had a good, precise mind. She was impeccable in her dress, as in her work and her relationship with her classmates, over whom she had a great influence. She radiated *joie de vivre* and good health, and was always ready to lend a hand. In my opinion, she represented all that is best in Iranian girlhood: subtlety, reserve, and astuteness combined with warmth and lasting friendship.

No doubt I had inherited something of my father's personality: honest, no-nonsense, and naturally inclined to be happy. But I most certainly owed the greater part of these qualities to my mother's great strictness; she did not let me get away with anything. Mother was very anxious about having to raise me on her own in a society that was particularly fussy about the way girls should be brought up. It's true that her brother, my uncle Ghotbi, had little by little taken the place of a father with me, but he was not concerned with day-to-day living; he was there to support me, teach me about life, and prepare my future. His wife, my aunt Louise, showed me unfailing affection. She thought I possessed every possible good quality, and with hindsight I now think that she is the person who loved me most after my mother. It was Mother who watched over me from day to day, and just a small step out of line could bring down her wrath and suddenly involve me in all kinds of drama. For example, I remember having failed an end-of-the-year spelling exam, which meant I would have to take it again in September. I must have been thirteen or fourteen at the time. Mother worked herself up into such a state, telling me over and over again that with everything she had done for me, I had no right to do that to her, that I soon felt I was a disgrace to the family. It was dreadful, I was shattered, and I can still feel some of that emotion when I think of it today. I shut myself in my room and cried all day long, as if this failure in spelling had really ruined my future.

On the national level, however, dramatic events of another nature were brewing at that time, events that would hasten my political awareness. It was 1952 and the government was at loggerheads with the British over the nationalization of our oil. The National Front, which represented Iranian discontent with the British, was led by Mohammad Mossadeq. The king had called on him to head the government and he had acted firmly and courageously, but his intransigence led the British to freeze our oil production: not a drop of oil was allowed to leave Iran and, as a result, the whole national economy was in decline. Our country at that time seemed to be losing on all counts: the international court was taking a long time recognizing Iran's rights, and the British embargo had precipitated a crisis that affected all levels of the population.

The king was said to be very worried. He was, of course, in favor of nationalization but thought that Mossadeq had gone too far by constantly refusing British offers to negotiate. Impoverishment and increased dissatisfaction naturally suited the communist Tudeh Party, which had never before been so much in evidence. Some people claimed that Mossadeq was unwittingly playing into the Tudeh's hands; others supported him in spite of the diplomatic failure, because his position was a tribute to national pride.

When the crisis took a turn for the worse, the king decided to let his prime minister go, but Mossadeq refused to leave, causing a deep division of opinion in Iranian minds and leaving scars that are still painful today.

The question of how best to achieve nationalization of our oil sowed discord in every family. Most were torn between supporters of the king and followers of Mossadeq. Our own household did not escape, and one evening I witnessed a memorable angry scene by one of my cousins, who came to the point of insulting one of our uncles, a fervent supporter of Mossadeq. At the time my cousin Reza leaned toward the pan-Iranist, monarchist party, which was also very anticommunist. Although only thirteen, he was a well-recognized authority on *The Book of Kings* at his school, and I remember that his classmates often used to ask him to write the beginning of their essays for them. I also felt deeply royalist and nationalist. Why? It was certainly because of my upbringing and also because, like Reza, I was immersed in Ferdowsi's ideas: only the kings were legitimate rulers in our country.

The debate also affected the classes at Jeanne d'Arc, where the students echoed their parents' point of view. But at our level the question depended mainly on how we felt, because, whatever side we took, we took it simply because it appealed to us emotionally. I personally could not understand how anyone could be against our young king: his sensitive but determined look touched me deeply. However, our confrontations in the school yard were limited to harmless battles with orange peel. We were all in agreement on the nationalization of oil, and I can remember how proud we were to translate BP (British Petroleum), the emblem of British power, as "*Benzine Pars,*" Iranian Oil.

Things took a more serious turn with the boys, especially in my cousin Reza's Alborz College. Militant communists of the Tudeh Party regularly came to provoke the students by hawking their magazine. Tempers rose rapidly and Reza, who was very worked up, set about tearing the papers to pieces. Those on the Tudeh side also became more belligerent, and one evening our worst fears came true: Reza was stabbed. We heard that he had been taken to the hospital. Luckily that day he was wearing thick clothing and the blade had not reached any vital organ.

Then a rumor went round the city that the king was thinking of leaving the country to prevent the various tensions from degenerating into civil war. Thousands of Iranians, especially young people, gathered in front of the palace to beg him to stay. People were worried. Once again Iran seemed on the edge of the precipice. I remember that tanks had taken up positions at the crossroads. Good Lord, what would happen if the king abandoned us? The prospect made me so anxious that I could no longer eat or sleep, and my uncle and aunt's despondency, together with Mother's silence, were not likely to reassure me. Every evening they rang one of my uncles, Ahmad Diba, whose house was near Parliament Square, to try to get the latest news.

The general agitation faded, and my nightmares disappeared, only to attack me again in the terrible summer of 1953. The family was on holiday at Bandar-Pahlavi on the Caspian Sea and I was about to celebrate my fifteenth birthday when the news reached us that the king had left Iran. No rumor this time. The radio confirmed it, saying that the king had dismissed Mossadeq, who had refused to step down, and that rioters had now taken to the streets in support of the prime minister. There was a Russian woman in the boarding house where we were staying, a White Russian who had fled the Bolshevik Revolution thirty-five years earlier. "That's it! We're going the same way as Russia!" she kept repeating. The poor woman was gray in the face and in despair. We knew that we were living through terrible times that could be fatal for Iran. Loudspeakers had been set up in the streets of the little seaside town to broadcast news hour by hour. People went about their business looking haggard and anxious. I can remember antiroyalists in boats already shouting "Anzali! Anzali!"—the old name for the port of Bandar-Pahlavi. It was only a symbolic admonition, but it was very significant. What would become of us? My heart was full of dismay and I was too sad even to cry.

Riots swept through Tehran for three days, leaving great confusion. Communists, Mossadeq supporters, and even religious men held the streets with violent slogans against the king. Before he left, the king had appointed General Fazlollah Zahedi as prime minister, replacing Mohammad Mossadeq. The army rallied to General Zahedi rather than obeying the orders of the former Prime Minister. At last the news that Mossadeq's house had been destroyed by a tank came as the first sign that order was being restored.

And in fact the next day the king returned to Tehran to great acclaim. His exile with Queen Soraya, which had lasted only one week, made me, like many Iranians very anxious the whole time. Twenty-five years later, when I had become queen and would accompany the king into a new exile, that happy outcome would help me keep alive the hope that we would return.

In the memoirs he wrote shortly before he died, the king referred briefly to that first exile:

> Being quite aware of Mossadeq's plans and ambitions, I had decided to leave Iran before a takeover by force. I wanted to avoid bloodshed and leave the country free to make its choice.
>
> There were three days of rioting, mainly in Tehran. The first two days were organized by the Mossadeq and Tudeh parties. It was only on the morning of the third day, 19 August 1953, that workers and craftsmen, students and members of the liberal professions, soldiers, policemen, even women and children, took an extraordinarily courageous stand against the rifles, machine guns, and armored tanks of the frenzied dictator, and reversed the situation. A single warning shot at the ex-prime minister's villa, fired by a faithful tank, put an end to three years of political madness....
>
> I immediately came back to Tehran, where I received an enthusiastic welcome from the people. It really was an overwhelming plebiscite throughout Iran. Before evidence like this, I had been only a hereditary monarch. Now I had the right to say that I was really elected by the people....
>
> The legal proceedings that followed the elimination of Mossadeq's system brought to light some strange facts about the events of 1951–53. It was revealed, for example, that the communist Tudeh Party, which had only 110 officers when Mossadeq became minister of war in 1951, had 640 by the time he left in 1953.
>
> The communist plan was first to use Mossadeq to overthrow me. According to papers found in the Tudeh Party, Mossadeq was to be got rid of two or three weeks after my departure. I have seen postage stamps of the People's Iranian Republic, which was to have been proclaimed....
>
> Released after three years in prison, Mossadeq retired to his estate at Ahmad-Abad, to the west of our capital, and died there in 1967.

Beyond the upheavals of recent history, I can maintain today that the king, who had enthusiastically supported Dr. Mossadeq at the time of the nationalization of oil, also had great respect for him. I feel sure that if Mossadeq had been less intransigent and more diplomatic with the British, as the king wanted, we would not have had such strife for so many years. My wish today is that all Iranians put an end to this fifty-year-old quarrel. It has no place in the Iran of tomorrow, which all of us should build together.

LIFE RESUMED A CALMER COURSE, in the country as at home. Under the leadership of Father Michel Goyaux, I discovered the Scout movement. Volunteers were needed to supervise the youngest members, the Cubs at the École Saint Louis (the equivalent of Jeanne d'Arc for boys), which was run by the Lazarist Fathers. As I was already captain of the basketball team, I soon became Cub mistress.

Scouting was my first experience of taking on real responsibility, and when I became queen, I often gave silent thanks to it. It's not easy at only fifteen to be responsible for thirty-odd children for one or two weeks at camp. One learns organization and self-sacrifice, patience and a cool head. One also learns, in those rare free moments, to think about one's mistakes, what would have been better to say or do at such and such a time in the rush and bustle of the day. Yes, as a young queen I would be grateful to the Scouts for having given me a sense of duty fairly early in my life. Even in exile I would correspond with Father Goyaux, who was in charge of the Scout movement at the time and a person we all liked for his energy, his openness, and his great generosity.

It was also thanks to the Scouts that I made my first trip to France in 1956. Two girls and two boys were invited to go to an international jamboree at the Château de Jambville near Paris.

However, we had to pay our own fares. The profits from a production of Marcel Pagnol's play *Topaze*, staged in a Tehran theater that had friendly relations with the École Saint Louis, made it possible for us to buy our tickets for France.

I was extremely excited at the idea of discovering Paris. The city had particular importance for my family: my father had studied there after leaving St. Petersburg, and he had looked forward to taking me there. His father, my grandfather Mehdi Diba, had been secretary of the Persian legation in France at the beginning of the century. Both spoke French perfectly, and my father had passed on to me his fondness for France and especially its capital.

As soon as we arrived, we set out up the Champs-Élysées to the Arc de Triomphe. I was dazzled and wild with excitement. I would have liked to take in the whole of Paris in that one afternoon. I was sure we would never have enough time. We went on to see the magical places whose names had been part of my earliest childhood: the Invalides, Saint Germain, the Sorbonne, Notre Dame, the Eiffel Tower....In the evening—we were staying with various families—I was very happy but my feet were covered in blisters, some of them bleeding.

And the metro! It had never seen anything like it. After glancing at the map, down we went and resurfaced under the fine August sky, but in a completely different area of Paris. Although we were Cub leaders, I remember that we were like children when we saw the machines that gave out candy or chewing gum for a few coins. We were especially fond of Pierrot Gourmand lollipops, which reminded us of the "sugar roosters" we used to suck when we were small.

Then we went to Jambville. Young people from all over the world shared stories about their country in one way or another: some sang folk songs, others improvised little shows. It was quite moving, as we managed to communicate with each other in spite of the language barrier. "Self-expression camp," as it was called in those days, was also intended to teach us to be group leaders. I learned how to speak in public, how to gain people's attention, and how to tell stories by controlling the suspense. Ten years later, with my own children, I knew in my heart as well as my head how important it is to be able to tell stories well.

After Jambville we were taken to Royan, this time to learn how to run a sports camp with a variety of activities such as swimming and rappelling. Finally, on the way home, we had a stopover of a day or two in Athens, where we of course visited the Acropolis. I remember that a friend and I sat on the marble throne of Darius, the great king of ancient Persia, in the Dionysus theater, and that we felt quite thrilled and proud.

UNLIKE MOST IRANIAN MOTHERS of those days, my mother refused to hear of an arranged marriage for me, and I naturally agreed with her. I know that certain members of the family were discreetly trying to persuade her in that direction. After all, I was approaching the age when, according to them, it was usual to look for a good match. But Mother and I believed that I should first finish my studies before thinking of marriage. Mother herself had passed her baccalaureate and was very well read. On the subject of marriage, which we discussed often from that time on, I remember I let it be known that I wanted to try and keep the name of Diba, which came from my father. I was very attached to this name and was afraid it could die out, since very few of my cousins had it. I would bring it up with my family and friends, saying, "If I go on to do major studies and become an outstanding woman, perhaps I'll be allowed to keep my maiden name. Don't you think so?"

In the end, having married the most important man in Iran, I more than anyone else, should have dropped my maiden name. As it happens, one of the little ironies in the footnotes of history decided the opposite: in many countries, especially in France, I am still called Farah Diba, while in my heart, legally, and historically, my name is Farah Pahlavi.

In any case, having also firmly decided to undertake a long and prestigious course of studies, I began tenth grade at the French Lycée Razi in Tehran to prepare for my baccalaureate. I have marvelous memories of my three years at Razi. It was a long trip by bus to get there every morning, but I liked crossing Tehran from one side to the other. There were already a lot of cars in the city at that time—the first traffic jams were occurring here and there—and I had plenty of time to gaze at some old houses I really loved, with luxuriant gardens and vegetation hanging over the walls. Then there were the Tehran trees I adored: plane trees, locust trees, magnolias. And oh, the smell of the honeysuckle in summer! On all the street corners, peddlers with little carts colored differently according to the season attracted small groups of passersby. The school was in a charming old building with colonnades and walls covered with mosaics. To change classes we had to go up and down a few lopsided steps or take winding corridors. One of my great regrets is not to have had the presence of mind, when I was queen, to save the wonderful building of the Lycée Razi, as I did for many others. Located in the southern part of Tehran, it was pulled down in one of the big urban redevelopments of the sixties and seventies.

The subjects we studied at Razi were taught either in Persian or French by both Iranian and French teachers. I was therefore able to continue learning about Persian literature. Although the school was a state school, we were also taught religion. The teachers already treated us rather like older students, respecting our autonomy, skillfully helping us to develop our personalities. All the pupils in my class actually were later accepted at the best universities in the world. We liked and respected our teachers a great deal, though it still made us giggle to hear one or another of them whose French was not as good as ours make a mistake.

The Lycée Razi was coeducational: a sign of open-mindedness, approved by my mother. I did not find it hard to adjust, because at Jeanne d'Arc we often organized outings with the boys of Saint Louis. And besides, I was used to being with boys of my age within the family and at Scouts. At Razi I especially liked lunchtimes when I sat with two girl friends in the shade of the old plane trees. As there was no canteen here either, we continued bringing our lunches. It was a time for discussions and much giggling. We were happy and full of confidence in the life that lay ahead of us.

In those days it was inconceivable to have a boyfriend and be seen with him. If you secretly had a crush on someone, as they used to put it, you would never have dared tell anyone, not even a best friend, and certainly not the person in question.

I lived with the same noisy intensity as all the other high school students of my age. We began to organize our first parties at each other's homes and took our first steps at dancing. I was mad about Elvis Presley, like all the young people in Tehran, and remember going as far as missing a class to see a film he starred in. We adored the cinema and loved to go all together in groups. It was a stampede to get in, as our generation had not yet adopted the virtue of waiting in line. Many films came to us undubbed, and screens of text giving a resumé of the plot were regularly inserted between the images to compensate for this inconvenience. We liked James Dean, Gregory Peck, Elizabeth Taylor, Montgomery Clift, and many others. As regards music, we were mad about American pop, of course, but I also liked Iranian music very much—the folk songs—while I found our traditional music too sad. Lastly, I enjoyed classical music—opera—and I remember our excitement on one particular occasion with Reza when we discovered a 78 rpm record of the Italian tenor Enrico Caruso among the jumble of goods in a little shop. Then, in quite another style, Tino Rossi and Jacqueline François struck an emotional chord with me, for as soon as I heard them, I could see my father again playing their records on our old gramophone.

Caught between her concern that I should receive a strict upbringing and her desire to let me know more of the world, my mother was not generous in giving me more leeway. She allowed me to stay out until midnight and always arranged for the parents of one of my friends to bring me home. If I was late, I'd find her anxiously standing in the street in her bathrobe. Poor Mother. If only she had known how sensible her daughter was in spite of it all, she would have gone to bed without waiting up for me.

But she worried constantly that I might leave the straight and narrow. Every new sign of emancipation on my part would plunge her into a state of anxiety. I remember that one evening for a party, one of my friends had put on lipstick. We were in raptures and, of course, the lipstick went the rounds. I was just looking at myself in a mirror, amazed and uncertain, when my mother suddenly came into the room to remind me at what time I should be back home. I saw the sudden look of horror on her face. God in heaven! How could I allow myself to do something so vulgar! Didn't I know that only married women could wear lipstick?

My uncle never took part in any of these scenes; I don't actually have any memory of him scolding me for anything at all. On the other hand, the question of deciding what studies I should pursue after the baccalaureate occupied his mind as much as it did my mother's. For a time I had thought of doing research in natural science. We had talked about it and I had given up the idea myself, realizing that I could not bear spending my life staring into a microscope in a laboratory, as I loved being outside so much. It was then that my liking for architecture came to the fore. To me architecture was a magnificent profession that merged the inside with the outside, combining solitary contemplation with the supervision of workers, and approaching the way people live with art and ingenuity. I wanted to be outside, on the work sites. I had seen my uncle working at his profession from my earliest childhood. At some times he would be bent over his drawing board, at others he would be directing a work site, coming home freezing cold or sunburned, but happy and obviously fascinated by what he was doing.

And besides, Iran, for all its rapid growth, had only one woman architect* for the limitless prospects of construction work to be done. What other sector would offer me so many opportunities to express myself while helping to contribute to my country's growth?

*Nectar Papazian Andreef

Chapter 4

Was I entitled to a scholarship to finance my architecture studies in Paris? I thought so and hoped to get one. As it happened I had just graduated at the top of my class and was accepted into the École Spéciale d'Architecture on the Boulevard Raspail, which had the reputation of being very selective and demanding. The obstacle course one had to go through to get the scholarship—which I never did receive—was my first contact with bureaucracy. At the Ministry of Education, where I wandered about for days, no one could explain what procedure I should follow, not even the minister himself, whom my family knew and I had the good fortune to see. Some told me I had to take an extra language exam, but they could not tell me who was responsible for it or how to enroll. Weeks went by, the summer ended, and somehow my application for the scholarship got lost among the various departments of the state education system. Classes had already begun in Paris, but during that time I was still being sent all over the place from one end of Tehran to the other. I was so angry that in the end I left for France, saying to myself that I would never set foot in this country again. It was a childish outburst forgotten within a week.

My aunt Louise Ghotbi, Reza's mother, was already in Paris. I have mentioned how fond we were of each other. We spent the first days of that autumn in 1957 in a hotel, then I obtained a room at the Cité Universitaire, near the Parc Montsouris. It was in the Collège Neerlandais, which had the reputation of being the strictest. It was forbidden in particular to visit boys and vice versa. Convinced that I was in good hands, my aunt then returned to Tehran.

I had scarcely arrived at the architecture school when I had reason to silently thank the Iranian bureaucracy: by making me miss the first fortnight of lectures, it had unwittingly spared me the worst of the traditional hazing. Some male students were so shocked by the violence and strangeness of this custom that they gave up and went home. The hazing was not as tough for the girls. It consisted mainly of making us freshmen act as servants to the students who were senior to us. At any time of the day one of them could give us an order and we had to obey immediately. It was usually to go to all the classrooms and ask for an imaginary object, such as a scroll compass. We novices had no idea that it did not exist, so wherever we went we caused great hilarity without knowing why. When we asked for the object, we were always solemnly told that it was in the next room or the floor above. If we refused to take part in these farces, we would immediately get "a mugful." In other words, you had to cover your chest with an apron, stand against the wall, and open your mouth wide. Thereupon one of the happy tormentors would throw a glass of water in your face. Then you had to say, "Thank you, oh most noble and venerable seniors," pronouncing all the words clearly and correctly. The boy or girl who did not say it properly received a second mugful. The worst thing to do obviously was to show that you were angry, for then you would suffer endless humiliation, or cry, which made you the very scapegoat they were looking for. As I was easygoing and used to group games, I came out of it fairly well.

There were several of us from overseas, and one day the seniors decided to make us talk in our own languages. They obviously wanted to create a kind of ridiculous, incoherent cacophony, which would no doubt be very amusing. Once again the "venerable seniors" had a good laugh at our expense. What I didn't know at the time was that they had recorded us. That could have caused me a lot of embarrassment in terms of diplomacy and protocol, for the day after the announcement of my engagement to the king, one of them sent this tape to a radio station in Paris, which promptly broadcast it. Luckily I had not said any rude words, which can be tempting when one is sure that nobody in the room understands your language.

There was a very different mentality here from the one that I had known at Jeanne d'Arc and the Lycée Razi. For years we had been taught solidarity and team spirit, but now we had to embrace the opposite to succeed. Individualism and elitism were the main values held by the students in my year, and I confess that for me, loving nothing better than harmony and concord, the atmosphere was almost harder to put up with than the hazing. The system was responsible for the students' attitude: only the best went on to the second year. School took the form of a competition, which meant that we were all prompted to rejoice in our neighbor's misfortunes. When someone came to ask me for help in math, for example, I gave it and could not imagine doing otherwise, but I could see that this was not done here, that people wriggled out of it. The worst thing was in the studio when all sixty students in the year were working at the table doing a drawing test. If one of us spilled a bottle of ink over the drawing or inadvertently tore the sheet of paper, we would hear him shout, "Shit!"—the others immediately responded, "Great! That's one less!"

I happened to be good at drawing, but I didn't know the technique that was taught in these special schools, which was a great handicap, as drawing was an important subject. And so I worked terribly hard at it, while being put down by the others and even my teacher. "You Orientals," he often said to me, "you know nothing about perspective." I remember how proud I was when through sheer persistence I managed to do a horse's head that was graded at 17/20 and was displayed in the school.

In the beginning I was fairly depressed by this atmosphere, all the more so because there were only five or six girls in our studio and the environment was very macho. Most of the boys made fun of us and put us down. "There's never been a girl who's become an architect worthy of the name." Or, "You girls just come here to get yourselves a husband." One day one of them turned on me in front of all the others. "And how many camels are you worth in your country?" He was a Frenchman. I was so offended that I never forgot him. When he wrote to me some time later in Tehran to ask for help, I didn't even reply. He is the only one to whom I never replied. I have corresponded with many of the others, even with "venerable seniors" who threw water in my face. But not with him.

My heart was full of homesickness for my family and Iran in those first months, especially as I knew that, for financial reasons, I would not be seeing them for four years. Four years! It was an eternity! Waking up when it was still dark, going down into the metro, where haggard, miserable-looking workmen stood hunched over, smoking, and then arriving at the school, putting up with continuous taunts—that was a lot for a girl who had until then been much loved and rather spoiled.

But I hid my homesickness from Sister Claire in this letter dated October 1957, which gives a fairly accurate picture of my life at that time:

> Dear Sister Claire,
> I have my own, very comfortable room in the Collège Neerlandais, looking out onto the boulevard. We had a small party here to help students get to know each other. This was fortunate for me, otherwise I'd never have spoken to anyone! I leave my room in the morning and come back to it in the evening to work. The others stay reading for a while in the foyer, but I don't have the time. At school we train for volleyball and basketball at different sports grounds. I didn't tell them that I had been a member of the championship Iranian team. The garden in the Cité Universitaire is lovely when the sun is shining! There's an amusing custom in the restaurant: if someone comes in wearing a hat or even a scarf on their head, everyone bangs on their plate until the person removes it. I sometimes feel such a strong desire to see my family and friends again. But the blues disappear with the friendly smile of a girl in one of the neighboring rooms.

I had given up on a scholarship for the time being, but all my basic needs were covered. At the beginning of each month, my mother sent me money for my expenses and I even had enough to buy restaurant meals or metro tickets for my friends. My only real luxury was a turntable and, at the beginning of the month, a bunch of flowers that I pampered to make them last.

The atmosphere, however, did improve at the school. Some boys became friendlier and also more appealing. I could see that they didn't believe me when I told them that I didn't have a boyfriend. They didn't understand that this custom was foreign to our culture. To be left in peace, I began to tell people at school that I had a fiancé at the Cité Universitaire, and at the Cité I told them I had one at the school. If that didn't convince them, or they found out the truth, I made up a fiancé in Tehran. They christened this unlikely suitor Mahmoud, and one day stuck a drawing on my desk of a man with a magnificent mustache and a turban, which is how they imagined an Iranian man looked, I suppose. Underneath was written, "Mahmoud, Farah's fiancé."

It was not long before current events gave them something to feed their wildest dreams. In the spring of 1958, we learned that the shah was separating from Empress Soraya. That evening I wrote in my private diary, "The Shah and Soraya are getting a divorce. What a pity." In the months that followed, the press announced that the shah, who wanted more than anything else to have a son to succeed him, was now looking for a girl to marry.

"And why wouldn't the shah marry you? You're pretty." It became the favorite joke of my contemporaries at the school. I remember that once we had finished work, we sometimes spent a while in the studio laughing about it. "Why don't you write to him," I said, "and try to convince him that there's a very suitable girl for him here." And they would say, "No, but just suppose. If you went back to Iran and became queen, what would you do? What would be the first thing?" "My first decision? I'd invite you all to Iran to see my country." I had an Afghan girl friend that year called Mermone, who also kept saying, "But you're marvelous. The shah should marry you." I have even kept a postcard she gave me when we were on holidays together in Spain. On it she had written, just as little girls do in school, "Farah Diba = Farah Pahlavi." She was therefore the first to link my first name with the king's family name.

The year finished less brilliantly than she predicted. Despite all my efforts, especially in drawing, I learned that I had been accepted…to repeat the year. There were many of us in that situation, and most of the seniors had been through the same agonies. That summer, to avoid giving in to feelings of depression and homesickness, I went exploring Brittany with some girl friends who were foreigners like me. What surprised me the most was watching the sea rise around Mont Saint Michel. We also went to the Île de Batz, where the beach would later be named after me.

My second year in France was definitely more pleasant. I knew Paris well and I had several good friends, both boys and girls. We went to the cinema together and, as it was frowned upon to see sentimental films, we went to art houses. I remember in particular the frightening impression Ingmar Bergman's *Seventh Seal* made on me. We also went to the opera and concerts, for which I had a Youth Music concession card. My favorite singers were Charles Aznavour, Jamshid Shaybani, Hamid Ghanbari, Jacques Brel, and Paul Anka.

Most of my activities were centered around the Latin Quarter and the Cité Universitaire. We favored the cinemas and cafés of the Boulevard Saint Germain. At the Cité, in addition to evenings spent studying, sometimes we had dinners organized by friends. The annual fête at the Cité was a real event: each country represented built its own pavilion. We Iranians had drawn two big replicas of the lions of Persepolis, made some typical dishes, and I wore a costume from Gilan.

Members of the family came to Paris from time to time, and then we would go out to a restaurant for dinner. I remember that one of my uncles, Manouchehr, took me to the Moulin Rouge and that I didn't like the show. No doubt I had simpler tastes: at that time we students were very taken with self-service cafeterias, which were just becoming popular. Some evenings I was invited to dinner at the home of some student friends who were already married and had their own apartment.

At the school I was now considered an elder, which exempted me from the hazing. On top of that, I was expected to be one of the tormentors. But I could never do it, being too sensitive or having too many scruples about doing to others what I had disliked having done to me. The only hazing I allowed myself was to have my drawing board carried to the metro station (it was really very heavy), to write my name on a stool that no one but me could touch, and to put a lock on my drawer.

That year I spent Christmas in Munich, invited by one of my Iranian girl friends who lived there. I have very happy memories of that city, its museums and galleries, our long walks through streets full of history, with occasional stops for a comforting cup of hot chocolate or tea. It was during one of these excursions that we were asked where we came from by some people who heard us speaking a language they didn't recognize. "From Iran!" This information seemed to surprise them, for their only response was to show us by gestures that they thought we were all cannibals! Thanks to student organizations, we were also able to visit the Universal Exhibition in Brussels and explore the Belgian capital at the same time.

That winter I had occasion to experience once again the uneasiness that communists made me feel. One of my Iranian friends* tried to convince me to go to a rally against the war in Algeria. This was 1958–59. She claimed we should show solidarity with the Algerians who were fighting French imperialism. I could understand her own feeling of revolt against colonialism, but it seemed to me out of place or improper for us to engage in a fight against France while that country was generous enough to welcome us. I was there to study and certainly not to engage in poli-

*This friend, an academic, would later go to prison under the monarchy as a member of the communist party and a partisan of armed struggle. She refused to let me intervene to free her, which does her credit. Many years later she

tics. She brushed aside my objections in the name of a so-called "international revolution," which was to restore the worth of the individual everywhere. But I had personally seen its swift and fairly unworthy methods at work in Azarbaijan and Gilan.

She introduced me to her sister and other friends of hers, all militant communists, in a café in Paris. The memory I have of that meeting is grim and deeply depressing. The world was a gloomy place to these girls and boys. They were so young, but already they seemed to be against the whole world, extremely sour and bitter. You would have thought that, in their view, there was nothing worth keeping on this planet, apart from the Soviet Union. With an alarming fervor that was almost religious, they described Stalin, who had died in 1953, as something like a prophet.

As I refused to join them in a demonstration against the war in Algeria, they scoffed at me, saying that I didn't have the courage to do it. Was it to prove the opposite to them that I did go in the end? Probably. I have no memory of that day, except of my astonishment when I noticed that most of the boys were hiding blackjacks or iron bars under their leather jackets. I thought to myself, "If it ever turns nasty and they throw us in prison, what will I say to Mother and the embassy?"

On another occasion these girls introduced me to a man who had come from East Germany. I describe this memory here because many years later I found myself once again in his presence by chance and under strange circumstances. While the king and I were watching a play in Gilan, one of the security men came to alert us that a shot would be fired on stage and he asked us not to be alarmed. And who should I see rushing on stage

wrote to me to express her sympathy after the death of my little Leila. I called her and we spoke together after so many years' silence. Both of us have known tragedy in our lives, but I know one day we will meet again.

brandishing the imitation revolver? The man from East Germany. I leaned over and whispered a brief account of the story in my husband's ear. Nothing happened, and the man left for parts unknown, taking his secret Communist past with him.

It was in the spring of that same year, 1959, that I was given my first opportunity to see the king. The Shah was coming on an official visit for talks with General de Gaulle and, as usually happens on these occasions, the Iranian embassy wished to present some representatives of our community in France. I was one of those chosen.

As I reread the letter I wrote to my mother on the evening of this meeting, I realize how excited and proud I was.

> I put on a black and white tweed suit with a camellia on the lapel of the jacket. We went to the Embassy. What a nice car! And how nice he is! His hair is almost white and he has sad eyes. I was so happy to see him close up for the first time! But the students rushed forward as usual, and in spite of my three-inch heels, it was hard for me to see him. Then Mr. Tafazoli, the cultural attaché, came and took me by the hand, saying, "Do move forward, come closer." But you know me.... I didn't move. I stayed behind where I was. I don't want people to say that I was pushing myself forward.
>
> A little later I shook his hand. I said, "Farah Diba, architecture," and he replied, "How long have you been here?" I said, "Two years." Tafazoli added immediately, "Mademoiselle is a very good student. She is first in her class and she speaks French very well." It's very nice of him to have said so many nice things about me. Then of course, there was a handshake and a curtsey, with my heart beating fast, as you can imagine...
>
> Of course my friends teased me straight away. "Farah, you spend the day at the hairdresser's, and when the Shah appears, you don't dare go up to him." A cousin who was present claimed that the

> King liked me. "When you left the room," she told me, "he watched you go." Of course, all of that is just talk.
>
> Later I heard Tafazoli complaining, "Really, some girls are very rude, rushing up to the King like that. I had to take control and make them stand back." Thank goodness I wasn't among them. By the way, I spoke to Tafazoli again about the scholarship business, and he has promised to try and help me.

The school year ended happily. I was admitted to the second year. I was just coming back from a walk on the Boulevard Saint Germain and was crossing the Pont Neuf when one of my classmates told me the good news: I also learned that I was to spend the summer in Tehran. Mother was giving me the airplane ticket as a gift. Nothing could have given me greater pleasure.

I spent those last days in Paris going shopping with my Iranian friend who was also going back to Tehran for the holidays. I'd never felt so excited. I wanted to take little gifts for everyone and have them see me looking like a real parisienne. I bought a floral silk blouse in shades of ivory and pale green; a narrow, straight skirt in the same ivory color, fuchsia-colored shoes with very high heels, and matching purse; and lastly a light coat in olive green suede. I never could have suspected that four months later I would be back in Paris, staying at the Hôtel de Crillon, going shopping again, but this time for my trousseau as the future queen.

Chapter 5

MY MEMORY OF TEHRAN airport had been of a very basic kind of building. If you were accompanying passengers, you went out of it and walked up to a low wall built only a few feet from the aircraft. The whole place was so small that it was reminiscent of the beginning of aviation. Now, in only two years, the runways had taken over a good part of the surrounding countryside, with a real control tower looking down on them, and they ended at a terminal with brand-new ticket desks. European and American aviation companies, which were very much in evidence, seemed to have discovered Iran.

And so, six years after the crisis brought about by the nationalization of oil, our economy appeared to be booming once more. Tehran itself was unrecognizable, more dusty than ever from the increase in construction sites, jammed with cars (what had become of the horse-drawn cabs of my childhood?), the footpaths crowded with little shops. I knew that we were no longer living in the apartment to which we had had to retreat after my father's death, and I was eager to see our new house. It had been built by my uncle Ghotbi who, after years of hard work, was now also reaping the benefits of the economic expansion and was able to house us in true comfort. The villa with its swimming pool stood on the heights of Tehran, very near Shemiran, where fifteen years earlier I had spent my holidays out in the country. What joy to join Mother, all my relatives and friends in this place, the scene of our happiest times together as a family.

I arrived from France with my head full of songs by Ray Charles, Sidney Bechet, Juliette Greco, and Charles Aznavour, whom I liked best of all. I naïvely thought that I was up with the latest hits, but I soon learned, at the first parties I attended, that people in Tehran now listened to the same music as people in Paris. It's true that nearly all of us—cousins, ex-pupils of Jeanne d'Arc and the Lycée Razi—were coming back at the same time from universities in the West.

As privileged children of a developing country, we were very Iranian but also open to other cultures, free of sectarianism, ready to listen and like anything, provided it carried us away. That summer we danced a lot at each other's houses, listened to a huge amount of rock, and went to various cinemas, as several more had opened during my absence.

For my second-year project, I had chosen to work on the architecture of the Shah's Mosque in Isfahan with its façade covered in dazzlingly beautiful mosaics. Wanting to reproduce part of the façade, I made my summer quarters in the Tehran Museum of Archeology so that I could draw and consult all available documents on the mosque. When I went home in the evening, I joined my group of cousins and friends for dinner on the grass at Shemiran or at a party somewhere in Tehran. Never in my life had I experienced such a feeling of fulfillment; I was happy in my studies, in harmony with my family and my generation, and reconciled with Tehran, though two years earlier I had sworn never to set foot in it again.

One day Sohrab, a cousin of the king and a friend of my cousin Reza, invited our little group of students to spend the day outside of Tehran in Shah Dasht, a magnificent property belonging to the Queen Mother Taj al Molouk. I remember our astonishment at finding ourselves within walls that had housed the royal family. We were thrilled and overawed. In every room one of us would invariably murmur, "Just imagine. Perhaps the king sat in this chair... perhaps the king slept in this bed..." It took our breath away.

I had been brought up to venerate the king from childhood. To me his mission gave him an aura that placed him high above the ordinary run of mortals. One of my father's brothers, Esfandiar Diba, was the king's chamberlain, and as such, every year at Now Ruz he received a small gold coin that was called a Pahlavi, because it had the king's portrait on it. My uncle gave me one and I remember that I thought it had heavenly powers. We generally considered everything coming from the king auspicious, and in those days, when people dreamed about him, they thought it was a good omen.

I still had to resolve the problem of my scholarship, for although my uncle Ghotbi now had a better income and my mother could provide for my needs, financing my studies in Paris for a further four or five years would nonetheless be a considerable strain on my family. I thought that I had a right to this assistance. The whole question still remained one of finding the right person to see.

We found out that the man who was now in charge of Iranian students abroad was none other than the king's son-in-law. That seemed a good sign to me! The king's son-in-law could not be one of those irresponsible bureaucrats who had nearly driven me to distraction two years before. I was all the more certain as he was Ardeshir Zahedi, the son of General Fazlollah Zahedi, who had been appointed prime minister by the king in 1953, replacing Mohammad Mossadeq. Ardeshir Zahedi had married Princess Shahnaz, the only child of the king's first marriage. In 1939, when he was twenty, the king had wed Princess Fawzia of Egypt, the sister of King Farouk.

My uncle Esfandiar Diba knew Mr. Zahedi, and so he was the one who took the initiative to obtain an interview for us. Ardeshir Zahedi received us in a charming old building in Tehran with a garden full of trees and shrubs. He was a young man and very pleasant. I could naturally never have imagined that he would be with us twenty years later, when we would know the suffering of exile.

He asked me about my studies, my plans, my life in Paris, my interests, and rather curiously, at the end of our interview, he said to my uncle that he would like to introduce me to his young wife, Princess Shahnaz. Accordingly, a few days later I received an invitation to have tea with the princess. The villa was a little further up than Shemiran, at Hessarak, on a wonderful site at the foot of the Alborz Mountains, with a magnificent view over the vast expanse of Tehran, stretching out in all directions like tentacles.

The princess also inquired about me in a very kind way. It was a strange and amusing situation, for although we were of the same generation—she was eighteen at the time and I was twenty—she performed her role as hostess with elegance and charm, while I had to make an effort to overcome my shyness.* Suddenly, there was the sound of voices and doors opening, and then someone arrived to tell us that the king was coming. Good Lord! I could feel my heart pounding. I was amazed and thrilled all at once. I was with the king's daughter, so there was nothing

*Princess Shahnaz already had a little daughter, Mahnaz, whom I would come to know later and whom I love dearly. Mahnaz, a little older than my elder son Reza, has remained very close to her uncles and aunts (my children).

really surprising in his calling unexpectedly to see her, but still, what luck that I should be there at the time! I thought with great delight that it was an extraordinary coincidence.

The king appeared, relaxed and smiling, rather different from the reserved and seemingly sad man I had briefly met two months earlier in Paris. The princess and Mr. Zahedi introduced me, and the king sat down with us quite informally. He began talking to me straightaway, but he did it with such warmth, smiling and nodding his head in approval as soon as I began to speak, that I immediately forgot my surroundings. I think I managed to speak very naturally, in spite of the intense emotion I was feeling. In reply to his questions I told him about my life as a student in Paris, and my memory is of an easy, happy conversation in which we both enjoyed our eye contact and our flow of dialogue, forgetting for a moment where we were. With hindsight, I think that it was really a blessed moment, and I thank heaven for it, for without the freedom of expression in this first interview, perhaps we would have gone our separate ways.

At the time I had no idea of what would come of our meeting. In my mind it was the result of a miraculous stroke of luck, and so when I arrived back home, sure that I had just had a unique experience that would never be repeated, I just exploded. I described it all to my mother, then to my uncle and aunt, and my excitement ran through the whole household. Spending an hour with the king was indeed a historic event that would leave its mark on the family for decades to come.

One or two weeks went by, which I spent working at the Tehran Museum of Archeology. Life was following its usual routine once more, my excitement had lessened a little but was still there within me like a buried treasure, when I received a dinner invitation from Princess Shahnaz. This time I had an inkling that some plan was being devised concerning me. What if the king had not come by chance the other day, but especially to see me? Could it be that after interviewing me, Ardeshir Zahedi thought I might appeal to the king? If so, he would have had the idea of organizing an initial informal meeting while I was with the princess. That could have been the end of it, but now the princess was inviting me again, not for tea but for dinner. The king was not mentioned, naturally, but I was sure he would be there. Then it all came back to me: the sad look in his eyes in Paris, everything I had read about his divorce from Empress Soraya eighteen months earlier, and what people had said about the king wanting to marry again, to secure the succession and have a family which, at thirty-nine, would bring him a happiness that life had refused him so far. I couldn't get over it. Why had our king's gaze suddenly fallen on me? As for me, I felt an attraction to him that I would never have acknowledged had he not given me this reason to do so. I found the king extremely attractive, naturally endowed as he was with all the intellectual qualities a woman could wish for in the man close to her heart. His gentle, serious look, which could still be indulgent and warm, and his lovely smile touched me deeply. And there were other details I liked: the way he held his head, his long eyelashes, which I found unutterably romantic, his hands. Yes, I was secretly won over, charmed by him.

He would tell me later that he liked my naturalness. I think that first casual meeting is what gave me the strength—or the lack of awareness—to forget my shyness and calmly enter a situation that could have paralyzed me with fear. At the dinner we once again fell into the familiar, playful, almost affectionate tone that had charmed both of us at that first meeting. During the meal I dared to ask him if he remembered having met me at the Iranian Embassy in Paris. The importance I placed on every detail obviously amused him greatly. For him, such tiny moments scarcely register in an official visit. He laughed, and so did I.

Then there were other meetings at the princess's house, in particular an afternoon when a lot of us were playing quoits and I, quite naturally and without making anything of it, went and picked up the rubber rings for all the others. Was that the day the king chose me to be his wife and the mother of his children? He considered it, most certainly, but still gave himself time to think it over.

We became friendly enough for him to invite me out from time to time for a drive around Tehran. Sports cars were his passion, one of the few material things in life that he cared about, together with watches. So we would leave town for an hour or two in a fast car, followed at a discreet distance by a security car. We got to know each other, he more than I, because I still did not dare ask him questions, but our conversations or our silences were always relaxed. He had a real gift for putting me at my ease with a word or a smile, and so I could just enjoy the pleasure of being there beside him. It was both easy and intoxicating at the same time.

One day he invited me to take the seat beside him in a small jet. It was known that he was a very good pilot. The airplane was a French Morane-Saulnier four-seater, and I think that Princess Shahnaz was with us. He flew us over Tehran, then we climbed up over the Alborz Mountains. It was magic. Then we suddenly dived down over the lake at the Sefid Rud dam, which he wanted to show me. My uncle Sa'adi worked there as an agricultural engineer. The plane went through a lot of turbulence, as that area is always very windy, but I was completely unconcerned about any possible danger. On the way back, when the airport was in sight, he unexpectedly increased altitude and circled over the suburbs of Tehran. Finally he asked me to take one of the controls that was between us and "pump." I did so without asking for any explanation, absolutely unaware of the situation we were in. A few minutes later he began his approach and made a smooth landing. It was then I noticed that there were fire trucks on the runway, and that several ambulances with lights flashing were also waiting there.

"Did something happen up there?" I asked.

"The undercarriage wouldn't come down," he told me calmly. "You got the wheels out manually. Everything's all right. Let's get out."

We could have been killed, but he remained completely calm through it all.

THE SUMMER WOULD SOON BE OVER. I learned through Mr. Zahedi that the king had asked my uncle for photos of me. There was no longer any doubt about it. The king had feelings for me that went beyond friendship. As for me, I was more and more in love with him. Everything about the man affected me, moved me deeply. These feelings, which were so strong and disturbing for a girl coming to know love for the first time, were mixed with pride at having been chosen by someone unique, the most admired and respected person in the land.

He let it be known that he would like to spend an afternoon with me in the palace to talk and take a swim in his private pool. I brought my swimsuit with me and we swam together. When I think of moments like these, I thank heaven for having given me a natural disposition and an untroubled mind. Without such innate sincerity and disdain for show, I think it would have been impossible to be able to stand calmly there in a swimsuit, at twenty years of age, in the company of the most important man in the country. The king himself found such naturalness surprising, and I remember saying to him that I fitted easily into whatever circumstances I found myself. It was a disturbing and delightful afternoon.

Then for several days—maybe it was two or three weeks—I heard nothing more. Why? What was going on? I felt upset, but what were my feelings compared with his responsibilities? Though he was already a large part of my life, I was well aware that the same was not necessarily true in his case. How much room was there for love in the life of a head of state? I thought only of him; he must have had so many problems of all kinds to resolve before finding the time to think of me. Perhaps he had forgotten me. It was September and the date of my return to the École Spéciale d'Architecture in the Boulevard Raspail was approaching. What should I do? Quietly go back to Paris as if nothing had ever happened? No, I decided to find out; I asked my uncle to inquire from Mr. Zahedi: could I go back to my studies in France?

Much later the king confessed jokingly that I had rushed him that summer, so that he would make up his mind quickly. But at the time the message was to wait, so I stayed where I was and let the date for the beginning of the semester come and go. Another invitation from Princess Shahnaz arrived at last.

There were a lot of us there with the king that evening, maybe twenty. I was happy and relieved to see him again. The conversation was light and the king smiled, showing nothing of the cares and tensions that must invariably have been on his mind. As we were in the drawing room, I suddenly noticed that the guests were leaving one by one. The King and I were there alone on a sofa. Then he told me very calmly something of his two former marriages: the first to Princess Fawzia of Egypt, who had given him his daughter Shahnaz, the young princess, and the second with Soraya Esfandiari Bakhtiari, who he had vainly hoped would give him a son. Then he stopped talking, took my hand, and gazing into my eyes, said to me, "Will you consent to be my wife?" Yes! I replied yes straightaway, because there was no need to think about it, because I had no reservations. It was yes, I loved him and was ready to follow him.

I did not really know what that yes implied: that by becoming his wife I would have to shoulder some very heavy responsibilities. "As queen," he added, "you will have a lot of responsibilities toward the Iranian people." Once again I agreed. I knew about responsibility. I had been raised in that spirit. My parents, my family, school, and Scouts had constantly worked toward awakening my mind to the suffering of others; they had taught me that the ideal should be to work for the common good. The king's warning did not therefore catch me unawares. I felt that I was just the right person to carry out that task. However, I had no idea on what scale: I did not realize the weight or the extent of the mission ahead of me.

IT WAS 14 OCTOBER 1959, my birthday. I was twenty-one and I had just said yes to the king. Yes to his love, and to the special destiny that love entailed. I was going to become queen for the best, and also for the worst, which I was far from being able to imagine. As he left me, the king asked me to keep the news secret for the moment. I couldn't hide it from my family. It was too much happiness, too much excitement. As soon as I got home, I told my mother and my aunt everything; I also told my uncle when he came home from the office a little later. Visibly overcome, Mother had a hard time hiding the apprehension behind her expressions of joy. Of course she shared my happiness, but she confessed to me later that she had immediately wondered whether my father would have approved. It was said that life at court was riddled with intrigue, with gossip about this one and that one, that the queen mother was like this, the princesses like that....Could a naïve, straightforward girl like me, my mother wondered, find her place among people raised in the court, used to power plays, double-talk, and the subtleties of diplomacy? She was worried, but what could she say or do? And what would be the use?

The same day, unable to calm down, I called my friend Elli.

"Come to the house right away. I've got something to tell you."

"What? Tell me now!"

"I can't tell you on the phone. Take a taxi and come over. Hurry! Hurry!"

"Farah! Are you mad! Tell me, what's the matter?"

"A great piece of news."

"You're getting married!"

"Yes!"

"But that's wonderful! Who to? Do I know him? Tell me his name."

"That's it. I can't. You'll find out when you come. You've already taken at least five minutes!"

"I'll never be able to wait." She began to reel off the names of all my cousins. "Reza. I bet it's Reza."

"Are you crazy? Reza's like a brother to me."

"Kamran?"

"Think again!"

"Parviz? Yahya?"

"No. It's not Parviz or Yahya."

Finally, after mentioning everyone she could think of, she said with a laugh, "Well, that only leaves the king."

"It's him!"

She dropped the receiver and for quite some time she could not utter a sound.

SHORTLY AFTERWARDS, the king told me that he wanted to introduce me to his family, and to the most important of them all, the queen mother, Taj al Molouk. As the second wife of the founder of the Pahlavi dynasty, who died in 1944, Taj al Molouk had given him four children: Princess Shams, born 27 October 1917; then Mohammad Reza, my future husband, and his twin sister, Princess Ashraf, both born on 16 October 1919; and lastly Prince Ali Reza who died in an airplane accident in 1954. The queen mother had the reputation of being a rather difficult person. It was said that people feared her outspokenness and also that she had had words with Empress Soraya, annoyed by Soraya's casual attitude, which was all the more pronounced because it hid the anguish Soraya felt at not being able to give the king—and the queen mother—the heir they hoped for.

This first meeting with a woman who was a historical figure and not to be crossed was intimidating. Even if it was not described as such, this encounter was a kind of final exam. The king had suffered from the tensions between his mother, his sisters, and Soraya; it would be a token of happiness for us all if good relations were established between his family and myself from the start.

When I entered the reception room, the king took me up to his mother, who was seated by herself on a sofa. After the customary words, the queen mother asked me to come and sit with her. I instinctively sat down on a little pouf so that I was close enough for her to talk to me but on a slightly lower level. Thus began our conversation, or rather a form of questioning with which I was happy to comply. She asked me about my tastes, my childhood, and my family (my mother and Aunt Louise had known members of the queen mother's family and had been at school with her sisters) and my aspirations. My future mother-in-law naturally wanted to know who and what I was. She was a small but imposing woman with pale green eyes. I would have liked my children to have the same. I was not alone with her which made things easier for a first meeting. All the people who were invited to this interview had eyes only for the girl that I was.

It is certain that on that day the king's inner circle saw me as an unaffected girl who knew nothing of their world of courtiers and diplomats.

PART TWO

Chapter 6

MY ENGAGEMENT TO Mohammad Reza Pahlavi, the Shah of Iran, was not to be officially announced until 21 November 1959, that is, more than a month after we had sealed our destinies in private. During this time it was agreed that I should unobtrusively return to Paris to put together a wardrobe suitable for my future position. Our ambassador to France, Nassrollah Entezam, was let into the secret and was naturally requested to give me every assistance.

And so, on 3 November I left for Paris, accompanied by my uncle Esfandiar Diba, his wife, Banou, and my aunt Louise, who had been so important to me all my life. Having them by my side was very reassuring: they would keep me company and would help me to put together this trousseau that was so very special and, to tell the truth, impossible to imagine for the thrifty student that I was.

The plane made a stop in Geneva, where we touched down in the middle of the afternoon. I had found out that the president of the Iranian Parliament, Sardar Fakher Hekmat, was on board, so I was not surprised to see a group of photographers gathered around the foot of the gangway. When I went down to the terminal where we were to wait awhile, the photographers took no notice of me. Then suddenly, when my uncle and aunts and I had almost reached the building, an unbelievable crush built up around us. Among the shouts and the crackle of the flashbulbs, I was astonished to hear my name being called—"Farah Diba! Farah Diba! Are you Farah Diba?"—and as I nodded, questions came at me from all sides. "When will the wedding take place? How do you feel about becoming empress? Where are you staying in Paris?"

I was stunned. I had been naïve enough to think that the secret of our engagement would be scrupulously kept and respected, and now I found that I had become a celebrity, not only without wanting to, but without having prepared myself for it in the slightest. I had never seen these photographers before, but they knew me—obviously not very well yet, since they had let me pass at first. Now my face, shot by a barrage of cameras, would go all the way around the world. From that moment my freedom to come and go as I pleased like any other woman became a thing of the past, although I didn't know it at the time.

"We can't say anything. We don't know anything. Please, let us through!" my uncle said, trying to make himself heard, but like me, quite overtaken by these events.

I felt immense relief as we boarded the plane again, this time protected by the airport staff. My uncle, aunts, and I exchanged our impressions of what had happened, thinking that we were safe at last from prying eyes and ears. However, I learned later that a journalist had managed to get a seat next to mine on the Geneva-Paris flight. Fortunately we had spoken nothing but Persian.

The reception at Orly, when we arrived in the evening, was on a very different scale from the one we had encountered in Geneva. This time the airport tarmac was swarming with journalists and photographers. I had never seen such a crush, and I could hardly believe that I was the reason for it, having left Paris from this same airport four months earlier without anyone taking the slightest notice. Every means possible was used to separate me from this frenzied trampling mob screaming my name. I was pushed and pulled; there were so many flashes I could see nothing; I had no idea where I was being led; I even lost a shoe on the grass at the side of the runway. It was only after a quarter of an hour of this shock treatment that I suddenly landed in the padded, protective interior of a luxury car, the official car of the Iranian embassy.

I was groggy but able to smile and laugh at the reception nonetheless. Once in the car, however, I scarcely had time to catch my breath, for as soon as the doors were shut, we were literally trapped. Flashes lit up the inside of the car, and as we could not move, I felt like an animal tracked by men who hunt at night to dazzle their prey. The driver finally managed to get us away. Then began a chase that nearly drove me mad. Pursued by photographers on motorbikes zooming almost under our wheels at breakneck speed, I was screaming, thinking that we would kill one of them at any moment. The result was that they took a series of photos of me with my mouth wide open and my face contorted with fear, photos they later made the most of when they claimed I was unhappy.

Under these conditions, my arrival at the Hôtel de Crillon did not pass unnoticed, and the following morning the people of Paris were informed that the future Queen of Iran was staying in this luxury hotel overlooking the Place de la Concorde. That news naturally increased the pressure from the journalists, and for the two or three weeks of my stay, I hardly ever left the hotel without being chased by an armada of cars and motorbikes. They managed to thwart everything we did to put them off the trail. How could they be everywhere at once? I began to understand when I learned that a journalist had bribed a bellboy into letting him put on his uniform so that he could get closer to me. This harassment by the press must have been in response to public expectation, for from the very first, I could sense people's natural curiosity, and above all their goodwill. Indeed, despite the journalists—or perhaps because of them—I had many wonderful and emotional moments throughout the trip. One cannot resist spontaneous affection, and the strong links I have had with France all my life, and with Parisians in particular, go back to these whirlwind days when everywhere I met nothing but smiles and applause, in spite of the traffic jams sometimes caused by nothing more than my presence.

The young sovereign of Iran had touched French hearts well before I ever came into his life. As I talked with people, I soon realized how aware they were of the difficulties he had encountered during his life. They remembered the troubled circumstances that had brought him, at barely twenty-one, to succeed his father, who had been forced into exile by British and Soviet troops occupying Iran. The French public had been touched by his separation in 1947 from the romantic and melancholy Princess Fawzia, who had spent the war years at his side, but finally returned to the Egypt she had always missed so much. Even more touching was the despair that descended on the king's second marriage, with Soraya Esfandiari, when it appeared that she could not give him the child he hoped for. A lot had been said and written in France about the obvious grief felt by the monarch right up to his divorce, when I was in my first year of architecture studies in Paris. And now, here was the king who had touched their hearts about to marry an ex-student of the Boulevard Raspail.

The fact that through love alone I went from my little room in the Cité Universitaire to the Palace of Everlasting Persia stirred the tender, romantic souls of the French and played a large part in securing their affection. The king was not marrying a princess; he was not giving in to the convention of arranged marriages between families of royal blood. No, he had fallen in love with a "little Iranian girl" and, as in the fairy tales, he was going to follow his heart. It was almost too good to be true. But not good enough, it seems, for some journalists, who saw in it an opportunity to revive the Cinderella myth. Consequently, they exaggerated the facts, and I was occasionally described as a shepherdess brought up in poverty. My uncle despaired of them. "In a while they'll tell us that you were born in the gutter! It's unbelievable! Unbelievable!" It didn't matter to me. I never thought that a person's worth came from birth or wealth, and much later when I was queen, and then in exile, I had ample proof of it. In any case, what could we do to establish the truth? Nothing had been said officially, and for the moment I was just a young woman royally accommodated in a suite in the Hôtel de Crillon, doing the rounds of the couturiers and the boutiques with the blessing of the Iranian embassy.

I remember one particular visit to Guerlain on the Champs Élysées. There was such a pack of photographers and cameramen on my heels that it had temporarily stopped the traffic on the most beautiful avenue in the world while I chose some perfume. It was incredible! But the worst was probably at the Carita sisters, who had been given the task of creating a new hairstyle for me. Maria Carita described the event to Lesley Blanch, who reproduced it in her biography of me.*

> One of the ladies from the Iranian Embassy made an appointment, as she often did, and then seemed very anxious that both of us should be around that day: she said she was bringing in a special friend—that it would be better to be in one of the private

*Lesley Blanch, *Farah Shahbanou of Iran,* Collins. London 1978

> cubicles. She seemed so insistent on that point—we wondered what sort of extraordinary creature she was bringing!…On the morning of the appointment, we heard the most alarming noise outside in the street, much shouting and confusion…it sounded like an angry mob. When we looked out we saw the whole entrance completely blocked by men and cameras—movie cameras too—all fighting for place. At that moment, our client and her mysterious friend got out of a car, and it was a free-for-all, as a police escort tried to force a way for the ladies through the mass of reporters. They were got inside, somehow, and we managed to close the doors on this roaring mob—though they continued to try to storm in, and some of them even found a way round over the roofs, and were getting in from the back. By then, we had learned who our new client was. It was very exciting, and of course we went to all sorts of lengths to protect her, in the days that followed.
>
> Madame Rosie recalled how shy, how silent this special client remained when the discussions over styles of coiffure, or nuances of maquillage, went on round her. 'She hardly spoke, but she did not seem at all unsure of herself—just silent, observing everything with an extreme concentration. She realized we knew what we were about, and she preferred to learn from our experience. We had to try all kinds of styles, chignons and braids, curls even, though that is not really her style. We had to reckon with the heavy tiaras and coronets she would be wearing too. They looked absurd on any everyday short hair style. She was such a pretty girl, beautifully made, with such lovely hands, and that intense, blue-black hair, like you see in the Persian miniatures…'

They had to put sheets across the windows, which immediately made us feel like creatures in a cage, yet one journalist succeeded in taking my photo from the building opposite, where he had taken up his post. That was the day the Carita sisters created that hairstyle for me with the parting down the middle and hair over the temples, which was copied all over the world. Women asked to have their hair done "like Farah Diba."

At Dior I was shown the collection created by Yves Saint Laurent. He was to design my engagement and wedding dresses.

During this whirlwind of activity I was able to go to the premiere of *Carmen* at the Opera Garnier. General and Madame de Gaulle were present, as well as several ministers and the whole of Paris society. It was a thrill to have a close-up view of the man who had saved France and whom my uncle Bahram admired so much, but I soon noticed, to my great embarrassment, that the general's entourage had eyes only for me. The future that awaited me was known, of course, to those at the highest state level, and no doubt they were curious to see what I looked like. I didn't suspect that two years later, as Queen of Iran, I would be so affectionately received at the Élysée Palace by the general and his wife.

It was during that stay in Paris that the great writer André Malraux showed me his interest and friendship by writing this inscription in my copy of his book, *The Voices of Silence*, which I had sent to him with a note a few days before my return to Tehran as a student.

> It is moving, Mademoiselle, that one of the most faithful admirers of the spirit of Iran should be in your mind at the time when you are leaving us. I hope that the student who was thoughtful enough to write to me will tell the empress that I love the great power of enchantment that in Iran today is associated with your destiny, and I heartily wish that the fairies of France, still very much alive, join those of Iran to watch over your happiness.
>
> —André Malraux, November, 1959.

The king called me every evening. The expectation of this contact lit up my day and gave meaning to everything I was doing, since it all basically had only one aim: to prepare for the life we were going to build together. I remember that my heart literally gave a jolt when I heard he was on the telephone. I was very much in love, and I had to make an effort to keep my voice from trembling with emotion. He was also moved; I could hear it. He would assure me, a long time later, that he had said "I love you" to only three women. "One of them is you," he told me.

OUR ENGAGEMENT WAS OFFICIALLY ANNOUNCED in a brief communiqué on 21 November: "Today, at five o'clock in the Ekhtessassi Palace, the engagement took place of His Majesty the Shahanshah Mohammad Reza Pahlavi, King of Iran, and Miss Farah Diba. The wedding will be celebrated in one month, on 29 azar 1338, according to the Iranian solar calendar, 21 December 1959, according to the Christian calendar."

When I returned from Paris, my lifestyle was completely changed. I no longer lived with my mother in my uncle's big house. From now on the king wanted me to stay within the palace compound. The queen mother had gone temporarily to her country house and kindly lent me her private apartments so that the king could receive me there.

I lived these last weeks before my marriage in a state of great excitement. Now the king was breathing and working only a few hundred yards from me, and I could see him from my windows. Bit by bit, I also discovered what the timetable of a head of state was like, and how few and precious were the private moments he could take. King for over eighteen years, although he was only just forty, the man who was to be my husband had perfect management of the different areas that made up his existence. I saw him receive the official visit of President Eisenhower during that month of December 1959, preside over all the ceremonies that had been arranged, and still find time to take a walk with me in the garden, or chat over a cup of tea, apparently calm and relaxed.

Autumn is my favorite season. The trees blaze with color in the slanting sunlight; the Alborz Mountains release that cool air we vainly long for all summer; one feels miraculously at one with nature. The king knew how I loved the light color of these blessed months, and almost every day we would discreetly flee the palace together in one of his cars. At that time security was not the ever-present worry it has become since, so only two bodyguards followed us in their own car. The faces of the people in the streets lit up the moment they recognized the king. They waved, they clapped, and he gave them a little wave in return. I was filled with wonder and emotion to be suddenly linked with a man who inspired such adoration. I remember when I was a child, holding my mother's hand and waving to him in similar circumstances on the roadside near the Caspian Sea. He seemed to turn a little in his seat and smile back at us. I told him about it once. Of course he had no memory of that moment, but he spontaneously smiled at me just as he had that afternoon.

It was during these weeks that I became better acquainted with the king's brothers and sisters, as most of them lived near the palace. With his first wife, Reza Shah had had a daughter, Princess Hamdam Saltaneh, whom I met. I have already mentioned Princess Ashraf, the king's twin sister, and Princess Shams, their elder sister, both children of Reza Shah's marriage with the Queen Mother Taj al Molouk. However, Reza Shah had had two other marriages as well, which produced six children. Gholam-Reza was born from his marriage with Queen Touran. From his marriage with Queen Esmat came Prince Abdol-Reza, Prince Ahmad-Reza, Prince Mahmoud-Reza, Princess Fatemeh, and

Prince Hamid-Reza. To me as a young student and a novice in matters of protocol, it could easily have seemed impossible to find a place among all these brothers- and sisters-in-law, who were all very concerned that their prerogatives and rank should receive due respect. When I became aware of these jostling interests, I had a better understanding of my mother's anxiety on my behalf: what would become of her daughter, who was still so naïve, in a court reported to be full of intrigue and power play? I did what I had done in my childhood. I refused to take part in the quarrels, spoken or unspoken, that inevitably arose, and I maintained the attitude that was part of my nature: to bring harmony wherever possible and turn a deaf ear to everything that tried to deflect me from it. I did not allow myself to be drawn into the pettiness and disagreements to which, unfortunately, no family is immune. During my life as queen, I would maintain this attitude, which had been firmly established from my earliest years. I believed that it would not be difficult, as I would have the constant support and love of the king, who disliked meanness intensely. As an Iranian, I have a natural respect for the family, and I knew that it was essential that the king, who had so much else to occupy his mind, should have harmonious surroundings in his private life. Today, I can say that I have constantly maintained good relations with all the king's family.

Chapter 7

WE ALL AWOKE at the crack of dawn on the morning of 21 December 1959. My wedding was to be celebrated in the early afternoon and, for that last night, I had gone back to my uncle's house to be with my family. The dress designed by Yves Saint Laurent was there on the hanger but, before putting it on, I had to put myself into the expert hands of the Carita sisters, who had come specially from Paris to do my hair. They seemed even more excited and nervous than I was, and so I set about reassuring them, which brought a little laughter. It would be a long, emotional day, and I wanted everyone to enjoy it.

The tiara was delivered after breakfast. As the crown jewels are the property of the state and guarantee the currency, they very rarely leave the vaults of the Central Bank of Iran. The authorization has to be countersigned by several people, including the Minister of Finance. I was to wear a tiara made from the Crown Jewels of Iran designed by Harry Winston. It was incredibly beautiful, but this priceless object had the disadvantage of weighing nearly two kilos.

That gives some idea of the challenge faced by my hairdressers: to set this marvel on a head unaccustomed to performing balancing acts, and even less to staying still. The task was all the more difficult as I had to wear the tiara until evening, travel several miles in a car, go up and down stairs, walk, smile, greet people....They worked for three full hours, and I don't think they really breathed easily until the next morning when they learned that nothing dreadful had happened.

As I put on my dress embroidered with Persian motifs in silver thread, sequins and pearls (imitation, of course), I had a kind thought for the dressmakers at the House of Dior in Paris. They had wished me all the happiness in the world, and I know that they had sewn one hem with blue so that the good fairies would at last give the king the son he so desired.

At last, at the appropriate time, Princess Shahnaz, whose affection had been so invaluable in those last weeks, Prime Minister Manouchehr Eghbal, and Minister of Court Hossein Ala arrived to take me to the king. The religious service was to be celebrated at the Marble Palace right in the heart of Tehran, and so we had a long way to travel from the wooded slopes of Shemiran.

Following the custom of Muslims, who place themselves under the protection of the Koran before any important event, I walked under the sacred book held by my mother as I left the porch. Then, as a last gesture of good luck, I freed some doves, which we watched for a moment as they flew up into the milky blue sky of that first day of winter. The Twenty-first of December in Iran is Shab-e-Yalda, the longest night of the year, which families celebrate by gathering together to read poems of Hafez and share melons, pomegranates, and dried fruits. Also on that day and the following day, we stay up late, as we are symbolically celebrating the conquest of light.

The cavalcade of cars slowly began its journey. Then I saw that the streets were thick with people. They had massed all along our route, and they had most certainly been there for several hours. Their faces lit up as we passed; everyone waved and clapped, and I heard the hubbub of my name being repeated over and over again. Naturally, I had never been the object of such enthusiasm, such fervor, and a lump came to my throat. The people of Tehran, from whom I came, were giving me their trust, adopting me, honoring me, although I had done nothing yet either for them or for Iran. I felt so moved and overcome that I promised myself I would do everything in my power for these men and women, and for the children I could see perched everywhere. It occurred to me only much later that I was replacing a queen they had loved and applauded in the same way, and in spite of everything they had come in the thousands. I thought they deserved to be thanked twice over. I learned later that my countrymen were happy that the king was marrying an Iranian. And the clergy, knowing that I was a Seyedeh, a descendant of the Prophet, said that in marrying me the king became the son-in-law of the Prophet.

The king was waiting for me at the top of the grand staircase of the Marble Palace, standing very straight and tall in his ceremonial uniform. As soon as I got out of the car, six little girls dressed in white with coronets of flowers fell in behind me, but one pageboy, my little cousin Ahmad Hossein, went before us strewing petals on the steps. I don't know who felt more emotion—the king or I. Our marriage would be celebrated in a few moments, and it was only then that I realized I had no ring for him! No one had thought of it, least of all me, but it is the bride who should bring the ring. Ardeshir Zahedi, the king's son-in-law, came to the rescue by giving me his, which a few moments later I put on my husband's finger. A few days later I gave him a wedding ring, and since his death I wear both our wedding rings on the same finger.

Only our families and a few members of the government had been invited. We wanted it to be an intimate ceremony, as is usually the case in Iran for religious weddings. According to custom, all the symbols of a fruitful, happy marriage had been laid on a carpet: a mirror and candles for light, bread for plenty, incense to ward off evil, candy for the sweetness of life, and of course the Koran. The Imam Jome of Tehran recited the verses that precede the union of two people. Then, raising his eyes, he asked me solemnly if I would take the man by my side to be my husband. Contrary to the tradition which requires the fiancée to be persuaded and not to agree until the third time she is asked, this time the imam did not have to wait: I answered yes immediately with a spirit and joy that raised smiles and murmurs around us.

Shortly afterwards two representatives of the civil state brought us the official register, and I thought to myself, as I wrote it for the first time, that Farah Pahlavi would be my signature from now on and forever.

When I saw the photos of the ceremony with all its moving moments, I felt slightly disappointed. Because of my train, I could not sit in an armchair like the king, and so I had been put on a stool, which made me half a head taller than my husband. There had not been a single person, among all those protocol people so experienced in what is proper and elegant, who had thought that it would have been more fitting, and also more harmonious, to have the sovereign at least on the same level as his wife.

After a short moment's respite with the family, we went on to the sumptuous old Golestan Palace—the former residence of the Qajar kings now used only for ceremonial occasions—where more than a thousand guests were waiting for us. I went through this magical reception in a haze, so my memory of it is dazzling but vague. All the faces around us seemed to share our happiness, whether they were close friends and relatives or officials.

A FEW DAYS LATER WE LEFT FOR RAMSAR, a small seaside town on the Caspian Sea. We traveled as far as Sari in the royal carriage, which is attached to a normal train for these occasions, then we went on to Ramsar by car. We had decided to spend our honeymoon in this region which we both loved, rather than abroad. I often used to tease the king about this, saying, "People realized, from the time of our wedding, that you had married a real Iranian girl."

I still have a vivid memory of this journey to Ramsar. For the first time as queen I was traveling through the interior, our arid mountains, then the verdant plain of Mazandaran. The train stopped at every village and people were waiting for us everywhere, dressed in their best, so proud and happy to greet us. The women touched me, kissed me, and I glimpsed a look of pride in the men's eyes at showing the king a brand-new school, orphanage, or factory that was soon to be opened. It showed me what faith the people had in the man to whom I myself had just given my whole life.

In all these public exchanges with welcoming crowds, he who was so attentive in private was always slightly aloof. Iranians would certainly not have understood or liked it if their sovereign had become familiar, but I saw that the king's reserve often kept him from expressing the warmth he felt for those who were welcoming him. Consequently, I frequently used to urge him to smile, certain that the expression would convey much more than words: "Smile for the photos. You're so handsome and people will see what's in your heart." A few years later, when I asked our second son, Ali-Reza, who was three or four, to do the same, he replied without moving a muscle, "No, I don't want to smile. I want to stay like Daddy." Those who were traditional Iranians liked that the king appeared serious on all occasions.

We got to know more about each other during this first holiday together. The king was a great sportsman and a particularly good horseback rider. Sport became something that we both shared and enjoyed. Here at least he was completely relaxed and regained a youthful sense of playfulness. We had never laughed so much before. I remember wanting to learn to ride a motor scooter: I went too fast and fell off. As a result, Her Majesty the Empress—this was the official title given to me on my wedding day—had skinned knees, which amused the king and the photographers even more, and gave a more natural, or at least a less formal, style to our everyday life.

We stayed in the Grand Hotel at Ramsar, the only hotel in the town. Built in the monumental style of Reza Shah, the hotel overlooked the main thoroughfare. The days passed pleasantly, with visits to tea plantations in the area, long walks, the parlor games Iranians like to play, and dinners with the family.

I remember having given a brief interview to the correspondent of the London *Times* during which I told him that I was going to devote my life "to the service of the Iranian people" and in particular to women, giving them the opportunity to study and work. Once back in Tehran, I realized how far I was from being able to be of service to anyone. Isolated in the palace, where the king worked from morning till night, I had no idea of the tools that had to be put in place to make action possible. The work of being a queen had still to be learned.

THE FIRST THING I FACED WAS BOREDOM. Only six months ago I had been feverishly preparing for my architecture exams. I had never been inactive since primary school, and suddenly, through force of circumstance, I was. The palace staff had no need of me in the running of the household. If I wanted a particular menu, I said so, but if I didn't, the chef managed perfectly well without my advice. Besides, if I ventured to suggest a change in the usual order of things, I was respectfully told that it had always been done in that way, and so I did not insist. Apart from my maid, Momtaz, whom I had known since I was a small child and who had come to the palace with me, and my nanny, Monavar, who came now and again, all the people around me had served the court for years and were much more experienced than I in the customs of the palace.

Little by little, as mistress of the house I would intervene in details for a reception, but it would never be a role that interested me. On the other hand, from the very beginning I wanted to do something concrete, to work for the country. But how should I go about it? That was the question that occupied my mind at that time.

Rereading the official diary of my first weeks as queen, I see that it follows the pattern of what was expected of the shah's wife in those days:

> 8 January 1960. The 17 day (Iranian Women's Liberation Day) was celebrated in the presence of the Shahanshah and H. M. the Empress.
>
> 9 January 1960. H. M. the Empress visited the Pasteur Institute.
>
> 13 January 1960. H. M. the Empress kindly visited the Institute for the Protection of Mothers and Newborn Children and inspected the various sections of the Institute.
>
> 16 January 1960. The Shahanshah and H. M. the Empress inspected the Farabi Hospital. On this occasion, Professor Shams presented the special ophthalmology Charter and respectfully requested H. M. the Empress to become chief patron.
>
> 17 January 1960. H. M. the Empress inspected the TB Hospital and the new building, which has 400 beds.
>
> 19 January 1960. H. M. the Empress inspected the various sections of the Shah Abad Sanatorium.

24 January 1960. The Centre for the Prevention of Tuberculosis on the Avenue Mowlavi was opened by H. M. the Empress.

28 January 1960. H. M. the Empress inspected Reza Shah the Great High School.

30 January 1960. The Festival of the Student Union of the University of Tehran took place in the presence of H. M. the Empress.

I inspected, I opened buildings and institutes, but while doing so, I watched, I listened, and I learned. At the same time I received a lot of correspondence. These letters were extremely affecting: the often awkwardly expressed accounts of tragic situations enabled me to learn about the problems of the moment. In the farthest provinces people were still suffering great poverty, infant mortality was high, schools were few and far between, children lacked hygiene and were weakened by malnutrition.

I could not remain unmoved by these appeals. I had to reply, to give them hope, but what could I say? The government might already have been working on the question, in which case I wanted to find out about it. If not, it was up to me to be the voice of these unfortunate people within the government. I quickly spoke about it with my husband. He knew the problems I had taken to heart and he had been working to resolve them little by little for years, but fortunately he encouraged me in this course of action. "I'll arrange for you to be informed of what the government is doing," he told me. And indeed, a few days later he sent me an outstanding man to act as my principal private secretary, Mr. Fazlollah Nabil.

As an ex-ambassador, universally respected and very knowledgeable about the workings of the executive, Fazlollah Nabil was just the man I needed. Thanks to his experience—he was old enough to be my father—I learned first of all how to get organized. Then, guided by him and the appropriate officials, I quickly began to familiarize myself with development projects already under way and reforms planned for the future. We could then begin the work of conveying information to my correspondents and proposals to the government. He also took over the arrangement of my daily schedule, and soon I began to meet ministers and a wide variety of representatives of civil life. Throughout my time as queen my door was always open to these men and women who guided me and later helped me create various associations for the promotion of health, hygiene, education, and also culture, which we undertook together.

My eagerness to work and help the king quickly encountered the most marvelous handicap: two months after our marriage, I found that I was expecting a child. My husband's face lit up when he heard the news. I had never seen him so filled with silent emotion. The thought that I would perhaps be able to give him that happiness he had vainly sought for twenty years also gave me the greatest possible joy. We decided to wait for a few more weeks before making the announcement, but from the first moment our lives were completely taken over by it. The king's habitual look, which had struck me as melancholy a year earlier in Paris, was now very different. His face lit up with a spark of joy as soon as he saw me.

We were the only ones to know the secret when we flew to Pakistan on 20 February. It was my first official trip and I was very excited about seeing that country for the first time. I was especially happy to accompany the king—we felt deeply close to each other from the very beginning of my pregnancy. I had, however, underestimated the severity of morning sickness, intensified by the overpowering heat in Pakistan. The worst moment, and in a way the most amusing in hindsight, occurred when I was traveling in a car next to the Pakistani president, General Ayub Khan. This charming man was telling me about various aspects of his country while I was wondering if I could hold out until we got to our destination. As soon as we arrived, I had to rush to the bathroom. There were so many times during that trip that I had to be urgently accompanied to our quarters! The king made sure that it was not too difficult for me, but people must have wondered what on earth was wrong with me all the same. That did not stop me from appreciating the affection shown by the Pakistanis—we had always had friendly relations with our neighbor—and enjoying the cultural evenings, especially those in the wonderful gardens of Lahore. This was where we heard readings of Eghbal Lahoori's poetry in Persian. My interest in culture and the arts was becoming known. Later, when I set up the Shiraz Festival, we naturally invited Pakistani artists.

On the way back from Pakistan, we stopped for two or three days at Abadan on the Persian Gulf, which at that time had the largest oil refinery in the world and was one of the prides of the burgeoning Iranian economy. I was very glad to see our installations and meet the thousands of workers and engineers who were helping our country to get moving.

There also I had underestimated my state of health. I like the smell of gas, which these days always makes me homesick for Iran, but the sulfurous fumes of Abadan and the scorching heat made my morning sickness worse. Now I was being honored by the people, who wanted to see me and embrace me; I just could not be ill. If there is any heroism in being a public figure, it would be that: the absolute resolution to be there and return the affection shown you, when you would really like to be in bed. I was struck, despite my discomfort, by the hard living conditions in some quarters of Abadan and, on receiving a group of women, I made no secret of it. "While visiting the working-class districts," I said, "I felt that these families needed more attention and compassion. We should do something to help them, and as quickly as possible."

These trips, together with the large amount of correspondence I received, allowed me to gauge people's expectations. In 1925 Reza Shah had been handed the reins of an almost medieval country whose provinces lived under the yoke of local tribal chiefs or bandits. He had passed on to his son, my husband, a reasonably centralized administration and the first foundations of a modern economy. In spite of the progress already achieved, we were still an underdeveloped country, notably in the vital areas of education, health, agriculture, and communications. The people in far-flung villages were suffering; we were aware of it; something had to be done quickly. The money from oil, which had slipped out of our hands for so long, was now flowing into the state coffers. The king was optimistic and wanted me to share his confidence. "It's not possible to do everything for everyone overnight," he said to me, "but we will soon be able to speed up growth."

The future looked full of promise for the country—and for us, too. My pregnancy had not yet been officially announced, but people were already becoming impatient, in Iran of course, but also abroad. Parcels arrived at the palace for me every day: little blue bootees or various good-luck gifts, such as a piece of netting from a cradle that had only rocked boys. Princess Shams had insisted on summoning a Swiss doctor, Professor de Watteville, who, it was said, could give advice on how to have a boy rather than a girl. He came, but fortunately I was already expecting. An old seamstress, who had worked for my family, had assured me that writing a prayer on your belly with earth that had been blessed would guarantee a boy. I read the following amusing, silly item in a book recently published in Iran: I had a boy thanks to an Iranian doctor who concocted a diet for me based on mandarins and oranges! That people are still going on about it forty years after this pregnancy says a lot about the impatience and the hope it inspired.

At last on 20 March 1960, the eve of Now Ruz, the Iranian New Year, the court spokesman was authorized to announce the happy event. According to custom, we had waited three months before saying anything. Ultrasounds did not exist at that time and doctors could not determine the sex of the child. There were only more or less fanciful hypotheses based on the shape of the belly and the baby's heartbeat. The sense of impatience increased noticeably in Iran, and so did the parcels of bootees and other encouraging tokens. As usually happens in our country, the most improbable rumors circulated. It was claimed, for example, that I was not really pregnant but had put a cushion on my stomach. The source of this kind of misinformation was generally the Communist Tudeh Party and its sympathizers. It was also said that the shah was not the father because he could not have children. Later a rumor went round that my son was mute, and to stop it we had to show a film on television of the little prince babbling in his father's office. Then there was the idea that I had the baby in the big public hospital in the south of the city so that the girl I gave birth to could be exchanged for a boy.

Reza was born on 31 October 1960, shortly before midday. I had decided to go to the Institute for the Protection of Mothers and Newborn Children, in south Tehran, a working-class area. Built by Reza Shah, this hospital gave free care to the most needy women. My husband agreed to this, and he drove me there himself when the first contractions began. Very soon the whole family joined us.

I think the entire hospital knew it was a boy before I did. Toward the end of labor I had to be given an anesthetic, and the anesthetist overdid it somewhat (which enraged the obstetrician who was attending me, Professor Jahan Shah Saleh), for when I woke up, the corridors were already buzzing with the event. I was told later that people were running everywhere to tell the news to the king, and my anxious mother was vainly asking them, "How is my daughter? Do you have any news?"

When I opened my eyes, the king was at my bedside, holding my hand.

"Do you want to know?" he said gently.

"Yes."

"It's a boy!"

I burst into tears.

The official photo of Reza was taken three days later, and you could see how much he looked like his father. Next to him are Professor Jahan Shah Saleh and the pediatrician Dr. Lioussa Pirnia, who would be with us even in exile.

THOUSANDS OF PEOPLE HAD BEEN GATHERING in front of the hospital gates since dawn. Iranian and foreign journalists had already been camped there for days. As soon as the obstetrician announced that the Pahlavi dynasty had an heir at last, a twenty-one-gun salute was fired. The crowd at the doors of the hospital increased, to such an extent that my husband, who wanted to go and pray at the holy place, Shah Abdol-Azim, and reflect at his father's grave, was unable to reach the mausoleum and had to give up the idea for the moment. As soon as the crowd recognized his car, it broke through the security cordon and swarmed around him. He would tell me that he had never seen such an outpouring of universal joy and warmth. People were laughing and crying; they wanted to kiss him and, torn between the desire to do him honor and stand back to let him pass, they actually lifted up his car! At the same time, Iranians throughout the country went out into the street to celebrate the great event. They began to offer each other special candies that every family had made at home. There was dancing in the streets of Tehran, Tabriz, and Shiraz and other cities. When I saw the pictures of joy in the papers, I was filled with an extraordinary emotion. To think that the cause of all this happiness was this softly breathing little boy in my arms.

The news obviously went all around the world, but once again the prize for the best welcome went to France, where one of the daily newspapers had the idea of writing the headline, in Persian: *Pessar Ast!* "It's a boy!"

A few days later I received a magnificent tribute from the people of Tehran. Knowing that I was leaving the hospital to return to the palace, people had lined the route, spread carpets and flowers on the roadway, and put up triumphal arches here and there. I asked the driver to go slowly so that I could wave to them. I would have liked to tell every one of them how grateful I was for their presence and their affection.

Chapter 8

REZA'S ARRIVAL BOUND us more closely together. The child was such a joy! I would have greeted a girl with the same happy tears, but the fact that he was a boy added a sense of calm to my husband's happiness. It also gave our love a new harmony that was lighter, free from expectation, and more confident of the future.

In a few weeks I saw the king change completely. He who was usually so modest, so reserved, did not even try to hide the tenderness and emotion he felt for his son. As I was breast-feeding Reza, he would steal away between audiences to be there. He checked that the baby was feeding well, asked the French governess we had employed, Jeanne Guillon, to tell him again what height and weight he was, and recommended that she take special care to avoid a particular germ that had been mentioned in the papers. His great worry was that his son would not be as tall as he hoped. "Farah," he asked me, "why are his legs so bowed and so small? Are you sure it's normal?" I reminded him of that much later when Reza reached six feet and was taller than he was.

Our family life was now organized around Reza. I can remember how thrilled the king was, and so was I, when Reza took his first steps in the palace garden. On Fridays, which is a nonworking day, the three of us would sometimes go off into the country above Shemiran, weather permitting. The king would roll in the grass with his son, making up all sorts of games for him. They already shared a love of cars and especially planes. I remember that coming back to Tehran in the evening, Reza would sometimes be restless, and all that was needed to calm him was to tell him that we would soon be passing a cinema called the Moulin Rouge. The sails of the windmill fascinated him, as airplane propellers would when he was older. Even in the palace he would often stop in front of the fans. "Make them go round, please," he would say. And his eyes would light up with pleasure.

Then we began to worry: he didn't seem able to roll the *r* as we do in Persian. It was a worry for a future monarch, who has to speak in public. Did he have a malformation of the tongue? For months I had him repeating words like Rrrreza, darrria (sea), derrrakht (tree), before realizing that he was simply pronouncing the *r* in the French way, like his new governess, Joëlle Fouyet. Then we discovered that he was left-handed like his illustrious grandfather, Reza Shah. However, this comparison was not enough to reassure my husband's doctor, who was a soldier, General Abdol Karim Ayadi.

"It's not good for the crown prince to be left-handed," he kept telling me. "He must lose the habit."

And my reply was "No, it's not important. When the time comes for him to do a military salute, he'll do it with his right hand!"

The doctor was not convinced; my husband just smiled.

The king was more relaxed and laughed more readily despite a very heavy workload. As for me, queen and now mother, I remember several times slipping out of an official reception, sometimes wearing an evening dress and tiara, to discreetly feed my baby.

Our lives at that time had a certain pattern. Rising early, the king generally spent breakfast time reading Iranian and foreign newspapers and various reports that came in locked cases. Then he went to his office in the Marble Palace on the far side of a small square. We saw each other again at lunch, which over the years became a work meeting, but in the early days of our marriage was still a short time when we could relax. At two o'clock he listened to the news. This was sacrosanct—nothing would keep him from it—then he made it a rule to take a short siesta before resuming his audiences. He kept a moment in the evening before dinner to look at the papers again and do some exercise—dumbbells or weightlifting—then his valet gave him a massage and we would have dinner. Later Reza, then his brother and sisters, would often come in during the massage session and lie down next to the king, who would affectionately tickle their backs or necks.

Monday evening was reserved for the extended family. As soon as I came to the palace, I worked on restoring good relations between the king and some of his brothers and sisters and other members of the family, who had sometimes become estranged through old differences over the years; at the same time I also encouraged his relations with my own family. As a good Iranian, I respect family ties and traditions, and that has always swept from my mind the misunderstandings and animosity that inevitably arise.

Friday in particular was devoted to friends. In addition, there were official dinners and those connected with work. But in spite of all, we sometimes managed to be alone together in the evening, and I remember how much the king and I enjoyed these rare intimate moments.

"Tell me what you did today," he would ask me.

Sometimes what I had to tell him was not at all amusing, but at that time I was still organizing my office and what I was experiencing could be quite funny. Besides, I have always loved telling stories, making everyday little adventures come to life. As a child, I had managed to bore my cousin Reza silly. When he couldn't stand any more of my chatter, he would run away, and I can still see myself running after him to make him listen to me. But the king didn't tire of listening. During this period I made him laugh a lot. In particular I told him about certain conversations I had had during the day, and knowing it amused him, I would add little stories to go with them.

We often ended these free evenings with a film in the projection room that had been built in the basement of the palace. My husband loved Charlie Chaplin, Laurel and Hardy, Jerry Lewis, and Bob Hope. I never saw him laugh so much as when he was watching Charlie Chaplin's pranks. He would split his sides laughing like a child, and I thought, "It's good that he has this tiny space to let himself go and have fun. He works so hard the rest of the time!" The pleasure of seeing him relax made me laugh much more than the antics of comedians who have never had me rolling in the aisles. When I was young, my friends used to be amused just looking at me sitting there unmoved while they were laughing uncontrollably. To the present day the only ones who have really made me laugh are Louis de Funès, Bill Cosby, Mel Brooks, Arham Sadr, Parviz Sayyad, and Shabadji "Khanoum." The king and I also liked historical films and war films for the heroic side of some of the characters.

As far as politics were concerned, the future also seemed bright for my husband after those very difficult years of the fifties. The economy was moving ahead again thanks to the compromise struck over the nationalization of oil. For the first time the government could invest the revenue from our oil fields in national development. The king would talk very enthusiastically about the nationalization with me, regretting that it had taken a twenty-year battle to achieve. But this time we had got it: never, since the great period of Reza Shah, had there been so many new projects under way. As the fifties gave way to the sixties, the first big dams were constructed, as well as irrigation canals, hydroelectric power stations, and chemical fertilizer factories. Plans were embarked upon to triple the railway network, pave 5,000 kilometers of roadway, and create 30,000 kilometers of secondary roads. Among other things, a 2,400 kilometer trans-Iranian pipeline was constructed. The king thought that he would soon have the means to start the peaceful revolution he had in mind, so that the country could finally emerge from its state of under-development. This revolution had been in his mind since he was a student in Switzerland. The first mainstay would obviously have to be agrarian reform, which met much resistance.

Wanting to show that large private land holdings were not tenable as long as small peasants had such difficulty eking out a living, my husband gave his own land to the government to be distributed starting in 1941. In 1955 a Bank of Agricultural Credit and Reconstruction was founded on his initiative: 200,000 hectares of land in the public domain had been shared out among 42,000 farmers. That was only a start, but one resented by the large landowners, among whom were clerics who drew most of their resources from their land. Confronting the Shiite clergy, whose influence was enormous throughout the country, was not the least of these difficulties. The king was well aware of their resistance, but he knew that the progress and democratic adjustments he wanted would necessarily involve changing people's outlook. The revolution he was planning would also take place on the cultural level. He could only do it, he said, if he had the confidence of the country, of a majority of the people, and at the beginning of the 1960s he felt he had that confidence. The enthusiasm inspired by the birth of the heir to the throne could only reinforce this impression.

ON 11 OCTOBER 1961, we went on an official three-day visit to France. My husband greatly admired General de Gaulle. Of all the living heads of state, he was the embodiment of the way the king saw his own mission: tough patriotism together with great clear-sightedness. "When General de Gaulle came through Tehran on his way to Moscow in 1942," he wrote in his memoirs, "I was a very young king. I was won over by his unusual personality from the moment I met him. Listening to him speak about France, it was like an echo of the ambitions I had for my country: to see it independent once more within its own borders. He had a subdued eloquence that made his faith in his country infectious." My husband therefore saw a symbolic value in meeting the general again just as he was preparing to involve Iran in a critical change for its future. All the more so because the esteem was mutual. The general appreciated the efforts being made to bring about Iran's recovery, and he showed his support for the king for the rest of his life. Much later, when the Islamic Revolution had brought decades of progress to nothing, his son, Admiral Philippe de Gaulle, subtly recalled the links between his father and the king by being filmed for a televised interview with a portrait of my husband clearly in evidence behind him. I am very grateful to him for the gesture, as he did it at a time when very few had the courage to express their opinion.

As for me, I was very impatient and excited to be in Paris again. Well before my arrival, the French press wrote many columns recalling the fact that I had left the country two years earlier as "a little architecture student" and that I was returning as "a queen and young mother." Nevertheless, beyond this carefully promoted fairy-tale theme, there remained a very real affection between myself and many French people, which made me feel almost as though I were coming home to an adopted family.

Quite apart from the pomp of their welcome, General and Madame de Gaulle reinforced this impression by showing a particular, almost parental affection toward the still young and inexperienced queen that I was at that time. Years later I was told that when the general was asked, "Of all the wives of the heads of state you have met, which one do you like best?" he had replied, "Farah!"

"What about Jackie Kennedy?"

"She is very pretty too," he replied, "but Farah has an impish quality, which gives her something extra."

My husband had a long talk with the general, while Madame de Gaulle showed me round the Élysée Palace. André Malraux, whose lovely dedication I still remembered, was kind enough to take me through some of the great museums in Paris. I was pleased to see our ambassador, Nassrollah Entezam, once again—the same man who had welcomed me to the embassy in March 1959, when the king had expressed a wish to meet some Iranian students while he was on a brief visit in Paris.

The French authorities had wanted our visit to coincide with the opening of an Iranian Art Exhibition in Paris to celebrate seven thousand years of our people's history. One of the high points of this trip came when the king, who was devoted to Iranian culture and civilization, signalled his vision for the future through his reference to his father, Reza Shah: "No man has ever had such love for, and faith in, his country as my father. He was so devoted to the land of his birth that he thought Persian culture surpassed all others in every way. And yet, no man had ever put such energy into reforming his country, in wanting to rejuvenate and modernize it, which seems at odds with his love of Persian culture. My father admired Persia's great past; he wanted to save those of our ancient ways that were not incompatible with progress. But he was convinced that unity of the land and the nation, as well as the happiness of the people, made rapid westernization a necessity."

The seeds of the gentle revolution the king was preparing were contained in those few sentences. The seeds of the various forms of opposition he would have to overcome were also implied in them. No one failed to understand, and I remember the words of Édouard Sablier, then an editorial writer with *Le Monde*: "When one has tamed the Greek conqueror, triumphed over the might of Rome, assimilated the conqueror, survived the Mongol, contained the Ottoman Empire and, almost the only case in contemporary annals, loosened the grip of the Red Army on a province, Azarbaijan, which had almost been lost, what is there to fear from the future?"

Six months later I experienced a very different welcome in the United States. We were invited by President Kennedy, who had only recently been elected, and I was thrilled at the idea of this trip; I dreamed of seeing America. For my husband, who had received President Eisenhower in Tehran in 1959, the object of the visit was to sound out his successor and pave the way for a relationship that was important for our economy. The king had traditionally had a greater affinity with the Republicans than with the Democrats, but he was sure he could convince Kennedy of the merits of his policy. The Kennedys were extremely warm and welcoming, Jackie taking me off on an informal tour of the White House, then a long walk through the gardens. I can still see her pushing little John-John in his baby carriage. However, the United States was host to a large number of Iranian students, most of them on state scholarships, which did not prevent them from belonging to the communist Tudeh Party or to other anti-monarchist movements, and so there were demonstrations.

This trip left me with the depressing memory of protesters yelling hostile slogans at the king. They were everywhere, sometimes within a few yards of us, to the point where my husband had to strain his voice when he needed to speak. We heard them shouting from morning till night, even below our windows at the hotel.

I had to constantly overcome my anxiety, so that I did not let any of it show, especially when journalists were present, but on the inside I was anything but calm. I heard the students' demands. It was true that the country still had a long way to go, but a great deal had already been done. To me these very Iranian students were living proof of that, since they were mostly financed by the state they were reviling. Many of them would soon be employed. They were not aware of how far we had come, what poverty there was before Reza Shah took over. They certainly did not realize how long it had taken the United States to reach the level of wealth and democracy they were now experiencing. In any event, that first trip to the United States remained a traumatic event in my memory. A few years later I refused to accompany my husband on an official visit there. Working twelve hours a day for the welfare of the Iranian people, I said to him, "If I go there only to be insulted again, I would be of much more use here in Tehran." I naturally had no idea that twenty years on, demonstrators would once again stand shouting and praying for the King's death—this time outside the hospital in New York where my husband, in exile, was battling serious illness.

Nevertheless, this early impression should not overshadow the memory of several fascinating visits: to the Metropolitan Museum, Lincoln Center, or the Hollywood studios, where we were given a very pleasant lunch in the company of Gregory Peck,

Red Skelton, Danny Kaye, Ginger Rogers, George Cukor, among others. There were some unforgettable meetings, in particular with Walt Disney, who gave us some original drawings for Reza.

In California I discovered how warm and friendly Americans can be, and that cheered me. It was during this trip that we formed a friendship with Lyndon Johnson, who was vice president at the time. His wife, daughter, and son-in-law still keep in touch with me to this day. Being still not totally comfortable with the English language, I remember the trouble I had trying to understand the vice president's striking Texan accent.

It was that same year, 1962, when he was being shouted down in Washington, that the king finished planning the first six great reforms, which he called the White Revolution—white because this revolution was intended to make Iran a modern country without spilling a drop of blood.

The first item on this program was, of course, agrarian reform, so longed for by the peasants and small farmers, so feared by the big landowners. As I have mentioned, despite the King's initiative, those who owned vast properties had not given up anything. In the middle of the twentieth century in Iran, 95 percent of arable land remained in the hands of a privileged few while our peasant class was just as badly off as the serfs of medieval Europe. That inequity could not continue. According to the new law those who owned several villages could keep only one and had to sell the others to the government which would parcel out the land to the peasants. At the time there were no land registers in Iran, so the village was the measuring unit used, although the size of the villages varied. Two years after the promulgation of the agrarian reform law, 8,200 villages (out of the calculated total of 18,000) had already been shared out among 300,000 families. And the movement would continue in spite of the violent opposition of the clergy, which I will describe later.

The second step: To finance the agrarian reform, it was decided to privatize a certain number of state enterprises. The king anticipated that rich Iranians, notably the large landowners, would decide to reinvest their fortunes in these enterprises now on the open market. This did happen, but very slowly, since the Iranian economic elite were initially timid and disinclined to support the king's efforts to modernize the country.

The third step: Nationalization of forests and pasture land—an indispensable adjunct to agrarian reform.

The fourth step was to help the workers by enabling them to participate in the profits of their companies. Later, twenty percent of all shares in Iranian companies were reserved for workers and managerial staff.

The fifth step, which also proved to be fraught with consequences, resulted in giving women the right to vote and to become candidates for election. A conservative and obscurantist section of the clergy quickly took offense. In 1936 Reza Shah, who was very anxious to give women the same rights as men, had already earned the wrath of the clerics by forbidding chador (veils) to be worn and, worse still, by requiring the police to remove the chador from women who persisted in wearing it. (He had applied this ruling to his own family and had the queen mother and her two daughters appear wearing hats and no veils.) This time the initiative was in no way meant to be seen as an attack on modesty, but rather as the opposite, as an elementary mark of respect for women. They were at last to be full citizens in their own right. As for the chador, my husband had long since abolished his father's edict and allowed women the freedom to wear it or not as they wished.

Lastly, the sixth step, essential for the development of the country, was the creation of a "Literacy Corps," made up of high school graduates whose mission was to bring literacy to country areas. At the beginning of the 1960s, the illiteracy rate in Iran was at 70 percent! How could we make up this huge amount of lost ground, when the number of primary school teachers being trained was scarcely enough to fill the needs of the cities? To use young recruits for this colossal task proved to be an idea of unique inspiration that rapidly won world attention. How gratifying that was! Twenty-five years later Iran would have practically eradicated this terrible handicap, thanks to these motivated soldiers and the Organization for the Fight Against Illiteracy. The country would have conquered the scourge of illiteracy.

Seeing the undeniable success of this method, the king would quickly extend it by creating in 1964 a "Public Health Corps" made up of medical and dental students who would bring first aid to villages and above all teach the elementary rules of hygiene to prevent disease. Then came the "Development Corps" to teach farmers modern methods of cultivation. Naturally all these young people were well trained before being sent out into the countryside, and they wore uniforms so that they could be easily identified.

The king, the government, and the people in charge were well aware of the difficulties ahead of them with this first raft of reforms. We talked about it at great length, and I was extremely proud to be the wife of a man who put such courage and clear-sightedness into the service of his country. I admired him and felt that he was about to contribute some essential pages to our history. It was exciting because I was certain that he had the right vision, and was totally committed to Iran. This pride went hand in hand with a deep happiness: at that time I was expecting our second child, due in March 1963. I had the feeling of living intensely, with great purpose. My private and public lives were in perfect harmony with this loving, generous, strong king. "I too am a soldier of the Revolution," I said to the king on a trip to a town in the south of Iran.

My husband had decided to submit these measures to the people through a referendum. The decision to use a referendum, the prerogative of modern democracies, shows clearly that the times were changing: the absolutism of Reza Shah had been necessary, indeed inevitable, to rapidly bring the country out of the backward state where it had languished under the Qajars. However, we were now entering a period when the citizens had a greater voice. In this matter my husband wanted to lead Iran gradually toward an open and democratic monarchy. Life had only left Reza Shah enough time to go half the distance.

Born in 1878 in Alasht, in Mazandaran, the young man who was then called Reza Khan followed the example of his officer father by joining the Persian Cossacks when he was eighteen. His strength of character quickly impressed both the British and the Russian officers who were rivals for power and influence over Persia at the beginning of the century. In 1919, with the rank of colonel, Reza Khan fought the Bolsheviks, who were threatening to annex the northern provinces of the country, Gilan in particular. But Iran continued to disintegrate: there was no central power, bandits and local authorities shared the provinces. As for justice, it was entirely in the hands of the clergy. For a patriot like Reza Khan, this was a heartrending state of affairs.

He became minister for war under the last of the Qajars, Ahmad Shah. He set out to reorganize the army, a prerequisite to the reestablishment of authority over the country. But Ahmad Shah, who was more often in Europe than Tehran at the time, did not seem at all anxious to assume the power handed to him by his minister for war. He came back to Iran but left again for Europe. Meanwhile Mustafa Kamal Ataturk was at work turning neighboring Turkey into a strong modern state. Reza Khan increasingly admired him and soon the two established relations based on mutual admiration and friendship. Kamal undeniably set an example for the Cossack officer, by then the commander of the army of a neglected country. This was the state of things when, on 31 October 1925, the Parliament voted to depose Ahmad Shah. It was a matter of urgency. A constituent assembly was immediately elected and handed the crown to the first of the Pahlavis. There were only five dissenting voices. Reza Khan would personally have preferred a republic, but it was the clergy that urged him to become king because monarchy and religion were the two pillars of Iranian society at the time. Having become Reza Shah, he chose the symbolic name of Pahlavi, which refers to the language and writing of the Parthian dynasty (250 B.C.–226 A.D.).

This outstanding man continued living like a soldier throughout his reign: he slept on a mattress on the ground, rose at five in the morning, and disliked flatterers. It was he who restored unity to Iran. I have already mentioned some of his achievements, notably the Trans-Iranian Railway. He also brought in compulsory primary education, increased the number of hospitals, founded the University of Tehran, and sent the first students on scholarships to the West (among them Mehdi Bazargan, who later became Khomeini's prime minister). Reza Shah was, in addition, the architect of Iran's secular justice system, giving Iran a civil code and criminal laws modeled on those of the great democracies. That reform naturally meant the clergy lost one of the tools of its authority over the people in addition to a major source of income through notarized deeds. During his reign, 90 percent of clerics lost their judicial functions and the social status that accompanied them. The mullahs, of course, expressed their discontent; they remained opposed to all proposals for reform. Yet the first of the Pahlavis was no less of a practicing Muslim. But, as my husband used to say, "He was too much of a believer to think of God as a kind of superior electoral agent or chief engineer of oil wells."

There were lots of stories about this extraordinary man, all of them showing his uncompromising character and dislike of sycophants. During one of his trips to Gilan, a young man ran up to him, prostrated himself, and asked to be appointed guardian of the Imam Reza shrine (these guardians did nothing but still received a salary). Reza Shah turned toward those who were accompanying him and said, "Take hold of this man immediately and send him on military service."

Another time, when he was visiting the construction site of a new palace, Reza Shah stopped in front of a workman who was busily sculpting a lion's head on a stucco ceiling. "Your animal is squinting," he remarked. "If you had as much weight on your back as he has," replied the sculptor, who had not recognized him, "you'd be squinting too." It is said that the king burst out laughing and arranged for the workman to be promoted.

The White Revolution continued and extended the work undertaken forty years earlier by that force of nature that was Reza Shah. To be sure that he remained in control of his policies and to avoid the risk of a gap between rich and poor, the king called Assadollah Alam, a close advisor in whom he had every confidence, to become head of the government. Alam came from a prominent family in Birjand. He was a man of great worth, experienced in political life, and he had the rare quality of not hiding the truth from the king. On the eve of a great battle, it is important to surround oneself with people who are exacting and clearheaded. Assadollah Alam, who was later appointed minister of court, remained with the king and myself until his death from cancer in 1978.

Chapter 9

A FEW DAYS BEFORE the referendum, the king gave a solemn address to the nation. He had carefully considered every word of his speech, had asked me to read it aloud to him, and had several times asked me to stop so that he could make a correction. He was sure he was serving the interests of the majority, and I could sense his emotion behind the words. I shared it; I supported him wholeheartedly. Later, when I heard him giving the talk, I was worried, wondering how the people would receive this revolutionary address.

"If I have decided to submit these reforms directly to the people's vote," he said, "it is so that no one can ever bring back the regime of slavery to which our peasants were subjected; so that a minority will never again exploit the wealth of our nation for its own profit; so that never again will the private interests of an individual or group of individuals be able to destroy or distort the effects of these revolutionary innovations."

On 26 January 1963, the people gave massive approval to the underlying principles of the White Revolution. Women did not yet have the right to vote, but the minister in charge of agrarian reform, Hassan Arsanjani, had encouraged them to go and vote, even though their votes and voices could not be counted; consequently special voting booths were opened. The press revealed a few days later that women had declared themselves in favor of the reforms by a large majority. As for the official vote, it was quite rightly called a plebiscite. The commitment of the Iranian people made it possible to launch the third stage of development (1963–68) with a good deal of optimism. "My final aim," the king said, "is to bring Iran to the level of civilization and progress of the most developed countries within twenty years. The backwardness of the country has decreased by half in the last ten years, but it is the second half of that gap which will be the most difficult to close." During the five years that followed, Iran made the most remarkable leap forward in its history with a growth rate of 8.8 percent, exceeding the most optimistic forecasts. Projects essential for the growth of the country were completed, such as the great Karaj, Sefid Rud, and Dez dams, while equally crucial industrial projects such as the Tabriz tractor factories or the Arak motor works were also launched. Buildings needed by the workers were always built next to the factories: living quarters, obviously, but also schools, nurseries, free health clinics, and so on. During the same period the country acquired the economic and social tools needed for future expansion. A bureau of statistics was established and the banking system modernized. Industrial centers were being created at the same time as universities. The road network and hydroelectric plants grew considerably.

All of that was achieved with the support of the people and the thousands of Iranians who took part in the fight like real pioneers, throwing themselves into it body and soul, taking no notice of how tired they were or how much time it took, and with no thought of financial gain. But the progress that was made was also against the wishes of segments of the clergy who tried, from the earliest months, to raise rebel movements in several towns. The most reactionary clerics gained support from the communists, whose ambition was still to overthrow the monarchy. The king called it "the accursed alliance of the red and the black." A short time before the referendum, a cleric we had never heard of, a certain Ruhollah Khomeini, had written to the king to make a protest against women's suffrage. He expressed the deep conviction of nearly all the clergy. What could one reply to men who denied women intelligence and the right to express an opinion on the life of the country? That we women were worth no more than goats? That we were no longer living in the Middle Ages? What was the use? The king was banking on the irresistible momentum of intelligence against backwardness and obscurantism.

Protests in the holy cities, especially Qom, nevertheless became more and more violent as time went on. As well as opposing women's suffrage, the clerics were against agrarian reform, as I have mentioned, because it would deprive them of the income from their large properties. They naturally found allies for this fight in the large landowners. In the longer term, the clergy also saw the Literacy Corps as a threat, for these young high school graduates went out all over the countryside and, by spreading knowledge and information, inevitably took minds away from the total influence of the mullahs. Maintaining the status quo seemed to be the only policy that suited our clergy. Later, however, when I was traveling throughout Iran, I saw that the people themselves wanted the Literacy Corps to come to their villages.

On New Year's Day, 21 March 1963, the police had to intervene in Qom to quell the unrest. The king feared that blood might be shed, but he was determined to stand his ground. He had an ally in his prime minister, Assadollah Alam, who was not going to let himself be intimidated by the forces of "black reaction." On 1 April, my husband flew out for a short pilgrimage to the Mausoleum of Imam Reza in Mashhad. I had just given birth to our daughter Farahnaz and so could not accompany him. In his speech, he referred to the sacred commandments of the Koran and criticized their interpretation by certain people "in the interest of their own pockets and against the principles of equality and fraternity in the holy book." "These people," he added, "hinder the march of progress and the development of the country. Fortunately the Iranian people are well acquainted with the reactionaries. If necessary, we will name them."

They named themselves, in particular the most inflammatory of them, Ruhollah Khomeini. He had lost his deference and now made angry speeches against progress and modernization, which he summed up as a "Westernization" of the country. At the beginning of June the unrest reached a peak when a policeman was killed by the crowd in the holy city of Mashhad, where the king had been two months earlier. In Tehran and Shiraz the rioters set fire to a municipal library, newspaper kiosks, and there were several instances of looting. As a result, the government decided to have Khomeini arrested. The tension was evident even in our immediate environment: this year the king had us go earlier than usual to the Sa'ad Abad Palace in Shemiran, far from the center of town. I remember that as I tightened my arms around our little Farahnaz, then only three months old, I noticed that the guards had put on combat uniforms.

The agitation led to the arrest of Khomeini and, sensing the danger facing the country, Prime Minister Alam asked the king for provisional authority over the army. He gathered the officers in charge and warned them that the city of Tehran could well be taken by the insurgents. He authorized them to shoot when in extreme danger. In order to protect his king, Alam had taken upon himself the responsibility for reestablishing order, stating clearly that if he failed, he would take the consequences. He succeeded, but there were fifty deaths in Tehran and the provinces.

There was a rumor that Ruhollah Khomeini risked the death penalty. The prime minister was in favor of a term of imprisonment, at the very least. It was the head of SAVAK (the State Security and Intelligence Organization), General Hassan Pakravan, a man of great culture, intelligence, and humanity, who pleaded clemency to the king. In his opinion it was necessary to calm people's minds, let the clergy get used to reforms gradually, and for the moment be content with exiling Khomeini. The king agreed. "He was neither sentenced, nor even tried," he wrote in his memoirs. "He was simply asked to exercise his inflammatory eloquence elsewhere." The cleric was sent to Turkey but later asked the king's permission to settle in Iraq, where he continued his slow, insidious, undermining work. One of the first people he ordered to be killed on his return to Tehran after the Islamic Revolution was General Pakravan, the man who had saved his life. The news reached us when we were in exile in the Bahamas. It upset me dreadfully. The general and his wife were very close to us, and they had been friends of my parents.

The failure of the reactionary uprisings of 1963 and the beginnings of the White Revolution were hailed in all democratic countries. The *New York Times,* in particular, wrote that the king had "joined forces with the workers and peasants against the conservatives and traditionalists."

FARAHNAZ WAS BORN ON 12 MARCH 1963, at the beginning of the unrest. I gave birth to her in the palace. There was a dentist's room in one of the basements, which was made into a delivery room for the occasion. I remember the wave of happiness that swept through me when I learned that we had a girl! It must have been contagious: when Princess Ashraf and my stepdaughter, Princess Shahnaz, heard the news, they let out such shrieks of joy that they nearly made a charming man who was bringing me the Koran lose his footing on the stairs.

The king and our young Reza together took Farahnaz in their arms. My husband was very happy to have a girl, which is hardly odd, because, as I noted in Farahnaz's record book: "Horoscope: great love for her father." And Farahnaz did in fact have a particular devotion to her father, who returned it. The two of them shared a wonderful mutual understanding.

Our family was growing and little Crown Prince Reza was nearly three. Decisions about his schooling had occupied our minds a good deal: should he go to a public school like any other child, or should he be taught apart? We realized very quickly that the first alternative was not feasible: being an object of curiosity and veneration wherever he went, Reza would not fit in at the local school, where no matter what we said, the teachers would give him special treatment. As for the children themselves, they became excited and fascinated as soon as he appeared. And Reza could not understand it. I remember how surprised he was, when we were visiting a school together, to see the children running behind him and stopping the moment he stopped. And yet we did not want to isolate him from his own generation. It was therefore decided to set up a kindergarten within the palace grounds, which would take children of his age from the families of those close to us.

Reza, then Farahnaz, Ali-Reza, and Leila all benefited from this tailor-made school system, which was both selective and open. From the emotional and psychological point of view, it also had the advantage of keeping them near us, contrary to the practice of many reigning families, who sent their children to prestigious private schools in Europe or the United States for the whole of their education.

As a small child my husband had tutors at first, then he was sent away to school. Despite his habitual reticence, one could sense that it had caused him some unhappiness. At the tender age of eleven he had to leave his family and go to the Swiss Le Rosey school at Rolle on the banks of Lake Geneva. In addition to his younger brother, Ali-Reza, who went with him, he asked to go there with one of his friends, Hossein Fardoust, a child from a modest background who did all his studies with my husband and stayed close to him throughout his reign.* Going to Switzerland at that time meant a very long journey. They left for Bakou from Bandar-Pahlavi, a small port on the Caspian Sea. From there they crossed the whole of Europe by train. "I want my son to grow up like an ordinary boy and learn to stand on his own two feet," Reza Shah had informed the school.

He spent five long years in Switzerland and could not grow up *exactly* the same as the other boys, for the good reason that he was destined to be a king. "I was like a prisoner," he wrote later. "During their free time my friends all went into town together, but I did not have permission to go with them. During the Christmas and New Year holidays, they went to dances and parties organized in hotels close to Le Rosey, but I could not join them. My friends enjoyed themselves, laughed and danced, while I stayed sitting alone in my room. I had a radio and a gramophone to keep me company, but that could not compensate for all the fun my friends could have. I think it was unfair." His only entertainment was playing football and ice hockey.

"When I went back in 1936," he wrote, "I didn't recognize anything: Bandar-Pahlavi was a modern, Western town. The old

*Hossein Fardoust eventually became a full general and was appointed head of the Special Information Bureau by the king. He had the confidence and the ear of the king, but would betray this long friendship by offering his services to the fundamentalist regime.

city walls surrounding Tehran had been demolished on my father's orders, and the city was beginning to look like a European capital." From those adolescent years in Europe, he nonetheless brought back an attitude and frame of mind that founded the White Revolution. "Those were the most important years of my life," he said later, disregarding the melancholy that was part of them. "It was there I learned what democracy is all about."

In Iran, as everywhere else, promoting an idea comes at a price. On 10 April 1965, when we had just celebrated Farahnaz's first birthday and Reza was three and a half, my husband and son narrowly escaped an assassination attempt. Every morning Reza accompanied his father to his office in the Marble Palace. They usually went on foot, holding each other by the hand. Then someone took Reza from the office to the kindergarten, which was close by. That April morning was an exception: because a new little boy was joining the class, Reza's governess had requested that he be there a little earlier than usual to welcome the new pupil. And so the king left on his own and in a car, despite the short distance. As soon as he appeared, one of the soldiers mounting guard began shooting at the car. According to accounts given by the valet and other security people, my husband got out of the car quite unruffled and went into the foyer of the building. During all that time the soldier continued firing at him. The two guards who were usually stationed at each side of the door to the Marble Palace had fled at the sound of the first shots. The valet had tried to shut the doors but had been shot in the hand. The gunman then rushed in behind my husband, who at that moment was calmly entering his office. In the meantime his bodyguards inside the palace had realized what was happening and had begun to return fire. There was a wild exchange of shots in which two security men died, Sergeants Ayat Lashgari and Mohammad Ali Babaian, while the killer was brought down. It then became apparent that a bullet had gone through the door of my husband's office and lodged in the back of the chair he usually occupied.

At that moment I was putting on my makeup in front of the mirror for a work meeting due to begin ten minutes later.

The phone rang. It was the queen mother, who lived in the grounds of the Marble Palace.

"Oh, my God, Farah *joûne* (darling)!"

Her voice was unrecognizable.

"What's wrong Mamman?"

"Someone has shot at the king!"

Then she burst into tears, incapable of adding anything more, and I felt as if I were dying myself, dying...she was crying and could not tell me if he was alive or dead. I could hardly breathe but made an enormous effort to get out the words, "But he...He...How...?"

"He's alive, thank God."

I remember hanging up and finishing my makeup, as if in a trance. Then I ran to him. Perfectly calm, he was giving instructions to the security officer and continued with his normal schedule.

What dreadful tragedy could have happened if the king had appeared to the assassin holding Reza's little hand in his?

Later the king asked that one of the accomplices of the gunman, who had just been arrested, be brought to the Ekhtessassi Palace. From the balcony above, I could see the man with his hands tied behind his back and my husband talking to him quietly. He was very young, standing there silent and ashamed. It was a moving scene; I was sorry for him and angry with all those who had dragged him into that folly.

It appeared that the young men implicated in the assassination attempt had been approached, then indoctrinated by an extreme leftist group close to the Tudeh. The brains behind it, Parviz Nickhah, was sentenced to ten years in prison, then pardoned by the king. The king often said that he could forgive those who had designs on his life, but not those who threatened the security and unity of the country. When he was released, Parviz Nickhah rallied to the monarchy and worked for Iranian television, which resulted in his being condemned to death and executed at the very beginning of the Islamic Revolution, on the instigation, I was told, of his former comrades of the Tudeh Party. Many years later one of his friends brought me this account by Nickhah of his period as a militant communist: "SAVAK concentrated all its attention on the communists and completely ignored the clerics. When I went into the villages to indoctrinate the peasants, the people would denounce me to the Security Organization, while the clerics could say what they liked against the monarchy. They never were bothered."

The king had already survived an attack on his life fifteen years earlier, on 4 February 1949. On that day he had come to preside over the ceremonies commemorating the founding of the University of Tehran and was later to present some students with their diplomas. It was a little after three in the afternoon when he took his place at the head of the official procession. As usual on these occasions, there was a pack of photographers crowding a few feet away from him. Suddenly one of them left the group and, with a gun hidden in his camera, fired at the king several times from less than three yards away. "Three bullets shot my cap off, grazing my skull," the king related. "The fourth hit me on the right cheek bone, made my head tip back, and came out under my nose. I had not taken my eyes off my attacker and I realized he was going to fire again. I had just enough time to turn around and lean over slightly, so that the bullet that should have hit me right in the heart caught me in the shoulder. He still had one bullet, but the gun jammed." My husband told me that the man then threw the revolver in his face.

At that moment, however, he was killed by the chiefs of the national police and the military police, who fired in unison. Probably stunned, no one had tried to intervene when the shots were being fired. The assassin, named Nasser Fakhr Araï, was discovered to be a member of the Tudeh. It seems that the day before the attempt he had received a press card in the name of a religious publication, *The Flag of Islam*, so that he could be among the journalists and get close to the king. In 1951, two years after having tried to assassinate the king, these same terrorists managed to kill his prime minister, General Haj-Ali Razmara, a remarkable man who had taken part in the liberation of Azarbaijan as chief of staff.

There was no basis for suspecting the king of apostasy, and what is more, he saw the benevolent hand of God behind the repeated failure of threats to his life, in whatever form they took. As a child he should have died of typhoid a few months after his father's coronation. After forty days of very high fever, the doctors announced that his end was near, and it is said that this was the only time the iron-willed Reza Shah, who loved this son more than anything else, gave way to tears. In the middle of the night he summoned a cleric and asked him to pray for his son's recovery. "The next day, the fever dropped," my husband told me, "and I recovered quickly."

A few years later, when he was going on horseback to Imamzadeh Davood, a place of pilgrimage in the mountains, he had a fall while riding at great speed, his head struck a rock, and those with him thought for a few minutes that he was dead. But after being unconscious for a short time, he got up, strangely unharmed. There again, he said that he felt he had been saved by his faith.

He had no other explanation for having survived a crash when he was a pilot at the controls of a two-seater Tiger Moth. He was going to a place near Esfahan to inspect some work being done on a river, accompanied by the general in charge of the area's army division, when an engine cut out. As he told it, what happened next made me shiver with fright for some time.

> I had to land as soon as possible. A quick look around showed that it would not be easy. There was a village in front of us, a mountain on my right, on my left newly plowed fields that would be impossible for a landing.
>
> And so I decided to veer to my right, keeping enough speed to stay in the air. Suddenly I saw that the mountain was cut by a deep ravine. I pulled on the joystick and we just got through. The only thing I could do then was land on the mountainside, which I did. I had only just made contact with the ground when a rock appeared ahead of us. There was no way to avoid it. The landing gear was ripped off and the plane continued on its belly, which fortunately slowed it down. A minute later the propeller hit another rock and the plane turned over.
>
> My traveling companion and I found ourselves hanging upside down. We managed to get out of our harnesses, not without some difficulty.

My husband was certain that he would not die until his mission on earth was finished, and that belief no doubt explains why he did not even try to protect himself from the bullets of that second attempt on his life in 1964 at the door of his office in the Marble Palace. He was a man of faith.

Chapter 10

YES, I CONSIDERED myself a soldier of the revolution because I believed with all my strength that the path mapped out by my husband was the right one. We had been an underdeveloped country, and although I came from a privileged background, I can remember the poverty of Iran in my childhood. Twenty years later we had earned the title of "developing country." Westerners do not realize the hope and pride that exists behind this simple semantic change. And we owed it all to the determination of the king and many other Iranians to advance, despite being hampered by closed minds and opposition within—the "red reaction" of the Tudeh allied with the "black reaction" of the clergy—as well as countless other obstacles from outside, the nationalization of oil, taken back from the British, being the outstanding example. I truly believed, as my husband so often said, that if we pursued our efforts with the same determination, we would reach an economic level on a par with Western European countries by the middle of the 1980s.

From that time onward, like all people of goodwill, I wanted to help wherever my position would allow me to play a part, in supporting initiatives, getting projects off the ground, removing obstacles. My husband had encouraged me in this work from day one; he had been my guide and my mainstay. He wanted me to be by his side and work for the good of the country. How? It was up to me to get the feel of things and find where I could make the best contribution. There are no doubt a hundred different ways of carrying out the task of being queen, depending on the personality of the woman concerned and, naturally, of the monarch. I was led to involve myself body and soul, not only out of loyalty to the man I loved, but also for the love of my country. I think that when I was very young my family passed on to me its love for Iran and its desire to serve. My father had learned these sentiments from his father, who had been an ambassador of the crown, and they had become second nature to me. I too wanted to serve my country, and I could not have imagined a better opportunity for service than the one my husband offered me.

The birth of Reza, then Farahnaz, had kept me away somewhat from the activities of my office. But the time was well past when I was struggling to get organized. At the beginning, there were even days when I had been a little bored. Since then, my office had grown considerably and my timetable was so heavy that sometimes I found it hard to take an hour off to have lunch alone with the king. I often had to skip the meal—too often. In fact, everything that concerned Iran concerned me. All subjects interested me, provided I felt able to bring some benefit to people's lives. Of course the king and the government worked enormously hard, but I sometimes brought the perspective of a woman and mother to certain questions, and perhaps things were resolved more easily in certain cases because of my intervention. Sometimes my presence or my support also allowed certain bureaucratic obstacles to be removed. I pleaded certain causes brought to my notice, and in which I believed, to the king or to the government.

This was particularly the case for the campaign we were about to launch against leprosy. I had heard about this illness for the first time at the École Jeanne d'Arc, where a Frenchman, Raoul Follereau, came to speak about the scourge and his commitment to fight it. I had no idea at that time that leprosy was rife in Iran. I had been so distressed by it that I talked of nothing else to my mother that evening. A few days later I read *Soledad with the Green Eyes,* the story of a young woman who caught the disease and was sent to a leper island. I could not imagine a greater misfortune than that: to be driven out of society, banished, exiled because of an illness.

Shortly after my marriage, Dr. Abdolhossein Raji, the former health minister, asked to meet me. I received him. He came with a lady, Mrs. Ozra Ziaï; they were both admirable people. They asked me if I would accept the presidency of the Lepers' Aid Association, which already existed. I naturally agreed straightaway. And so, scarcely ten years after the shock of Mr. Follereau's lecture, fate brought him to mind again. Now I could do more than just sympathize; I had the means to act.

As president, I quickly decided to visit the Leper Center at Tabriz (there was another at Mashhad). And there I was shocked a second time, and much more deeply than the first. For the first time I saw those ashen, disfigured, ragged faces, and the deep distress in their eyes. The milder cases survived in reasonable buildings, but the others were relegated to dark little rooms which gave out a terrible smell. Cakes had been brought for them, and I suddenly saw my guide throw these cakes to the afflicted as if throwing bones to dogs. I don't think I had ever experienced such a feeling of humiliation and horror. I cried, "Good heavens, how could you? How dare you? They're human beings!"

The poor man didn't know what to say, he was so afraid of catching the disease.

Immediately afterward I met the few people in Iran who devoted themselves to these unfortunates: Iranian and foreign doctors—in particular Dr. Baltazar, a Frenchman who directed the Pasteur Institute in Tehran—but also nuns and priests. (I learned later that none of our Muslim religious men nor any members of the clergy worked in these establishments.)

As a result of this visit we began discussions with specialists about what could be done to improve conditions for the sick. It became apparent, first of all, that our doctors did not have the necessary training to detect leprosy at the start. They took it for some sort of skin complaint or eczema and so lost the opportunity to arrest the infection, for which treatment did exist. Our first initiative was therefore to work out a program of early detection and teaching for medical students and doctors.

Then a study was undertaken to find out where in our country the disease appeared and why, so that alert, trained doctors could be sent to those regions. France helped us a lot in this study by sending a team of epidemiologists, geographers, and hospital doctors, as part of a technical cooperation agreement.

At the same time we were trying to determine the best way of reducing the isolation of the sick, and even more importantly, of reintegrating those who were cured but still showed the marks of leprosy—patients who were in the clear, as the saying goes. Our ideal solution was for them to be admitted to general hospitals. It had been explained to me that leprosy is far less contagious than is generally imagined but that the doctors themselves were afraid of it. There was a lot of opposition, which meant more information sessions, but by the end of the seventies, we had managed to persuade some hospitals to admit lepers.

On the other hand, we gave up the idea of encouraging people who were cured to go back to their villages, as the World Health Organization recommends. The staff in Geneva could not feel the fear that this disease inspires in a small rural community. When one member of a family has it, the whole family has to leave. That led us to plan a village specially for those cured of leprosy and their families.

I asked the king if he could grant us a site on his own property, and he agreed. Thus we received enough land in Gorgan province to house a community of more than a thousand souls. During the seventies, Beh Kadeh had three hundred houses, a fifteen-bed hospital, a primary school, a cinema, a police station, a restaurant, a factory, a joinery, storehouses for agricultural products, several wells, vegetable gardens, and so on. The village was such a success that integration took place the other way round: it was the inhabitants of neighboring towns who came in ever-increasing numbers to work there or take advantage of the restaurant or the cinema.

History did not leave us enough time to build other Beh Kadehs, but I think that in twenty years we managed to make Iranian hearts respond to the fate of leprosy sufferers and those who had been cured. I remember in particular the film made by one of our great women poets, Forough Farrokhzad, *The House is Black*, which was a great help in influencing public opinion. During all these years I paid regular visits to places where leprosy sufferers were accommodated, and each time it was an overwhelming experience. The women kissed me and touched my face, then their own, as if I had the power to cure them. It was sometimes very hard for me to hide my feelings when faced with such suffering and expectation.

Lastly, in the 1970s we received the help of some extraordinary doctors—Pakistani, Indian, Swiss, and French—who came and worked for nothing, rebuilding the faces of some of our former sufferers. They reconstructed noses, implanted eyelashes and eyebrows, and often also opened hands that the disease leaves stiffly clenched. I will never forget the joy of a man whose face had been operated on, when he came to tell me of his impending marriage. He was so happy! As I listened to him telling me how his life had been given back to him, I silently blessed the surgeons who had wrought this miracle.

Recently one of the things that has touched me most was a greeting from one of those former sufferers whose fate had concerned me so much. An Iranian doctor with the WHO had met him and brought back the message whispered in his ear: "If you see the lady, say hello to her for me. We haven't forgotten her." Some words have the power to heal, like balm on a wound. Those words gave me the strength to hope that one day the truth will be told. I believe in my heart that a seed planted with love never dies.

CHILDREN'S LIBRARIES WERE ONE OF THOSE SEEDS. That enterprise began through the visit of a childhood friend, Lili Amir-Arjomand, who had come back from the United States having just finished her studies in library science. We saw each other informally, and the idea of providing Iranian children with something to read came out of our conversation. We had come across very few books intended for our age when we were young. We were told ancient stories in our oral tradition, but most of these tales had not been written down. As for the contemporary illustrated stories available in the West, one didn't even dream of such things. We had been brought up with the writings of only one author, Mr. Sobhi, who told a story for schoolchildren every morning on the radio, beginning with the words, "Good morning, children!" (*Bacheha salam!*) A few episodes had been published—that was the extent of our literary world. It was really very little. We imagined the extraordinary cultural horizons we could open for children if we could introduce books into their daily lives. Books must surely be the best way of discovering other lives and projecting oneself into the future. After all, we must have a dream first before we can embark on any new life. Yes, if we could get our children to read, we would help them enter the modern world, have less trouble accepting new ideas, and acquire a sense of morality and responsibility.

The first thing that had to be done, before putting anything into place, was to test the level of schoolchildren's interest. We decided that Lili and Homa Zahedi, a woman member of Parliament, and two other volunteers would go into the working-class areas in the south of Tehran with a few boxes of books to observe the children's reactions. It was beyond our expectations: they fought over these illustrated stories as if they were candy.

From that, the Organization for the Intellectual Development of Children and Young Adults was formed, and to launch it, we began going from door to door. We needed a great deal of money, which meant we had to involve some large institutions in our project, such as the Ministries of Education and Culture. We received the support of both. When asked, the National Iranian Oil Company also agreed to help us. All that remained was to gain the backing of publishers—who were obviously enthusiastic—artists, academics, and a certain number of private individuals likely to help us with money and ideas. For the latter, two young American experts came and gave us the benefit of their knowledge. One of them, Dan, who lives in California, still sends me a little packet of flower seeds for Now Ruz in memory of those other seeds—the books and libraries—that we sowed together.

For the location of our first children's library, we naturally chose Tehran, which had the greatest number of potential readers. As a budding architect who loved the profession, I personally saw to the esthetics of the first building and of all those we built later. I wanted them to express the fun side of reading. We set the first in the middle of a park, so that the children could go from games in the open air to books and vice versa. To preserve the parks, the only development permitted was for the libraries and later museums and theaters. The libraries obviously had to be available to all free of charge, from nursery school to age sixteen, and we would need talented staff members for each age group. For the very youngest children we had to train real childcare nurses who could also tell stories. For the older ones we wanted people capable of advising their readers and therefore enthusiastic enough about books to have read a lot themselves.

That left the essentials: the books. They had to be created or translated, since we did not have any. Convincing our authors to write for a young readership was not too difficult; finding illustrators certainly was. We had very good painters but no tradition of artwork for children, so we had to be innovative. Czechoslovakia was doing remarkable work in that field, so several of our artists went there to acquire the skill. While there they also learned the technique of animation and cartoons. We were later able to hold an International Children's Film Festival and to win some awards and prizes.

For my own pleasure, but also as a symbol of my involvement in this project, I translated and illustrated Hans Christian Andersen's *The Little Mermaid.* Reza must have been two or three at the time, and it made me very happy to think that he would soon be of an age to appreciate this tale and my drawings (the book also came with two phonograph records for those who could not yet read). As it bore my name, it naturally sold very well, and the profits helped to partially finance the publication of other books.

Some of these books promoted political opinions different from ours, although I didn't know it at first. Eventually I had to weigh the workings of democracy in a country where some ideologies, such as communism, were banned. There were authors, probably close to various leftist movements, who brought us eloquent texts that had, for example, little birds finally ridding themselves of an extremely savage lion through solidarity and courage. The editorial committee was not sure whether these tales should be published: we knew the communists' liking for indoctrination. In the end they came and asked me my opinion. I favored freedom of expression, convinced that the further we advanced, the more the Iranian people could judge for themselves what was good or bad for them. Besides, I was well aware that any refusal on our part would be used against us.

That actually happened with a book containing a very clear message, *The Little Black Fish.* It told the story of a little fish that kept swimming against the current. The organization was reluctant to publish this book, as it would be difficult to support such a message, but then it gave its permission and the book was printed. However, this background became known and the little black fish was immediately endowed with all the virtues of the resistance. It became the symbol of opposition to the monarchy, so much so that when its author died, a rumor went round that he had been killed by the secret police. We had unintentionally given the book an impact that it certainly would not have had if it had been allowed to go on its way from the beginning.

I was very much involved, in a general way, in the production of these books for young people. I looked at layout and illustrations; I listened to cassettes.

The organization built several libraries in the main cities of the country and, as a result of the children's enthusiasm, we decided to quickly add both classes introducing them to music, and craft and theater workshops. Ardavan Mofid, who was a wonderful storyteller, took charge of the theater and later the traveling theater. Oral and physical expression was a natural extension of reading. Through it, the world of the imagination could come to life and the element of play become part of the exercise. The children dressed up and painted their faces, and even for those who were too shy to try, just seeing the others helped them to come out of themselves. Lastly, cinema workshops were opened where children were taught to film in 8 mm and where they learned about cinema.* The Children's Film Festival would bring a new dimension to this experiment.

Our great ambition, however, was to reach the entire country, even the furthest villages, and for that the organization created traveling libraries. Depending on the terrain and the state of the roads, we loaded the books onto trucks, jeeps, or even mules, if mules were the only means of transport that could get through. After a few days, or sometimes only once a month if the distance was great, our librarians would go to pick up the books and distribute new ones.

The mobile libraries soon worked in tandem with the young teachers of the Literacy Corps, who also reached into the most distant villages. This worked so well that we saw more and more examples that gave hope for the future, such as children reading in households where both father and mother were illiterate. We also had a traveling theater, which went from village to village. Many Westerners who came to Iran for the festivals envied this initiative.

MY PARTICIPATION IN PRIVATE ORGANIZATIONS for education, health, culture, and sport had helped me to better fulfill my role as queen. In the beginning, when I was overwhelmed by the hundreds of letters that arrived for me at the palace, I sincerely thought that I could help everyone and relieve the most desperate and inextricable predicaments. I sometimes offered my own money. It took me a while to accept the fact that this thin scattering of aid was useless. My

*The great filmmaker Abbas Kiarostami began his career in the workshops.

very tight budget would not stretch to cover everything, and even the money of the state itself was not inexhaustible. Listening to one's heart resulted in doing charity, but charity basically changed nothing in the way people lived. If I wanted to be useful, I had to concentrate my energy on a few matters that needed the most attention and bring them to fruition.

In the mid-sixties, five years after my marriage, I finally felt that I had found my bearings. It was then that the king and his new prime minister, Amir Abbas Hoveyda, decided to appoint me as regent, which meant that if the king died, until Reza was twenty the fate of Iran would rest on my shoulders. I never thought for a second that it could ever happen. Not for one second. I was twenty-eight, my husband was only forty-six, and I was expecting our third child. We were extremely happy, more confident than ever in the future of the country, the king had no particular ailment, and God did indeed seem to be protecting him from the fanatics who wanted to kill him. I therefore took this decision as a purely formal tribute, even if it was officially ratified by the Parliament. I saw it as proof of my husband's esteem and the confidence he had in me. It made me feel very proud and happy.

Then I realized the symbolic significance of this act: the man who had urged the country to give women the vote had just potentially handed the reins of Iran to one of them! It was a remarkable initiative to take in a Muslim country. I did find out that certain members of Parliament had vigorously opposed this new revolutionary change in our customs. A few years later the king would go even further by deciding to crown me at his side at the time of his coronation. There was no precedent for this honor in the long history of Persia.

"A woman today in Iran," he explained to the country, "is totally different from what she was a few centuries ago, or even only a few decades ago. As all walks of life are open to her, so is the throne. Moreover, the empress has played such an important role among her people during recent years, she has been such a support to me and has fulfilled her task with such fervor and passion that she has richly deserved this honor. Yes, she has done a great deal for all men and women, unstintingly, and will continue to do so, for our task is far from complete."

My favorite photo of the king.

Being held by my father who adored me and was so afraid of losing me when I was very young.

My father, Sohrab Diba, officer cadet at Saint-Cyr in France.

My paternal grandfather, Mehdi Diba Choaeddoleh (seated), around 1870.

My favorite photo of my parents, in the mid-'30s.

With my cousin Reza Ghotbi, who grew up with me and was like the brother I never had.

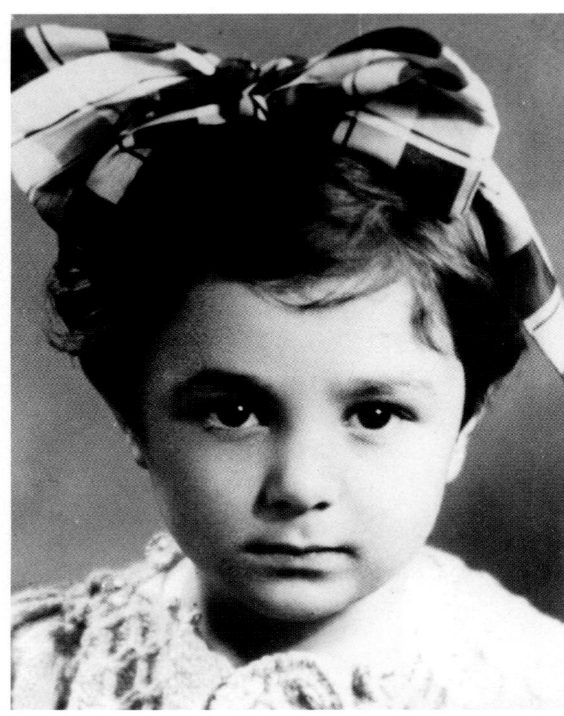

At three or four years old. When I look at this photo today, I feel I am seeing my granddaughter Iman.

I loved spending holidays at Zanjan with my father's sister, my aunt Aziz.

My first school, the Italian school of Tehran. (I am standing to the left of the trees.)

Wearing number 10, I am captain of the Tehran basketball team, which won the championship. Since then I have always had an affinity for players wearing number 10.

My position as cub scout leader earned me my first trip to Paris for training camps. These cubs have become successful men and some still keep in touch with me.

My student card at the Special Architecture School (ESA of Paris), renewed for the 1959 academic year, which I never completed, as I was entering another world. . . .

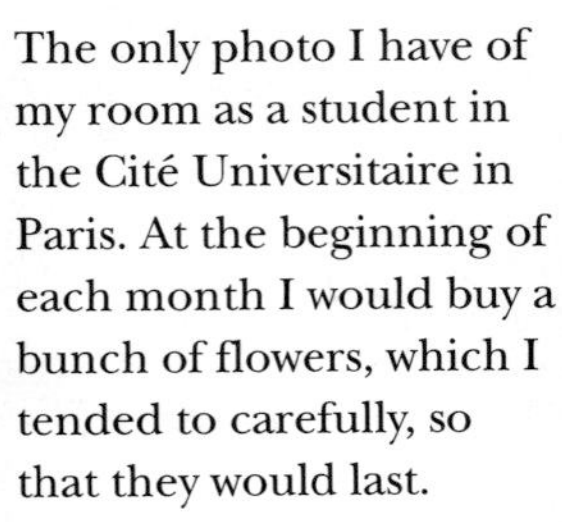

The only photo I have of my room as a student in the Cité Universitaire in Paris. At the beginning of each month I would buy a bunch of flowers, which I tended to carefully, so that they would last.

My engagement to the shah aroused great interest in France. Here at the theatre in Paris, in November 1959, I had exchanged my student's braid for a new hairstyle created by the Carita sisters.

I immediately replied "yes" with such joy and enthusiasm that those around us whispered and smiled.

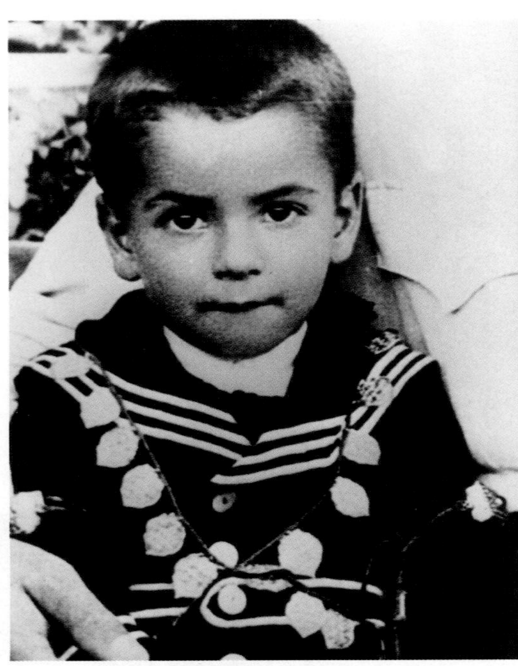

My future husband with religious medals around his neck to protect him. Leila looked like him when she was very young.

Reza Shah the Great with his children. From right to left: Prince Ali-Reza, Princess Shams, Princess Ashraf, Mohammad Reza, the Crown Prince (my future husband), and Prince Gholam-Reza.

Reza Shah the Great accompanied by my future husband, the Crown Prince, whom he included in all his activities.

7 January 1936. The Queen Mother and her two daughters, the Princesses Ashraf and Shams, going out in public for the first time without the veil. This date marks the day of women's emancipation.

Our elder son Reza was born on 31 October 1960.

Farahnaz, born on 12 March 1963, in her father's arms.

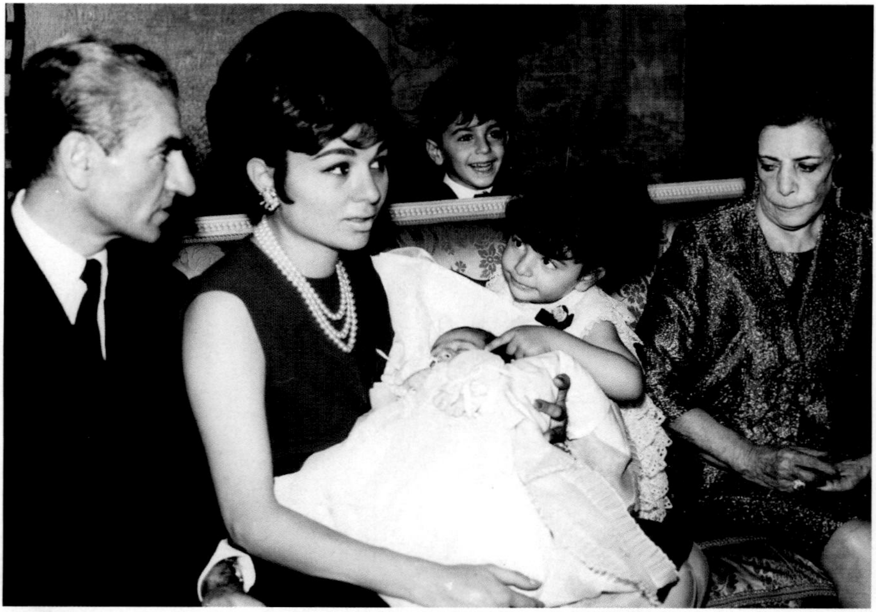

Ali-Reza, our third child, born 28 April 1966, under the benevolent gaze of the Queen Mother, Taj ol Molok.

"Leila's birth on 27 March 1970, marked the realization of our ideal family. We had wanted four children and God had given them to us. . . ."

Reza with his friends at a scout camp on the shores of the Caspian Sea.

. . . and greeting his father returning from a trip.

In the gardens of the Niavaran Palace. Leila takes her first steps toward her father's outstretched hands. He was so proud of her.

Our official portrait.

Reza at the controls of a jet: the pride of his father, who was also a pilot.

The whole family came to see Ali-Reza's first solo flight (in the flying suit). His sisters and brother were as excited as we were.

We have just celebrated Farahnaz's birthday and she wants to show us one of the books she has received.

Chapter 11

ALTHOUGH HE HAD been on the throne for a quarter of a century, my husband had constantly postponed his coronation ceremony. To those who pressed him to assume the crown, he would reply gravely that he would do it when he felt that the country was well advanced on the road to progress, but that in the meantime he did not feel particularly proud of being crowned before a population that was still poor and partially illiterate. From 1965, when he could see the first results of the White Revolution and above all the way it had mobilized enthusiasm throughout Iran, the king began to officially consider his coronation. All the more reason as Reza, the crown prince, who was almost seven, could now be part of this very symbolic act, as my husband wished.

As the birth of our third child, Ali-Reza, was expected in the spring of 1966, the coronation ceremony was put forward definitely to 26 October 1967, the date of the king's forty-eighth birthday, which he would celebrate at the same time. He envisaged his coronation as an event that would be shared by all Iranians, since it marked the beginning of a new era. It was therefore essential that it should arouse wide interest. A Coronation Committee was set up to organize this historic day presided over by a former companion of Reza Shah, a man who had supported the dynasty from its beginning, General Morteza Yazdan Panah. He would be assisted in this task by Mehdi Samii, the governor of the Central Bank of Iran, which is the custodian of the crown jewels.

Reza Shah had assumed the crown on 25 April 1926, also when he was forty-eight, six months after being chosen by the Constituent Assembly. The ceremony took place in the Golestan Palace. At the end of the proceedings, my future husband, who was in his seventh year, was officially proclaimed crown prince.

The Coronation Committee once again chose the Golestan Palace for the ceremony, and so, forty-one years after his father, my husband would perform the solemn rites of monarchy, appointing Reza as his successor; and Reza himself would also be in his seventh year.

Because a crowd of several hundred people would be there beneath the mirrors and stucco decorations of the Golestan Palace, it was decided to make a thorough inspection of the building. When a huge portrait of Reza Shah was taken down to be dusted, it was discovered that the palace was almost on the point of collapsing: there was an enormous crack across the wall. Architects sent immediately to the site confirmed that the supports were shifting under the weight of the roof. Over the decades, too much earth had been put on the terraces without taking the weight into account. It was more than time to reverse the damage: the whole edifice could crumble on top of the guests at any time. Work was begun immediately, and I thought it was a good sign that the coronation should come to the aid of our ailing Golestan Palace.

The crown my husband would put on, which was State property, was kept in the vaults of the Central Bank. Reza Shah had ordered a Persian jeweler called Seradj-ed-din to make it in the style of the Sassanian crowns.* For me, everything had to be created from scratch—the crown, the robe, even the protocol—as none of our monarchs had ever crowned his wife. Although there were enough jewels in the treasury coffers, a designer had to be found to make the crown in a relatively short time. I naturally wanted my crown to be in the same style as my husband's; they had to be related. The first sketches were disappointing, and it was finally the Parisian house of Van Cleef and Arpels that managed the best fusion of Persian design, elegance, and femininity. Mr. Pierre Arpels came to Tehran in person to choose the stones and, as they are not allowed out of the country, he came back with experts from his workroom to set them.

As with the crown, there was no model on which we could base a design for the robe. I did not want it to be like those worn by queens in the West but, on the other hand, I had no ancient picture to provide a typically Iranian style to be followed. That is why, in the end, it was simple and white. Marc Bohan from Christian Dior designed it and also the cloak, which was to be embroidered with Iranian motifs. They were both made in Tehran, at the Officers' Club, the only place in the capital that had tables long enough to spread out the train.

For the embroidery, I turned to a former neighbor from the time when we lived in the flat with the big terrace after my father's death. The first thing that impressed me about Pouran was her piano playing. I envied her: she was a very good pianist. Then I discovered that she did wonderful embroidery, while her sister, Iran, was a painter. I later bought some of her paintings. Pouran agreed to do the artistic work, photographs of which were seen all round the world. Several Iranian dressmakers plus two from Switzerland worked by her side.

*The Sassanian dynasty ruled the Persian Empire 226–651.

The day of the coronation was declared a public holiday throughout the land so that everyone could take part in the celebration. We left from the Marble Palace to go to the Golestan in antique horse-drawn carriages, one for the king and myself and one for the crown prince. At the Golestan, every one of our movements, almost down to our breathing, had to follow the choreography strictly laid down by the uncompromising General Yazdan Panah, the grand master of ceremonies. The little prince entered first, preceded by his guard, advancing through the silent crowd. A little chair for him had been placed to the left of the throne. He sat down on it and waited. Then I appeared, followed by young girls carrying my train, and escorted by ladies-in-waiting. The king arrived last. Then came his coronation, then mine, for which I had to kneel before him. When he crowned me, he had to be careful not to crush my chignon and, most important of all, he had to set the jeweled crown elegantly on my head.

We therefore had to rehearse each of the actions that the Iranian people and beyond them millions of television viewers would see on the day. Reza did the same with his governess. She told me later that he was highly excited at the beginning of the rehearsal, running here and there, until she thought of dressing him in the uniform he would be wearing for the ceremony. "Then," she said, "he immediately became aware of the role he had to play and behaved exceptionally well." These rehearsals gave me the opportunity to try to clear up the various problems of precedence that arose among the king's brothers and sisters, as they did with my ladies-in-waiting. If we were not careful they could lead to resentment and disputes. These quarrels were a source of great annoyance to my husband, and they wore me down also. However, people had to be placated, so I placated them. On the other hand, we had some marvelous times choosing the music to accompany the coronation. During dinners with the queen mother, Minister of Culture Mehrdad Pahlbod played us various works by Iranian composers, and my husband and I finally chose movements that combined feeling and solemnity.

The nearer we came to the day, the more exhausted I became, for all of this preparation was done in addition to my usual daily workload, which left me little breathing space at the best of times. I lost weight, and I can remember the king joking about it affectionately one evening. "You've done it on purpose," he said, "so that you will have hollow cheeks and prominent cheekbones on the day of the coronation!" He knew that I was not very fond of the full, round cheeks of the young woman he had proposed to eight years before.

A DENSE, BRIGHTLY DRESSED CROWD lined the avenues down which we would travel to the Golestan Palace on that 26 October. It was a bright sunny day. As soon as they saw us, the people broke into a joyful chant: *"Zendeh bad Shah! Zendeh bad Shabanou!"* Long live the King! Long live the Queen! Looking into their faces from the carriage slowly drawn along by eight horses, I saw that they all wore an eager and radiant expression. My countrymen had generously given me their affection from the very first, but now we knew each other, and I hoped that I had been able to show them through my work that I loved them in return. In any case, there seemed to be a real connection between us from that time, and I was sure of it that morning as I received their waves and kisses, which I returned with all my heart. "The empress has done a great deal, and she will do a lot more, for our task is still far from complete," the king had said. I was happy at the thought of those words. Yes, there was still a long way to go, but the confidence was obviously there, and we had the time and energy to see it through, or so we thought.

Traveling through the center of Tehran was a wonderful experience, full of laughter and flowers. The little prince following behind in his carriage with the Commander of the Imperial Guard General Mohsen Hashemi-Nejad beside him, brought bursts of youthful enthusiasm from the crowd. He had diligently listened to all my advice, had learned how to wave to the crowd, and rehearsed what he had to do, but I was worried because he had woken up with a cold and slight temperature. The first to enter the Golestan in all its pomp, with the cameras of the whole world upon him, he was a model of solemnity and restrained emotion. The international press would write that his bearing throughout made him the "star" of the ceremony. And indeed, when I viewed the film of the event a few days later, tears came to my eyes as I looked at him.

My entrance, followed by the king's, also took place without a hitch. I had time to give my little Farahnaz a quick smile as she sat quietly with the family to the right of the throne. My husband wanted the ceremony to be strictly Iranian in character, which is why foreign royalty and heads of state had not been invited, apart from Prince Karim Aga Khan and the Begum Ommeh Habibeh, because of the respect and affection between us—ties that would continue during exile. The ambassadors of all the countries represented in Tehran were there, of course. The queen mother, however, had not wished to be present: Rumor had it she was dead, we wanted to hide the fact that she simply never went to official functions.

The trumpets sounded and the coronation began. The Friday prayer Imam began with a prayer, then presented the Koran to the king, who kissed it. Then the imperial accoutrements were brought forward and my husband put on the saber and then the cloak that his father had worn. The crown was presented; he took it firmly and put it on his head while the cannon roared outside the palace.

A moment later the king sat down on the throne that now passed to him and read the following profession of faith. It has a heartrending resonance today, after all the suffering that Iran has endured.

> I thank God, who has allowed me to be of use to my country and my people in every way within my power. I ask God to grant me the power to continue to serve as I have done to this day. The sole aim of my life is the honor and glory of my people and my country. I have but one hope: to preserve the independence and the sovereignty of Iran and advance the Iranian people. To this end, if needs be, I am ready to lay down my life.
>
> May Almighty God allow me to bequeath to future generations a happy country, a prosperous society, and may my son, the crown prince, also remain under divine protection in carrying out the heavy task that lies ahead of him.

Then it was my turn. I came and knelt at the king's feet, and when he put the crown on my head, I felt that he had just honored all the women of Iran. Only four years earlier we had been in the same legal category as the mentally handicapped: we did not even have the basic right of choosing our representatives. This crown wiped out centuries of humiliation; more surely than any law, it solemnly affirmed the equality of men and women.

I was not seeking any further power, nor did I feel any more important the following day than I had previously. It's not in my nature. Power was only important to me insofar as it allowed me to do something to improve the lives of Iranians; I had no desire for it personally. I remember coming out of a film that had been made about me and hearing an American journalist say, "She doesn't belong to this world." I didn't understand him until much later when I was in exile and a few people tried to caricature my role and show me as a power seeker. Perhaps it is normal to pursue power and money, but I can honestly say that it has never crossed my mind.

A YEAR AND A HALF BEFORE THIS HISTORIC DAY, on 28 April 1966, I had given birth to Ali-Reza. Two days later I had written in his baby book, "He looks very like his father; he will have a clear complexion." God was very good to us: after Reza, so conscious of the responsibilities that awaited him, and so admired by all for his seriousness; after imaginative, warm-hearted Farahnaz, who concerned herself with the problems of the underprivileged and would spend hours out in the open petting animals; God had just sent us the most mischievous little boy. Of course we didn't know it yet, but we would soon find out.

Unlike Farahnaz, who expressed herself very early in a delightful babble, Ali-Reza took his time, but when he did decide to talk, he spoke perfectly and with a sense of humor that would often make us burst out laughing. One day when he was urging me to get dressed so that we could go out into the garden, he remarked, "People will say, what kind of majesty is this still in her bathrobe!" On another occasion when he was having lunch and we were all talking around him, one of my cousins stole a piece of potato from his plate. We saw him turn and look around for the man who was waiting on table. "Alain," he said to him, "would you please bring a fork for Miss Jaleh."

He was scarcely three at that time, and he wanted to be called either Toutoune, the nickname his governess had given him, or Pilot, because he dreamed of piloting one of those American Phantom fighter planes that fascinated him.

"Toutoune, you're a naughty boy!"

"No," he replied, "I'm Pilot."

We were in the heyday of the hippie era, and one evening I heard him say to his governess, who was vainly trying to get him to the bathtub, "I don't want to have a bath. I want to stay a dirty hippie."

Another day, right in the middle of dinner, he informed us that he liked "free love."

A few months later he entered nursery school at the Lycée Razi, where I had done my baccalaureate. The high school had considerably expanded since then and had moved to a new location in the north of Tehran. It had grown in order to accommodate very young children, so Ali-Reza was able to go there, unlike his two elder siblings who had been taught for a while in the palace after kindergarten. He liked it so much that when school was over on the first day he refused to leave and told the chauffeur who was waiting for him to go back without him.

These childish stories amused the king as much as they did me. We would relate them in our rare moments alone, and I would see his face relax and light up almost miraculously. He adored having the children with him when he was exercising late in the afternoon. They talked and laughed together and often made quite a rumpus. Ali-Reza would get on his back and play horses, the bigger ones would throw cushions, and for a quarter of an hour it was a real pillow fight.

A government minister, Abdol-Majid Majidi, told me that one afternoon when he was in the middle of a meeting with the king, he saw him suddenly look at the door that had creaked. "The king had stopped listening to me," he said, "and so I stopped talking and waited until he was ready to come back to what I was saying. But instead I saw him smile. He was suddenly a thousand miles away from our discussion. Then I also turned toward the door. Little Princess Farahnaz was standing in the doorway, waiting for her father to ask her to come in, and there was such a flow of affection between the two of them that I was the one who got up and made a discreet exit."

The children were conscious of the power they had over their father, and for his part my husband knew how to delight them and with just a few words restore the closeness interrupted by official trips away or long working days at home. "You are much better than I am at talking to children," I would say to him. When we interrupted their dinner to kiss them before leaving for a reception, their governess lost all control over them as soon as they saw him. It was as though the rules of discipline were suddenly abolished for the time that he was with them. I can still see Ali-Reza, who was being told by his nanny to eat his spinach, spitting it out again and bursting out laughing when his father came in. It was difficult: I tried to reassure these poor ladies who went to a lot of trouble to teach our children manners, but at the same time I was very happy at this understanding between them and their father. That too was a gift from heaven.

My husband accepted the fact that the governesses had to be strict, but he would not tolerate their being aggressive or unfair. I remember how angry he was one evening when he discovered Farahnaz in tears, having been sent to her room. I was still in my office, and I saw him come in, white-faced, holding his daughter in his arms.

"Tell that governess to go immediately! Immediately!"

He could understand someone losing her temper with Ali-Reza's pranks, but he could not bear injustice. Farahnaz was so sweet, already so thoughtful of others, that he could not bear to find her upset.

He had a special intimacy with each of his children. Farahnaz's love of nature and her tomboy side delighted him. When she was older, she loved driving up the steps of the palace on her motorbike, to the great displeasure of the protocol people who obviously feared she would disturb the king. But he would come out of his office smiling and invariably say, "Let it be, let it be." Then he would stand there for a moment watching her do her tricks. With the boys, it made him feel quietly proud to see in them all the signs of his own passion for sports cars and planes. "Look at Reza," he would say to me. "His wrist is hardly bigger than my thumb and he can drive wonderfully well already." Later, with our fourth child, Leila, he would have conversations about the drought that worried him so much. As he kissed her before bed, he would often say to her, "Pray for rain, Leila *joune*." Drought was an enormous problem for our agriculture. Little Leila, no longer with us today, would often say, "I like it when the sky is gray." And I would think, with some emotion, "Her father has passed on his love of rain to her. Forever."

WITH THE ARRIVAL OF ALI-REZA, we were forced to seriously consider moving. The Ekhtessassi Palace, where we had lived since our marriage, was now definitely too small to accommodate us all. It had only two bedrooms: one for the king, the other for me. We had put Reza in a small villa next door and had added another floor to it for Farahnaz. We could not do the same for Ali-Reza, and so I gave him my office next to our bedrooms. But that could not last either. It was stifling. The Ekhtessassi Palace, which in Reza Shah's time was an oasis of fresh air and greenery, found itself over the decades in the center of a hugely expanding Tehran, permanently surrounded by a noisy, polluting stream of traffic. And besides, the garden was not very big.

We had already thought several times of moving to the Niavaran Palace, then one of us would be caught up by our work and the idea would be put aside. Built in the sixties to house temporary guests, the Niavaran Palace had the great advantage of being situated on the slopes of the Alborz, at an altitude of 5,500 feet, well above the grimy rush and bustle of the town, and in addition it was in the middle of large, beautiful gardens. I looked it over and had work begin immediately on the alterations that were needed for the children and for the receptions that were an integral function of a head of state. Careful as I always was not to incur too many expenses for ourselves, and since I spent part of my days trying to find money for the various organizations I presided over, I gave up the idea of installing air conditioning, given also that in the summer we usually went to Sa'ad Abad Palace, which was cooler. It was a silly thing to do. The architect said as much, but I insisted, feeling good about giving up that luxury. The palace was very badly insulated and we suffered from the heat there, which gave the king an opportunity to tease me about my "exaggerated sense of duty."

I preferred Niavaran to Sa'ad Abad, which was dark and gloomy with a rather overgrown garden. Niavaran was modern and light. There was a magnificent view over the city to the south, to the north were the Alborz Mountains, and to the east you could see the Damavand volcano with its mantle of snow. That being said, Niavaran was functional and welcoming, but it did not have the splendor one imagines in the palaces of Europe. I well remember the writer Lesley Blanch's surprise when I received her there for the book she was writing about me.* "The first impression is surprising," she wrote,

> at first sight it surprises, for it has none of the concomitants of a palace, in terms of size or splendour. But though it may not possess the legendary grandeur of Windsor, nor the size and studied

***Farah Shahbanou of Iran.*

> perfection of Versailles, nor the haunting drama of any of mad Ludwig's Bavarian splendours, it is, in its own right, interesting. It is an essay in *simplified* Royal living, expressed in contemporary terms, while in no way resembling an informal Royal holiday pavilion. The uncompromisingly four-square lofty white cube, strangely windowless on the side approached from the gates, is very modest-looking to house such a monarch as the Shahanshah, and its portico, with soaring tubular pillars, does not impress. But if the exterior has no outstanding features, the interior is agreeably personal and inviting. Round the four sides of the cube which forms the entrance hall or foyer, a wide, railed first floor gallery gives on to the private apartments.

I really liked my private library, which I had built in a wing adjacent to the palace. It was the only place that had been planned exactly according to my specifications and decorated according to my personal taste. There was also an open balcony on the first floor. Sculptures and objects both ancient and modern were there side by side. In this vast, bright room I had gathered together the works that meant the most to me: writers from all over the world and Iranian poets, art books and antiquarian books, paintings and sculptures by contemporary Iranians such as Zenderoudi, Oveissi, Mohasses, and Tanâvoli, with works by Andy Warhol, César, and Arnaldo Pomodoro. As for the garden, the tall plane trees reminded me of my childhood holidays in the old village of Shemiran, which was now part of the city.

An old building of the Qajar dynasty, the Jahan Nama Palace, had been restored to house my husband's offices. It was situated within the garden and had a view over the whole town below. It was there, twelve years later, that the king witnessed the uprising of a people for whose welfare he had devoted all his energies.

Chapter 12

AFTER MY FIRST two children were born, I began to travel extensively on my own throughout the country. I wanted to meet people in the furthest provinces to get a better idea of their problems and expectations and to see what had been done by the government and the various organizations that I headed. In that way I would also have a better opportunity to know my country, my fellow countrymen and -women and their different cultures. In Tehran, although I was snowed under by reports, I could not experience situations firsthand or talk directly to farmers, workers, and officials—all those people far from the capital who were involved in the development of the country. The White Revolution was proceeding, bringing new expectations and inevitable frustrations. These trips were an opportunity for me to register these numerous reactions and report them to the king. He also traveled, but I had more time, as he had to attend to both international and domestic affairs. Moreover, I considered myself the best ambassador to give him a faithful report of what was being said far from Tehran and what life was really like in the provinces. It's the same in every country: some ministers and civil servants prefer to report the positive side of things and often hide the real situation for fear of offending the head of state. And, of course, when something is going well, it reflects well on them and justifies their role, while the opposite can perhaps cast doubt on them. I could say anything, and it was my duty to do so, to my compatriots as well as to my husband.

The choice of going to one particular region rather than another depended on the correspondence I received—my office dealt with an average of 80,000 letters a month—and on what I was told by the people I met. Of course my desire to visit a region I wasn't familiar with influenced my choice, as did requests from the king or the government. The people had quickly understood that I was sensitive to their plight and they did not hesitate to ask me for help. The letters were analyzed, the problems classified, and expectations grouped according to region. I then discussed them with the relevant ministers, and if I felt that my presence could be beneficial to all, I set plans for the trip in motion. The ministers concerned usually accompanied me, as did the directors of the National Gas Company and academic experts in subjects of importance to the province we were about to visit. I also always had with me my chief secretary, Karim Pasha Bahadori, who organized everything. His place was later taken by Houshang Nahavandi.

In spite of fatigue and difficulties, I can say today that these meetings with my countrymen and -women from Azarbaijan to Khorasan, from Gilan to the Persian Gulf, from Kurdistan to Baluchistan, not to mention the desert plateaus of the center, are among the best memories of my life as queen. The emotion was palpable from the start, as soon as I entered these towns or villages. An open car was usually made available so that the crowd could see me and wave to me and I to them. Many of the people who lined the streets had written asking me to come, and now that I was there, not only did they give free rein to their joy, but they also wanted to touch me and kiss me. Others intended to personally give me a letter, for it is a custom to give a request directly to the king or queen, and also they may not have trusted officials in the administration to give me their correspondence. Their eagerness always resulted in the same scenes, which both touched me profoundly and upset me at the same time: people threw themselves on my car, disregarding the speed and the Imperial Guard escort on motorcycles, to have a chance to get close to me. I begged the driver to keep to a walking pace—I was so afraid of causing an accident—but the security people feared that some fanatic might take advantage of that to attack me. To dissuade people from rushing forward, the motorcycle guards made their engines scream, and with the incessant roar and permanent fear of an accident, I had my heart in my mouth. In the end I had to ask the guard to change motorcycles. More practically, realizing that many people were prepared to risk their lives to give me their letters, I asked my ladies-in-waiting to go before me or after me in open jeeps, just to gather the letters. Slowly the word spread, and the villagers more confidently and calmly gave their letters to the ladies.

The security men had great difficulty coping with my way of traveling. As soon as I got out of the car, I liked to talk face to face with the people who had been waiting for me and take time to listen to some of them. Women would invariably throw their arms around my neck, kiss me, and hold me close. It was a constant strain trying to stop the police from dragging them away and having to order these men, sometimes sharply, to let me go about my work in my own way. In the evening I apologized and tried to explain how important these informal conversations were for me. I would say to them, "I can understand you protecting the king in that way—we can't take the risk of anything happening to him—but I'm not indispensable to the future of the country, and if I'm to be killed by an assassin, well, I'd prefer it to happen while I'm doing my duty. For pity's sake, let me go about my work in my own way." They agreed, but the next day they would start again, and I would lose my temper again. I imagine it's the same with security services everywhere in the world.

Then I would preside at work meetings with the governor, the mayors, the representatives of different sections of the population. When the ministers were there, they heard the proceedings for themselves, but I still asked my chief secretary to take minutes. In one village the people might ask for clean drinking water or the construction of a new road; in another it could be for a decent school building or a public bathhouse; elsewhere, a medical unit. What I found deeply moving every time was that I could see their love for the king in spite of their poverty; and they also showed me great affection. They asked me to tell the king how often they thought of him. I felt that they were aware of his total commitment to Iran and aware that although we were doing everything possible to help them, we could not make up the backwardness of several centuries overnight. In all these travels, I never once heard any mention of the clerics' opposition to female emancipation or agrarian reform. The mullahs,* who would later plunge the country into war and backwardness, greeted me everywhere with words of praise for my social work and with smiles that I took to be sincere. No doubt some of them were. The head Shiite clerics did not shake hands with me, but the Sunnis did. They all made requests for the restoration of holy sites. They knew how interested I was in these sanctuaries, where I liked to go and meditate.

*Representatives of the religious minorities were also present to welcome me on these trips.

Depending on the region I was visiting, I would travel by small plane, helicopter, car, or even bus, if the state of the roads permitted. We sometimes reached villages that were still so lacking in facilities that mothers took advantage of my presence to ask for immediate assistance. Several times I was able to make the helicopter or the plane available to these mothers to take a sick son, a wounded husband, or a handicapped child to the nearest hospital. Of course I knew that the same conditions would prevail after my departure, but at least there was hope: the young recruits of the various brigades would slowly cover the whole country, and we were training more and more doctors.

I was sometimes away for more than ten days, for example in Azarbaijan or Kurdistan, stopping in almost every village. Knowing that I would be passing by, the people ran to the sides of the little roads to greet me. Sometimes I only lowered the window to wave, but their joy was often so touching that I asked the driver to stop for a moment. Then it was very difficult to get on my way again. They had a thousand things to tell me; they could not understand that others were waiting for me, and that my schedule was very heavy. And farther on there they were, a crowd with radiant faces, families dressed in their best, and more of those exchanges full of affection and sincere words.

Meeting ordinary local people, meeting with officials to plan work, and visiting sites went on throughout the day. I had to be constantly available, listening attentively and catching the slightest detail. I was sometimes so exhausted that I lay down on the floor for five or ten minutes with my legs against the wall to get the blood circulating and the energy level reviving a little. The relentless activity made me more aware of what the village women endured. On top of all their other difficulties, they often had to walk several kilometers to fetch water. Thank God my health was good enough to handle these marathons. In the evening, if there were no official reception, I had dinner with the people who were traveling with me, we talked about what we had learned from these exchanges, and then we relaxed. Knowing my liking for poetry and music, the governor would often organize a dinner in a garden or by a river and, sitting on mats, we would listen to people reading to us from Hafez, Ferdowsi, or another of our wonderful Iranian poets. Or we would listen to the traditional music of the region. That also delighted the director of the Iranian Red Cross (Red Lion and Sun), Dr. Hossein Khatibi, who was usually with me because the organization had centers almost everywhere. Dr. Khatibi was an outstanding man, very cultured and able to recite from memory poems praising the beauty of the regions we were in or exactly illustrating the situations we were experiencing. The finance minister and future prime minister, Jamshid Amouzegar, who sometimes joined us, had the same astonishing talent. On other evenings I would suggest parlor games like riddles and the guessing games I liked so much. Then I would see these very serious gentlemen—the divisional commander, the minister for agriculture, and the governor—relax completely, regain their youthful high spirits, and burst out laughing. And I was the first to enjoy it. Working side by side, sharing enthusiasm and fatigue, created a mutual understanding that cast aside, at least for a while, the usual rules of protocol.

I loved the unexpected things that happened on these trips, for then I knew that I was in touch with the real Iran. When I was traveling by helicopter and we were flying over a village, an oasis, or countryside that suddenly inspired a particular response in me, I would ask the pilot to land. I remember once—this was also in Azarbaijan—I had insisted on landing by a lake, which I thought very beautiful. The place was completely deserted and the pilot could not understand what attracted me to it. The helicopter had scarcely touched down when we saw women, children, then men on horseback rushing out of the hills toward us. We were both astonished to see each other there. The local people couldn't believe their eyes: I had literally fallen from the skies in the last place they would have expected! And I was thrilled to have this meeting due purely to chance. A quarter of an hour earlier, neither they nor I had had any idea of it, and now here we were face to face. Some of the men knelt, but most of the women let out cries of joy. It was a wonderful moment that made all the fatigue disappear immediately. They kissed me and pressed me to their hearts as if I were one of their own returning home. Many of them covered my head with their veils, in that familiar gesture of our country, and their saliva on my cheeks was a living sign of their affection.

Once in Gilan, as we were flying over some buildings under construction, the governor accompanying me whispered in my ear, "Here we've made a model farm for raising silkworms, with the help of Japanese."

"Well, let's go and take a look!"

"But it's not on our itinerary, Your Majesty. No one is expecting us."

"All the more reason. The people are in there working. Let's give them a surprise."

The helicopter made a rather bumpy landing somewhere near the farm. Suddenly the people realized that I was inside. Then there was an immediate rush toward us, men and women running out everywhere. A worker lent us his jeep to drive over to the farm, but meanwhile a wildly excited crowd had packed around the car. There were joyful cries of "Long live the King! Long live the King!" and hands outstretched, so much so that we could go neither forwards nor backwards. The governor stood, shouting at the top of his voice to no avail, both of us covered in white dust blown up by the helicopter. The people were obviously in no hurry to see us leave, only too happy to keep me there. We began exchanging a few words, and once again I heard their expressions of affection. I, too, wanted to tell them how dear they were to me and that I would pass on their greetings and good wishes to the king. At last the pilot persuaded some men to join the governor to open a path for us. We advanced step by step in the midst of a sea of nothing but friendly, smiling faces. When we reached the buildings, they tried to shut the gates behind us to stop the whole population from surging in. It was a waste of time: no sooner were they closed than the gates gave way under the pressure from the crowd.

And I myself began to think that perhaps the governor was right in warning me about the hazards of unscheduled stops. I was not frightened for myself but for them as the crowd and the excitement kept increasing. So I shortened my visit and, taking every possible precaution, we got back to the helicopter. But once there, we found it impossible to take off, for the people crowded right under the rotor blades with no idea of the danger. The governor begged them to move back, but they just kept chanting the king's name as if it were a ceremony.

Then, standing on the landing skid, I described the moment we had shared; I told them how much I was touched by the feelings they had expressed, how much I would love to have more of these spontaneous exchanges, to come more often to all the villages, among families, in the factories… "And now," I told them, "I would ask you to stand back and sit down, so that this meeting is not marred by an accident."

They understood and did as I asked. We took off above a forest of waving arms and scarves.

I really valued these genuine, spontaneous moments. They justified the sometimes discouraging and thankless hard work my husband was doing in Tehran. They were proof that each of the government's initiatives would finally achieve its distant goal because the people believed in their king.

Some of these unusual encounters stand out in my memory and still move me when I think of them today. One day I was driving a little jeep myself with just one other woman companion and a few guards in another car. We went past a woman walking along the side of the road carrying a very heavy load. I stopped and asked her if I could drive her anywhere. She did not recognize me, so we could talk woman to woman. She told me about the difficulties she faced in her everyday life, seriously but without bitterness. We were in Babol, in the north of the country. After a while she asked me where I was going and who I was. I told her, naturally, and this woman who lived a life of poverty—this was in the mid-sixties—took my hand with such warmth and fervor that this simple gesture expressed all the words she could not find. She had no house; a short time later I helped her to buy one.

Another time I happened to go into a tiny candy shop in the town of Dezful. It was evening and I had only a friend with me (two security men were following me), and as we were simply dressed, we could pass for two city women on holiday. The woman selling the candy needed little persuasion to describe her already long life. She had worked in a *hammam* and known the insecurity of the dynasty in its early years. Suddenly she said, "I thank God and the king every day for giving us security. Every morning I come to work very early and no one ever bothers me." Then one of her neighbors came in, a young sergeant who lived above the shop. He listened to us for a moment, then he suddenly recognized me. He was covered in confusion, as was the candy seller, but I tried to keep the simple, familiar tone of the conversation we had been having a moment earlier. The young man slowly found his voice, to the point of asking me if I would have a cup of tea with himself and his wife upstairs.

"With pleasure," I told him.

The apartment was one room where his wife and children were sleeping on a mattress on the floor. He woke his young wife. Not a very easy situation to find herself in, woken up like that to find me there. But we kissed and I sat with them around the samovar. She talked about her children and he about his work in the army. They were both from Azarbaijan and wished to go back there. At least that was one wish I could grant without having to move heaven and earth.

One other evening in Rasht I knocked on the door of a house at random. This time they recognized me immediately, and there was instant excitement. It only took a few minutes for the news to go round the village, and soon people were climbing over the fences and crowding onto the porch. They all wanted to tell me what was troubling them, what was wrong, what has to be done, and those who did not dare speak ran up with letters. One wanted to send his son to study overseas and asked me to get him a scholarship. One young man insisted on seeing me in private: a heroin addict, he begged me to send him to a hospital. A woman could not put up with her husband's violence any longer...

People also knew about my interest in our national heritage and, in the course of every visit, they would try to drag me off to see hidden treasures that even the specialists in the Ministry of Culture had never heard about. If I was in the bazaar, they would say, "Farah, Farah, come this way," or "Shahbanou, come and see the terrible state of our poet's grave. Something must be done to help us restore it." I felt how important it was to comply, because the poet was the pride of their little town, the cultural symbol that united them and which they wanted their children to admire in their turn.

Sometimes, if we were not too far from the desert, I would ask to go there in the evening. The desert is a place of grace, of meditation, on the fringe of civilization, and after the intensity of the day's experiences, I needed its silence to regain a certain serenity.

A fire was built, and we would gaze at the vast expanse of the sky and the magic of the stars, which in the desert, and only there, suddenly seem to fall only a few hundred meters away. One of my great regrets is to have not taken the time to cross the desert by camel as I dreamed of doing, accompanying the nomads on their route for a few days. I told myself that I would have the leisure to do it later, and so I put it off year after year. We always longed for cool breezes and green countryside, but now that I live in the United States and Europe, I badly miss the rocky arid mountains of the desert. I miss the dust and the flies. I even miss the smell of gasoline, so noticeable in Iran.

Another regret of mine is having decided not to wear the traditional costume of the regions I was visiting on special occasions. I always wanted to, but did not dare, for fear that the gesture might be misinterpreted. Today I think that dressing like all the women who were honoring me would have been a better way to show them how much I felt myself to be one of them and how thoroughly Iranian I felt. One never loses that feeling of belonging to a community, and every day in exile some aspect of daily life brings a painful reminder that I am not among my own and that my roots have remained in Iran. The flapping of a pigeon's wings in the courtyard of a building takes me back to Tehran, like an unexpected waft of honeysuckle or lilac while taking a walk. A piece of feta cheese on a slice of bread with a mint leaf on top or a few apricots that a friend brings me from home fill me with indescribable nostalgia. And the boiling hot tea accompanied with mulberries! When these mulberries are dried in the sun, they still have a little bit of sand that crunches when you chew. Recently, eating some of these little fruits that the king and I liked so much I found that one of them had a few grains of sand. I thought I had broken a tooth, but at the same time I felt a surge of happiness at having swallowed a little bit of Iranian soil.

I came back from my trips full of energy and confidence in the future. All the Iranians I met were dignified in spite of the difficulties they experienced, full of integrity, clear-sighted about what should be done. They were examples of courage to me. I had only to think of any number of women I had met, and fathers, workers, peasants, and soldiers, to keep myself smiling.

THE PLACE OF WOMEN IN OUR SOCIETY, especially within the family, was a constant preoccupation of mine. Many women had been campaigning for years to have their rights recognized. I am thinking in particular of Hadjar Tarbiat, who fought for women under Reza Shah, and also of Mahnaz Afkhami, who was the first minister for women's affairs. Now we were one of the few Muslim countries to have legislation making men and women equal under the law, but everyone knows how wide the gap can be between the spirit of the law and its practice! Yes, women could vote and be elected to Parliament, study, enter a university, and pursue the career of their choice, but what did these possibilities mean far from cities, in a rural society that was still for the most part illiterate and traditional in outlook? To a large number of peasants, they still meant nothing. The mullah remained the only moral authority in most villages, and the efforts of the government, backed by various associations for the protection of women's rights, encountered great difficulty in making another voice heard. The girls wanted to go to school, the women wanted the reforms, but the men were dragging their feet. In these conditions—they were extremely difficult—women turned to me in ever-increasing numbers. By appointing me regent, then crowning me queen, the king had clearly shown them the way, and it was surely easier to tell their sufferings to another woman than to complain to the king himself or to officers of the administration.

Many women told me personally or by mail of their distress at having been cast aside for a younger wife. What should they do? In theory they could have demanded a divorce, as polygamy was now forbidden. In practice the situation was not so clear-cut, as pressure by the clerics had obliged the legislature to retain a limited form of polygamy: if the first wife could not have children, or if she had a serious illness, the husband could take a second wife with the first wife's approval.

Despite the law, it was very difficult for both sexes to be treated equally with respect to divorce. It had been a strictly male prerogative for a long time: the man could repudiate his wife without even consulting her. The poor woman often only learned of it by a letter informing her that her marriage had been dissolved. Now women could also file for divorce, and the law had set up family courts where, theoretically, the couple could come and state their case. But what could these courts do, when most of the women I talked with felt that men were all-powerful?

And indeed, not everything had been reformed. For example, the law still insisted that a woman have the signed permission of her husband if she wanted to travel, just like a minor. One can imagine the humiliating or ridiculous situations this caused for certain women academics, lawyers, or engineers. I spoke about it to my husband and to the ministers concerned, but it was one of the many vexing questions with the clerics, who saw in it a way of legally maintaining women's dependence on men. We wanted to go forward, and I was particularly insistent on it for women, but we had to pay attention to different mentalities, being careful not to precipitously do away with solidly held customs, not to shock people, and I tried to propose some adjustments in each case. Many other women were working toward the same goal, in particular Princess Ashraf, who brought all the women's associations together and did a great deal for the standing of women.

The Literacy Corps, which originally consisted of volunteers to go and teach in the country, now had as many women students as men. The idea had been suggested to me by some young women when I was having lunch at the Pahlavi University in Shiraz. "Why couldn't we also take part in literacy programs?" they said. And they were right, doubly right, for in some regions we came up against parents who refused to send their daughters to school if the teacher was a man. The Women's Literacy Corps, which my husband enthusiastically approved, would allow us to overcome this problem in particular.

I say in particular, for these young women also helped us spread the word when we tried to get people to accept family planning. The government had consulted the clerics, who opposed it at first, but finally agreed to it with a *fatwa*, a religious decree. (After the Islamic Revolution, they would do away with family planning, claiming that the king had only brought it in to decrease the Muslim population. Then, faced with a birthrate that was rising at an alarming rate, they had to bring it back.) Having received the clerics' consent, we now had to tackle the hardest task—convincing rural populations that taking control of the number of children they had would bring them and the country a better life. The circumstances in which they lived made them think exactly the opposite: the more children we have, they assured us, the more manpower we have. Some also told me that they would produce soldiers for the crown prince. They could not imagine the progress of mechanization, nor a different future for their children through increased access to education, better health, and social security. It was our job to inform them and make them understand. For the moment, the rate of infant mortality seemed to plead their case, but the rate would rapidly diminish thanks to the Health Corps, the opening of dispensaries, vaccination, and free meals in schools. The menace of polygamy followed the same lines: women had a child every year for fear that the husband might leave or take a second wife. We could see that it was absolutely imperative to explain the modernization of the country to the people.

One of the women who did a great deal of work to change people's ways of thinking was, without doubt, Mrs. Farrokhrou Parsa, who was minister for national education. Her own mother had been one of the pioneers of women's emancipation. I had known Mrs. Parsa at the École Jeanne d'Arc, where she had been my science teacher. She was also a doctor and deeply committed to the double mission of education and health. When I was queen, my friendship and admiration for her was strengthened through her work. I cannot think of her today without a great deal of emotion and sadness. Knowing the role she had played, for women in particular, the mullahs condemned her to death and shot her in a way that I cannot describe without feeling ashamed—ashamed that Iranians could have done such a thing. They put her in a sack so that when her body fell, it would not arouse her torturers. Thousands of women were executed in the same way, and those who were virgins were raped before being killed because according to religious text virgins go to heaven.

THE SORRY PLIGHT OF ORPHANS was another of my tasks. I had taken over the presidency of the organization responsible for these children. There were about ten thousand members throughout the country and, apart from the manager, Fatemeh Khozeime Alam, my chief associate here was my mother. This organization, which had been in existence for many years, did not have enough centers in the various regions of the country to house everyone, and so our first concern was to build more.

Then we realized that apart from the principals, the women who worked in these centers had no special training. The children were clothed, fed, and well cared for, but they did not have enough psychological support.

We therefore decided to train young men and women to be educators. France gave us very valuable aid by setting up a special school. People throughout the country offered to help by taking responsibility for a few children. Other, wealthier Iranians gave us land or buildings to provide for our needs, which were enormous.

Each time I visited these children, I felt how much they needed to be seen as individuals, apart from the group. Little girls would run up to me and say, "I'm So-and-so." Their uniforms made them all look alike, and quite often the little boys had their heads shaved because of lice. The looks on their faces were heartbreaking. The uniforms had to go, and we had to make the staff realize that every child is an individual who needs to be acknowledged as such if he or she is to blossom. It was a change of thinking that took a lot of patient explanation.

In the beginning, when I arrived at some orphanages, I sometimes felt that everything had been specially set up for my visit, that they had cleaned everything and carefully hidden anything that was not right, even sick children or those who were very upset, whom they preferred I did not see. That sometimes led to some lively exchanges. "If I take the trouble to travel and come from so far away," I would say to the staff, "it's not so that you can conceal the most distressing situations or the things that don't work. On the contrary, I'm here to help you, and I want to see the difficulties you face every day. And then it's very bad for the children. Don't you think they can see that you're lying to me?" Making them understand that even though I was queen, I had to come into contact with reality, with life as it was in order to be able to make good decisions. And that too meant changing their way of thinking.

After a few years, when we had provided respectable homes and an enviroment where the children were as well adjusted as they could be—they went to school like other children and were more integrated now that they no longer wore uniforms—we could then think of the next step. This involved creating holiday centers where they could get to know another part of the country and, above all, participate in cultural and sporting activities, they had never before known. I went door-knocking once again. A gentleman gave us some magnificent land in Shemiran, not far from the Niavaran Palace, and with the money we had collected, we could build our first two holiday homes, one on that site and the other by the Caspian Sea.

I personally supervised the architecture and interior fittings of these buildings. The architects we had employed were concerned for the children and sensitive to their needs. I vividly remember the lively discussions we had over every detail: the right proportions of the bedrooms, the color of the beds, the orientation of the kitchen, so that the cook could take advantage of the view over the sea while peeling the potatoes. Our work was amply repaid when the children saw the sea for the first time.

We had special centers in Tehran and some other towns for children abandoned at birth. Individual women in the organization would look after one or two newborn babies and take care of their emotional and physical needs. My mother had "her children," whom she looked after as she had looked after me. When an opportunity arose for them to be adopted by Iranian or even foreign couples, we discussed it, gathered information about the adoptive parents, and if this information was favorable, we granted the adoption. We thought that if these little ones had the chance to live with a Swiss, Norwegian, or Danish family, why refuse it? The woman in charge of the organization kept in contact with the adoptive parents.

Several of the adoptees, who had become Europeans, wrote to me after the Islamic Revolution, and I have corresponded with some of them. Today most of them are happy, well-adjusted young adults, but there is a little corner of them that still feels Iranian. Some would very much like to know their country; others dream of finding their birth parents. I am their link with the Iran they have never known, a maternal link, and I find that very touching indeed.

However, the great majority of children abandoned at birth stayed in Iran. We tried to help them with the transition to adult life in the best way we could. For some we found temporary accommodation, for others it was work. Everyone tried hard. And when one of them got married, it was a real celebration.

THE FATE OF HANDICAPPED CHILDREN had concerned the government and authorities for some time. I had accepted the chairmanship of the National Society for the Protection of Children, which had been formed many years earlier. The organization had a center for the mentally handicapped and was engaged in research to find the causes of retardation. Consanguinity was frequently a cause and in this area I remember the outstanding work of Senator Mehrangiz Manouchehrian, who was the author of a law obliging young engaged couples to have a medical examination before marriage. This woman was also the driving force behind the setting up of children's courts and a prison law forbidding the incarceration of minors in the same place as adults.

Several schools had been opened to teach the blind to read and write and, for those who had the talent, learn music. I regularly visited these centers and had great admiration for the devotion and competence of all the teachers. Our aim was obviously to make it possible for these young people to find work despite their handicap, and I remember that many of them were successfully employed as switchboard operators. The same effort was being made for the deaf. A center had been set up in Tehran to teach them to speak. Some could be employed in the noisiest industries, which showed that society could have need of them.

We wanted to give all these young people, handicapped or not, the opportunity to play sports. I was among other things the president of the Sporting Federation for the Deaf. The government and the king believed strongly in the benefits of sport, and they saw to it that every town had the essential facilities.

Chapter 13

WITH LEILA'S BIRTH on 27 March 1970 we now had our ideal family. We wanted four children; God had given them to us, equally divided between boys and girls. During an interview at the very beginning of my pregnancy, I said, "I have a feeling that my fourth child will be a girl. The king and I want to call her Leila." I kept the interview and, full of joy after the birth of my little girl, I placed it in her baby book. It is still there. A few pages further on, I read these few words I wrote on 27 March 1971, for her first birthday: "A lovely nature, happy, sociable, wrinkles her nose when she smiles. Loves to laugh..."

Despite a heavy schedule, we had more or less managed to create a family life. It had begun ten years before with the amazing discovery that we were both in love, with the tastes we had in common and the laughter we shared. It had blossomed with Reza's birth, which reassured the king about the future of the dynasty and allowed him to enjoy a full, serene happiness that he had never known.

The holidays were a godsend for us. They seem today like marvelous periods of calm on a constantly stormy sea. We could get together at last relatively free from other people's cares and expectations, from the incessant intrusion into our daily lives of the affairs of Iran and the rest of the world. I say "relatively" because whether we were at winter sports or the seaside, I never saw my husband spend a day without at least meeting with the prime minister or Cabinet members or receiving a foreign dignitary visiting Iran. In any case, he worked every morning.

Basically, we were never able to live as a normal family and give the children as much time as we would have liked. While they have a certain understanding of what our responsibilities were, the children remark on it to me today, and if I had my life to live over again, I would give more time to them and to my husband. For a mother, the happiness and well-being of her children is the most important thing, and if I have one piece of advice to give to women, it is this: If it is not essential, minimize your work and be available to your children. In heading a host of organizations, I feel I contributed to the well-being of my fellow countrymen and -women—and in so doing I was thinking of my own children's future in that country—but that cannot replace the daily show of affection and the presence that I would have liked to give them.

At the beginning of our marriage we went to Babol on the shores of the Caspian Sea for our holidays. There was an old, picturesque little palace from Reza Shah's time set in the midst of the type of garden that I love—lush, overflowing with plants typical of the northern provinces of Gilan and Mazandaran: reeds, orange trees, lemon trees...I loved walking there, away from everything, letting my mind wander. The king would go horseback riding. We played petanque together and, in the evening, there were the parlor games, guessing games that were sometimes silly but so funny. I loved to see him laugh. He was so serious and full of care for the rest of the year. We went to Babol by train for a fortnight at the Iranian New Year, 21 March.

In the summer we spent a month in a kind of bungalow built on piles at Now Shahr, also on the Caspian Sea. That house was nothing like a palace. It had only one bedroom, a small drawing room where the king received government officials or his guests, a dining room, and a covered verandah where we sometimes had lunch or saw a film in the evening. There was also a room for the security people and some bathing huts. No, it certainly was not a palace, yet we had the best times of our lives there; it was there that we were happiest. I can remember the astonishment of Professor Georges Flandrin, the king's French doctor, when he first saw our summer residence. He later described it:

> The port of Now Shahr was formed by a small inlet hemmed in by steep banks. You entered on the left after going past a guard post manned by the Imperial Guard when the king was in residence. At the end of the pier was a low single-story wooden building standing with its feet in the water like the fairly ordinary place of a swimming instructor on some Normandy beach. The first time I went there, I saw HM in the morning. He received me dressed in a bathrobe over his bathing costume, in a room with very simple wooden chairs covered with cushions. There were perhaps two or three rooms, one of which was a bedroom, all with direct access to the water, with a motorboat and all the equipment necessary for waterskiing. At first I naturally thought that it was just the departure building for that sport, but then I realized that what I saw was actually the whole royal summer residence. It was fairly spartan and far from being the Château de Chambord.*

In many ways it was a poor old building; everything was out of alignment, including my bed—I had to be careful not to fall out

*The letters of Georges Flandrin to Jean Bernard, November 1987–January 1988.

of it—and yet it gave us the simple pleasure of being together and sharing our everyday life.

As there was no room for the children, they stayed in a house on the shore. Ali-Reza even spent a summer there in a caravan. As for the other visitors, the uncles and aunts, cousins and friends, they had to make do with hotels.

The days were filled with the pleasures of the seaside, especially waterskiing. Our teacher was one of my brothers-in-law, Commander in Chief of the Air Force General Mohammad Khatami, a great sportsman and always ready to try the impossible. After the mono-ski and the ski jump, he introduced us to flying: hanging from parachutes that take you up twenty or thirty meters above the water. Now Shahr is a port that dealt with a lot of Soviet cargo ships at that time. The water was not very clean, but we didn't worry about it. When I think back on it today, I wonder how we were not all sick.

Later we somewhat neglected the Caspian Sea and spent the Iranian New Year on the island of Kish in the Persian Gulf instead. It was a magnificent island, almost in its native state, with only a small local population and a bazaar. The only modern building at that time was the radar station built by the air force. The government intended to develop Kish as a free port for a rich clientele from the Emirates, who liked to hunt in Iran but preferred Lebanon for other leisure pursuits. First a residence was built for us, followed by a hotel, a casino, other villas, and a modern bazaar. The architecture was contemporary, but it blended in with the look of the island, and the old village was restored.

Kish was an ideal site for all kinds of sports. The children had grown, so we all learned diving together. Reza and I were fascinated by the colors and the harmony of the underwater world, although I was constantly wary of sharks and sea snakes. We sometimes passed fairly close to them. My husband often went for long rides on horseback with his elder son and sometimes with Farahnaz, who was a very good sportswoman even though still young. He also liked riding motorcycles, and little by little I came to like it too. We even organized some races with a few friends. I loved the speed, but I probably was not a wonderful driver, and one day the inevitable happened: I went off the road, me one way and the bike the other. It's not usual for a queen to be seen sprawled on the ground, and I remember the consternation of my security officer. I was groggy and could not get up; he could only think of how I looked.

"Get up, please, Your Majesty," he begged me. "It's not right for people to see you in that state."

A little later, when I was apologizing to him, I had to tell him that monarchs are no less men and women who have hearts and react to physical shocks. He agreed, but I'm not sure that he believed me. Well after the Islamic Revolution, the spot where I had my accident was still called Farah's Bend.

The holidays at Kish gave the king the opportunity to look more closely at the way this part of the Persian Gulf was progressing. He met representatives of the administration, inspected facilities of the marines and industrial operations on the coast, and judged the state of fisheries and agriculture. The idea of adopting a more decentralized form of government arose in this context. Minister of Court Assadollah Alam thought it important that the king have residences in various regions of the country to make it convenient for him regularly to spend a few days there to inspect state installations and motivate local authorities.

As for the winter holidays, we could choose between skiing on the slopes above Tehran or at St. Moritz in Switzerland. I was opposed to our having any residence beyond the borders of Iran; I also opposed taking our holidays abroad. At a time when we were appealing to the country to make an effort to catch up with other countries, it seemed out of place to me—and did not show much solidarity with our people—if we escaped to the advantages offered by Europe. The only exception I allowed myself was St. Moritz, for two weeks a year. Of course I enjoyed skiing in our mountains, but I couldn't relax there as I did at St. Moritz, where one could mix with the other people on holiday. At home, even in a ski suit, I was on show in spite of myself, always an object of curiosity, even when I was not being filmed or photographed by our journalists. Also, whenever we were in Iran, I felt responsible for everything, from the running of the resort, to the mood of the skiers, including the way the ski lift operators were dressed, the state of the slopes, and the living conditions of the local inhabitants. For me such concerns were a constant tension, a kind of extension of my work. For example, I can see myself trying to make sure that people did not jostle each other in the queue or that my bodyguards did not organize things one way or another for me to go first. Yes, St. Moritz was like an oasis, and I needed that brief respite so that I could energetically fulfill my role for the rest of the year. We had to stop going there, however, from the winter of 1976, as the Swiss authorities informed us that they feared for our safety. With cause, as I was to find out after the Islamic Revolution: an attack on the king's life had been planned by some communist leaders working with European terrorists of the extreme left.

Of course the children had other activities outside of these family holidays. Reza had joined the Scouts very early; the happy memories I had of my years as head of the Cubs had certainly counted for something in our decision, and besides, the king was head of the Scouts in Iran. Reza loved going to camp, living in a tent, and spending evenings around the campfire. It had no doubt been difficult for him, being singled out from other children of the same age and looked on as someone unique, but at Scouts he was treated like the others. His presence did, however, make police surveillance necessary for the whole troop. Unfortunately this kind of protection was essential. In 1973 Reza and I narrowly escaped an abduction attempt when we were attending the Children's Film Festival. Ten people or so were arrested. It was a plot organized by the extreme left.

Reza shared his father's passions, first for cars and then for planes. He was only thirteen when his instructor thought him capable of flying a Beechcraft F33C Bonanza on his own. My brother-in-law, the commander in chief of the air force, agreed with the instructor: Reza was perfectly capable of flying solo. I was very worried at the idea. At the same time, I knew that neither my brother-in-law nor the instructor would have taken the slightest risk. If they agreed to this flight, it was because they were absolutely sure of him and of themselves. Yes, I knew that, but I also knew that the unexpected can always happen in human activities, all the more so in the still immature mind of a thirteen-year-old. What would happen if he suddenly panicked, or if for some reason he lost control of his plane? My brother-in-law dismissed my anxieties with a wave of the hand. He had sent his own son up on a flight at twelve and a half, and everything had gone extremely well. We talked about it at length with my husband. Reza begged to do the flight and, since his cousin had done it before him, we had no reason to forbid it. Our only valid argument concerned his position as crown prince: as such, he did not have the right to endanger his life. We both agreed to waive that consideration. Reza, who had a very strong sense of duty, already submitted to all the obligations his position imposed upon him, and it would have been unfair to deprive him of this exploit on that pretext. The king decided that the matter was closed and gave his permission.

The test would take place at the army base. My husband seemed his usual serious, serene self that morning at breakfast. When we got to the base, we saw the little plane and then Reza appeared in his flying suit. I could hardly bear the thought that he was going to take off alone. I tried not to let it show. He smiled at me, solemnly greeted his father, then disappeared up to his neck in the cockpit. And in fact, from the first few moments, his handling of the plane reassured us. He took off very smoothly without a hitch, and I felt my husband relax. The whole flight was completed with the same elegance, like a ballet that had been rehearsed a hundred times, and when I saw him approach at the end of the runway to make his landing, I had to bite my lip not to cry. As for the king, he had that discreet little smile that showed the pride and pleasure he was feeling.

This was just the beginning, as it turned out. Our son's love of airplanes delighted his father, but always pained me, for as much as I loved to hear them compare notes, it always caused me much anxiety. At sixteen Reza wanted to take up an American F5 fighter plane. This first solo flight in a jet plane took place at the Vahdati airforce base in Dezful. My husband could not be present, but I was, and much more worried than I had been for his first flight three years earlier. He did all the maneuvers extremely well, and all the officers standing with me, as well as his instructor, gave him a warm round of applause when he landed. But that didn't save him from the traditional bucket of water over his head when he got out of the plane. Reza went on to receive his license to fly Boeing 707s, 737s, and 727s, as well as Falcon 20s. When a head of state came on an official visit to Iran, it was customary for his plane to be escorted by our fighter planes as soon as it entered our airspace. I remember my husband's intense pride the day Reza joined the escort to welcome King Hussein of Jordan, especially when King Hussein learned that the crown prince had just flown with him.

Then, when he was twelve, it was Ali-Reza's turn to climb into the cockpit of a Beechcraft Bonanza. The whole family turned out for his first flight. His brother and sisters were as worked up as we were, knowing that this experience was something of an unavoidable rite of passage that absolutely had to be mastered. Ali-Reza was so young, so small, that they had to ballast his plane with sandbags. The flight went perfectly, but just as he was about to land, the nose of his craft dipped slightly. I remember letting out an "Oh, my God!" but the instructor, who was in permanent radio contact with him, had warned him, and Ali-Reza very calmly leveled his plane before coming in to make a smooth landing.

As he grew up, Ali-Reza lost nothing of his mischief and his humor. He was known around the palace for the silly things he did. He was also much loved, as his antics were always amusing. When he was five or six he was discovered in pajamas during a reception, throwing bread pellets down on the heads of the guests from the galleries above the entrance hall. (It is true that his two older siblings had done it before him.) At roughly the same age, when the terraces were being waterproofed, he cheerfully climbed into a barrel of tar up to his neck. At school he created a scandal by systematically puncturing all the basketballs. The headmistress, shocked, assembled all the students for a kind of trial, to show how serious the incident was. But when she asked him why he had put a hole in all the balls, he made everyone laugh by replying, "Nobody had told me not to."

Reza and Ali-Reza had given me a lot of frights, especially with their flying, but unconsciously I must have thought that frights were inevitable with boys—like a necessary good or evil, I'm not sure which—for when Farahnaz asked my permission to do parachute jumping, I flatly refused. I thought two pilots or even three, counting my husband, were quite enough in one household without adding a parachutist! I regret it in hindsight. In a way, Farahnaz paid the price for her brothers. I was really too frightened: the girls at least wouldn't put me through that. So Farahnaz had to wait until she was thirty-five to make a parachute jump, without my permission but with the help of Ali-Reza, who was doing free-fall parachuting at that time. He encouraged her to jump in tandem to reduce any risk.

She, and later Leila, gave me the affection that the boys were careful not to show. I felt the need to make a fuss over my children, to cuddle them, and Farahnaz liked that. She was a docile little girl, always smiling and amazingly generous. For example, she was always very thoughtful to the palace staff, the people who worked for us, as if she were aware of their difficulties. If she came across people in the street who were poor or unhappy, it always affected her, and I could feel that she was disturbed and upset. As a child she would often position herself at the palace gates, which looked out on to a public park, and watch the people walking there, the children and the families. She told me that she tried several times to get out to play with the young people of her own age. Much later, when we were exiled and Farahnaz was in Switzerland, a young man approached her and said with great feeling and respect, "You are Princess Farahnaz, aren't you? I remember you very well. I was one of the little boys you used to talk to behind the palace gates." Yes, you could see that from an early age she always wanted to be with others. Later, after studying psychology, she did her graduate studies in social work. Poverty always disturbed her. I can remember during the 1980s in New York, she got to know the homeless in her area and brought them clothes. I can still hear Leila saying to her with amusement and disbelief, "You know, Farahnaz, I saw a guy in the street wearing your pullover." And Reza would smile affectionately. "You have a Mother Teresa complex," he would say to her.

When she was an adult, Farahnaz tried to join various nongovernmental organizations so that she could go to the countries most in need, but she was never accepted because of her name. A UNICEF official even refused to see her when he learned that she was called Pahlavi. She was very hurt by it, and it made me very sad: in what way was she at fault? Was she to be refused the right to help her neighbor on the pretext that she was the daughter of the Shah of Iran?

While waiting to be able to help her fellow humans, Farahnaz as a child opened her heart to animals. She could spend hours grooming her dog, petting her mice. My mother never dared go into Farahnaz's bathroom, because the mice were housed there. We had kept a few cows, which she also loved, and from time to time, to her great joy, a new boarder would arrive, courtesy of a head of state. At one time we had a little lion from the animal park at Thoiry, a gift to Reza from France, which delighted the king as much as Farahnaz. I also remember a fox that only appeared at mealtimes and was almost tame.

My husband more easily expressed his affection to his daughters than to his sons. Deep down, he probably wanted the boys to be like him. He was delighted with Farahnaz, who had boundless affection and admiration for him. I loved to hear them talking together: she would question him about a visitor she had seen, and her father would explain who the man was. Farahnaz would listen seriously, nodding her head.

Leila's arrival filled us all once again with the wonder of new life. The king had just celebrated his fiftieth birthday, the country was awakening; its situation had never been more promising. This fourth child, we thought, would know the Iran we were building for the future: a country open to the outside world, happy, fulfilling its potential.

Chapter 14

As a child, my husband had known Iran under the economic and political sway of foreign powers, with Great Britain, who exploited our oil, at the top of the league. He was there when our national identity was restored, led by the iron will of his father, Reza Shah. However, when he succeeded his father in September 1941, everything seemed to be back to square one, for British and Russian troops had just taken advantage of the Second World War to invade Iran. Who on the worldwide stage was concerned about this inexperienced, twenty-one-year-old king reigning over a country that the Allies had turned into a backup base to support the USSR war effort? In the nineteenth century, right up to the beginning of the twentieth, Czarist Russia had fought with the British Empire for hegemony over Iran. Fifty years later Russia had become the USSR, but there were fears that our country could be divided up again as in the dark days of the Qajar dynasty. Then Azarbaijan, which had been occupied by the Tudeh with the help of the USSR, was fought over and won back again in 1946. Having been exploited for so long, our oil was returned to us in 1954 after a memorable wrestling match with British interests. Once our oil was secured, the king started the country on its road to development. He did it by launching his White Revolution with a referendum in 1963. But he also did it by traveling the world to form alliances with numerous countries great and small, capitalist and communist, always with the aim of developing our economy and giving Iran a respected place on the world stage.

I accompanied my husband on these trips, which were so different from the moving experiences I always had on my trips inside Iran. Now I came into close contact with the discreet world of diplomacy. Given my nature, I was obviously more attracted to the warm, enthusiastic contacts I had with Iranians in our provinces, but I still have some vivid memories from those foreign travels.

Strangely enough, we went most often to the USSR, that prickly neighbor with whom our relations were always running either hot or cold. On my first visit to Moscow and Leningrad at the beginning of the sixties, we were shown the historic buildings, notably the palaces where the czars had lived. I remember wondering, "If one day we were chased from Iran, would people be shown around our bedrooms, our drawing rooms, as they do here? Would our private life be put on display for the curious to inspect?" Unlike the Chinese leaders, who had the delicacy to spare me the vestiges of their last emperors, the Russians seemed to take pleasure in presenting the palaces of Nicholas II to us, even to the places where his collaborators were executed. The situation in Iran was still fragile: the White Revolution had only just begun and activists on the extreme left and some feudal landlords were opposing the policies of the regime, so the Soviets' rather perverse insistence on the subject increased our constant anxiety about them. But by the seventies I was so sure that we were on the right track, and I felt that my husband had such confidence in the future of the country, that the repeated allusions of the Soviets no longer gave me the least concern. Actually, it was precisely within this context of improved conditions in Iran that agitation grew. And today, as presaged by the sinister foreboding I had then, the Islamic authorities have opened to the public some of the residences where we lived as a family, notably Sa'ad Abad and Niavaran.

My personal background led me to take an interest in Russia. My father had done part of his studies in St. Petersburg and had spoken Russian fluently. Then there was my grandfather who had been Iranian consul in Georgia and then had followed his love of art and architecture by doing research in Leningrad in the thirties. One of his books is still in the Hermitage museum today. However, in spite of this motivation to learn Russian, I found our first official visits to the USSR deeply depressing. I had never been to a communist country before and found the empty avenues disturbing. On the few anonymous faces we passed, there was an expression of sadness or stony silence that I have never seen anywhere else. So many buildings had been put up, so many schools, so many trees planted: I desperately waited for some humorous note, some lighthearted comment, which never came. I had the feeling of being surrounded by robots and, as the hours and days went by, it weighed heavily on my spirits. My husband coped with it much better than I did, and in the evening we tried to joke about it. I wondered, deep inside, whether it was conceivable for Russia to become a noncommunist state once more, which would allow us to have genuine friendly relations. I liked the country so much, its language, its music, and its literature.

We were staying in the Kremlin and were very limited in our movements. As we were sure of being listened to, we went out into the gardens to talk. Sometimes when we were inside, we heard strange noises, and our ambassador, Ahmad Mir Fendereski, who was a very humorous man and spoke Russian extremely well, claimed that it was the KGB people feverishly turning the pages of the dictionary. Once, on a semi-private visit, I had proof that they recorded our conversations. I had said to someone in my entourage, "This is a surprising country: they have marvelous palaces but don't think of putting nice furniture in them." The next day, during a conversation, one of the Soviet ladies turned and said to me with a strange look in her eye, "Unfortunately we don't have outstanding interior decoration, but everything is very clean!" I was rather embarrassed, but it made me smile all the same.

When the leaders themselves did attempt to be humorous, they were dismal. I remember one evening at the ballet sitting beside Alexei Kosygin. It was *Swan Lake*. When the black swan appeared, Kosygin leaned over to us and said with a tight-lipped smile, "It makes you think of NATO, doesn't it?"

I was tempted to reply, "It's more like the Warsaw Pact," but of course I said nothing.

It was different in August 1968: when the Warsaw Pact troops crushed the Prague Spring, I expressed my anger to my husband in no uncertain terms. We were once again on an official visit to Moscow. This move by the Soviets seemed shameful and inhuman to me, all the more so because I had a great liking for Czechoslovakia. "I can't bear to stay a day longer smiling at these people as if we were the best of friends," I said to my husband. I was very affected by it. He understood and let me do as I thought best. I gave the excuse that my sister-in-law was ill and flew to Paris. I remember in the plane catching myself wondering once again about the unlikely possibility of a revolution that would overthrow the dictatorship of communism over half of Europe. The evolution of the Eastern Bloc was one of my husband's main concerns. Although we belonged to the opposite camp, we shared 2,500 kilometers of border with the USSR and, in point of fact, my husband was constantly trying to emphasize what brought us together rather than what set us apart, in the face of constant perfidy and provocation from Moscow. Didn't Khrushchev, who was supposed to be more open-minded, say that one day Iran would fall "like a ripe apple" into the hands of the USSR? In spite of all that, we managed to cooperate, and the great steel works built by the Soviets in Esfahan are the best example. (Our allies in the West had always refused to help us in that field.)

Russia remained a mythical country in my mind, and after several of these strangely soulless official visits—although to be fair I should say that on each occasion there were warm and friendly encounters with private people, especially artists—I asked my husband if it would be possible to organize a "private" visit, where I would be freer to come and go as I pleased. Besides, the official visits always took place in the summer months, and I wanted to see Russia under snow, the eternal, legendary Russia.

The Kremlin agreed. I landed in Moscow in the middle of winter, accompanied by a few close friends and relatives, including my mother. The king was not with me. I was happy to be there, in fact so happy that I took our little group out into the snow-covered streets of the town. Our Russian security guards thought we were mad. There was not a soul out of doors.

The next day we visited the little town of Zagorsk, near Moscow, where the churches have fortunately been preserved. The people very quickly discovered who we were; even on a private outing we could not stay unobserved for long with the security men around us. I can still see the smiles and the look of wonder on the faces of some old women in one of the churches. They jostled each other to get close to us, and I heard them exclaim, "Good heavens! Please let us look at a living queen!" I had worked on my Russian, and as I had a good accent, people thought that I understood everything, which was unfortunately not the case. In one of these churches we were able to hear a choir. The hymns of the Orthodox Church are very moving; we had tears in our eyes. For me, it was like suddenly finding myself in Tolstoy's Russia. Afterwards the priests invited us to lunch.

In Leningrad we experienced a very different atmosphere. My friends could joke and laugh quite freely, but even though I was more relaxed, I always had to watch what I did and said. I was able to follow the trail of my grandfather and imagine my father at fifteen walking the lanes of old St. Petersburg, from the Alexandrovski Kadetski Corpus military college to the Neva embankment, where he had a room. Then, when we were visiting the summer palace of the czars, I thought how nice it would be to go and see one or two villages in the surrounding countryside in a troika, which is scarcely seen these days. The troika was ostensibly a symbol of czarist Russia, and one would think that the authorities would not look kindly on the Queen of Iran traveling over Soviet territory drawn by three horses like the aristocrats of old. Not at all. The Soviets were so well disposed toward Iran at that time that we had our troika and all the necessary arrangements for our trip. On the other hand, I never did manage to see Tchaikovsky's grave. The composer of *Swan Lake* is one of my favorites, and I had long wanted to sit and meditate beside his tomb. The Soviets found countless pretexts to prevent me from going there, and I never did receive any explanation for their refusal.

I met the same lack of cooperation when I asked to hear some Gypsy music, but this time we knew why: the Gypsies were considered resistant to communist ideology and their music, so full of yearning, a degrading relic of a counterrevolutionary past. Our ambassador managed, nevertheless, to organize a musical evening where we were staying, but in the presence of several representatives of the Kremlin. The group playing for us must have been conscious of expressing the wandering and the sadness of a whole people, for every note was charged with emotion. When it finished, the singer came to me and took my hands with such feeling, wishing that God would protect me and my husband and children, that I was afraid for her. The Soviets were obviously displeased, and the icy look one of the generals gave this woman sent a shiver down my spine.

During this trip we visited the capital of Tajikistan, Dushanbe, which held great interest for me because the Tajiks spoke Persian. Then we went to Baku, the capital of Soviet Azarbaijan, over the border from our province of Azarbaijan. The Soviet Azarbaijanis knew my father came from that region, and I felt that the memory created a special affinity between us. We could see that the people in the street were very curious about us; they wanted to talk to us and find out what things were really like in Iran. Evidently the Soviet authorities wanted to avoid these contacts and informal discussions. For so-called security reasons, they separated us from the population with rather suspect haste. We found some explanation for this zeal when we were looking at an exhibition of watercolors and drawings. Some showed farmers plowing with obviously medieval oxcarts. Above it was this succinct commentary as a caption: "On the other side of the border…" The people were not really fooled by it, especially since Soviet Azarbaijan had taken in numerous Iranian communists who had fled Iran in 1946, when we drove out Jafar Pishevari's troops, which were supported by Stalin. Some of these Iranians, who had had their fill of communist ideals, now wanted to come back to Iran, their families, and the freedom they no longer enjoyed. They tried to approach us and to give me letters requesting permission to go home.

I did draw the king's attention to the situation of these people. The government naturally looked on them with great suspicion. Had they really changed their views? Wouldn't they work undercover for the Soviets or join some extreme leftist movement dedicated to overthrowing the monarchy? It was later decided to demarcate a border zone where they could meet their families while awaiting permanent reentry. Now that the communist regime has fallen, some ex-militants of the Tudeh Party have written or said how miserable they were in Soviet territory after expecting to find paradise on the other side of the border.

WE MAINTAINED RELATIONS with all the countries of the Communist Bloc and were therefore received by them all (with the exception of Albania, Cuba, and East Germany, whose invitation we had to refuse at the end of 1977 because of the tensions in Iran). I found these visits difficult as they were spoiled by a great deal of hypocrisy. We were well aware how much these regimes disliked the monarchy, and we had fought Soviet hegemony for long enough to harbor a great mistrust of communists. When we arrived in Czechoslovakia, for example, we knew that in spite of the flowers and red carpet, this country had a radio station that supported the Tudeh and broadcast insults about us daily. It was the same in the USSR, where my translator, Dagmara, with whom I got on well, regularly spoke on the radio against Iran. Embarrassed, she apologized to me, saying that she could not do otherwise; she had been ordered to do it.

All the leaders of the communist countries had the same mechanical way of referring to "the great achievements of socialism," and one had to go into raptures over factory chimneys and dismal dormitory towns. The empty streets and the empty shops, however, revealed the poor conditions in which the populations of these countries lived. It hurt me to see how much the word "comrade" and a superficial familiarity were used to hide the deep inequality of regimes that claimed to serve the workers. The leaders made a show, for example, of sitting beside their drivers and being called "comrade," but the look on the driver's face showed the fear inside him. I thought of my driver in Iran, who certainly did not have the same familiarity, but I knew his wife and children, and he did not hesitate to ask for my help if any difficulty arose.

To catch a few honest words, one had to wait until the Party members left. I remember one evening in Czechoslovakia after the Soviet invasion in the summer of '68. The leaders left and suddenly the people began to tell jokes.

"Your Majesty," my neighbor said to me, "have you heard the latest story that's doing the rounds of Prague?"

"No. Tell me."

"Two men are having a discussion on the terrace of a bar. Suddenly a car goes past. 'Oh, what a fine Russian car!' one of them exclaims. The other says, 'Come on, that's not a Russian car! Don't you know the make of that car?' 'Yes, I know it,' the first man replies, 'but I don't know you.'"

In Czechoslovakia I had the great pleasure of meeting with an eminent scholar of Iranian studies, Professor Ripka, who had worked with my grandfather in Iran. Back in Tehran I still had a photo of the two men on the site of Persepolis. There were historical links between the two countries forged by the Qajar kings. They had liked the thermal waters of Czechoslovakia and had left reminders of their times there, notably at Karlovy Vary, the old Karlsbad, where you can find Persian carpets and chandeliers of Iranian crystal. I thought, with some relief, that despite its frenzy of destruction communism had not been able to wipe out all traces of the past.

I went back to Prague after the fall of the Berlin Wall, and I was there the day Václav Havel was elected. On the Charles Bridge people were selling all the badges and medals that had been the glory of the Red Army for one or two dollars. It was a cruel irony, and very sad for the men who had earned these decorations, but one couldn't help feeling that there was justice in it: the people of Prague, who had been crushed and humiliated in 1968, were now selling off their invaders' medals for the price of a packet of cigarettes. In the same spirit, pictures of all the old party chiefs of the Communist Bloc had been hung up in the main street of Prague like outlaws. "Well," I said jokingly to my host when I saw them, "you've put my friends on show." And I had actually met them all.

But it warmed my heart to find traces of Persian culture here and there in those countries. At the university of Krakow in Poland, where Aricenna's teaching on medicine had been included in the curriculum, we came across manuscripts which were said to be by him. Still in Poland, we saw some of the Persian carpets woven with gold and silver that had been ordered in Iran by the kings of Poland, and which were called "Polish carpets" in our country at that time. Yet I can't describe this trip to Poland without remembering the horror I felt when I visited the concentration camp at Auschwitz.

Surprisingly, another place we met Poles was in New Zealand. Besides the official reception at the airport, there was a touching surprise: a group of about a hundred Poles waving flowers and banners with "Welcome to the Shah of Iran." These people wanted to thank the king for having accepted them into Iran thirty years earlier. From 1942 to 1943 my husband had indeed opened the frontiers to a large number of Poles who were fleeing Stalin's troops. Many had established themselves in our country after marrying an Iranian; others had gone to settle in New Zealand. But they had not forgotten.

IN SEPTEMBER 1972 the responsibility fell to me to mark the official restoration of our relations with China to offset the growing influence of the Soviet Union. The silk route in itself had long symbolized the commercial links between Iran and China, abruptly broken off by the revolution of Mao Zedong. The king was very anxious to reestablish diplomatic relations with that great country of the East. In 1970 he had sent an important emissary to Beijing: his own sister, Princess Ashraf, who was then chairperson of the Human Rights Commission at the United Nations. The Chinese leaders were favorably disposed to these overtures and, when China was admitted to the UN in 1971, Princess Ashraf was the first to invite the Chinese delegation to a lunch at the residence of the Iranian ambassador to the United Nations.

The king would willingly have gone to Beijing himself, but there was a protocol problem: Chairman Mao Zedong was ill and could not receive him. Under these circumstances, the mission to lead our delegation for a ten-day visit fell to me.

It was very exciting. In centuries past, the vagaries of history had sometimes brought our two peoples together, such as the time when the Sassanian princes took refuge in China from the Arab invasion; several centuries later China had imported our carpets and we, in turn, had gone there for such precious commodities as silkworms, tea, and porcelain. In a way I was coming to reopen these old routes that time had gradually erased from our maps. Certainly, I had never before had as many people with me as I did for this journey: Prime Minister Amir Abbas Hoveyda was by my side, as were several ministers including Minister for Cooperatives and Rural Affairs Abdol Azim Valian, and Minister for National Education Farrokhrou Parsa, who had taught me at Jeanne d'Arc and whose tragic death at the beginning of the Islamic Revolution I have already described. A few members of the court and my office were also present, my chief secretary Karim Pasha Bohadori, and also my mother and my cousin Reza Ghotbi, now director of Iranian National Television, and Shoja Eddine Shafa, Deputy Minister for the Court.

Premier Minister Zhou Enlai was waiting for me as I left the plane, and all around us were thousands of young people with shining faces, wearing brightly colored clothes, all waving banners and singing. I thought that was the official welcome but I was wide of the mark. When we arrived at Tiananmen Square, I was asked to use an open car. It was then that I saw that thousands of men and women, all in the same gray uniform, and young children in colored clothes, all waving banners, had crowded the length of the avenue we were about to go down. I could hardly believe my eyes. As we began driving, immediately there was music and singing: bands and enormous drums had been stationed at regular intervals. I soon realized that the whole city had been mobilized for us, since the crowds extended for kilometers, just as big, just as smiling. The Chinese told me that only Ho Chi Minh had been welcomed with such ceremony.

The first official dinner in the evening was just as impressive as this extraordinary reception. More than a thousand people were seated around a vast number of round tables covered with colorful and delicious dishes. I was on the right of Mr. Zhou. He referred to the old friendship between our two countries, tactfully declining to dwell on our current political differences, and I thought to myself, "I wonder how long it has been since he said the word *empress*, a word that must be anathema to a man who was on Mao's Long March?" I had been reworking my own speech until the last minute. I was thoroughly convinced that only sincerity and declarations from the heart could bridge our ideological rifts. In China as in Iran we had been struggling for half a century to help our respective countries emerge from backwardness and underdevelopment. We had taken very different roads to achieve it, but we still shared this same ambition. I had the feeling that beyond the diplomatic smiles and the polite applause, a certain warmth was beginning to flow between us. I was struck by Zhou's intellectual refinement throughout the reception. He even tried to teach me how to use chopsticks, which made him smile with amusement. I was told later that it was one of the rare official dinners at which none of the guests left in the middle of the speeches in a show of disapproval.

Later events confirmed this first impression. Despite a very heavy schedule with visits to factories, model farms, and museums, as well as political meetings and receptions, a good climate was created, which was not without its humorous side. We were all actually very happy to be in China, sincerely eager to see new methods and innovations, and charmed by the hospitality shown to us by the leaders at every level. We were staying in a villa full of poetic charm nestled deep in a garden of delicate flowering plants. I have a very fond memory of our welcome on the first evening. A middle-aged lady, whose gentle eyes contrasted with the severity of her uniform, did the honors and showed me around the house. Every room had been prepared with particular care, and my hostess had obviously overseen every detail. I marveled at the house and she was visibly pleased. I only realized at the end that it was Madame Zhou Enlai in person.

However, no matter where we went, we always met this same automatically expressed fervor for Mao, the same cult of the personality. In a school or a factory we would congratulate a young woman or a worker: all would reply with almost the same words, "I do it for my country, for Mao, the sun of Beijing." In schools the children welcomed us by singing with their fists in the air, and once again it was about "the sun of Beijing." We were, of course, aware of the enormous conditioning that such uniformity must have entailed, but behind the slogans there remained nonetheless a lust for life and an obvious confidence in the future. It was tremendous but also disturbing.

One of the most impressive things we saw was an operation using acupuncture instead of anesthetic. It was in Shanghai. As we watched, the surgeons opened the skull of a patient, who remained perfectly conscious throughout, and could see and speak. They even asked him several times to eat, only bananas. How was it possible? We were fascinated. When the operation was over, the surgeons tried to answer our questions. They admitted that they did not have all the scientific explanations we were eager to hear, the origin of acupuncture being empirical. Then a man from the Revolutionary Committee suddenly gave this response, "We will have to put the question to the masses." We looked at each other with alarm, and the conversation ended there.

Our hosts nonetheless treated us with remarkable sensitivity. When we visited certain museums where objects belonging to their former emperors were exhibited, unlike the Soviets they were careful to walk us quickly past any showcases that could have caused us embarrassment. They never made the slightest unpleasant innuendo and, when I met Madame Mao over a cup of tea, the same restraint was evident throughout our conversation. That did not stop me from imagining how much this severe woman must have detested me.

One of the most moving moments in this long trip occurred when I phoned my husband from Xian, the gates of the old silk road. It was a symbolic reopening of the route between China and Iran. The king could hear how I felt and shared my excitement.

Then came the return journey, and I remember that the moment the pilot announced we were entering our own airspace, we all spontaneously broke into applause. I could see then how much each of us—I most of all—had felt oppressed by the uniform way of thinking and the indoctrination so characteristic of communist regimes and how relieved we were to be in our own country again.

The chairman of the Chinese Communist Party, Hua Guofeng, would be the last person to make an official visit to Tehran under the monarchy. I remember that his arrival coincided with the appearance of a picture of Ayatollah Khomeini on page one of the daily paper *Keyhan.* Rightly or wrongly, I took Mr. Hua's visit during those turbulent days as a gesture of support for the king.

Chapter 15

AT THE BEGINNING of the sixties, the king had rejected the idea that had been suggested to him by one of his cultural advisors, Shoja Eddine Shafa, a great Iranian scholar, to celebrate the foundation of the Persian Empire by Cyrus the Great twenty centuries earlier (between 550 and 530 B.C.). "Too early. We'll see later," he had said quite definitely. At that time he did not want anything to distract the country from the White Revolution he was preparing to launch. Ten years later he thought the time seemed ripe for the celebration because Iran had largely emerged from being an underdeveloped country.

He was not the only one to think so. Praise was coming from all the capitals of the world for the phenomenal leap forward that had occurred in a decade. Cambridge professor Peter Avery wrote in the UNESCO *Courier* in October 1971:

> Modern Iran has resources, it has regained its self-confidence lost in servitude during the period of foreign domination and exploitation. It began in 1722 when the Safavian dynasty lost power, and it characterized the whole of the nineteenth and the

> first years of the twentieth centuries, when British and Russian expansionism strangled Iran and almost killed it. Now Iran once again commands respect on the international stage. It can and does play a real role in world affairs. As a member of the United Nations it shows the way to other developing countries. It has become the ideal meeting ground for the preparation of international agreements, debates on current problems like food, agricultural development, illiteracy, women's rights. Once again it is the hub of ideas and techniques.

The French journalist Édouard Sablier, returning from a long journey throughout the country, published the following picture of Iran in *Atlas*. In hindsight, the conclusion of this passage seems amazingly prophetic:

> This is a fast-developing country. Towns have grown like mushrooms after a storm. Construction sites and new roads are everywhere to be seen. Fifteen-story buildings surround the center of the capital; villas and bungalows have covered the slopes of the formerly aristocratic Shemiran for some time.
>
> In twenty years Tehran had gone from 800,000 to 3 million inhabitants. The number of cars on the road causes some of the best traffic jams I have ever seen. And few vehicles are more than ten years old.
>
> Although they do not equal Tehran, the other towns in Iran are developing at a rapid rate. Tabriz, Shiraz, Ahvaz, Esfahan have become industrial centers. Everywhere the shops are well stocked, the people in the street quite well dressed. The standard of living keeps improving; industry is growing at a rate only surpassed by Japan.
>
> The golden rule of their foreign policy is national independence. Granted Iran, like Western Europe, is in the American sphere of influence, but its government retains the

initiative in its day-to-day diplomacy. Relations with the USSR are excellent; they are even developing at the moment with China.

Persian nationalism has reason to be glad. The Persian Gulf is slowly becoming a sphere of influence for Tehran. Kuwait, Bahrain, all the Emirates and even Saudi Arabia are aware that Iran is a country to be reckoned with, just as in the time of the Great Kings, the Hellenic world recognized the importance of Persia.

All that is on the credit side. Iranians of all classes I have been able to meet generally agree, although with more or less hesitation. I have not seen any more of those fanatics who used to attack the regime at every turn. I even met some happy Iranians.

But the general impression has some gloomy overtones. Naturally a nation cannot develop without encountering along the way the drawbacks, the frustrations, and the unrest that are part of modern times. That is why the progress of this vast country, as everywhere else, comes up against the ignorance of some, the resistance of castes and clans that do not want to disappear, and the impatience of the young, who think that the current methods are taking too long.

The "resistance" of some (clerics and large landowners) and the impatience of others (students and intellectuals), although from opposite ends of the spectrum, would together fuel the growing discontent from 1976 to 1977, leading to our departure and the coming of the Islamic Republic. But in 1971 these reactions did not worry the king: he thought they were usual in a country undergoing profound change and he put his faith in the fruits of progress to free our society, satisfy expectations, and reconcile extremes.

To him the main goal of celebrating the founding of the Persian Empire was to bring the nation together in recognition that its identity had been restored and its pride regained after two centuries of humiliation and great poverty. He wanted this highly symbolic festival to allow everyone to forget their little daily frustrations and discover "where we are coming from and where we are going."

I climbed on the bandwagon, although when the king gave his consent for the planning of the various events, I was getting ready for the birth of Leila, our fourth child, an event that forced me to slow down my activities for a while.

An organizing committee was immediately set up. There was no discussion about the site for the celebrations: it would obviously be Persepolis, the first royal city of the Achaemenian Persian Empire, with its vestiges of the palace of Darius I, the wise successor of Cyrus the Great. Monarchs and heads of state of the whole world would be invited there, yet the site was in the middle of the desert, with no facilities, and sixty kilometers from the nearest town, Shiraz.

We were less than a year away from the festivities, scheduled for mid-October 1971, when the organizing committee asked me to preside. I accepted because I had the greatest belief in my husband's plans and said so publicly: "We must go hand in hand, united, to prove that the times we are living in now, the Pahlavi era, is a period of renaissance for Iranian civilization." But what I discovered went against my Iranian sensibility: a host of foreign suppliers had been contacted, and among the most expensive, when we could have hired Iranians in certain areas.

I was upset. How did it happen? Was it still possible to cancel these arrangements? I was told that the given time frame necessitated using European expertise, that Iranian businesses were still too new and inexperienced to be able to provide those services at a high-enough quality and on time. "Well, let's wait until they are no longer inexperienced," I replied. "Let's give ourselves the time to do these things as they should be done. We've waited twenty-five hundred years, we can wait a few more." But it didn't take me long to realize that, practically speaking, it was too late, and I worried. Knowing what journalists are like, I suspected that they would latch on to these foreign contracts as a pretext to criticize, and soon they would not see the forest for the trees; that is to say, they would not see everything that the festival of Persepolis would bring Iran, in terms of both infrastructure within the country and influence on the outside world. At that stage all I could do was accept the choices that had already been made.

Of all the tasks that fell to me in the preparation for the festivities, coping with that misstep was the most difficult and the most depressing, for just as I had predicted, a wave of acerbic criticisms about expenditure on luxuries slowly arose from the West. The journalists got on this hobbyhorse and rode it again and again. What kind of monarchy is dressed by Lanvin and eats at Maxim's when its people still sometimes lack food and schools? Although this image was a caricature meant to appeal to the masses, it circulated widely and was naturally taken up by the Iranian opposition. In the end it partially perverted the meaning of the celebrations at Persepolis, although I tried constantly to explain to foreign correspondents how unfair it was to attack us in this way after so much had been done over so many years to help those most in need. What was more, our efforts had earned the unanimous praise of countries throughout the world. It was unfair to remember only the price tag for the celebrations marking the reawakening of Iran.

The attack was all the more unfair because most of the money spent for amenities considerably increased Iran's assets: 2,500 schools were opened for the occasion, electricity was connected to remote villages, hotels were built, roads paved, all of which remained after the ceremonies as permanent improvements. Finally, as far as public relations were concerned, we got a huge press campaign absolutely free. Festival committees were set up in the major capital cities of the world. All these cities held exhibitions of Iranian art and culture, concerts, and lectures. To have paid for all the films, books, and articles on Iran released during this period, or for the TV and radio reports broadcast all over the world, would have cost us millions of dollars. There were many people in 1970 who probably could not find Iran on a map and for whom this was a first lesson who at the time first learned about its geography and history. Who could put a figure on the benefits that flowed from it, especially from the development of tourism?

But that was the angle the international press adopted, and the negative reports continued to dominate to the very end, ignoring everything that the festivities at Persepolis gave Iranian hearts and minds: a feeling of pride and gratitude that cannot be expressed in monetary terms.

NO DOUBT IT WAS THE FIRST TIME in the long history of Iran that monarchs and heads of state would be honoring the historic capital of Persia with their presence. The invitations had been sent out; acceptances piled up rapidly on the desk of the minister of court, Assadollah Alam. We were expecting the sovereigns of Denmark, Jordan, Norway, Nepal, and Belgium. Queen Elizabeth of England would be represented by her husband, Prince Philip, and their daughter, Princess Anne; similarly, Queen Juliana of the Netherlands would be represented by her husband, Prince Bernhard. Emperor Haile Selassie of Ethiopia would make the journey, as would the emir of Qatar; the emir of Kuwait; Sultan Kabus of Oman; the president of the United Arab Emirates, Sheikh Zayed; the emir of Bahrain; the princes of Monaco and Liechtenstein; the grand dukes of Luxembourg; Prince Juan-Carlos and

Princess Sofia of Spain; Crown Prince Carl Gustaf representing the King of Sweden; King Constantine of Greece and his wife, Queen Anne-Marie; Victor-Emmanuel of Italy; and Princess Bilqis of Afghanistan and her husband, Sardar Abdul Wali. There were even more heads of state and government, since we were expecting the presidents of Finland, India, Turkey, Pakistan, Yugoslavia, Austria, Bulgaria, Poland, Romania, and Senegal. The United States would be represented by Vice President Spiro Agnew, the USSR by Nikolai Podgorny, and France by Prime Minister Jacques Chaban-Delmas, accompanied by his wife.

While laborers and engineers worked on the tent camp that would shelter these illustrious people for three days, each section of the organizing committee tackled its own particular task: some oversaw the installation of a security system network, others the organization of transport between Shiraz and Persepolis, while still others addressed the many questions of protocol. I had to keep an eye on everything, in addition to regularly welcoming all the journalists who came to check things out in Tehran and Persepolis. The wife of each head of state would be assisted and guided during her stay by a lady-in-waiting who spoke her language and was well versed in the rules of protocol. These women had to be found and trained. The same applied for the aides-de-camp provided for kings and presidents. As for the gifts the guests would take home with them, the committee had decided to order carpets from the artists in Azarbaijan with a portrait of the head of state as the central motif. In addition guests would receive a copy of the edict of Cyrus the Great that had been found on a terra-cotta cylinder in Babylon and kept in the British Museum. This idea made me feel very proud, for in this text intended for the vanquished people of Babylon, Cyrus outlines the basis of what will become, many centuries later, the Declaration of the Rights of Man. He forbids pillage, orders the release of prisoners and the rebuilding of houses, and, showing an amazing religious tolerance for the times, demands respect for all the gods and establishes equality for all through the abolition of slavery. Following his principles, his successors sent the Jews back to Jerusalem and allowed them to rebuild their temple.

Yes, I was proud that this "earthen cylinder," the basis of great Persia's humanist principles, would become a reality again in the eyes of the world. Our clerics would see it as yet another snub and suspect the king of trying to downplay Islam, adopted by the Iranians after the Arab invasion in 637 A.D. They forgot that Persia existed well before this invasion and that, although it was defeated, it was able to turn its defeat into victory. Persian literature, philosophy, civil administration, medicine, and art would become the basic elements of Islamic civilization from the earliest days of the conquest, and Iranians would later bring Islam to East Asia without violence or bloodshed.

In the eyes of the most fundamentalist clerics, the ceremonies themselves must have increased this cause for vexation—without our being really aware of it—since they began on 12 October 1971 at the tomb of Cyrus the Great, with this homage from my husband, spoken in a voice shaking with emotion:

> O Cyrus, Great King, King of Kings, Emperor of the Achaemenians, monarch of the land of Iran. I, the Shahanshah of Iran, offer thee salutations from myself and from our nation.
>
> At a time when Iran is renewing its links with history, we come here to show you the immense gratitude of a whole people, immortal hero of history, founder of the oldest empire in the world, great liberator, worthy son of humanity.

As a sign of tolerance and open-mindedness, the representatives of major religions from all over the world had been invited to this tribute: Roman Catholics, Protestants, Zoroastrians, the Orthodox Church, Mormons, Shintoists, Buddhists, Sikhs, Jews, representatives of the the Native Americans, and of course, Muslims. On that day not one Muslim present expressed the slightest reservation.*

Today, more than twenty years after the Islamic Revolution, the king is no longer there to watch over the continuity of this timeless heritage, but Iranian identity, embodied in our people, is always present, and I know that it will survive obscurantism.

WELCOMING THE GUESTS took up most of the following day, 13 October. The regular arrival of planes at Shiraz had been timed to one almost every fifteen minutes. The king's brothers or members of the government received the guests as they disembarked. The dignitaries were then driven with escort to Persepolis, where we received them officially. The king then said, "In the name of the empress and of myself, I welcome you to Iran on the occasion of the twenty-fifth-hundred anniversary of our monarchy." Our guest was then invited to stand on a podium with the king and listen to the national anthem of his or her country played by the Imperial Guard. Then the offi-

*Another aspect of these celebrations was the International Congress of Specialists in Iranian Studies, which was held from 14-16 October 1971. It was attended by more than 300 Iranian and foreign specialists in Iranian history and civilization. They were presented to my husband and me on the evening of the inauguration, and we expressed our gratitude to them for the services they rendered to Iranian culture. The Congress was entirely devoted to the history of Iran, more particularly to Cyrus the Great. About 1,000 papers had been collected by the Congress secretariat from scholars all over the world, making this the most complete study of Cyrus in existence. Unfortunately we learned later that it had been destroyed by the Guardians of the Islamic Revolution in the very early days after they took control.

cer in charge of these presentations read out the names and titles of the honored guest and invited him to inspect the guard.

I was full of admiration for the officer in charge of introductions, Major Karim Shams, who through all those exhausting hours did not make one mistake in pronouncing the names or stating the titles, which were often extremely complex. That evening I took him aside to congratulate him. He was exhausted but very affected by his role.

In anticipation of these days, for the first time in my life I asked my doctor to prescribe some tranquilizers for me. Anxious and overwhelmed by work, I had lost a lot of weight in the last few months, and I also dreaded something happening to spoil the festival. The Iranians created a spirit of mutual aid and of solidarity that I had never seen before. I saw some of our ministers, members of the court, generals, other officers, and ambassadors, all usually sticklers for their prerogatives, carrying the cases of a guest or even sleeping on the floor to offer their bedrooms to unexpected guests. I saw educated members of prominent families simply pick up an iron to help housemaids who had more work than they could handle. Everyone joined in without being asked, even Reza, our elder son, whom I saw delivering breakfasts in a golf buggy to the back of the tents.

The day of 14 October began with a procession showing warriors from all the different periods of Iran's history. Soldiers numbering 1,724 had been mobilized for this parade, led by General Fathollah Minbashian. Lesley Blanch gives a colorful description of it:

> the tight crimped beards of the Medes and the Persians; the small pointed beards of the Safavids, or the fierce moustachios of Qajar troops. Shields, lances, pennons, broadswords and daggers of earlier

> warriors, all were there. Beneath a scorching sun, but shielded by parasols provided for those in need, the guests, who were seated on a rostrum below the pillared ruins of Cyrus' might, watched this impressive procession. Achaemenian foot guards, Parthian warriors, the cavalry of Xerxes, litters, chariots, tanks, Bactrian camels, Fath Ali Shah's artillery, warriors from the Caspian or the Persian Gulf, the Air Force, the new Women's contingents of the armed forces...all were there at Persepolis; all attested to Iran's glories, past and present.

The afternoon was set aside for tours of the site, for those who did not mind the sun, and there was a gala dinner in the evening.

The dinner was served in a tent sixty-eight meters long and twenty-four wide, set up in the middle of the camp. We knew practically all the monarchs and heads of state and government present, but some better than others. Some were real friends, like King Hussein of Jordan, whom we regularly saw on private visits, and the kings of Greece, Belgium, and Afghanistan. Hassan II of Morocco, a particular friend of my husband's who had been unable to get away, sent his brother, Prince Moulay Abdallah, with his wife, Princess Lamia. The pleasure of seeing each other again was very real in spite of protocol, and this pleasure went beyond the circle of friends. I had already met Nikolai Podgorny: and several times during the dinner I exchanged a few words and even a joke with him in Russian. There was a lot of banter going on around us. Later I heard that Prince Rainier of Monaco expressed surprise to find himself seated between Prince Philip of England and Prince Bernhard of the Netherlands. (There were not enough women to go around.) Prince Philip replied to him, "Haven't you noticed, my dear man, that we are the only two male queens in the whole gathering?"

Others took advantage of this occasion to engage in more serious discussions, which continued during the next afternoon in the cafeteria, where the atmosphere was cordial and relaxed but apparently also earnest. Men and women who would never have been able to speak to each other officially, because of their political differences, had an opportunity here to exchange points of view far from the eyes and ears of the press.

For us there were all the comings and goings behind the scenes that never seemed to stop. The kitchen staff had to be kept happy, given a helping hand, and sometimes comforted, and catastrophes had to be averted. Before dinner my presence was discreetly requested. I hurried over to find the pastry chef in tears: his cake had broken in transit! In double-quick time I consoled him, found a way to put it together as best we could, and then, when it was all over, tried to have a laugh about it. "Don't worry, we'll present it sideways, no one will notice a thing, and anyway the main thing is all the love of fine craftsmanship that has gone into the cake, and I'm sure the guests can't fail to notice that..."

The evening ended with a sound and light show followed by a fireworks display. Both were the work of French specialists. It was a great success, spectacular, and yet the anxiety was still there: "I just hope that the noise doesn't frighten the dozens of horses and buffaloes from this morning's procession. If one begins to kick or becomes agitated, the whole lot could start and the frightened animals could surge down on our guests..."

The third and last day was less formal, and the choice of activity left to the guests. Some went on an excursion into the desert; most took the opportunity to have discreet talks with this guest or that. The American vice president, Spiro Agnew, received King Constantine of Greece, who had been in exile since the colonels' coup in April 1967. My husband had a long conversation with Presidents Podgorny of the USSR and Sunay of Turkey. Emperor Haile Selassie received President Tito of Yugoslavia. King Hussein gathered together a few Arab rulers for a friendly talk.

The evening's entertainment was purely Iranian. We had brought in artists and artisans from all the regions of the country for this event. Musicians, painters, weavers, and cooks responded to our invitation; this dinner was designed to show everyone the cultural richness of Iran, beginning with its cuisine and its crafts. One of our ambitions was to get this sector flourishing again, especially the export of village-made carpets. I regularly tried to persuade the hoteliers of the country to furnish their rooms with objects of Iranian arts and crafts. This time we were going to appeal to rulers and heads of state to make our artisans known to the whole world.

Some of our guests left the next day; others wanted to visit a particular town or the Caspian Sea, and so stayed longer. The ceremonies officially closed with the inauguration of the Arya Mehr stadium in Tehran, which seats 100,000 and of the Memorial to the History of Iran, the Shahyad, a modern triumphal arch built to the west of the capital. A final fireworks display was held on this occasion and, in the last group photo, I can clearly be seen giving a sigh of relief.

Chapter 16

One of my growing concerns in the second half of the sixties was not to forget culture in the march of progress. The king wanted the country to develop toward democracy once it had caught up economically. In my opinion there is no better stimulus for a democracy than a flourishing culture. On the one hand, we had to help our artists, improve their standing, and make them better known at home and abroad; on the other, we needed to open our borders to creative men and women from other countries.

I asked my cousin, Reza Ghotbi, director of national television, to think this over with me, and from our discussions came the idea of holding a great international festival of the arts. From the very beginning we wanted this festival to feature contemporary theater and music but also traditional and ancestral works, while avoiding the popular, touristy, folklore side of the genre.

The minister of culture subscribed to the idea and we quickly formed a founding committee made up of writers, artists, journalists, and government representatives. The first decision to be made was a geographical one: where should the festival be held? Shiraz was the unanimous choice. Two things recommended it: its proximity to the site of Persepolis—we could already imagine what the theater people could do with that—and its proximity to the desert. And of course Shiraz already had a claim to fame: it is the city of the two favorite poets of the Iranian people, Saadi (1213–91) and Hafez (1324–89), whose tombs are there. For a long time it was considered the literary capital of Persia. Shiraz, an oasis of nature and culture, a jewel box of roses, nightingales and love—it was the ideal choice for a festival devoted to inspire creativity. On a more prosaic level, it already had several hotels, and their number would increase thanks to the festivities at Persepolis. Better still, there were university dormitories that could provide rooms.

The Shiraz Festival was there on paper; now the real work began: finding and gathering artists, not only from all over the world, but also from throughout Iran. We knew a great deal of the creative work that was being done in Iran in the sixties, but we wanted to seek out lesser-known artists. The festival team, led by Farrokh Ghaffari, its future director, sent people out to the distant reaches of the country, and what they brought back still endures as a source of wonder and a hope for the future of our country. In the poorest and most far-flung villages, everywhere, there had survived or appeared storytellers, bands, little theater or marionette troupes, and naturally, poets. We found ourselves curators of these treasures, which had styles typical of their regions. Now it was up to us to draw up a list of them and decide whom to invite and on what criteria. It was an embarrassment of riches.

The same procedure was followed for other parts of the world. Members of the committee, Farrokh Ghaffari and Bijan Saffari, went to Asia and Europe to observe what happened at other festivals. The festival at Royan in France was very helpful for the theater, and the international festival in Nancy was a mine of information. One of the main people we found there was Robert Wilson, the American avante-garde playwright, who would come to Shiraz.

At last, in September 1967, we timidly opened our first grand cultural event. We had chosen September so that students, who were still on holiday during that month, could take part in the festival. It is also the best time of the year in Iran, neither too hot nor too cold, and it is possible to stay out of doors at night. Yehudi Menuhin's attendance helped bring many others.

The following year Yannis Xenakis and Artur Rubinstein came to play at Shiraz. And in 1969 the festival had an international influence, thanks to the theme of that year—"percussion instruments throughout the world"—which brought us the Persian *tombak*, the Indian mridangam, the Balinese gamelan, the Rwandan drum, and many others. Yannis Xenakis came back and the Italian composer Bruno Maderna also participated. The festival became more and more successful from that time until it was held for the last time in 1977.*

Even though the festival was my idea, I limited my involvement to opening it and seeing some performances at the beginning and at the end. I would have liked to see everything but my schedule would not allow it. Fortunately the event escaped excessive bureaucratic supervision and answered only to a committee of imaginative, open-minded artists. I loved the atmosphere at the festival: the people were obviously all happy to be there; you could feel the Iranians' thirst to discover the music or theater of another land, as well as their own, and the artists were delighted to be received with such warmth. The whole city of

*In 1976 we set up the Dialogue between Cultures, an organization whose aim was to establish fruitful exchanges between cultures throughout the world. The first seminar took place in Iran in 1978 and included European countries, Japan, and Egypt.

Shiraz saw to it that all the guests felt at home. Everyone contributed—the governor, the mayor, the local army commander. I, too, didn't hesitate to carry chairs or drag benches if they were needed and I often lent a hand.

The artists were invited to stage their shows wherever they wished. They had only to ask and the committee went out of its way to facilitate the performances, providing cars, trucks, and equipment. In 1972 Robert Wilson came and put on a performance, *Ka Mountain*, that lasted 168 hours, seven days and seven nights without interruption in the hills overlooking Shiraz. Others chose Cyrus's tomb in the desert as their site, or the caravanserai in the bazaar, or an old house they had seen in town, or one of the many parks. *Alice in Wonderland* was put on in a melon shed, and I watched it sitting on a carpet on the ground. In 1971 Peter Brook came to direct *Orghast at Persepolis*, written by Ted Hughes. It nearly turned into a real-life drama, and this time my presence was useful in sorting things out. Planning to see the performance, I headed out to Persepolis probably one or two hours after Mr. Brook. Suddenly we came upon an unusual group of people. The driver of our bus slowed down and stopped. Out of the crowd rushed Minister of Education Manouchehr Ganji, ashen-faced.

"Your Majesty, you have arrived just at the right moment. Mr. Brook is furious."

"A soldier on guard duty refused to let him pass. He's canceling the performance and wants to go back to Europe immediately."

"Where is Mr. Brook?"

"In the little café over there. He won't listen to a thing."

"I would like to speak to him."

A moment later I saw him appear, and he was very angry.

"Mr. Brook, he was just an ordinary soldier doing his duty," I said to him. "He didn't recognize you. It's not his fault, it's ours. Please don't hold it against us."

Our famous guest looked inscrutable and said nothing. And so I continued, with a little humor, "In this conversation, Mr. Brook, it seems to me that I am the one who is acting like an artist and you like an empress."

He looked at me and suddenly his face lit up. "That's a nice picture! All right, let's resume our own roles, if you will."

In 1974 Maurice Béjart, who has since become a great lover of Iran, took part with a ballet specially created for the festival: *Golestan*, the name of Sa'adi's masterpiece. Knowing this, I had asked my husband to make the trip to Shiraz. We were dazzled from the very first notes: Béjart had taken his inspiration from the traditional music of Baluchistan, a province in the far southeast of the country. The moment when his dancers appeared under the starry night sky at Persepolis was definitely one of the finest in the history of the festival. The performance ended with traditional Iranian music accompanying the marvelous voice of Razavi reciting poems of Rumi. Béjart came back in 1977, the last year of the festival. Then the Islamic Revolution brought our collaboration to an abrupt end, but when we saw each other again in New York in the mid-eighties, the reunion was so emotional that neither of us could hold back our tears.

In 1975 the No Theater of Japan honored us with their presence. It was an unprecedented cultural event: the theater had never before left Japan. They had agreed to come because they had been assured that I would come to the performance. I often went with my children, especially the two eldest, Reza and Farahnaz, who were interested in some of the productions. But for the first night of the No, there was only my little Leila with me. She was only five, but she watched the whole thing, delightfully attentive. The strange beauty of the No captivated us both.

Alongside the international events, the festival led to a revival of Iranian theater.* I'm thinking in particular of directors such as Arbi Ovanessian, Bijan Mofid, and Parviz Sayyad. Inspired by the festival, many troupes of young actors worked on plays all year, then came and presented them in Shiraz. Musicians, for their part, unearthed old traditional melodies, and we would gather in the evening at Hafez's tomb to hear them. Seats, carpets, and cushions were laid out in the lovely gardens, and as night fell, little candles were lit on each side of the path. So many came to listen that people would even be sitting out in the street. I liked these evenings best; foreign visitors and Iranians would come together, communicating deeply through the music, with the great feeling that we were witnessing the rediscovery of a hidden part of our soul. Much later, Mahmoud, a fighter pilot who had been in the war with Iraq and had then gone into exile in the United States, confided to me, "My affection for you, Your Majesty, goes back to the Shiraz Festival, one evening at Hafez's tomb. I was sitting on the footpath in the street listening to our traditional music. At some point I stood up and I caught sight of you. You were in the crowd in front of me, and you looked so happy to be there with us. Quite apart from what you represent officially, I felt at that moment how close we were, how we were united by our cultural roots."

Many young people have told me subsequently that without the festival they would probably never have thought of studying cinema, theater, or music. They had found their vocation at Shiraz by coming into contact with creative works from Iran and elsewhere.

The main part of the festival was devoted to the traditional arts of Iran and elsewhere, but Shiraz was also a testing ground for ideas that could shake up people's attitudes a little, to the

*The Ta'zieh (passion play) was put on for the first time in an international festival.

extent that some people later would even claim that the festival paved the way for the Islamic reaction and was therefore one of the causes of the overthrow of the monarchy.

Of all the festival's productions, there was only one, put on by a Hungarian group, that shocked people. I did not see the offending show, but the incident was exaggerated—especially after the Revolution—by members of the opposition who were looking for any pretext to criticize. Members of the security force, who resented the freedom enjoyed by the festival directors, also complained, as well as people who were against me personally.

It is likely that the festival was an opportunity for political trends to find expression. Some foreign theater groups expressed opposition to the king and in a fairly provocative way, claiming to plead the cause of liberalization of the regime. For example, an American troupe, Bread and Puppet, put on its play under the walls of a fortress in Shiraz, representing a prison. We allowed them to act in their own way, and denounce what they wished, even if it did not please some people in security. Some Iranian artists took advantage of the occasion to spread criticisms of the monarchy. We also left them alone. Roundtable discussions with the playwrights and directors were organized at the university the day after the performances. I was told that Jerzy Grotowski, a Polish director, was taken to task at one of these roundtables, by an Iranian student who asked him if he was aware that, by taking part in the festival, he was sanctioning "a dictatorship." "If you really believed what you say," Grotowski replied in so many words, "you'd be up there in the mountains with a machine gun, rather than talking calmly here with me."

Some European journalists also arrived in Shiraz very wound up about the monarchy and ready for a fight. As they knew about my commitment to culture, they often asked to meet me, and our conversations invariably began with some aggressive questions. I took the time to explain the king's intentions, to remind them how far Iran had lagged behind Europe, and I asked them to compare only those things that could be compared. I noticed that little by little they began to understand me. We had interminable discussions, sometimes until two or three in the morning, sitting in the Bagh-e-Eram Garden (Garden of Paradise) around little candles flickering in the warm wind from the nearby desert. We met from year to year, and several of these journalists even became friends.

In the eyes of some ministers and advisors to the king, the Shiraz Festival symbolized too great a desire for openness to the outside world. Thus Minister of Court Assadollah Alam, whose culture and intelligence I much admired, reproached me in his memoirs for my "misplaced liberal ideas." Many others like him saw a divergence between my husband's political line and the one I followed. My husband and I actually had no basic differences. He believed that Iran's economic awakening was still too fragile to survive a complete liberalization of society, a Western-style liberalization. "The country still needs a decade of stability to get to that stage," he would say, "but I want my son to reign in a different way from me." He had hoped to pass on to Reza a state that was ready for democracy. We often talked about it. I understood that he was racing against the clock, and that is why it hurt me so much to hear, both within our borders and without, that there was no freedom in Iran, neither political freedom nor freedom of expression. This attack on the king was quite unjustified. How long did it take France to find the calm waters of democracy after 1789? Nearly a century. And Iran was asked to move straight out of the Middle Ages into the democratic refinement of contemporary Europe. It seemed to me that my mission in this area should be that of a goodwill ambassador between the expectations of some people and the position of the king. I understood what the king required, I admired his tenacity and his strength, but I also understood the frustration of some of our intellectuals and politicians who were disheartened because they could not see the reasons behind that firmness.

People knew what motivated my work, and they did not hesitate to write to me or to ask to see me. Some were artists I had met at Shiraz, some academics, teachers, and students. They had written something against the monarchy or had demonstrated, and now they had problems with the police. I looked into the charges, if they were not serious I asked the king to help, and he never refused. He was always ready to wipe the slate clean and to forgive. Sometimes I acted alone, and most of the time the person concerned was released.

The police were quite often heavy-handed, as happens in most developing countries, where everyone tries to wield the small amount of power he has and instead of serving the regime, undermines it. For example, I was about to open an art gallery when SAVAK agents created an incident, so that the next day people talked much more about that than about the new gallery. SAVAK had asked me for a list of people invited, which I gave them, but on the day of the opening, they questioned some of the guests or prevented them from entering. That placed me in a very awkward situation. I would say to them, "You have seen the list, and you have raised no objections. And now that this person is here, you cause difficulties for him on the grounds that he has written something against the state. Don't you understand that by acting in this way, you just reinforce his opposition?" Then they would apologize, saying that they had mistaken him for someone else, but the damage had been done.

The police sometimes acted rashly. I can remember that at the beginning of the seventies, the Iranian painter Zenderoudi came back to Tehran for an exhibition. He was already well known and lived in France. Like many Western artists at that time, he had long hair. Ostensibly for this reason alone, he was questioned in the street and his head was shaved. Furious, I spoke to my husband about it. He removed the Chief of the National Police Force from office for this degrading act.

Another time I learned that an executive, who had been received at the palace with other business leaders a few days earlier, had now been arrested. He had very freely expressed his opinion about what was wrong and, in particular, he deplored the way a certain minister had acted. It was a time when the government was trying to control price increases, and to that end had sent students into the bazaar to observe the merchants. Now this executive, who was very close to people working in the bazaar, told me how badly this method affected the merchants and how humiliating they found it. I understood what he was saying and thanked him, and then the police came and arrested him. Consequently, he could well believe that I disapproved of his frankness. Feeling angry and humiliated, I told the king, "It's incredible! An Iranian comes to your house, has tea with me, and tells me honestly what is worrying him. Then the very next day the SAVAK people come and arrest him. It's terrible. I see these people so that I can talk to you about what they've said and lighten your load. It's intolerable that they should be in trouble later." The king naturally had the business leader released immediately, but once again the damage had been done.

The zeal of the police was matched by that of the administration. The minister for information thought he was being conscientious when he censored an article because it was too familiar. The journalist had interviewed our daughter Farahnaz, who naturally enough referred to us as "Daddy and Mummy," just as she called her elder brother by his first name rather than by his titles. "It's forbidden to speak of sovereigns like that," the minister informed him. The journalist happened to know my mother and called her. We were on an official visit abroad at that time. My mother managed to contact my husband, who found this kind of stupidity very annoying indeed. "Call the Ministry," he said to his chief secretary, "and ask them to apologize to the paper. It's ridiculous!"

We knew that these reactions would gradually disappear. One morning the governor of a province called me at the palace. "Your Majesty," he said to me, "the population of one of our villages is getting ready to open a small public bathhouse. They would like to name it after the king, and I don't think it's proper." I agreed with him; it was ridiculous. A dam or a city square, yes, perhaps—I didn't really want too much of that either—but public baths did not seem appropriate. I don't know the words the governor used to let the villagers know that they would need to find a different name, but the fact remains that a few weeks later a report from SAVAK made its way to my husband's office casting serious doubts about this governor who had "refused" to allow a public bathhouse to bear the king's name. The poor man had already been in some difficulties, which my husband had had to take the time to put right. He tried to make light of it, but such overreaching by the authorities actually offended him as much as it did me. Such actions could only harm the monarchy.

The journalists themselves, encouraged by overzealous bureaucrats in the ministry of information, found it very difficult to get beyond this authoritarian way of thinking. I would chat with them when I was traveling in the provinces or when I was officially opening something. I would say to them, "Don't put my photo everywhere. We're here to open a new hospital, so talk about the hospital rather than me. People are much more interested in that. They don't need you to know that I'm this or that kind of queen. Let them make up their own minds."

Having my husband's picture displayed everywhere was also excessive. It was understandable that his portrait should figure prominently in state institutions, but not elsewhere. I talked to him about it. In the same spirit I asked for an inventory to be taken of all the buildings and places bearing his name, so that the number could be reduced. The pressure was strong in all the villages, because the king's name was used to obtain subsidies. People said, "How can it be that this street is called Pahlavi, and it's not even paved?" My husband thought that time would change their way of thinking, for in this battle of images we also came up against the rigid mentality of some security agents.

Created in 1957 to combat communist subversion in the troubled years following the war, this policing agency had fulfilled its role perfectly. At that time the USSR and its satellites, as well as some radical Arab countries, kept agents in Iran to stir up trouble. It was imperative to forestall them and if possible arrest the agitators. The king himself had been the victim of assassination attempts by radical Islamic groups close to the communists and three of his prime ministers were killed by the fundamentalists. The Tudeh openly wanted to make Iran a Soviet republic, which would serve the interests of the Kremlin.

Some SAVAK agents no doubt went too far and it is said committed indefensible acts. Were they aware of it? The trouble is that by abusing their power, perhaps unintentionally, they harmed the moral authority of the king and the monarchy. But many members of SAVAK honestly contributed to the security and stability of the country. In the seventies, my husband began progressively to reform its scope of authority. Some of its powers were withdrawn and given to the gendarmes and police. If the king had been given enough time, SAVAK would have slowly become the equivalent of the American CIA or the British intelligence service.

PART THREE

Chapter 17

IN THE SPRING of 1977, Professor Abbas Safavian, Chancellor of the National University of Tehran, asked to see me. I was in Paris at the time, and he was also on a visit to the French capital. His request was nothing out of the ordinary, as we knew each other well and the professor regularly discussed various problems concerning the university with me. This time what he had to say left me greatly perplexed: he asked me to please consult three eminent French doctors, Professors Bernard, Milliez, and Flandrin. What they had to tell me was a secret of such importance, he explained, that it was out of the question for me to receive them at the embassy. I should meet with them in a place that was strictly private, where no one could overhear our conversation.

As soon as Professor Safavian left, I began to feel vaguely apprehensive. But there seemed to be no cause for it: our four children, who were regularly checked, were in perfect health; as for the king, although he was tired now and then, he was amazingly energetic and robust for a man of fifty-seven.

One of my aunts lived in Paris. Through Professor Safavian, I let the French doctors know that I would meet them there. When I left the Iranian embassy, I was careful to sit right back in the car, knowing that journalists could be watching my movements.

I can still feel the icy fear that filled me at that meeting. Time has not erased it. The doctors revealed that my husband had a disease of the blood, Waldenström's disease, they said, a serious illness but one that could be treated, if not cured. Who mentioned the word *cancer* for the first time? Perhaps I did when I was questioning them. They didn't want to worry me too much, and they assured me that there were means of fighting the illness. And to tell the truth, they had not waited to begin the battle: the first symptoms had appeared in the autumn of 1973!

This second revelation added confusion to pain: these doctors had been treating my husband for four years, but I had been kept out of the secret at his request. This meeting itself had been decided upon against the king's orders by the doctors alone, because in their opinion, they said, I could play a beneficial role with the patient in the future.

I knew my husband's courage and willpower. He had wanted, and still wanted, to protect me from this ordeal. As I returned to Tehran, all my thoughts were of him and the family we had started after our wedding, eighteen years earlier. Something had frozen within me, but the doctors had not destroyed my confidence, quite the opposite.

IT WAS ONLY THROUGH THE ACCOUNT GIVEN TO ME by Professor Georges Flandrin many years later that I discovered the hidden story of my husband's illness in detail. This man, who stayed by the king's side until the end and whose competence and extreme loyalty I greatly appreciated, undertook to write down his account of the illness in three long letters to his esteemed teacher, Professor Jean Bernard.

I was completely overcome by these letters. No other document could better depict the seriousness and the emotion of these clandestine visits to the king, which began in May 1974 and continued until we went into exile. They show the vital role played by the minister of court, Mr. Alam, in introducing the French doctors to the king. Assadollah Alam was himself being treated for a blood disease that caused his death in 1978.

> And so it was on 1 May 1974, that we went to Tehran for the first time. You had contacted me on Sunday evening at home and we left on Tuesday morning, both canceling that morning's outpatient consultations at the last minute. "Well, Flandrin is also canceling his Tuesday consultations, like the chief," your secretary commented. We were only able to take precautions at the last minute, that is Monday morning, after you had explained to me in your office what our trip was about. Dr. Abbas Safavian had telephoned you, asking you to come to Tehran and bring your "head of laboratory," as he called it, using the old terminology. He had made it clear that we would have "no contact with local medical people and that we would have to bring with us any equipment we thought necessary." When you passed on this information to me, I thought, as you did, that it was a huge undertaking...still hoping that we would be confined to our area of specialization, hematology.
>
> After giving it some thought, I told you that essentially, anything was possible, apart from taking a microscope with me—one would have to be found there. Experience would show me that I could have risked it after all, since a few months later I make a trip to Switzerland with a microscope in my hand luggage, without attracting any attention....Admittedly, airport inspections in 1974 were not as thorough as they have become since. The Air France planes going to Tehran still left from Orly Airport, and that is

where we were on Tuesday morning, trying to guess the reason for this mysterious request. The previous evening we had collected prepaid tickets in first class and, just before boarding the plane, I said to you rather sheepishly, "What if it is a practical joke?" to which you very sensibly replied, "In my experience, practical jokes don't come with first-class tickets!" And so that was the first of many Paris-Tehran flights I made in your company. At Mehrabad two cars with flashing lights were waiting for us at the foot of the gangway, and we shook hands with some gentlemen we had never met but whose faces we would regularly see at our arrivals in Tehran. We were taken to the government pavilion where we were welcomed by Dr. Safavian, who had been waiting there for us. Dr. Safavian was a French university aggregated Professor and dean of one of the Faculties of Medicine, of which he later became rector. Safavian shook my hand, saying, "Flandrin, you obviously don't recognize me!" It took only a few words to refresh my memory. We had indeed been externs together under Professor Gilbert Dreyfus at the Hôpital de la Pitié. Safavian remembered it better than I did, but perhaps he had also changed more. After our passports were handed back to us, we left for a grand hotel in Tehran, the Hilton, where no particular discretion seemed to be required. Once in our room, Safavian explained to us that we would be examining His Excellency Assadollah Alam, minister of the court. You already knew about his health problem as Professor Milliez had sought your advice about him earlier. You pointed out to me as an aside that so much mystery seemed out of proportion to the minister's problem: it was a simple one and we knew all about it. We then met Mr. Alam, who informed us that we would be seeing His Majesty the Shah. I remember very well that the minister of the court told us that we would be taking care of his "boss's" health—that is the word he used with his best smile. From his house we were driven to the Niavaran Palace and taken in to H. M.

Speaking for myself, I had a feeling of déjà vu, as you do with some landscapes—as I did when I saw Machu Picchu or the Great Wall for the first time. Being surrounded by so much of the world on television takes away the mystery and fascination that travelers of the last century must still have felt upon seeing famous things for the first time. Their only information came from engravings in shops specializing in exotic bric-a-brac. This was the realm of the predictable: here before us was indeed the man we expected both in face and figure. The only small surprise was his voice. It was soft, and he spoke perfect French, without any accent, but with a very particular timbre, which was slightly nasal. Standing beside his master was a small man dressed in a military uniform; apart from this he did not look very much like a soldier. It was General Ayadi, H. M.'s personal physician. We all sat around a table and it was H. M. himself who explained his problem, telling us that a few months earlier, that is to say at the end of 1973, when he was on the Island of Kish, he had noticed a curve on his left hypochondrium. He had palpated himself and made an accurate self-diagnosis: splenomegaly. Of all the consultations we had subsequently, this first one was perhaps the strangest. In answer to one of your questions and to show how sure he was of his own anatomical diagnosis, H. M., matching words with gestures, opened his jacket and pulled up his shirt, then hooked his fingers under his rib cage and breathed in…according to the book! We could then examine H. M. ourselves. He lay down on a narrow bed in a kind of alcove with a small oil painting by Renoir hanging above it. The spleen was indeed large, the only physical symptom and without adenopathy.* We were looking at a man who was still young: H. M. was fifty-five (I was forty and you were sixty-seven at

*Professor Flandrin's medical vocabulary is retained for the purpose of historical accuracy.

the time). Physically, the subject was athletic, and it surprised me when I put on the cuff to take his blood pressure. Once the clinical examination had been made and the necessary samples taken, we went into an office near the bedroom.

Up to this point, everything had been relatively simple; now I had to come up with some technical innovations. From the shoulder bag that served as my hand luggage I took the various tiny pieces of equipment needed to count platelets, leukocytes, hemoglobin, and to do the basic staining of the blood and marrow smears. No doubt you can also still picture H. M.'s office, where we carried out our work. In the course of the thirty-five trips I made to Iran in the years that followed, I became very used to this room and my way of working there, with the microscope and my equipment all set out for me.…It was a relatively small room, well lit and looking out on the Niavaran Palace gardens with a curtain of great oriental plane trees filtering the bright light of that spring day. The room had a desk which would be our laboratory bench, where we had already set up the microscope General Ayadi had provided. The desk sat on a carpet which was actually a reproduction of the most famous and most ancient Persian carpet, the Pazyryk carpet with its famous border of horses. It was in this very new kind of laboratory that I had to carry out my work…with drips or spots! I needed water to stain my slides and for the first time in my life I did a Giemsa's stain in a marble-tiled bathroom with gilt taps.

We both looked at the stained slides under the microscope. As we know, H. M. was suffering from a chronic lymphocytic blood disease, which we diagnosed at that time. It was therefore a slightly unusual form of chronic lymphocytic leukemia with enlarged spleen. We kept General Ayadi informed from our very first consultations. The piece of information that stuck in his mind was the word leukemia, and he declared that it definitely must not be used: as far as he was concerned, H. M. had to be told that everything was fine! That was a lot to ask, all the same, as we had just diagnosed a lymphocytic blood disease, which admittedly was chronic, but it would ultimately become malignant! In addition to that, there would have to be treatment that we could hardly prescribe without some explanation. During this first visit we did not yet have the result of the serum immunoelectrophoresis, which would show the presence of a "monoclonal immunoglobulin M peak" characteristic of Waldenström's disease. As the patient's state did not give serious cause for concern, we decided to keep our practical recommendations until we returned to Paris and all the tests had been completed and checked. Later then, when we had all the results in hand, we chose the terminology "Waldenström's disease," knowing that it was not the typical advanced form, for the immunoglobulin M peak was not pronounced in this case. Our personal reasons for using this term coincided with General Ayadi's wish not to dramatize the situation, and we were simply adopting the attitude that we would have taken for any other patient.

When we left the palace after this first visit, our impressions were mixed. I remember back at the Hilton you made the following remark, "Tomorrow American doctors will be consulted and they'll be here where we are now." Which shows that anyone can be mistaken, because your prediction was not borne out by the facts. We still had a lot to learn, and we had not reckoned with the personal and psychological strength of the patient. Having you come to Tehran, and me with you, was a deliberate and considered choice made by H. M. He had understood at the very least that his splenomegaly indicated a blood disease, and he got you here via Mr. Alam. This was the person H. M. saw after his discovery at Kish, saying to him, "Ask your Paris doctors to come here." Mr. Alam told me that later. It seems certain that everything was organized between H. M. and Mr. Alam so that nothing would go further

> than a very tight group, since H. M. consulted almost no other doctors after 1974. Accordingly, in the beginning five people knew about it: the "hard core" comprised the two of us, as we had all the information and a precise awareness of the causes of the problem. General Ayadi was the third. He had all the information but found it difficult to accept the conclusions; H. M. had the information in so far as we could get it through to him, since Ayadi vetted it first. The fifth was Mr. Alam, who organized what we did, although we did not give him a precise account of the medical results.
>
> Once we were back in Paris and had communicated our conclusions, nothing happened from 1 May until September 1974. As is the rule in similar medical situations, we had decided to begin with supervision but no treatment. To our surprise we were asked to return to Tehran on 18 September 1974.

From 24 to 29 June 1974, my husband and I were on an official visit to France on the invitation of the newly elected President of the Republic Valéry Giscard d'Estaing. The French president received us with splendor, organizing a lavish reception in the salons of the Palais de Versailles. The king was happy and proud of the recognition Iran now received from all the great countries of the world. So much had been accomplished in half a century, and the two architects of this spectacular recovery were Reza Shah and my husband whose triumph I watched with a feeling of gratitude and joy. Nothing led me to suspect the illness that was beginning to undermine him.

The country had never been in such an encouraging position as it was that year, 1974. Our production of crude oil had risen from 73 million tons in 1963 to 302 million tons, making Iran the fourth most important oil-producing country, behind the United States, the USSR, and Saudi Arabia. In 1973, the oil agreement of 1954 had been entirely recast under the personal guidance of the king.

From then on, the entire oil infrastructure, from production to sales to research, was controlled by our national company. The foreign companies who used to belong to the consortium became the main buyers of Iranian oil. The price for crude oil had just quadrupled—it was the 1973–74 boom—giving us a 64 percent growth in our oil revenue in one fiscal year. A rise like that allowed us to hope for an annual increase of 26 percent for the next four years. These were staggering figures but in line with the modernization promised at the beginning of the sixties. This outlook was quite evident in Tehran, where investors and businessmen were pouring in from all the great capitals of the world. Our hotels were full, with some visitors prepared to rent a bathroom for the night. It was like a gold rush: people said that the gutters of Tehran were flowing with dollars. As a result of this enthusiasm, prices rose considerably, especially rents. And so, while some Iranians became rich, others began to suffer from the country's economic expansion.

We had taken off in all sectors, and the hope of joining the developed countries seemed within our reach in ten or fifteen years. Our efforts in the area of education had achieved remarkable progress: from the 25 to 30 percent who could read and write in 1962, the number had increased to 55 to 60 percent. The number of schools had gone up from 7,900 to 21,900, providing schooling for more than 5 million children, up from 1.5 million in 1962. Eight universities and numerous colleges and technical schools had been set up in the main provincial cities. I remember, as a symbol of this cultural revolution, the emotion of a grandmother who came to tell me that now she could read the letters her grandson sent her from abroad and reply to him. She had waited more than sixty years for this "miracle" of literacy.

On the industrial level, all the great construction projects launched at the beginning of the sixties had been finished, in particular the trans-Iranian gas pipeline; the Kharg oil terminal, the biggest in the world; the steel works at Esfahan; the aluminum factory at Arak; the chemical complexes of Shiraz and Abadan, and the Dez and Karun dams. Agriculture had also made a leap forward through the increase in irrigated land made possible by these dams. A few figures show how extensive this leap was: between 1957 and 1964 only 1,156 tractors had been sold, while 3,000 were bought in 1968 alone, and by 1973 there were 30,000 tractors in our rural areas. At the same time the private sector was stimulated and now booming. The automobile industry, textiles, and electricals were developing at full speed to satisfy the new demands of a population that was gradually discovering comfort and leisure.

Yes, the king had every reason to feel satisfied and optimistic. He was close to fulfilling the commitment he had made to the people when he launched his White Revolution twelve years earlier. And Iran owed this success to its own people, to the men and women, workers, engineers, researchers as well as leading political and elected officials, who, seeking to ensure a better life for their children, had fought body and soul to develop the country and open it to progress in all areas: health, education, and family life.

On the cultural level, the country had opened up remarkably: Iranian artists were working throughout the world, our painters were exhibited, our poets translated, our cinema directors recognized and rewarded. Conversely, foreign artists and academics were being welcomed all the time in the larger cities of Iran. I noticed this recognition by artistic and intellectual communities more and more as I traveled in other countries. I was warmly received by universities and in artistic circles, and I felt sure that through me they wanted to honor young Iranian creative artists. In this regard, France paid particular tribute to our artists and our desire to be open to the rest of the world when it received me into the Académie des Beaux-Arts as an overseas member on 25 June 1974.

I have not forgotten the words of welcome spoken by the President of the Academy: "When they return to their country of origin, travelers who have visited Iran and spoken with its rulers declare how wonderfully well Your Majesty assists your husband, the shah. It is the same in the huge work so courageously undertaken by him and by yourself to make Iran into a modern state."

"I am sure that through me," I replied, "it is all my collaborators and the whole of the Iranian people whom you wish to honor. For without the participation of the former and the support of the latter I, as organizer, could not have accomplished the heavy task I have had to undertake."

From the beginning of our economic expansion I had suggested to Prime Minister Hoveyda that we should take this opportunity to buy back from other countries a selection of Iranian artifacts that represent our cultural past. The government took action and soon we were able to set up several museums, including the carpet museum, the Negarestan Museum of Qajar works, the Reza Abassi Museum for pre-Islamic and Islamic works, the Khormabad Museum with its collection of Luristan bronzes and the Abguineh Museum housing ceramics and glass. The Museum of Contemporary Art as well as three cultural centers were also founded at that time.

As the leader of an Iran bustling with activity, an Iran to which he had dedicated his life, was the king aware at the time how serious his illness was? He did not seem to worry about it, for he let the summer of 1974 pass by before replying to the diagnosis of the French doctors by asking them to come back and see him in Tehran on 18 September. The previous evening we had both opened the second Tehran International Exhibition, and on the day itself we were due to fly out for an exceptionally long tour, three weeks in five different countries: Singapore, Australia,

New Zealand, Indonesia, and India. On that 18 September he had to see the doctors early in the morning, while I was busy with last-minute preparations.

"On this second visit," Georges Flandrin continues in his letter to Professor Jean Bernard,

> We were no longer two French doctors, but three; we were no longer five people in the secret, but seven...or was it eight? Between these two consultations, Professor Abbas Safavian, who was among other things Mr. Alam's doctor, had been let into the secret, which was reassuring as he supplied a necessary high-standard medical presence on the spot. Safavian, perhaps not wanting to be solely responsible for such a secret, thought reasonably enough that he should let his French mentor, Professor Paul Milliez, know about it also. That made seven. The eighth, who perhaps was not in on it but who did know why we were there, was someone close to H. M. and Mr. Alam, who put us up on each of our many trips at his sumptuous, out-of-the- way residence in the Shemiran quarter. It was there, after the second consultation in the palace, that we all met: yourself, Paul Milliez, Abbas Safavian, and me. I can see us walking in the garden on that sunny Sunday morning, discussing at great length so as to agree on the attitude we should take. Safavian insisted that everything must be kept in the strictest confidence. He feared in particular that H. M. might say something imprudent, as the king, it seems, would often talk about his health problems and could inadvertently let someone in his entourage into the secret. Medically the patient was still in excellent physical shape, but his spleen had grown larger. We decided to begin immediately with the appropriate classic treatment, 6 mg of Chlorambucil, with the usual monthly hemogram check. We thought that our task would end there and that we had no need to go into the practical details of carrying out these simple directions. What actually happened was very different.

After we left, it seems that the patient received only a week's treatment, when a hemogram test was ordered by General Ayadi. A week was too short a time to wait for this test, which ostensibly showed (and this seems very doubtful) a significant drop in white cells. There was panic and the treatment was stopped! As a result we only saw H. M. for the third time on 18 January 1975, and it was only then that we learned he had not been receiving treatment!

This third consultation took place once again in the presence of the same doctors—Ayadi, Safavian, Milliez, you, and me—but this time it was in Zurich. H. M. happened to be in Europe at that time, having just been skiing at Saint Moritz, where he was a regular visitor. We were staying at the Baur au Lac Hotel in Zurich and we went to see the patient at the Grand Dolder Hotel. I had made inquiries beforehand about the equipment I would have there, and I learned that the Tehran microscope was not in the luggage. I therefore set off from Paris with a little Carl Zeiss microscope, a replica of the one I had in Tehran, dismantled in my shoulder bag. He was looking fit, in fact very fit, for I made him tell me again how many times in a day he had gone down the Diavolezza trail. As a skier myself, I admired the feat, but I was horrified, imagining what a bad fall could have done, as his spleen had become enormous. We discovered in effect that the prescribed treatment had not been applied, the splenomegaly had grown, and the organ was now clearly visible as a bulge in the left hypochondrium. Treatment had to be administered and the Chlorambucil was once more prescribed. On the Iranian side, which should have been in charge of monitoring the patient, there was a total impasse, by both Ayadi and Safavian. It was explained to us that there was no way that hemograms could be done regularly and properly and the whole thing remain secret. I tried to convince Safavian to find an old aunt or a fictitious cousin to provide a fake identity; he told me it was impossible and would immediately be discovered. No doubt he knew for a fact what he was saying, and the unfortunate, uncoordinated attempt at the first check that had been left to General Ayadi did not encourage us to repeat it. And that was the moment when the trap set by fate closed around me. All eyes turned to me, and in those eyes I was becoming "the right man for the job." It was as simple as that...Indeed everything was simple the first time, and it seemed difficult not to simply say yes: I would only have to come back to Zurich for a few hours to carry out this test, as H. M. was staying another month in Switzerland....After that, we would see! That is what I did, and this is what we saw: having taken the first step with this blood count in Zurich, the logical result had me setting off in quick time to Tehran 19 February 1975, 18 March 1975, 19 April 1975, 20 May 1975, 20 June 1975, 7 August 1975, 13 September 1975, 1 November 1975, 14 December 1975, etc.

Sometimes with you and sometimes alone, I became a frequent visitor to the airports of Roissy and Mehrabad on Saturday mornings, almost every month until my last trip to Tehran at the end of December 1978. It was the same procedure every time. There was the departmental meeting chaired by you at Saint-Louis Hospital on Saturday morning from 9 to 10:30, a ward visit for you and to the laboratory for me, then alone or with you a quick escape around midday by car or taxi to Roissy and usually the Air France Paris—Manila flight via Tehran, first class, front row if possible so that we were not too visible, left side window if possible to see the Bosphorus and the Golden Horn. Arrival in Tehran usually at night, first out of the plane with the same cars with flashing lights at the bottom of the gangway, the same handshakes and the same anonymous smiling faces, the same cups of tea in the government pavilion while waiting for passports to be stamped. From there a car with silent driver, which was sometimes changed en route, arrival at the same house, delicious Iranian meal, male servants but no words or music, difficulty sleeping due to all that tea at the airport, and departure on Sunday morning at dawn for the palace. Quick trip back to the house, a long wait, reading or endless Sunday boredom, as it would have been unwise to show ourselves outside, return on Sunday night, and back at work at Saint-Louis on Monday morning.

At the palace, the interviews were often brief. Once the biological examinations had been done and the results conveyed to General Ayadi, we waited until the patient had been informed. We were usually not asked to see him again afterwards to comment on the results. Between January 1975 and December 1975, biological developments proved to be remarkably favorable. The spleen had gone back to its normal anatomical limits and the anomalies in the hemogram had been corrected; the monoclonal spike had also totally disappeared from the serum. In spite of this improvement, the treatment was maintained at the same dose and frequency, as is usually done in these conditions. For the checkup in February 1976, I went alone to see H. M., who was on winter holidays in Iran at a ski resort in the north of Tehran. I remember him seeing me looking out the window of his bedroom and asking me if I wanted to go skiing, offering to lend me whatever I needed. It was very kind, but not very prudent, and I politely declined his offer. He seemed particularly relaxed that day, which was mostly the case when I was alone. I think that he was rather in awe of you, or at least with an important person like yourself he maintained a semi-official reserve, which he gradually lost with me over time. When you were not there, he joked with me a little, and during 1975, having learned that I had passed the agregation examination, he greeted me with a mocking smile, saying to me, "Well, now I'll have to call you Professor!" He was probably amused by my difficulties and the blunders I made with protocol and the use of the third person.

Nevertheless, on that day in February 1976, I was unpleasantly surprised when I felt his spleen again and once again saw abnormal cells in his blood, when he was still supposed to be receiving treatment. It made me think that the illness had flared up and would already need more aggressive treatment. However, it was only a false alarm. This is how it happened. We had decided not to use the name Chlorambucil, which would have been the best way to give the game away: the diagnosis of the recipient of the product, or at least something approaching it, could have been worked out from the presence of this medicine alone. It was Mr. Milliez who suggested substituting a harmless patent medicine, Quinercyl, sold in the form of white pills very similar to those of Chlorambucil. I was the only provider of the product, and I bought the two drugs in Paris, taking the Chlorambucil in Quinercyl packets to Tehran. We also agreed to substitute the word Quinercyl for Chlorambucil in our reports. Our subterfuge worked very well, but at the same time it had an untoward effect. H. M.'s faithful valet, thinking that his master might one day make a long trip to distant parts, took the praiseworthy precaution of stocking up on the medicine he gave H. M. every day. He therefore bought a supply of the real false medicine, i.e. Quinercyl, and for more than two months the patient used the supply of real Quinercyl, thus interrupting his active treatment, without his or our being aware of it. Seeing our surprise at this early "flare-up" of the disease, Safavian made careful inquiries and, after talking to the valet, understood the mistake that had been made. The real treatment was begun again in April 1976, and in September 1976 a complete hematological normalization was achieved.

In the end, this unintentional "therapeutic window" had a beneficial, if unintentional, effect for future treatment. Until this experiment demonstrated the need for continuing dependence on this medication, H. M. was not convinced that the course of treatment we were prescribing had any real effect. He had his own opinion about his state of health, in particular about the size of his

> spleen, which he thought he could detect increasing, decreasing, then reappearing again from the false sensation he felt when palpating it himself. He thought that these supposed variations happened independently of our treatment, which gave rise to some exchanges that were occasionally rather sharp. Once I had to say to him, "Your Majesty, in matters concerning the spleen, I'm the one in authority!" He laughed but seemed to keep his own opinion. The reason was, above all, that our course of treatment looked so ineffective: it was only those three little pills, taken without side effects, which did not seem to him capable of delivering any therapeutic potency. According to General Ayadi, a great purveyor of a variety of drugs, the patient had a lifelong habit of taking various medicines prescribed or recommended by people, whether doctors or not, and in the course of his life he had crossed the paths of a charlatan or two who, for honest or dishonest purposes, had supplied him with various pills. Consequently another three little tablets made very little impression on him. The mistake with the real-wrong medication was explained to him, the wrong-real medication begun again. The demonstration of its positive effect was made all the more obvious to him because the relapse was accompanied by tiredness and the remission by a renewed feeling of well-being. His logical mind accepted this demonstration, and since that event, H. M. always fully complied with the advice we had occasion to give him.

Although I still knew nothing of the king's illness, I did notice a symptom that worried me at the beginning of 1976, a symptom directly linked to Chlorambucil's having been discontinued, as I found later when I read Professor Flandrin's letters. One morning I noticed that my husband's upper lip was abnormally swollen. When General Ayadi was consulted, he diagnosed an allergy, and that reassured me. As a child, the king had had typhoid fever and malaria, and these illnesses had left him with an extremely sensitive liver. He was allergic to certain things, especially fish. Then everything returned to normal, and I immediately stopped worrying.

It is true that in the middle of the 1970s, the effects of rapid development and the ever-increasing number of projects meant that our activities had spilled over into our family life, to the point of depriving us of much of the time we used to spend together. We were both feeling the effects of not seeing the children enough and when the two of us dined alone, it was still to bring up some project that was overdue, or some letter of protest that had been sent to me, confirming the fact that despite the increased rate of progress, expectations were becoming more and more urgent.

Paradoxically, it was during these very years, 1975–76, that a murmur of discontent began to make itself heard throughout the country. I had personally known about it from the conclusions drawn in an economic and social survey that the king had asked a group of academics to undertake. The chairman of the survey was Houshang Nahavandi, a professor at the University of Tehran and later to become my chief secretary. They had conducted their research for several months in the provinces and suburbs, and the picture they drew of what Iranians were thinking presented a distinct contrast to all of the positive accomplishments that had been made. People said that they were indeed aware that their living conditions had improved in the space of one generation, but they spoke more about the disappointments or the frustrations that this leap forward had brought them.

Corruption, which they suspected in the new ruling class, was a large part of the cause for this disenchantment or gloom. They claimed that it was rife even in our entourage. I had actually heard certain things and regularly spoke to the king about them. I felt that these rumors did us a great deal of harm. Neither my husband nor I had any interest in money, and each time that the king was informed of a possible misappropriation of funds, particularly through contracting, I know that he did what was necessary to restore equity. We thought that the court set an example of complete integrity, for instance not evading customs on the pretext of being a minister or the king's brother, stopping at red lights like any other citizen. The suspicion of corruption was not new: as early as 1958 the king had had to decree a raft of rulings to discourage corruption, either actual or alleged, in order to restore calm. The survey led by Houshang Nahavandi at the king's request showed moreover that every reform had given rise to new resentments and set this or that social group against the monarchy. The agrarian reform had offended a number of large landowners, who since then felt increased hostility toward the king. At the other end of the scale, some small farmers thought that the law could have been even more generous to them. By redistributing a part of the land held by the clerics, this same agrarian reform had alienated a not insignificant part of the clergy for a long time to come. The emancipation of women and the opening up to other cultures had only increased the hostility of the mullahs. At the same time, young people, the main beneficiaries of this openness, demanded more freedom of thought and expression—to the great indignation of our conservative clerics—and the most violent opponents of the monarchy were precisely these young people who had received state scholarships to study in the United States or Europe. Lastly, within and without the country, the clandestine Communist Party and the extreme left continued recruiting young idealists or fanatics who wanted to overthrow the regime and install a popular dictatorship on the Soviet or Chinese model.

This report should have been worthy of the government's attention; it would have alerted them to the dissatisfaction. The king handed it to the executive, who did not take it seriously enough. It is true that many reports landed on the desks of the various ministers concerned.

However, I too was aware of a certain malaise. As I traveled around or visited various establishments, I was always welcomed with the same warmth, but I sensed that things were not going as well. People still came to me, as they always had, but they focused on what was wrong rather than what was right. I reported what I had heard to the king, and I often thought that all I passed on to him now were complaints. He worked tremendously hard, and when we met in the evening he was tired, and there I was with only bad news to give him. As my pessimism did not seem to be shared either by my entourage or by the government, I finally thought that I was taking everything too much to heart and being too idealistic. No, the complex workings of a state could not function perfectly; no doubt one had to accept a certain amount of imperfection.

At that time, Amir Abbas Hoveyda had been prime minister for ten years: he had been appointed in 1965. He had the absolute confidence of the king and also his friendship. As for me, my relations with him were similarly trusting and friendly. He never refused government involvement in the various social and cultural organizations that I headed. In return, I kept him informed of what we were doing. Through the years Mr. Hoyveda and his wife had become part of the small circle of our close friends. We liked going to their house and we sometimes went to their villa on the Caspian Sea for a visit or for dinner. From a modest background, intelligent and cultivated, but distrusting honors and ostentation (he didn't have a chauffeur and drove an Iranian car), Mr. Hoveyda had all the necessary qualities to make an excellent head of government: great ability in all areas, both economic and diplomatic, together with a natural affinity with the people and great personal integrity. He was one of the few people who had the ear of the king, in the same way as Mr. Alam, and he could thus have been useful in helping to break the isolation my husband had to endure, like most rulers and heads of state. Strangely enough, Mr. Hoveyda took rather the opposite view, and tended to smooth things over so that he could give the king a constantly reassuring account of the state of the country. Did he underestimate the importance of the discontent? No doubt. His tragic death robs us today of an essential perspective.

One can see with hindsight how strongly the aftereffects of the euphoria from the rise in the price of crude oil in 1974 affected Iran. From 1975 onward the situation deteriorated and our forecasts, which had looked so encouraging, had to be revised downward. On the one hand, the oil-buying countries, the West and Japan, reduced their imports in favor of more economical sources of energy. On the other, the price of industrial products and food products that Iran imported from the West rose considerably as inflation spiraled out of control in those countries. Our income fell and our expenses kept increasing. Under these conditions, a good many undertakings and promises made by the government had to be put off or even cancelled, and a climate of disillusion progressively filtered through to all levels of the population.

We did not have a clear idea of this dissatisfaction at the time, and if the king had any worries about it, the optimism of some people in our circle influenced us. The discontent must have been noticeable, however, for I was surprised at how many security people we had around us when we traveled to the provinces. Security constantly got in the way of my direct contact with people, as I have described, but with time the guard had learned to be a little more adaptable.

On 21 March of 1976, we were celebrating the fiftieth anniversary of the Pahlavi dynasty. Particularly on that day I felt that something had changed between the people and the monarchy; I could feel it in my bones, like a sudden icy wind. There seemed to me to be an intangible shadow over the harmony and the confidence between us. Nevertheless my husband repeated his dedication to the people of Iran at Reza Shah's tomb; then he said these words, which today fill me with infinite sadness: "We stem from this people, we were born on the sacred soil of Iran, and we will be buried in this earth."

Was this unexpected reference to his death linked to the illness he was hiding from me?

The next day we left for a few days' rest on the island of Kish, and it was there, I think, that the swelling of his upper lip worried me for a while.

When I look back on it, I see that in the following months he made a decision that seems to me to show the worries he had at the time: he began to instruct me in the affairs of the country with our elder son, Reza. Several times a week Reza and I were taken to confer with the prime minister, then with each of the ministers involved in current matters. We also received the chiefs of the armed forces, representatives of different institutions, and particularly those of the Parliament. I found it a difficult and delicate situation, for I didn't imagine for one second that I would have to succeed him one day, and yet I obviously had to take this "training" seriously and question him as if he were going to die.

As I write these lines, I recall that the king had already taken a step in that direction three years earlier. On 22 October 1973, according to my archives, he had called the prime minister, members of Parliament, and the chiefs of the armed forces to the palace to deliver to them, in my presence, a kind of political will and testament.

This is, in essence, what he said to them: "I could die at any time. If this should happen when the crown prince is not of legal age to succeed me, authority will go to the queen and the Regency Council. The armed forces should remain loyal to the queen and later to the young king. Orders can come from a woman or a young man; they should be obeyed. Our security and our lives depend on it." Today, with the benefit of Professor Flandrin's account, this first initiative can be seen in a new and serious light: the king had probably just learned that he was suffering from Waldenström's disease.

The prospect of being regent sometimes worried me. "I hope that the Good Lord does not wish it, but if something happens to you, what should I do? What should I do first?"

He gave that barely perceptible little smile of his. "You will manage very well."

I smiled too. I was so sure that it would never happen. He was still young and Reza was not far from his twentieth birthday, the requisite age to ascend to the throne.

Informing me of the king's illness was the subject of lengthy debates among the doctors, who only decided to do it in the interest of their patient.

Professor Georges Flandrin recalls:

> At that time, apart from Mr. Alam and General Ayadi, Safavian was the only Iranian with whom we could discuss the whole subject of this problem of imposed secrecy. Such secrecy was much heavier for him to bear than for us, because it seemed obvious to him that one day or other he would be reproached, if only by the patient's family, for not having told anyone of facts which he knew had possible political consequences. After we discussed this subject many times, it seemed to us that logically we should inform the patient's wife. This met with some objections, but it is the decision we made. Before speaking to H. M. the Queen, who knew nothing about it, we had made some approaches to H. M. to try and convince him to speak about his health to his wife, but each time H. M. had avoided the question. Perhaps we were making a debatable decision there, because medical secrecy should even apply to a patient's close relations, in this case, his wife. What drove us to do it was that we felt it was in the best interest of his

health. Ensuing events showed us the importance of Her Majesty the Queen in taking responsibility for her husband's medical problem, in particular at the beginning of their exile and as long as she was able to. Fearing a foreseeable deterioration of the disease, we wanted his wife to be informed, so that she could be morally and psychologically prepared for what would inevitably happen one day. And so we had a very difficult message to give her, and what is more, it had to be done with absolute secrecy and, if I may be so bold, behind the backs of the patient, his secret service, our families, and our friends, not to mention our enemies and anyone else who might be naturally curious. Aggravating the situation was the fact that we could not talk about our decision either to H. M. or to Mr. Alam, our usual facilitator, who for once could not be asked to open doors for us.

Abbas Safavian and myself had to plan the scenario of a very strange and very secret meeting. Paris had been chosen as the only possible location. Tehran had been rejected, for unless Alam organized it, there was no hope of secrecy. I therefore remained rather vague about the conditions for this meeting. As I am sure you remember it was a very emotional time. We were there, all four of us, yourself, Mr. Milliez, Safavian, and I. The conditions laid down for this meeting were unusual, and H. M. the Queen still did not know precisely why we were so keen to see her and why it was so secret. Safavian, now rector at the University, had met her on university matters and had convinced her how important this meeting was. You probably remember this first conversation with H. M. the Queen, since you were the one who gave the information we had to convey, followed by Mr. Milliez. I only made a few comments, when asked, on certain precise points of medical testing. It was a hard thing for her to hear. Her husband, who seemed so healthy, had a blood disease that was chronic but serious. In addition to that, he knew it and had not wanted to say anything

> about it. All this had to be understood, if not accepted in such a short time, and then kept to herself. More difficult still: how was she going to tell her husband that she now knew all about it? The only way was for her to obtain permission to have an "official talk" with the French doctors, without having to say that she had already seen them in secret. She finally received permission, and when we were next in Tehran, with the king's knowledge, we were invited to meet the queen. One more person was now in the secret, and the circle of people who knew stayed the same until clinical worsening of the disease occurred in the Bahamas, and especially in Mexico, before his departure for New York.

Back in Tehran in that month of June 1977, how did I get the king to tell me about his illness? He spoke to me about it in fairly innocuous terms, saying that he had a problem with platelets and red corpuscles and that the medication he took corrected the anomaly. As secrecy no longer existed between us, he had no hesitation in mentioning his illness in the months that followed. But he did it rather casually, making me think that he did not know its seriousness, or that he did know but wanted to shield me from it. He would feel his spleen in my presence, commenting, "Well, it seems a little swollen today. Tell me what you think." I would try for myself and say, "Yes, it is a little" or "No, it's better than yesterday." But our conversations never went beyond these superficial exchanges, since I was supposed to know nothing apart from what he wanted to tell me: just a slight malfunction in the composition of the blood. It was therefore very hard for me and very sad: I had to bear this heartbreaking anxiety alone, feeling awful at not being able to help him. "If only he would let me know everything," I thought, "we could talk about it freely; he would not have to bear this burden on his own; I could help him, give him some of my energy."

I write this, but still today I do not know how aware he was of his illness in that second half of 1977 and during 1978. During this time the French doctors asked for a second interview with me, this time in the Niavaran Palace. They told me that they felt they had to tell him how serious his illness was, and as I showed some surprise, thinking that the king already knew all about it, they confessed that they had never actually mentioned the word "cancer" to him, only "Waldenström's disease" or "lymphoma," the vague term physicians often used with nonmedical people.

If I understood them correctly, I now actually knew more than my husband. That put considerable moral and political responsibility on my shoulders. I told them that they had to tell the king the true state of affairs without delay. "He has the strength and the courage to hear it," I stressed to them, "and his responsibilities make it essential that he have an accurate picture of his state of health." I added that in my opinion it would be easier for him to cope with the shock today, when he was feeling well, than when his strength was declining. At the end of this conversation, the doctors assured me that they would try to talk to him, but a few hours later they told me that once again they had not used the word "cancer" with him.

Is it possible that the king did not understand? I doubt that a man of his intelligence, who was also very careful about his health, could not have had, from the beginning, a clear picture of the unavoidable tragedy that awaited him. What he said to President Giscard d'Estaing, who met him in St. Moritz in the winter of 1975, confirms my feeling. When the French president expressed his surprise at the speed of growth in Iran, my husband confided to him without any explanation, "My problem is that I haven't enough time. I won't be remaining in power for long. I intend leaving in seven or eight years. I will be well over sixty. I would prefer to leave earlier, but my son is still too young. I will wait until he is ready, but I want the essentials to be in place before he takes over. He will have a lot of difficulties in the beginning. It's up to me to bring about the transformation of Iran. I am determined to do it." He always managed, however, to avoid giving me the feeling that he knew about his health, so to this day I have never stopped wondering how much he knew.

The doctors were also holding back, as Professor Flandrin reveals in his long correspondence with Jean Bernard. He describes the meeting during which they wanted to inform the king:

> That same morning you tried to bring the conversation around to his illness, to its possible course, with all the precautions and nuances that one owes to the patient. The king then made a comment which, in my opinion, completely rules out the assumption that he had not understood what we wanted to tell him. At the time his elder son was in an American air force academy. "I am only asking you to help me maintain my health for two years, enough time for the Crown Prince to finish the year in the US and spend another in Tehran." (Why a year in Tehran? He told us, but I have forgotten.)
>
> Much later, however, when I was with H. E. Alam at his Birjand domain in the mountains in eastern Iran, he talked a lot about himself and the king. On the subject of his master's personality, he described some paradoxical traits, which were no doubt equally real. He told me one day, for example, "It's strange to think that this man who has risen to such power could still be naïve enough in some ways to trust what people told him." On the other hand, he also said to me, "Used to assuming a role since childhood—the king has an amazing ability to completely hide what he is thinking and what he knows." He told me that he had often had proof of

> this when he came to give the king some information that Alam knew the king had already heard. The King was capable of not showing the slightest hint of it. That is why I have always thought that we could not rely on our own impressions to know if the king had really understood what we were telling him about his health.

It seems likely that, knowing his time was now limited, my husband was preparing the country for his successor. He had repeated many times that his son would not have to govern in the same way as he had; inheriting a country that had finally emerged from its underdevelopment, Reza's task would be to open Iran up to democracy. In the spring of 1977 demands for the liberalization of the regime were beginning to be more urgently voiced by the political opposition and by intellectuals and in particular a journalist who later supported Khomeini and the mullahs. In an open letter to the king, the journalist asked him in particular to rule according to the constitution and to give the country freedom of expression equal to that in Western Europe and the United States. Shapour Bakhtiar and Mehdi Bazargan also spoke out on the same issue.

The king planned to speed up the liberalization of the country. To make it clear to the country that the time for change had come, in the middle of summer 1977 he replaced Mr. Hoveyda as prime minister with a brilliant, cultivated man of great integrity, Jamshid Amouzegar.

"He had the well-earned reputation of being a truly honest man," my husband later wrote in his memoirs, "and in addition he was the secretary general of the Renaissance Party, which meant he could count on the support of that movement. My decision to change prime ministers in no way cast any doubts on Mr. Hoveyda's ability. Quite the opposite, this perceptive, cultivated man had served his country well for thirteen years, but positions of power are very wearing and he himself had thought of standing back a little from affairs of state. To show that I still had complete faith in him, I made him my minister of court so that I could keep him near me and speak with him daily. As soon as the new government was constituted, I declared myself in favor of the principle of liberalization, on condition that it could be done without bringing about the disintegration of the country."

The task of the new prime minister was indeed a delicate one, for he would have to oversee the opening up of the country at the same time as discontent was rising, due in particular to the disenchantment that had followed the oil boom. The Sixth Development Plan, which had seemed so promising, had to be abandoned in favor of a harsher economy, and that could also increase the atmosphere of gloom.

Demands for liberalization and the opening up of the country were not new, but they became stronger with the arrival in the White House of a Democratic president, Jimmy Carter, in November 1976. My husband had maintained close relations with his Republican predecessors, especially with Richard Nixon, who had remained a friend. He had the feeling that the Republican administration understood the immense difficulties he encountered trying to bring Iran out of its underdevelopment and knew that he could not do it without wielding a certain amount of authority. The chief American diplomat, Henry Kissinger, who knew Iran well, had a great admiration for what had been accomplished in the space of a decade. During the whole of his campaign, Jimmy Carter had proclaimed the theme of Human Rights, the freedom of the people, which in reality has to be treated with caution, taking the economic and cultural context of each country into account. The Iranian opposition saw an ally in Carter for future struggles, and the rush of demands in the spring of 1977 would doubtless not have been so great if another man had been elected to the White House.

The naming of the new prime minister did not calm the demands for liberalization. In October 1977 the Union of Iranian Authors organized poetry evenings in the Tehran Goethe Institute, which at the height of these demonstrations gathered up to 15,000 people. Above and beyond the words, the message was clear: the intellectuals were impatient to enter a new era.

In November we flew out for an official visit to the United States, an important visit because my husband was going to have talks for the first time with the new president. Would the two men be on the same wavelength? One was just beginning the business of governing; the other had reigned for thirty-seven years.

Our arrival at the White House was a difficult moment. Demonstrators had gathered behind the security cordons, some to applaud us, others to insult us, and when the two heads of state exchanged their first words on the lawn, in front of an audience of journalists and officials, violent fights broke out among the demonstrators, so that the police had to intervene using tear gas. The gas even reached us, and TV viewers the world over could see the extraordinary scene of the president of the United States and the king of Iran coughing and wiping their eyes while continuing their speeches as if nothing had happened.

We then went into the reception rooms. President Carter and his wife begged us to forget the incident—they were truly embarrassed—but I thought to myself that in Richard Nixon's time the demonstrators would never have been allowed to come so close to us. Didn't this permissiveness show a desire on the part of the new administration to embarrass us? The first talks between my husband and President Carter allayed this unpleasant impression. The king, who was in great form that day, spent some time explaining his view of the balance of power in the world and then spoke about the role Iran wanted to play. The president and his advisors later admitted that they were convinced and impressed by the king's analysis. Moreover, Jimmy Carter gave an enthusiastic eulogy of my husband, who was moved by it, as it was quite unexpected. On the following day the king told journalists that his first day had brought "tears in the morning and tears in the evening."

Outside, however, the hostile demonstrations continued, right under our windows. The demonstrators seemed to have gotten hold of our private schedule. As a result, when I arrived at a clinic in Minnesota for some medical checkups, I had the unpleasant surprise of finding about twenty opponents brandishing banners hostile to the monarchy. Much later a countryman who was then part of the opposition admitted to me that the American administration had indeed given them information that should have remained confidential.

It was during this official visit that I was amazed to see the picture of one of our clerics being waved by a group of students. They were demanding more freedom, which I could understand, but I could not understand how they could see a mullah as a symbol of liberalization and modernity. If there was one sector of society that had been heavily involved in blocking the king's efforts at opening up the country, it was the most conservative group of the clergy! From women suffrage to agrarian reform to literacy, my husband had constantly met opposition from certain clerics (although he had very good relationships with others, notably the Ayatollahs Behbahani and Khonsari). They had held sway over people's minds for centuries, and they saw progress and openness to the outside world as a threat to their hegemony. And so I asked the name of this mullah who was idolized by our young demonstrators and whose defiant look meant nothing to me. "The Ayatollah Ruhollah Khomeini," was the reply. His name recalled a distant memory. After making inflammatory speeches against the emancipation of women and inciting crowds of the faithful against the White Revolution, he had been arrested, pardoned by the king, then exiled. He had not lived in Iran for more than ten years, and had I not witnessed his reappearance on banners brandished in the streets of New York, I would surely have said that the country had forgotten him, as I had myself.

A few weeks later President Carter and his wife, on their way to New Delhi, made a stop at Tehran to celebrate the new year of 1978 with us. This fact in itself showed the strong impression the king had made on the new American president. After having recently welcomed the election of a Democrat, my husband thought the concern that Mr. Carter showed him was a good sign for the future.

We entertained the American couple at dinner on 31 December 1977 in the Niavaran Palace. On the eve of that year, 1978, which would prove to be such a dramatic one, the king expressed a confidence in the future I cannot forget. "According to an ancient tradition in our country," he said, "the visit of the first guest of the new year is a portent for the whole year. This evening's guest is a person of such energy and goodwill that we consider his visit as a most excellent omen."

Then Jimmy Carter rose with extremely laudatory words for the monarchy. No American president had ever paid such tribute to a sovereign:

> Iran, whose destiny is so remarkably well guided by the shah, is an island of stability in one of the most troubled regions of the world. That is a great tribute to you, Your Majesty, and to the great task that you are accomplishing in Iran, and to the respect, admiration, and love that your people bear you.
>
> Driving through the beautiful streets of Tehran today with the shah, we saw literally thousands of Iranian citizens lining the streets

> to show me their friendship. And I also saw hundreds, perhaps even thousands of American citizens who had come to welcome their president in this nation that has adopted them, and where they feel at home....
>
> Your people and the leaders of our two nations share the same deep attachment to the cause of the Rights of Man.
>
> No other nation of the globe is as close to us in the military organization of our mutual security. No other nation is in such close consultation with us on the problems of the regions which concern us both. There is no other head of state with whom I feel on friendlier terms and to whom I feel more gratitude.

King Hussein of Jordan had arrived in Tehran two days earlier to meet with my husband, and he had extended his stay to talk with President Carter. After the official dinner he therefore joined us in the library, where we had invited President and Mrs. Carter to celebrate the New Year in a more intimate setting. I have a happy memory of that evening, which was peaceful, friendly, and warm. King Hussein, President Carter, and my husband could relax, talk, and get to know each other, while Reza saw to the music.

Less than two years after that meeting, the Guardians of the Islamic Revolution violated the extraterritoriality of the American embassy in Tehran and took hostage the seventy American staff who were working there.

THE FIRST DEMONSTRATIONS BROKE OUT on 7 January 1978 in the holy city of Qom. On that day, the theological students used the pretext of an article insulting Ayatollah Khomeini, published in the daily newspaper *Ettela'at*, to take to the street. Qom was the town where the Ayatollah had taught until 1963. That year there had been uprisings on his instigation to protest against the reforms adopted by the referendum. We learned later that since his exile some of his former students had kept his legend alive. This article, which dragged him through the mud, was just what his faithful needed: they could cry blasphemy and call for action in his name.

The movement quickly got out of control, and on 9 January, the demonstrators attacked public buildings. They attacked everything they saw as a symbol of modernity: cinemas, restaurants, girls' schools. The police had to intervene and calm was restored but only after eight people had been killed: six protesters and two police.

"From that moment," the shah writes in his memoirs, "every forty days the 'mourning tactic' allowed those who manipulated the crowds to mobilize them for new demonstrations which, because of their violence, had every chance of degenerating into new revolts and claiming new victims. In this way, the anger of populations that were both credulous and fanatical would rise to its peak. It is a fact that, according to Muslim tradition, the parents and friends of someone who has died should go and meditate at his grave forty days later. I do not think that a person's death has elsewhere been so shamelessly exploited for political ends."

On 18 and 19 February, that is, forty days after the tragic events at Qom and ostensibly to mourn the victims, large demonstrations were organized in Tabriz, the capital of Azarbaijan. For the first time the political opposition, students, and the merchants in the bazaar joined the clerics to demand more freedom of expression and a raise in salaries. This coalition seemed quite inexplicable to us. How could people who wanted a more rapid "Westernization" of the regime and of society in general march beside mullahs and theologians who demanded exactly the opposite: the return to strict religious principles, the closure of Iran to the "immoral" cultural influence of the West, the obligatory wearing of the veil for women, and so on? Once again the protests turned into riots. The demonstrators attacked and burned everything that the mullahs regarded as symbolizing "corruption"—cinemas, liquor outlets, luxury shops—as well as state buildings such as the youth hall and the offices of the Rastakhiz political party. Unable to cope with this wave of hatred and violence, the police had to call out the army, and once again the confrontations ended with deaths on both sides. The army was extremely well trained for the defense of the country, but it had not been set up for urban police operations. I recall, in relation to this, that the American administration had made this task more difficult by refusing to supply us with rubber bullets and tear gas.

Having publicly come out of hiding for the first time, Ayatollah Khomeini, having taken refuge in Iraq, expressed his pleasure at this tragedy in cynical terms, which filled me with fear: "Our movement is still a fragile plant that needs the blood of martyrs to become a strong tree." What was this man's heart made of to want the death of his own people?

On 29 March 1978, using the pretext of mourning the Tabriz victims, new demonstrations took place in several towns and notably in Tehran. My husband had given strict orders to those in charge of the forces of law and order, the police and the army, to avoid bloodshed for the third time at all costs. But "martyrs" were needed, and so they were produced.

"The cynicism of the agitators knew no bounds," the king said later. "I received reports of cases where the bodies of people who had died a natural death or from an illness or accident had been taken as they arrived at the cemetery, hoisted onto the shoulders of a few ringleaders, who paraded them through the town, yelling, 'Here's a victim of the regime! Another crime committed by security forces!'"

Comments by Mohsen Rezai, chief of the Guardians of the Islamic Revolution Army, confirm those reports. He sums up the rebel strategy used during the whole of 1978: "Organization of sham funerals to be widely reported in the media. The coffins should contain weapons, especially knives, that can be used immediately if the forces of law and order intervene. Mourners of both sexes permanently stationed in cemeteries as a politico-religious weapon in the triumph of the Revolution. Use of red-stained clothing as psychological, political, and propaganda tools to bring out the people and make an impression on public opinion."

Witnesses reported to me that they had seen students at the university "making a martyr." One of them lay down on a stretcher and was covered with a white sheet. Blood from a bottle was spilled on it, then the group hoisted the stretcher onto their shoulders and went off through the streets shouting, "They've killed again! They've killed again!" Generally speaking, we had the impression that the revolutionaries were remarkably well organized and efficiently financed: the demonstrations were extremely well prepared and managed. They had everything: megaphones, masks, two-way radio transmitters, and later, weapons.

As the weeks went by, it became clear that "liberals" and leftists, many of whom had nothing in common with the mullahs, adhered to their movement for access to the wider population. And so religion was shamelessly used as a tool to stir up the people, in particular by the communists, who had the banning of religious practice as one of their aims if they came to power. Each component of this heterogeneous revolutionary coalition—religious, liberal, Marxist—had an opportunistic interest in allying themselves with the others, but it was obvious that if one day they took control of the country, none of them would stop until they had eliminated their former associates—which is exactly what happened.

For the time being, however, the coalition was holding , and it soon had regular backup from the merchants in the bazaar, a middle class that was wealthy, religious, and extremely influential in the towns. The oil boom and economic growth in general had helped them become rich. Feeling penalized by the severity of the Amouzegar government's, economic measures and unhappy with the new anticorruption measures, which hampered their business, they came down on the side of Ayatollah Khomeini, some of them, as was revealed later, bringing him considerable financial support.

Manipulated by these strategists with their various agendas, young people lent their strength and their influence to these unscrupulous leaders. "They needed troops," the king wrote, "and they found them in the universities and soon even in schools. They had set themselves to work our youth up to a state of real intoxication. Unfortunately they succeeded. Of course I did not expect young people to be conservative. In every country they turn to ideals that seem the most noble to them. One can do great things in the name of justice, but also the worst."

Watching these repeated demonstrations, which grew bigger every time, I alternated between disbelief and anxiety. The most difficult thing to understand was that everything positive that the monarchy had done for Iran was suddenly being described as negative by the world media. The very ones that had been most flattering to the king in the early 1970s now condemned his work. And those Western journalists, who were so punctilious about respecting freedoms, seemed to see Ayatollah Khomeini as the incarnation of the spiritual over the material. One Iranian philosopher even spoke of a new Gandhi! To we who knew the underlying sentiments and ambitions of this man, that was beyond belief. "The mistake I made," the king said later, "was not to have used our own media to fight against this incessant indoctrination."

The intellectual and political elite of the country asked to see me, and I received them all, hoping that doing so might help my husband. Academics, former political leaders, sociologists, clerics, and journalists came and went in my office one after the other. They too were stunned by the recent turn of events. When I got to the point of asking them the practical question of what they thought we should do to calm people's minds and regain the initiative, the reply was always the same: "The king must call on a prominent person who is beyond reproach. Someone popular, honest, intelligent, who rallies everyone to his name." I agreed, then I would say, "Whom do you have in mind?" They would invariably suggest some great men from the past. "I understand you, but whom do you suggest among the living?" And that brought nothing but a long silence. The fact is that through the years the opposition had discredited the whole political class by accusing some of corruption, others of supporting the United States or England. During these meetings, a former minister who had become bitter and afraid reproached me somewhat aggressively with having contributed to the annoyance of the clerics by turning Shiraz, a place of culture, into a place of perdition. "Minister, is that all I have done in twenty years?" I replied. All he could do was mumble, apologize, and the next day send me a copy of the Koran! People had lost confidence and they were beginning to lose their heads.

As I went about my usual activities in hospitals, schools, and libraries, I could feel the climate worsen. The time when I could give my security guards the slip and approach enthusiastic crowds was a thing of the past. Now I could clearly see that it was no longer possible. Some people greeted me with encouraging words, others stood aside and I could feel their hostility. Any dialogue with them had been broken off, and that was very worrying. I would go back to the palace desperately trying to find a way of restoring confidence.

When he crowned me on 26 October 1967, the king made me feel that he was crowning all the women of Iran.

Agrarian reform. The king makes a gift of the title deeds of his own lands to the peasants.

On a trip to the interior of the country, the crowd rushes to the car with a spontaneous show of delight. Everyone wants to give me a letter.

In Luristan. By the side of a waterfall some girls affectionately wind the traditional turban around my head. It is made up of at least seven scarves.

With the leprosy sufferers.

With the children from a school for nomadic tribes.

A moving welcome from women after an earthquake.

During one of my visits to an orphanage. I wonder what has become of these orphans.

With Maurice Béjart at the Shiraz Festival in 1976.

My first trip to the United States,
with the President and Jackie Kennedy.

President Richard Nixon and his wife on an official visit in Tehran.

My first official visit to Paris.
We were received by General and Mme de Gaulle at the Elysée Palace.

On an official visit to India. We are welcomed by Indira Gandhi, whom I greatly admired.

Prince Juan Carlos and Princess Sofia visit us in Tehran.

King Hassan II in Tehran.

With King Hussein of Jordan and Queen Sofia during the celebration at Persepolis.

I am given the mission to renew the ancient links that had existed between China and Iran, by going to Peking in September 1972 at the head of an impressive delegation. . .

16 January 1979. We leave Iran. Emotion grips the king.

President and Mme Sadat greet us at the airport on our arrival at Aswan. During the whole of our exile, they will be the only ones to offer us a helping hand. A year after my husband's death, Anwar el Sadat, who was like a brother to me and an uncle to my children, was assassinated by a fanatic. We are all grief-stricken once again.

In our room at the Oberoi Hotel, Aswan.

Exile. After being separated for several months, we are joined by our children in Morocco at last.

Cuernavaca in southern Mexico. Reza, who has come from the United States to see us, takes this picture of us back with him. He took the photograph himself.

On Contadora Island near Panama City in 1979. While the doctors squabble, the king's health deteriorates and I am terribly worried.

The last photo taken of us as a family. The children had joined us in Cairo before my husband's first operation. He is still smiling despite being so ill.

State funeral in Cairo, 29 July 1980.
In the front row on my left: Leila, Farahnaz, Ali-Reza;
on my right: Richard Nixon, Reza and President Anwar el Sadat.

In the Kubbeh Palace, Cairo, 31 October 1980.
Reza is twenty and officially succeeds his father.

Still in the Kubbeh Palace, shortly after my husband's death.
I am inundated by mail.

Farahnaz, who studied psychology at Columbia University, has just received her degree.

Columbia. Ali-Reza (in the second row) has just received his Masters Degree in Pre-Islamic Iranian History.

My last photo with Leila.

In front of my house in Greenwich, Connecticut, Reza and Yasmine release doves, which are a symbol of good luck for their marriage on 12 June 1986.

In the United States with Noor, one of my granddaughters. Despite appearances, she has just burst out laughing.

My mother. I am so happy that she had time to get to know her great-granddaughters.

My daughter-in-law, Yasmine, smiling between Noor and Iman on the day she received her diploma on completion of her law course.

Cairo, July 2000.
We commemorate the twentieth anniversary of the king's death.
The little ones see the tomb of their grandfather for the first time.

Together in New York to celebrate Ali-Reza's birthday.

Noor and Iman, whose smiles light up my life.

Surrounded by my family to celebrate my sixtieth birthday in Greenwich, Connecticut. Around me are Noor, Reza, Ali-Reza, Yasmine, Leila, Iman and Farahnaz (clockwise from top left).

The king was silent and serious but nonetheless continued to work from morning till night. He had lost weight and seemed weaker. That worried me more than anything. Was this deterioration due to the progress of his illness or to worry over the country's problems? Every new outbreak of violence affected him deeply. "Why are they doing it? Why?" he said again and again. He felt that he had been in communion with the people for a long time and could not understand how they had suddenly succumbed to the confused prophecies of an obscurantist cleric.

The Grand Ayatollah Kazem Shariatmadari shared my husband's dismay. Disapproving of Khomeini's fanaticism, he sent messages to the king asking him to arrest the most extremist clerics, supplying a list of names. He thought that the popular movement would fade out once these people were silenced. I saw the list and remember that the name of Sadegh Khalkhali was on it. The king would not agree to the arrests, favoring a political solution that would enable dialogue to be reestablished.

In June three prominent people from the National Front—Shapour Bakhtiar, Dariush Forouhar, and Karim Sanjabi, a university professor—published an open letter to the king asking him once again to reign according to the Constitution. They asked for the end of the one-party system introduced in 1974, freedom of the press, the freeing of political prisoners, and the formation of a government comprised of elected officials having received the backing of the people. This way of publicly appealing to the king was new—it was not done in Iran—and I had a strong feeling then that these people were acting in that way because they had the support of the United States, the new Carter administration. But that was not all: reading what these three men had to say, one would think that the monarchy had not accomplished anything positive for Iran, while the country had made an undeniable leap forward in all areas during the last twenty years. Shapour Bakhtiar was to be the last head of government appointed by the king. The two other signatories of the open letter joined Khomeini, before ending their days tragically. Dariush Forouhar, who was a minister for a time under the Islamic Republic before going over to the opposition, was murdered with his wife in appalling circumstances. Karim Sanjabi died in exile.

After more clashes in Qom in May, then in the holy city of Mashhad in July for the mourning of the "martyrs" of Qom, the king decided to speed up liberalization even more and, on Constitution Day, 5 August 1978, announced that parliamentary elections open to all political groups would be held in the spring of 1980. This was all the opposition had asked for and it should have fulfilled their wishes, but it was interpreted as a sign of weakness on the part of the king and immediately exploited by the revolutionary leaders.

On 11 August new confrontations broke out in Esfahan, and martial law was proclaimed in the city.

It was then that the disaster at the Rex Cinema in Abadan occurred, no doubt intended to intensify anger, inspire hatred, and mark a point of no return in the disintegration of the country. On 19 August the film had just begun in the largest cinema in Abadan when fire broke out. Four hundred people were burned alive. Having no doubts about the political mileage that would be made out of this tragedy, I immediately called Prime Minister Amouzegar to inform him of my intention of going to Abadan to be with the victims and their families. He persuaded me not to do it, and as I listened to him, I suddenly felt that he had lost confidence, confidence in the king and myself as symbols of strength and harmony in the country. I felt that he no longer had the same image of me, the image that had allowed me to talk freely and sincerely with all Iranians over the last twenty years. No doubt he was right to talk me out of that trip, for in the hours that followed, Ayatollah Khomeini went beyond the unbearable and accused the government of being behind this heinous act.

Since the beginning of the troubles, almost fifty cinemas had been burned down by the Islamic fundamentalists. If the fire at the Rex was a criminal act, there is every reason to believe that it was once again the work of the same fanatics. The inquiry would confirm it, but the perpetrator—a nineteen-year-old member of the Jamshid commando group, specializing in sabotage operations—fled to Iraq, then was saved by the Islamic Republic. In the meantime, the unfounded questioning of the regime in relation to this dreadful tragedy aroused further opposition to the monarchy.

"At the end of August," my husband writes in his memoirs, "the chief of security, General Moghadam, came to see me after a conversation he had had with a very important cleric whom I obviously cannot name. He reported to me what this person had said. It was, in essence: 'Sire, I beg you, do something spectacular. All our interests depend on it.' General Moghadam repeated several times the adjective the dignitary had used: 'something *spectacular*!' I could not remain unmoved by a message like that, but given the situation we found ourselves in at that time, what spectacular thing could we do? It occurred to me that only a change of government could fulfill this expectation, a government to which I would give complete freedom of action."

The choice of the new prime minister preoccupied the king, who confided in me about it. He should be a man of action, modern, open-minded, so that he could widen the basis of the government, and be morally beyond reproach. I proposed my chief secretary, Houshang Nahavandi. He was a French-trained economist, a convinced liberal, a man who could make decisions, and a former rector of Tehran University with many friends among the intellectuals. Lastly, I had been told that he had always wanted to be prime minister.

The king preferred Jafar Sharif-Emami. Mr. Sharif-Emami had extensive experience of political life, having already led the government and been the leader in the Senate for fifteen years. He also had many contacts within the clergy. However, his first declaration to the country was to say that he was no longer the "Sharif-Emami of old," which was not very astute.

The change of government did not produce the anticipated electric shock, and on Thursday 7 September, the end of Ramadan was the excuse for a new demonstration in the streets of Tehran. For the first time, the rioters demanded the king's departure and the return of Ayatollah Khomeini. Because an appeal was issued to carry on the demonstration the following day in all the large cities of the country, the new government decided during the night to impose martial law in the eleven cities, including Tehran, which was placed under the command of Lt. General Gholamali Oveissi.

When I heard about it, I was worried straightaway and asked the king how people would be warned about the martial law. As it implied both a ban on demonstrations and a curfew, this was a fundamental question. If the government did not find the means to warn the population, people ran the risk of being in the street illegally the next day without realizing it, and facing General Oveissi's troops. He was not known for laxity. I was told that the news would be broadcast by radio in special newsflashes, every half hour.

In reality the information was not given before early Friday morning, when hundreds of demonstrators were already on their way and many others who had stayed in the street since the day before could not be warned. Perhaps a minority would have gone home, and they at least would have been protected, for this Friday, 8 September, "Black Friday" as the revolutionaries called it, would be yet another tragic day for our country.

The army, which was waiting for the demonstrators in Jaleh Square in southeast Tehran, had received strict orders from General Oveissi. The clash was even more unstoppable because each side was armed: camouflaged Palestinian independents, both in the crowd and waiting on rooftops, opened fire on our soldiers, who returned fire. Twenty-one protesters died and seventy from the forces of law and order.

A week later, as if to confirm the fact that Iran was sinking into the worst of nightmares, there was a violent earthquake in Tabas, in the eastern province of Khorasan, killing 25,000 people. I knew Tabas well. It was a small town, classified as a historic monument, and I had followed the stages of its restoration.

I had the physical sensation of staggering under these blows. When would it stop? The suffering endured could be seen on my husband's face. Given the present tense situation, he thought he could not leave Tehran, and so I decided to go to the stricken population of Tabas alone. I spoke to the prime minister about it, and he asked me to wait for a while. Listening to him, I had never before had such a strong feeling of how precarious the government was and what a crisis of confidence he had to deal with: Mr. Sharif-Emami did not know how I would be received; he doubted how the population would react. The government had in fact lost direction. It was bombarded with differing opinions from politicians, clerics, and the army. I flew to Tabas with a heavy heart. The clerics were already there and very organized. Although the Red Lion and Sun organizations had rushed aid to the spot, the clerics had brought additional aid. I had to face the discontent and even the anger of these suffering people. An obviously false rumor had been spread, claiming that the king had allowed the Americans to do underground bomb tests near Tabas, which explained the earthquake. Some said that the disaster was due to the wrath of God! I spent the day there, trying to help as best I could and allay people's fears. Local dignitaries took advantage of my presence to express their feeling of helplessness.

The demonstrations continued in the days that followed this terrible Friday. The king had already responded favorably to demands to open up the country but now calm had to be restored so that the liberalization of the regime could be put into effect. Nothing could be put in place in such a state of disorder. It was obvious that the leaders of the insurrection had no desire to see these reforms applied, especially the promised elections.

"It is clear," the king wrote later, "that if martial law had been rigorously applied, the courts would have been sitting day and night. Martial law was actually nothing more than a warning that hardly disturbed the troublemakers. Our soldiers only opened fire on arsonists, looters, or members of armed commando groups."

Orders given to these commando units came from the mosques, and it was the mosques that were doing the liaison work. Agitators at the time could be seen declaring that there was no incompatibility between fundamentalist Islamism and Soviet-style socialism. This surprising theory had been imported by the People's Combatants (Mujahedeen-e-Khalq, or MEK), trained in Lebanon and Libya.

The leftist press in Western countries referred to the terrible regime, but made no mention of the terrorists. According to these papers the terrorists were the creation of the police and SAVAK. If these same papers were to be believed, more than 100,000 opponents of the shah were still in his prisons. The reality of the situation is this: there were never more than 3,164 political prisoners. In November 1978 there were only 300, all with criminal records.

Clearly the prerevolutionary situation we were now facing had been carefully planned. Guerrilla groups had been formed in the largest cities, where martial law remained in force. They had automatic weapons and explosives, the indispensable equipment of urban guerrilla warfare. They were soon given the order to attack embassies and government services. The goal was to bring the country to the brink of chaos as quickly as possible.

My husband consulted endlessly, tirelessly, asking each person for suggestions on how to reestablish contact with the various communities of the country. Many of those he spoke with recommended force, which he refused, reminding them that a ruler cannot open fire on his own people without losing his legitimacy.

As a result, he decided to address the nation, from the heart rather than from the head, since the protesters had became deaf to reason. The king's address was moving, going so far as to admit that he had made mistakes. At the time I felt sure that he would be heard and understood. Instead, his speech was immediately interpreted as another confession of weakness. Exhausted by the tension that had lasted for months, we were probably in no state to gauge the violence and determination of our adversaries. We were reaching out to people who had already condemned us to death.

In October I wrote these few lines in one of my personal notebooks: "I have the feeling there is no hope anymore. We have to fight on all fronts. Not that the situation is so bad today, but I'm pessimistic. And so tired! I still do what I can. I have to stay strong; it's the only way to keep going."

"I'm worried about the children." And a little farther on: "We must somehow set up a dialogue with people. There is no other solution. But it's as though all of us Iranians have gone mad, that we've caught a fever, that we're raving. I'm on the telephone from morning till night, receiving information, passing it on. We make plans. When the fever passes, surely there will be a way out of this nightmare?"

It was during that very difficult month of October that I received a very friendly letter from Mrs. Carter repeating her expressions of affection which touched me.

On Sunday, 5 November, thousands of demonstrators surged through Tehran. Bruised by the experience of the deaths in Jaleh Square two months earlier, this time the king ordered the forces of law and order to contain the rioters but to fire only if absolutely necessary. The soldiers and police were overwhelmed and the demonstrators vandalized everything in their path: cinemas, banks, public buildings. The Ministry of Information was looted and the British embassy partly destroyed by fire. The U.S. embassy, protected by the army, narrowly escaped the same fate.

That same evening, Jafar Sharif-Emami offered his resignation to the king, who accepted it.

In mid-October the Abadan refinery went on strike and, from Neauphle-le-Château in the suburbs of Paris, where he had found refuge, Ayatollah Khomeini now called for civil disobedience and a general strike. His call was relayed by the French media and the BBC in Persian. (After Khomeini arrived in Paris, France consulted the shah to seek his opinion as to what to do with Khomeini. My husband, thinking that the cleric would cause less harm in France than in Libya or Algeria, told the French to allow him to stay.) English radio diligently broadcast all of Khomeini's messages. The guest of Neauphle-le-Château actually admitted that "the BBC is my voice." In 1941 this same radio network had run a campaign urging the departure of Reza Shah, and the king had stepped down; Iranians remembered and consequently said in that autumn in 1978, "If the BBC campaigns against the shah, it's the end of the monarchy." In any case, the possibility of the country's degenerating into a state of paralysis made the king decide to form a military government. The economy could not be allowed to collapse; the country had to go back to work.

The choice of a general who could avoid this danger was the subject of many consultations. Some urged my husband to call General Oveissi, well known for his severity. I was not in favor, but the choice belonged to the king. Several members of the family phoned me when Oveissi was finally rejected, regretting the fact that he or someone else had not been selected. I said to each of them that if the king had chosen one man rather than another, he had his reasons for doing so, and that he was acting in the best interests of the country.

My husband finally asked General Golam Reza Azhari, chief of general staff, who was appointed head of a provisional government to give the king time to work out a political solution. General Azhari, a thinking, cultured man, was considered a moderate who was open to dialogue. One of his first initiatives was to order the arrest of the former prime minister, Mr. Hoveyda, whose detention was being demanded by many people even in the army. He thought that Mr. Hoveyda's trial would remove the misunderstandings that fueled the agitation. "I was not convinced that this argument was valid," my husband writes, "but Mr. Hoveyda, for whom I still had great esteem, was one of the opposition's favorite targets. In fact I am the one they were trying to attack through him."

No, my husband did not want him to be arrested; it went against everything he felt. The decision was made in a meeting attended by several members of the government and high ranking army officials. They were all in favor of Mr. Hoveyda's being taken in for questioning, and in the end the king gave in to their unanimous opinion. A little later he told me that the person he had on the phone during that meeting was General Moghadam, head of security, who had told him that, in his opinion, "Mr. Hoveyda's arrest was more important than our daily bread."

I was present at the meeting, but I did not speak out against Mr. Hoveyda's detention, although it broke my heart. It was generally thought that we had to try the impossible to protect the country in this hurricane that was capable of blowing everything away. The political and military officials who were there thought that Mr. Hoveyda could defend himself and would come out of this trial with his head held high.

Today I see the dreadful death of Amir Abbas Hoveyda, murdered in prison by the Islamic Republic, as a tragedy. But no one of us could have supposed that his detention, which was a purely political move made in a climate of great confusion, would end in that way. The unforeseeable cruelty of history does not in any way lessen my grief.

The appointment of a general as the head of government had an immediate beneficial result. Work resumed at the Abadan refinery, demonstrations ceased as if by magic, and for a few days, the streets of Tehran looked almost back to normal. The general strike called by Ayatollah Khomeini for 12 November was a failure.

During these terrible weeks, I was nevertheless able to gauge what a tragic influence this cleric had over people's minds.* Two young soldiers who had joined the cause of the

*On 18 November 1978, I left with my daughter Farahnaz and my son Ali-Reza for Karbala and Najaf, the two holy places in Iraq revered by the Shiites. I was going there to meet the Grand Ayatollah Khoi, who had great influence with the Shiite community. He received me in a small room where he lived very simply, and gave me a cornelian ring engraved with prayers as a gift for the king. He asked me to tell him that he would pray for him and for success in his service to Islam and Iran.

Islamic fundamentalists, Sergeant Abedi and Private Salamatbakhsh, opened fired on a group of officers in the mess hall of the Imperial Guard Garrison. I was told that quite a few of them were badly wounded—there were thirteen dead and thirty wounded—and I immediately went there to help and comfort as I could. It was deeply distressing. I cannot forget, in particular, how one of the men looked at me with such loyalty in his eyes as I held his cold hand. He died a few hours later. The two killers were executed. I was shown a copy of the last letter Private Salamatbakhsh wrote to his wife. "I did it on the orders of the Ayatollah Khomeini," he wrote, "and I will go to heaven. But don't worry. I will not look at the houris [female angels, virgins]. I will wait for you there."

During the same period, the fundamentalist insurgents certainly won over a lot of simple or naïve minds by publishing a list of about a hundred notable pro-monarchists (senior officers, businessmen, politicians) showing how much money each of them had taken out of the country. The exaggerated figures were obviously all phony, but they were enough to arouse public opinion. The new prime minister, General Azhari, trying to rapidly neutralize this propaganda, replied with a communiqué announcing that the people on the list were forbidden to leave the country! That was falling into the trap, giving credence to nothing but a lie, and the effect was obviously disastrous.*

*With the same aim of deceiving the people, a tape recording appeared one day of the Shah meeting with his military advisors; one heard him giving the order to fire on the crowd and asking that oil be kept in reserve for Israel. I listened to the tape myself: it was a perfect imitation of his voice saying these incriminating words; the rest were extracts of actual speeches my husband had made. We sent the cassette to an American laboratory to be analyzed, but by the time the proof of this deception arrived, the harm had already been done.

The respite after General Azhari's appointment did not last long. At the beginning of the month of mourning of *Moharram*, 3 December, the country erupted again. From Neauphle-le-Château, Ayatollah Khomeini had managed to flood Iran with cassette tapes of his inflammatory speeches.* Now, in thousands of homes, people listened religiously, as though to divine admonitions, to this fanatical man calling them to destroy everything until a new Islamic order was established. On the evenings indicated by the Ayatollah, at 8 P.M. sharp, people began to climb on roofs, shouting out together: *Allahu akbar* ("Allah is great"). For me, ever since I had been a little girl, this prayer had had a calming effect; I thought then that whenever I heard it in the future, it would send a shiver down my spine. Men who could do that, I thought, change a prayer into a cry of hate, could not be sincere men of God.

On 9 and 10 December, for Tasua and Ashura, the anniversaries of the martyrdom of Imam Hossein, Ayatollah Khomeini called for demonstrations throughout the country. Once again we were faced with the question of how to react. As martial law was in force, General Oveissi was in favor of forbidding the rioters to go down into the streets. He said he was ready to engage in a confrontation, but faithful to his beliefs, my husband refused. The army therefore withdrew its tanks from the center of Tehran, only maintaining a discreet presence near public buildings. The crowd occupied the city, and for two days chanted calls for the overthrow of the monarchy. Rioters' demands for the establishment of an Islamic Republic were heard for the first time.

"Then began the strikes that were to bring the country to its knees," the king recalls. "The electricity was cut off for several hours, there were transport strikes, strikes of water and oil; then

*Khomeini had several telephone lines at his disposal; his cassettes, which were recorded in Paris, were brought to Tehran by Air France or via East Germany.

banks, ministries, all the key sectors were jammed, one after the other or all together, paralyzing the nation, throwing out-of-work crowds into the streets and turning the mood sour. The ringleaders had threatened the workers and other strikers with harm to themselves or their families. We know very well that it takes only a few people strategically placed in big electric power stations for the power to fail. We know very well that the same applies in oil pumping stations. This small number explains how the insurrectionary strike could be so perfectly coordinated."

At the end of December, General Azhari, who had been prime minister for only six weeks, abandoned his post after suffering a heart attack. The country was then completely paralyzed and close to strangulation: our oil exports had stopped on 26 December, and since then not one barrel had left Iran.

The king then thought of inviting Gholam Hossein Saddighi to head the government. He had been minister of the interior under Mohammad Mossadeq, and he was greatly respected in all quarters. Mr. Saddighi accepted but wanted two weeks to form his government, which was much too long given the urgent situation of the country.

At this juncture General Oveissi and General Moghadam, who was head of security, asked to have a meeting with me. They told me that the situation was extremely serious and that, in their opinion, if the king did not appoint a new prime minister in two or three days, the revolutionaries might attack the palace. They put forward the name of Shapour Bakhtiar, indicating that they thought he would accept. I reported their suggestions to the king. He was not opposed to this choice, the leader of the National Front representing the group in the opposition that remained faithful to the Constitution. Certain people had already approached Mr. Bakhtiar, but it seemed that, for an initial meeting, he did not want to come to the palace. I therefore suggested to my husband that I see him myself at the home of my aunt, Louise Ghotbi, who belonged to the Bakhtiar family. The king agreed and the meeting took place. I did not know Mr. Bakhtiar, who straightaway began speaking about corruption and lack of freedom. I pointed out to him that the country was in great danger. He told me that one of the conditions for his acceptance to lead the government was the freeing of Karim Sanjabi, one of those closest to him at the head of the National Front. I reported our conversation to the king, who ordered the release of Mr. Sanjabi, whose first act, sad to say, was to praise Khomeini before flying out for Neauphle-le-Château.

This pre-condition satisfied, Mr. Bakhtiar came to the palace.

"And so I received him," my husband relates. "I think it was General Moghadam himself who brought him to the Niavaran Palace one evening outside of the usual audience hours. We had a long conversation. Mr. Bakhtiar made repeated displays of fidelity to the monarchy and embarked upon proving to me that he was the only person capable of forming a government in the critical times we were now experiencing. As he declared that he wanted to respect the Constitution, his proposition seemed acceptable to me."

At the same time,* some important people, including the ambassadors of the United States and Great Britain, were urging the king to leave Iran for a while, thinking that his departure

*At that time General Robert E. Huyser arrived in Tehran (5 January 1979). There was nothing out of the ordinary as such in his coming, as Iran was a member of CENTO (Central Treaty Organization). I later learned that his task was to ask the army to remain neutral. Many years later, General Alexander Haig, the chief of NATO, told me that he had resigned in protest against General Huyser's mission. In his opinion, the army should have acted to prevent Iran from sliding into chaos. General Haig thought that it was essential to maintain stability in the region.

would help calm things down. Mr. Bakhtiar was also of this opinion. It became known very quickly, particularly among the leaders of the armed forces, of whom the king was the commander in chief. Having already been harassed for months, our officers and soldiers had seen a large number of the country's officials and administrators flee the country. They thought it imperative for the king to stay at his post. In particular Chief of General Staff General Abbas Gharabaghi told me, "If His Majesty leaves, the army won't hold out." Some officers, including Generals Badrei'i and Manouchehr Khosrowdad, suggested that the king simply go to the island of Kish while they rectified the situation. They were dedicated and ready to sacrifice themselves, if necessary.

I also received a delegation of members of Parliament who pleaded the same cause. Some of these elected representatives, in a panic at the thought of the king's leaving, even suggested they could rally and arm the people of their regions to march on the rioters. During these last weeks, most of these officers and members of Parliament had received death threats to themselves and their wives and children. Some would be murdered in the first months of the Islamic Revolution.

I really did not think that the king's departure was the solution for defusing the blind hatred being expressed day after day, but my husband became convinced that it had to be accepted if it avoided further bloodshed. What thoughts could be filling the head of a man who, for thirty-seven years, had dedicated every moment of his life to his country and his people, who had given so much to bring Iran out of its underdevelopment, and who now saw himself so unjustly rejected? What is more, he was exhausted by the battle he had had to wage on two fronts for the whole of that terrible year, 1978: publicly against an enemy, the Ayatollah Khomeini, all the more inflexible because he was hiding his real agenda; privately, against his illness.

IN SPITE OF INCREASING DIFFICULTIES, Professor Georges Flandrin had not stopped his trips to Tehran. Rereading today what he wrote to Professor Jean Bernard takes me right back to the terrible atmosphere of those last months in Iran.

> Chronologically, it was in 1978, after the death of Mr. Alam, that the situation began to get complicated. On our last trip there together, you will certainly remember the difficulties we had getting back to the palace; the meeting when we were waiting for our friend Safavian; waiting in the street hoping for General Ayadi's car that was supposed to get us through the picket of guards.
>
> On my subsequent trips, until the end of 1978, this kind of problem, and others, became more and more frequent. Mr. Alam's death, then the withdrawal of General Ayadi resulted in the progressive breaking down of the organization that had served us so well and so discreetly up to that time. The basic pattern remained, however, and all the usual details involved in our arrivals and departures at the airport were always there, proceeding automatically. However, these stays became more and more difficult as I no longer had access to the discreet residence where we used to stay, I had to go to the hotel and try not to leave my room very often. The worse events became, the less I wanted to put my nose outside, for the disruptions, the electricity failures, the street demonstrations—sometimes bordering on riots—made even the short visits I had to make to the palace quite a problem.
>
> As for the patient, he remained as courteous as ever, but the visits were brief and, especially at our last meetings, one could feel that he was extremely tense and preoccupied. On the medical level, the discussion was basically concerned with the types of neuro-sedatives that should or should not be prescribed. Our friend Safavian was usually, but not absolutely always, at my side

during these last consultations in Iran. My last trip, at the end of December 1978, was the thirty-ninth visit to H.M. (thirty-five of them in Iran).

On that last occasion, the patient was almost unrecognizable, visibly suffering from apparently dreadful tension. He would not stop listening to the news on the radio while I examined him that Sunday morning.

Yes, the king was exhausted. He had now made the definite decision to leave the country for a while. But I was greatly touched by the dismay of his faithful followers, especially the army. That led me to ask him if I could stay in Iran.

"I won't do anything," I told him, "I won't receive anyone, but I'll be there in the palace, as a symbol of your presence."

"You don't have to be Joan of Arc," he replied sadly, and asked me to stay by his side.

January came, and snow started to fall heavily over Tehran. "The last days," my husband writes, "were agonized days and sleepless nights. I had to continue working, knowing that our departure was approaching." Deep distress slowly descended over the whole palace. People went about their business as usual, but like robots, and sometimes I came across one of them weeping silently. I told them that we would be back. They wanted to believe it, just as we did, but deep down we all felt the same chill in our hearts. What dramatic upheavals did history have in store for us?

PART FOUR

Chapter 18

We left Tehran in an icy wind. When we landed at Aswan in midafternoon on that 16 January 1979, there was a gentle, almost springlike warmth wafting over the city. President Sadat, his wife, and daughter were waiting for us on the tarmac. Knowing how distressed we were but unaware of the king's illness, they received us with particular affection. When my husband had finished slowly descending the ladder from the plane, the Egyptian president came forward and embraced him. "Rest assured," he told him, "that this country is your country, that we are your brothers and your people." The king, who was obviously exhausted, then revealed some of the great emotion he felt and, for a moment, the two men stood there looking at each other. Then Jehan Sadat kissed me affectionately with warm words of welcome and, as her daughter Jehan flung her arms around my neck, I suddenly felt I had found the kindness of a real family after months of tension and heartbreak.

My husband's ties with Anwar Sadat went back to the seventies when the Egyptian president, making a break with the diplomacy of his predecessor, initiated a rapprochement with the

United States that led to the Camp David Accords. Before that, President Sadat had taken the initiative of going to Jerusalem in November 1977 on a visit that has since been considered an historic event. The king favored the establishment of a lasting peace between the Arab countries and Israel and had constantly been in touch with President Sadat throughout the seventies. In the spring of 1975, he persuaded Israel to give back the Sinai oil wells to Egypt. Furthermore, Iran had regularly supported Egypt's development by making several significant grants of aid, notably for the reopening of the Suez Canal, to which our son Reza was invited. And I had come to know Jehan Sadat through our official meetings, to the point that, apart from our official activities, we had become real friends. We had telephoned each other regularly all through the autumn of 1978, and it was she who issued the invitation to come to Aswan. "Farah, come," she had said very simply. "We are here, waiting for you." I liked the particular way she said my first name: it had warmth and real affection.

Showing great consideration, President Sadat wanted our coming to have all the appearance of a normal official visit. The Egyptians had therefore been asked to welcome us, so there was a large crowd lining our route. The flags of our two countries were waving everywhere and people were holding portraits of the king as they had done during our last visit. That same evening the Sadats gave a dinner in our honor.

Where were we going? How long would this stop in Aswan last? President Sadat wanted us to stay in Egypt as long as the situation demanded it. Could we do that without causing him serious difficulties with his own fanatical fundamentalist opposition? I did not want to stay in the United States or Great Britain; I thought that the Iranians would take it badly and I feared that in the United States we would find the same demonstrations and insults coming right up to our door. Here, at least, the population received us like friends. Yes, I hoped to stay. I wrote in my notebook in the middle of that first night: "It's terrible not having a schedule, not knowing where to go. How long will we be wandering? A month? Two months? And if we don't go back to Iran, where will we go? What will become of the children?"

At that time the four of them were in the United States. The two youngest, Leila and Ali-Reza, had left Tehran on 15 January, only one day before us. They had flown out in a C-130 military transport accompanied by my mother; Leila's governess, Miss Golrokh; and an officer, Colonel Hossein Hamraz. As the plane was not equipped to take passengers, they were put in the cockpit, behind the pilots, and the palace cook had prepared a pot of rice for them, which was served on coffee cup saucers because there was no crockery on board. It was a very long flight for a C-130. They touched down at Madrid, where the officer got out to buy some food at the airport. Then they went on to New York. From there they went to Lubbock, Texas, where Reza had been living for several months while he was doing a fighter pilots' course. Farahnaz had joined Reza at Lubbock a month earlier to spend the Christmas holidays with him. They were in Hawaii with the Iranian ambassador, when they learned that we had left Tehran. They first tried to speak to us from their hotel; then once they found out what had happened, they returned immediately to Lubbock to welcome Leila and Ali-Reza. By that time the house was besieged by journalists, photographers, and cameramen. Fearing hostile demonstrations, the American authorities decided for the time being to house our four children on the army base where Reza was training.

We were put in the Oberoi Hotel, built on an island in the middle of the Nile, and from there we were at last able to contact the children. We were anxious about them, and they tried very bravely to reassure us. The two eldest were worried about us, as they had clearly seen the hostility of the United States toward us. "Don't come here," Farahnaz kept saying, "it's not safe." The king, who had worked all his life, right up to the last minute, now sat silently, dumbfounded and deep in thought. To the few people who called on him, including former president Gerald Ford, he gravely put the same question, "Why?" King Constantine of Greece and Queen Anne-Marie also came to show their friendship and warmly bring us comfort. For my part, I continued the task I had begun in the plane: to write and call on the world to help our people. Then I tried to contact those closest to us in Iran, but the country had broken down, making communications very difficult. There were hours of waiting, and I can remember the red handset at the end of a long cord, which we passed from room to room.

During these first days, spent in something of a stupor, Professor Flandrin, so remarkably dependable, came back to see my husband. I had forgotten his visit, which came back to me when I read the account he wrote to Professor Jean Bernard:

> H. M. had left his country. Safavian told me that we should go and see him at Aswan. It was on 20 January, only four days after his departure from Iran. We both set off for Cairo, in rather dubious circumstances, but that was only the beginning of a variety of comical travel adventures. To make my visit more discreet, Safavian had not arranged anything for me and, as I arrived at night, I had to go from hotel to hotel in a taxi to find somewhere to sleep. By giving a suitable bribe to the receptionist at the Meridien, I was finally given one of the bathing cabins around the swimming pool of this hotel on the banks of the Nile. After meeting Safavian at his hotel the next day, we took a plane together to Aswan. Once there, we had to cross the arm of the Nile to the island where H. M. was staying at the Oberoi Hotel.

Now, nothing had been arranged to get us there, at least not discreetly. You could hardly say that the requirements for confidentiality were coordinated! A number of Egyptian soldiers were stationed along the Nile, and in front of the hotel we could see military men in ceremonial dress with big red coats awaiting President Sadat's arrival. In addition we learned that ex-President Ford was also expected! It seemed that all we could do was reveal our presence or leave. Doing me the rather dubious honor of judging my English better than his, our friend Safavian told me that I was the one who should telephone. We had decided that the only way was to call H. M. the Queen, the only person who could arrange things without the word getting around. And so from the telephone box of a little local bistro I called the reception desk of the hotel, saying, "May I speak to Queen Farah?" It was no more difficult than that and, a few moments later, I recognized a very distinctive voice, which immediately recognized mine, and said, "Ah, you're here!"

I replied, "Yes, but we are on the bank and can't get across."

"You have to take the boat!"

I pointed out to her that there was little chance of the military cordon letting us through without some papers. H. M. saw the point and laughed, saying that she would send someone to pick us up.

An Egyptian officer came in a small motorboat and escorted us under the eyes of the guard of honor into the almost deserted foyer of the hotel. Safavian immediately made contact with the Iranians in the royal entourage and shot upstairs, leaving me in the foyer with my small hand luggage. I stayed there for a long time, perhaps an hour.... Someone came at last to tell me my room number and take me through the almost empty hotel. I had to stay there once again for quite a long time without any information about what was happening. I remember most of all that the room was very cold. I opened the window and went out onto the little balcony facing upstream. The winter sky was amazingly clear, in bright sunshine, but the rays did not reach me. I was frozen and annoyed, but it was like living in a disjointed dream. I watched, fascinated, as a pair of ospreys wheeled around and around, then suddenly dove into the water. I even remember that one of them dropped its prey as it rose into the air again. Then someone came to fetch me without telling me where we were going, and I found myself in H. M.'s room. Our friend Safavian was already there.

This is one of those moments when I have some scruples about describing my memories, as they concern the private personality of the man opposite me. I had an extraordinary impression, which totally surprised me. It was caused by the sight of this man, whose face lit up with an unmistakable look of joy when he saw me enter the room. I had the impression that he was truly happy to see me there; Safavian told me later that H. M. had feared that his doctors might also abandon him. According to what I was told, it took only a few days for defections from his ranks to make themselves felt. Technically, there was not a lot for me to do, and there was nothing new to say about his treatment. We talked and I had the feeling that H. M. was checking that we were going to follow the medical plan begun five years earlier. The tense, faraway look I had seen on the face of this anxious man a few weeks earlier had now disappeared. I think he spoke to me for longer than he ever had done before.

On 22 January 1979, only six days after our arrival in Egypt, we flew to Morocco. King Hassan II's invitation had come as a relief to my husband, who did not want to abuse President Sadat's hospitality, even though the president had renewed his invitation. He pointed out in particular that Egypt was closer to Iran for setting up the resistance he had in mind. One of the few heads of state to see Khomeini for what he was right from the beginning, President Sadat already considered him an impostor.*

We had warm and friendly relations with Hassan II and his family. In addition to official visits, we had invited the children of the Alawite** ruler to stay with us on the Caspian Sea; they knew our children well and they got on well. King Hassan's solicitude toward us was no doubt inspired by these ties. And his wife, Lalla Latifa, was with him—a big exception to Moroccan protocol—when he welcomed us affectionately at the Marrakesh airport. He put us in a beautiful modern villa with a big garden, built in an oasis outside the town, at the gateway to the Atlas Mountains. King Hassan's mother, his two sisters, and his brother were waiting there to welcome us. From my window I could see palm, orange, and olive trees and, in the distance, mountain peaks covered with snow. This quiet setting suited my husband, who had been weakened by this last move; in spite of the burden of recent events, I was almost happy to see him drop off to sleep. We had to take whatever good the moment offered and not give way to anxiety, which sometimes cast me into the abyss.

I set about writing and telephoning Iran again. What had the Bakhtiar government done? What was the man in the street thinking? Were the demonstrations still going on? What were they saying about the king now? One day I learned that a large constitutionalist demonstration had been organized in Tehran, and the news suddenly filled me with hope. I said so to my hus-

*On 4 January 1979, Jimmy Carter, President of the United States, the German Chancellor Helmut Schmidt, the British Prime Minister Leonard Callaghan, and the French President Valery Giscard d'Estaing met in Guadeloupe, where they decided to support a regime change in Iran.

**Name taken by the dynasty that began ruling in Morocco in 1666.

band who gave a slight smile. What was he thinking deep inside? Did he think that he could still return to finish his work and set Iran firmly in the 20th century? When President Sadat suggested bringing our fighter planes to Egypt, he gave a firm no, with the simple comment, "The air force belongs to Iran." It was clear that he would not do anything to regain power by force but would wait, faithful to his principles, until the people called him back.

People were now talking of the imminent return of Ayatollah Khomeini. One of the officers who was with us came to the king with the proposal that the obscurantist leader's plane be taken down before it reached Tehran. My husband refused categorically. This idea was not new: some air force officers had suggested the same plan to the king when we were still in Tehran, and he had already rejected it.

On 1 February we heard on the radio that the "guide" of the revolution had arrived in Tehran. I wanted to call some people in Iran immediately, but Hassan II asked me not to do anything, to remain silent for two days, which was very hard to do. My husband observed that the prime minister was still at his post, and that the armed forces were loyal to the constitutional government. Would the Ayatollah content himself with guiding souls? It quickly became apparent that he would not. Ignoring Bakhtiar's offers of conciliation, the cleric appointed his own government with Mehdi Bazargan, an ex-comrade of Bakhtiar, at its head. Demonstrations supporting this first Islamic government began on 7 February. Shapour Bakhtiar replied by calling Khomeini's program "archaic and medieval." But on 11 February the rioters broke into the barracks and seized weapons, and the soldiers, who had been severely tested for a year, began to desert. The next day Lt. General Abdol-Ali Badrei'i, Commander of Ground Forces, and Major General Amin Beglari, acting Commander of the Imperial Guard, who were deeply opposed to the neutrality of the army, were gunned down at their headquarters. Caught in the insurgents' fire, Shapour Bakhtiar managed to flee to France, where he would be brutally murdered ten years later (6 August 1991) after fighting tirelessly and courageously against the Islamic Republic.

On that 11 February the king and all the Iranians with us were listening to Radio Tehran in the villa at Marrakesh. As I was crossing the entrance hall, I heard, "The revolution has won, the bastion of dictatorship has collapsed." For a few seconds I thought that we had won. To me, we were the good ones and they were certainly the bastion of horror. Unfortunately they were the ones who had just won: they had overturned the last government appointed by my husband.

The first news about the massacres of officers in the street and the executions ordered by religious fanatics started coming through the following day. The king was shattered and retreated into silence for some time. A bit later, I managed to contact by phone a dear friend whose husband, Air Force General Nader Jahanbani, had just been executed. Insulted by one of the guardians of the revolution, he had had the courage to slap him in the face before dying. She was sobbing and I, who should have been able to find words to comfort her, could do nothing but cry with her. That evening, in deep despair, I wrote these few lines in my notebook: "I don't feel I have strength in me to go on fighting. I would prefer to die for my country with honor rather than be dragged toward death by the depression that is overtaking me. Dear God, if you are there, give me the strength to go on."

Realizing of course that a new chapter had begun and that we no longer had any hope of returning to Iran for some time, the king called together the military crew of the Boeing 707 that had brought us from Tehran to Marrakesh and released them from their mission. He also released some members of the security personnel who wanted to go back. He wanted the plane to be returned to Iran and besides, all these people had left their families behind. "We don't know when we will be back," he told them, "but it is now time for you to go home. If there is any trouble when you arrive, I authorize you to say that you were forced to accompany us at gunpoint." He said the same thing to the other people who had come with us, and some decided to go back to Iran, others to seek refuge in Europe or the United States. On their arrival in Tehran, the crew did not have to suffer for having transported us. The pilot, who was the son of a general, later joined the Mujahedeen. However, before that, in a twist of historical irony, he was the one who got two former allies of Khomeini, Abol Hassan Bani-Sadr and Masoud Rajavi, out of Iran.

Summary executions after mock trials nevertheless increased in Iran, and there were soon calls for our return so that the king could be "tried." Given this situation, could we continue staying in Morocco? When we learned on 14 February that the American embassy in Tehran had been besieged by the Guardians of the Revolution and occupied for several hours before being freed at the request of Mr. Bazargan, we realized that the gates open to us in exile would become harder to find. Would the United States, where our children were already staying, still extend their offer of hospitality? What country would be brave enough to welcome us if the new regime in Iran threatened its nationals in that way, both in Tehran and within its own borders?

The king, who spent his time reading, listening to the radio, and meeting people, avoided talking about our future when I was with him. We tried to comfort each other by not letting our personal fears show through. I was deeply affected by his courage. Thin and worn by illness and the endless tragedy of what was happening, he never uttered a word of complaint. We spent some time together and, as I silently gazed at him, I realized how much I loved him and how painful it was to see him suffer. We had lived twenty years in a continuous whirl; if fate suddenly brought us close to each other again, it must be to let us face this ordeal together. Telling myself that helped me to accept our new life as it happened and also to define how I would act: whatever happened, I had to stand firm and give the man whose love was so precious to me all the strength I could muster.

During these difficult days, he was very touched by visits from former King Umberto of Italy and the Comte de Paris. Nelson Rockefeller, who was going to come, died just a few days before the date set for his visit.

The children's arrival in Morocco just before our New Year was an unexpected joy for us. Our meeting was an extraordinary moment: our convoy had been late leaving for Marrakesh airport, so we crossed the children's path halfway there. All the cars stopped, and we fell into each other's arms in the middle of the road. I had not kissed the two youngest ones, Leila and Ali-Reza, since they had left Tehran with my mother two months earlier. As for Reza and Farahnaz, it had been longer still.

We left Marrakesh immediately for a marvelous palace in Rabat, which King Hassan II had put at our disposal. These few days of happy family life, an interlude in that period when dangers grew worse and more frequent, had an extraordinary effect on everyone's morale. The king's features relaxed, I heard him laugh again, and he even played with Leila in the grounds. We celebrated Farahnaz's sixteenth birthday and the New Year at the same time. King Hassan's children joined us and, one evening when his brother screened *The Mad Adventures of Rabbi Jacob* with Louis de Funès for us, I had the pleasure of hearing my husband burst out laughing again—something he had not done for more than a year.

They were moments stolen from the heartrending tragedy that surrounded us. There was a little zoo on the grounds of this palace, and I remember in particular a poor wild sheep that stood with drooping neck and battered body. Far from nature and freedom, its hooves had grown so much that they turned in on themselves. I could identify with it and see myself in its skin, now that I was a prisoner in a space that grew smaller every day, surrounded by fences that hurt me.

Alexandre de Marenches, the head of French Special Services, had actually seen my husband in Marrakesh to tell him of the risks our host, the King of Morocco, was facing because of us. These risks were naturally of a diplomatic but also of a private nature since, according to Mr. de Marenches, Ayatollah Khomeini had ordered his fanatics to kidnap members of the royal family so that they could then be exchanged for us. Mr. de Marenches had informed King Hassan II, who had replied with great courage, "It's abominable, but that does not change my decision in the slightest. I cannot refuse hospitality to a man who is going through a tragic time in his life."

Given this situation, it was now becoming urgent to find another refuge. France withdrew: according to Mr. de Marenches, it could not guarantee our safety. The same went for Switzerland, which did, however, perhaps foresee some possibility for the future, and for the Principality of Monaco, where our son Reza had gone. The principality had originally said yes, before withdrawing its offer under pressure from France. "Later, perhaps" was basically the reply from the United States. At the beginning of our exile we had received a message from Great Britain that Margaret Thatcher would accept us following a win at the elections. But later, having become prime minister while we were in the Bahamas, Mrs. Thatcher did not follow up her undertaking. She was under pressure, we were told, from Foreign Affairs Minister

Lord Carrington and from Anthony Parsons, the former ambassador of Great Britain in Iran, who convinced her that taking us would harm UK interests.

We had had relations with most of the countries of the world—close, friendly ones with some—and now they were all turning their backs on us. In those terrible days some comfort came from the letters sent to us. Some came from Iranians, who did not sign their letters for fear of reprisals, others from strangers who loved Iran and had seen the progress made in twenty years; some rulers and heads of state also wrote to us personally. All these letters were extremely touching, full of feeling and warmth.

King Hassan II had put his own plane at our disposal, and all we needed to take off was to know our destination. It was then we learned that the Bahamas would accept us, but only for three months. This invitation was obtained at the last moment by the combined efforts of David Rockefeller and my husband's friend, Henry Kissinger. Kissinger was scandalized by the ingratitude of the Carter administration toward the king. David Rockefeller had taken action because of the ties between my husband and his brother Nelson, who had just died suddenly. The two men had succeeded in convincing the president of the archipelago of the Bahamas to offer us temporary hospitality on Paradise Island, where a villa had hurriedly been found.

And so, on 30 March 1979 we took off for Nassau, the capital of the Bahamas, accompanied by my mother, the children's pediatrician, Dr. Lioussa Pirnia; Colonel Jahanbini, in charge of the king's security; Colonels Nevissi, Nasseri, Hamraz, Mohammadi, and Kambiz Atabaï; Leila's governess, Miss Golrokh; and lastly the king's valet, Mahmoud Eliassi.

A SMARTLY DRESSED MAN, Robert Armao, was waiting for us at the airport. We knew him. Because he was a specialist in public relations and a former colleague, Nelson Rockefeller had sent him to Tehran at the end of 1978 to try to limit the devastating effects of the opposition's propaganda. But it was already much too late to launch any kind of public relations campaign, and after a few days with my husband, Mr. Armao had gone back to New York.

So there he was again to help us, at the behest of the Rockefeller family and Princess Ashraf, this time to facilitate dealings on the diplomatic level with the authorities of the Bahamas, and on the practical level with questions of security and everyday life. He would also be our link with the American government. He was accompanied by one of his colleagues, Mark Morse.

The villa that he had been allowed to rent for us at great expense—now, just at the sound of our name, prices would go up five, even ten times—only comprised a sitting room and two bedrooms. We settled in as best we could. It was too small to hold our luggage—fifteen cases for the whole family—so they had to be stored in the courtyard under a tarpaulin. Bungalows in the area or hotel rooms had to be found for the people with us.

The two months and ten days we were to spend in the Bahamas were among the darkest times of my life. We had not been there long when we heard about the execution of Amir Abbas Hoveyda. After a mockery of a trial, the former prime minister had been dragged into the prison yard and killed with several bullets to the head and neck. This news filled us with indescribable despair. The king went out of the room to weep alone; I was overcome with grief. Good Lord, when would the horror end? I managed to phone New York and talk to Mr. Hoveyda's brother Fereydoun, who had been ambassador to the United Nations, to tell him how genuinely we shared his sorrow and how shattered we were.

The authorities in the Bahamas had only accepted us on condition that we did not express any political opinions, which had surprised me because the Bahamas had no relations with Iran. But how could we say nothing in the face of such crimes? We had loved this man, and he had given so much to this country, now in such an abject state. How could we remain silent? In a burst of impotent rage and despair, I said to my husband that the only thing left was to hire a boat and send a message into international waters, condemning in the strongest possible terms this regime of bloody murderers supposedly inspired by God!

Paris-Match added a new dimension to the cruelty of this imposed silence by publishing a week later a photo of Amir Abbas Hoveyda's body surrounded by his killers still with guns in their hands and, on the opposite page, another of the king on the beach at Paradise Island. It suggested that the king was enjoying himself while his former colleagues were being massacred. Many people believed it, and among the terrible letters that I received shortly afterwards, one absolutely got to me. It came from Saïdeh, the daughter of General Hassan Pakravan, who had just been executed. This poor grief-stricken woman was furious, writing to me that while we were enjoying ourselves on the beaches of the Bahamas, her father was being shot. Saïdeh later visited the king in Cairo shortly before his death. I also saw her as I was nevertheless touched by her gesture.

The children had not left us since Morocco—there was no room in the villa, so we had to rent bungalows for them—and as Ali-Reza's birthday was approaching, I decided to summon up all my strength to celebrate it in spite of everything. I am telling this story because it shows the state of mind we were in at the time. I bought what was needed and did what I could with the tiny house, then decided to dress as if it were a real party. My mother, who had joined us with the children, tried to help me.

I'm sure she did not realize the significance of what she was saying, but when she saw me come out of my room more elegantly dressed than for an ordinary day, she whispered to me, "Try not to laugh too much; don't look too happy; it would not create a good impression." That finished me. It had taken a great deal of willpower to organize my little boy's birthday party, and I should not have done that, not even that! How could my own mother think that I could feel any happiness in this nightmare we were going through? I was so hurt that I immediately went and shut myself in my room and took a tranquilizer. When the children came knocking at the door, I could not leave the bedroom.

Living became an unbearable burden. My chest was tight with anxiety day and night, and I felt that although the king never complained, he was going through the same agony. Seeing this man who had been so active all his life trying to survive the silent, stifling, muggy days in the company of Dr. Pirnia and my mother broke my heart. His illness was exhausting him. At night I prayed that he would fall asleep, and when I heard his regular breathing, I would get up again. I couldn't sleep anymore. I would go out and have a cigarette or walk up and down in the tiny courtyard where the luggage was piled up. I waited for the first light of day to fling myself into the pool and swim furiously up and down, trying to restore some energy despite the endless nightmare, to keep going and present the image of a strong woman to the king, as a reflection of his own courage. I remember that the radio kept playing the Gloria Gaynor song, "I Will Survive," and I clung to those few words to keep from giving in.

Princess Ashraf wrote a letter to President Carter asking him to accept the king. Armao showed it to my husband who fortunately did not want it to be sent. We would not lower ourselves to making an appeal to President Carter.

I found these lines from my notebook written at that time:

> What are we doing lost in the middle of the ocean, with no homeland? I'm sitting on a sand dune by the water. It's very calm, very beautiful, the sun will soon be setting and you can hear the seagulls crying. I'm looking for the words to describe my anguish, and yet I feel embarrassed to be here: I am thinking of the two American guards standing behind me, stationed there for my safety, and I fear that they must be so bored. I think of Iran and I choke with grief. How did it come to this? Death, blood, fear. And this dreadful silence! Not a voice raised to denounce the horror. Where are the journalists, the academics, the artists, the world organizations who care so much about human rights in Iran? Where are the students who marched for freedom of speech, for democracy? Poor children. It's as though a black pall has fallen over our young people.
>
> I must not listen to the radio or read the papers anymore. What is happening is so monstrous. They are murdering the best people, those who have given their lives for the common good: the soldiers, the intellectuals, the administrators.... The countries who were so quick to criticize my husband in the past now have nothing to say. Only Switzerland has expressed its indignation.

Then Great Britain informed us through its former ambassador to Tehran, Denis Wright, who came to the Bahamas, that it did not want our presence on its territory either. I'm told that Sir Denis was unrecognizably disguised in a mustache and hat, probably for fear of being questioned by journalists and having to explain publicly the reason for his visit. Yet, while the capitals of the world turned their backs on us one by one, we received extremely touching letters from everywhere. People we had never met offered us hospitality, in Canada, Mexico, Germany. Other more humble folk offered their own homes. These letters were our only comfort.

In the depths of this misery, learning that Sadegh Khalkhali, the cleric who ordered Hoveyda's execution, had just condemned us to death at least raised a sad smile. The thought of our own death seemed less painful than learning, day after day, of the execution of those we loved. In the summer of 1979 Khalkhali reported with a sneer of satisfaction, "Some nights the trucks would take about thirty bodies, if not more, from the prison." That bloodthirsty hatred was the true face of the Islamic Revolution. Khalkhali declared that he would send killers after us and, in the meantime, he promised a reward of $143,000 to anyone who would get rid of my husband. Later he would add these words: "If Farah kills him, she will get the benefit not only of the money, but also of an amnesty, and she may come back to Iran."

Some friends did, however, get in touch during this long night. King Hussein of Jordan had the consideration to send General Khamash with a message of friendship and comfort. King Baudouin and Queen Fabiola called us. Women who were old childhood friends, the faithful of the faithful, made the journey to assure us that they would always be there, no matter what happened.

The king's illness grew worse. Professor Flandrin, who had seen him twice in Morocco, agreed to come to us on Paradise Island. Once again I am using the account he gave to Professor Jean Bernard:

> On my first visit the medical situation seemed stable, but a few weeks later the patient found a mass above the clavicle. Even on the telephone the diagnosis was not difficult to predict, and I left with everything needed to do a chemotherapy treatment if necessary. From a lymph node differential cell count I made the diagnosis of

large cell lymphoma. There was a discussion about what treatment to pursue, and you probably remember that I consulted you by telephone at that time.

Contrary to what may have been said later, I am sure that the patient was perfectly aware of his medical condition. In any case, I was obliged to explain it to him quite bluntly: given the therapeutic consequences I was recommending, he deserved an explanation for my change in attitude and the escalation of his treatment. I therefore explained to him that, following normal medical practice, he should have gone to a well-equipped, special medical center to have a biopsy of the lymph node that I had just tapped, radiological investigations, very probably a laparotomy with splenectomy, even before additional chemotherapy followed by radiotherapy could be begun. The other choice was to do three series of additional chemotherapy without wasting time on investigations, and to assess the state of the lesions after those three months; then there would probably still be splenectomy and radiotherapy on the site of the Richter's syndrome that had just been discovered.

The situation became difficult for me to manage as a personal dimension came into the discussion. H. M. immediately asked me to risk the second solution, and he did it quite consciously and in full knowledge of what it involved. His reasons went beyond the simple health problem, and he told me quite clearly, "At a time when they are killing officers faithful to me in my country, I cannot reduce them to complete despair by revealing my state of health." He asked me for those three months and promised me that after the three monthly series of chemotherapy I wanted him to have, secrecy would be abandoned so that more normal medical practice could be resumed. The decision was a terribly hard one emotionally for H. M. the Queen to make and accept, being also aware of the reasons for her husband's choice. I must confess that I

> did not put up too many objections to what seemed to be the definite wish of the patient; in addition, the strategy we were going to adopt had some good arguments and advantages in favor of it...
>
> H. M. the Queen had the courage to overcome her distress and, at the end of a long discussion, she reminded me that in the last analysis it was up to me to make the decision. Above all, she had to have the courage to accept the fact that the continued necessity for secrecy meant that she could only call on me, my conscience, and my supposed knowledge of the problem. One can easily imagine how difficult that must be for people who, in other circumstances, could have had recourse to the most eminent medical specialists.
>
> I therefore began to apply the additional chemotherapy by drip, in spartan conditions, with only Her Majesty the Queen as nurse. I continued to carry out my usual biological tests with the equipment and microscope that had followed H. M. since Tehran. The patient's solid constitution allowed him to come through the beginning of the treatment remarkably well. To do the treatment on day 1 and day 8 of the monthly series, I had to go to Nassau two weeks in a row, while trying in the meantime to keep up the appearance of being fresh and alert in Paris.

About three weeks before our visas expired, the authorities in the Bahamas informed us that they would not be renewed. Where would we go? Embassies had refused us one after the other. Only Anwar Sadat courageously repeated his invitation, commenting in passing how pitiful he found "all these people who are too afraid to offer refuge." But President Sadat had just signed the Camp David Accords, setting a large part of the Arab world against him, and my husband thought that that was enough for him to cope with.

Finally it was Mexico that offered us hospitality at the request of Henry Kissinger. The king had met and liked President José López Portillo when he was finance minister, and no doubt these former ties counted for something. But we also had the feeling that on this occasion Mexico was not unhappy to give a lesson in political ethics to the United States.

Robert Armao had continued to do his utmost to make things easier for us during the whole of our stay in the Bahamas. He immediately flew to Mexico to find a suitable house for us. "For two years," he would confide later, "I lived only for the shah. I ran all around the world to find him a home. I dashed to Paris in the Concorde for dinner, came back the next morning, and immediately jumped into another plane to join him. Not an hour went by without my seeing him. I was close to him when he awoke and in the evening when he went to bed." This time Mr. Armao was accompanied by Colonel Jahanbini, who was more and more worried about the death threats against the king. He wanted to make sure of security in our next residence.

Their choice fell on Cuernavaca in southern Mexico. The house was a villa situated at the bottom of a cul-de-sac, which was very convenient for surveillance. Coming from the Bahamas, where we had suffered from claustrophobic accommodations and a host of other irritations, we were agreeably surprised at our new residence. A tropical garden hid it from the street, and it was large enough to lodge the people who were with us. However, as it had not been lived in for some time, it was damp and covered with mildew, and I had something of a shock to find scorpions on the walls. That did not worry the king, who exclaimed as he inspected it, "We'll be able to come alive again at last!"

He gave signs of it by starting to write his memoirs as soon as we had moved in. It was a brave undertaking in his situation. His strength was considerably diminished, and he did not have any documents to support his recollections. As for meeting people who had worked with him—at least those who were still at liberty—that was an impossibility. With a few exceptions people no longer wanted any contact with us; they fled from us like the plague, knowing that the Tehran assassins could strike anywhere in the world.

For my part, I started learning Spanish. Dr. Pirnia joined me in this endeavor and we employed a teacher to come to the house. The first sentence in our textbook was "*Dónde está la embajada americana?*", and we agreed that history sometimes makes allusions no one could imagine. I had wanted to learn Spanish for some time, and Mexico seemed inclined to offer us long-term hospitality. And so my husband and I both took up intellectual activities again, outside of the upsetting situation that was part of daily life, and it did give us the momentary feeling of coming alive again.

Several times we were invited to dinner at the homes of some of the prominent people in Cuernavaca, which also helped to restore some normality to our situation. We even plucked up the courage to make a few tourist trips; we were curious to see this country we had visited officially a few years earlier. There was the furtive pleasure of an outing together, as if snatched from the gloom, and also the emotion I felt on seeing my husband smile again and enjoy the beauty of things and the warmth of the air. I remember in particular our visit to Oaxaca and the pyramids of Mexico City.

The king bravely took every care to hide the constant pain and exhaustion caused by his illness. When he took his bath, I would sit in a corner and we would chat. We naturally spoke of what was happening and of the children's future. I tried to be always positive and strong and to show him that I still believed that better days would come again. The word "cancer" was never mentioned between us, so that we could each maintain the illusion of a possible imminent cure, especially to the other. But one evening he slipped this taboo word into the conversation. Was it accidental or did he do it on purpose to show me that he knew and had little hope? Recovering from the shock, I told him that I was sure that he would conquer his illness, even if it was cancer, and he had the kindness of heart to agree.

At the same time we began to look at houses with the prospect of staying for some time in Mexico, which apparently did not respond to the Tehran clerics' threats. These inspections were proof that my husband believed in the future, that his appetite for life was definitely still there. I found them both a comfort and deeply depressing. Seeing this man who had borne the fate of Iran for nearly forty years suddenly reduced to comparing kitchens and looking at wardrobes made me indescribably sad. It was the same when someone made him wait: he showed no irritation, he stayed unmoved, very upright as usual, but it really upset me.

Luckily the children joined us for a few days. They knew nothing of their father's illness. We enjoyed some happy times together as an affectionate family, forgetting the misfortune that threatened on all sides. Those were our last moments of really happy family life, for the sudden decline of the king's health would soon force me to tell them. In September the three youngest would be going to school in the United States, with Reza studying political science and English literature at Williams College in Massachusetts. The preparations for the start of their schooling had not been easy. Leaving the Bahamas in May with my mother and a few officers, they had moved into a townhouse belonging to Princess Ashraf in New York. An English teacher had been found so that they could quickly follow their classes in that language, as well as a Persian teacher to ensure they would not forget their own language. At the same time Robert Armao had set about finding schools, and this proved to be another trial for them. Schools would accept them, then very quickly withdraw their offer, saying that the parents were worried about the safety of their children. This was very hard on our three youngest: they visited the schools, were happy to learn that they had been accepted, then discovered that they were not wanted, that people avoided them like the plague. In the end we managed to enroll each of them, and they could now relax a little.

Richard Nixon also made the trip to Cuernavaca. He talked with my husband for several hours, but more than words, the fidelity of the ex-president of the United States touched the king deeply at a time when almost all the world turned its back on us. Henry Kissinger and his wife Nancy also came to visit us in Mexico.

Shapour Bakhtiar telephoned us from Paris. He had managed to get out of Iran safely. We were eating when he called. The king refused to speak to him. "Do you want me to go?" I asked. "If you like." The former prime minister told me that he now intended to fight the clerics who had taken over the country, and he asked me to convey his respects to the king.

At the beginning of summer Sadegh Khalkhali had announced that his assassins were en route to Cuernavaca. We therefore expected that they would appear in one way or another, and that expectation almost caused a drastic misunderstanding. One day Reza wanted to go flying, so he went to the aeroclub with Mark Morse, Robert Armao's assistant. An hour later, the sound of a helicopter set off a general alert around the villa. We were having lunch in the garden at the time. A commando coming out of the sky had certainly been foreseen as a possibility, for as soon as the helicopter came in sight the security guards began to fire at it. As it happens, it wasn't a killer at the controls but our son, who was happily coming down toward us so that we could see him. Realizing the mistake, I ran toward the security men, shouting at them to stop firing. Good Lord, what new tragedy would have befallen us if the bullet had hit its target? Sadegh Khalkhali would nonetheless have claimed that he had sent a commando to Mexico.

The king had been working on his memoirs for almost three months when he felt very ill again. Professor Flandrin, who had already come to Cuernavaca to give the second series of chemotherapy, was to come back shortly to give the third. In the meantime I had called on local doctors, who, obviously knowing nothing of the king's illness, thought it was a bout of malaria. My husband received the appropriate treatment, but his state did not improve. Consequently Robert Armao, who felt responsible for the king's health while also knowing nothing of it, took the initiative of getting an American specialist in tropical diseases, Dr. Benjamin Kean, to come to Cuernavaca. The arrival of Dr. Kean, arranged with the best of intentions, led to a period of diagnostic cacophony that ended in what Professor Flandrin later called "a whole chain of disasters."

The American doctor rejected the hypothesis of malaria in favor of a problem with the pancreas—the king had strong pains on his right side—and told his patient that he intended taking a blood sample, which my husband refused outright. He had complete confidence in Professor Flandrin and still did not want to break the secrecy surrounding his real illness. Dr. Kean went back to New York, not pleased but certainly intrigued by the restrictions his patient imposed.

I also called Professor Flandrin again, and I will let him relate what brought us to the New York Hospital rather than the Mexican hospital my husband and I would have preferred:

> When I arrived, I was not informed that Dr. Kean had just been there before me and only learned of it later. After I explained the changed medical situation to the patient and H. M. the Queen, it was agreed that hospitalization for investigation and treatment should take place without delay. I think that was a Sunday or a Monday. H. M. was to leave for New York on the following

Thursday (or Friday). Less than a week separated these two dates, but a lot would happen in those few days. The history that is being written about that crucial time has now brought to light the "inter-American" political battles that were a backdrop to what only appeared to me then as a medical discussion. The first problem we debated was where the hospitalization should be. When I mentioned the possibility of the United States, H. M. replied in no uncertain terms, "After what those people have done to me, they could beg me on their knees and I still wouldn't go." It was a Monday. On the following Thursday it was decided that he was going to the United States! I think I can say that all the arguments for the decisions were no longer in his hands, and that his original wishes had to give way to arguments that were beyond him.

On that Monday then, it was decided that I should find out what facilities were available in Mexico City, and I left immediately with a person from his entourage. I spent the night there and was taken to meet the head of a hospital medical department, Dr. Garcia. I explained my problem to him, asking him not to request the identity of the patient in the first instance. I wanted to know the possibilities of admitting a patient with an acute medical condition, needing particular security arrangements, and for whom we would need all modern facilities for radiological and surgical investigations, and the best technical equipment for radiotherapy. I gave your name [Professor Jean Bernard] as a referral to get him to accept these difficult requirements. Dr. Garcia had received me in his office in the afternoon. He seemed neither surprised nor curious, but he did not reject my request out of hand and made another appointment to see me the next day in his department at the hospital. He chose for the hospitalization a small annex that was separated from the body of the main hospital building. The conditions seemed suitable from a security point of view, as this annex was practically unoccupied. The only drawback was its appearance from the outside. I looked at all the technical facilities and paid particular attention to the radiotherapy equipment, which I considered essential for later treatment. I was able to have a personal talk with the Mexican radiotherapist, who had trained at the best centers in Canada and gave all the guarantees I thought desirable.

I then returned to Cuernavaca, where I gave a favorable report on the possibilities in Mexico City. Some people from the entourage went to check the security conditions, and according to what was said later, it would seem that they did not find them satisfactory. The fact remains that, with H. M.'s permission, I telephoned Dr. Garcia, telling him who the patient was and asking him to join me in Cuernavaca for a consultation. We saw the patient together, and he came to the same conclusions as I did: etiologic diagnosis of febrile obstructive jaundice to be done as soon as possible, certainly leading to surgery. The situation, medically speaking, was not complicated at that time, but what followed will show that it would never be simple again.

I quickly became aware that the American team did not like the idea of staying in Mexico. I presented all my arguments to Bob Armao, telling him that the facilities available in Mexico City seemed suitable and adequate. I did not defend Mexico City against the United States, I simply gave an answer to the question that had been put to me: "Can it be done in Mexico City?" My answer was, "Yes, it certainly can." Armao replied in effect that, "For a patient like this, the fact that it can be done is not good enough. It has to be the best and only the United States can provide the best."

It was quickly confirmed that enough arguments had been presented to convince H. M. to accept going to the United States, despite the emphatic declaration he had made to me a few days earlier. I was informed that the decision to go to the U.S. was still being made. Thinking that I still had the power to make medical decisions, I turned my attention to which medical team I should choose for him. (As Kean's first visit had been kept from me at that time, I could not suspect that an option had already been adopted.) It seemed obvious that we needed a well-known team that could bring its experience to bear on this therapeutic problem of a severe lymphoma, whatever the exact nature of the acute complication now apparent. I thought of some possibilities: on the West Coast (S. Rosenberg), on the East Coast (E. Frei). Having telephoned you to ask your advice, you recommended I try to contact Burchenal if New York was likely to be the choice. In the few hours I had left, I tried to act independently of Armao by endeavoring to contact these people by phone. I did not manage to speak to them directly and I could not leave an explicit message, other than asking them to try to phone me. Everything was happening very quickly, as I was told a New York doctor had arrived. It was Dr. Benjamin Kean (who had come back), but he was introduced to me as coming for the first time.

I therefore spoke to Dr. Kean, showing some surprise, and when I looked into his medical field of expertise, I protested that I did not need a specialist in tropical medicine and that handing over my responsibility to him did not seem sensible to me. I had been led to believe that the New York doctors I wanted could not come but that he was sending one of their assistants; in fact it was Kean I found. When I protested, they gave me all kinds of verbal reassurances, promising me that the specialists in New York would be called immediately. The further I went, the more the medical discussions I had with Kean absolutely amazed me. To my mind this man, who was going to take control of the situation, did not have sufficient command of hematology or modern oncology. All of that made me extremely irritated and pessimistic. From the medical standpoint, I was looking at a runaway of the lymphoma that was relapsing in the supraclavicular and, in my opinion at that time, it was probably at the subdiaphragmatic stage, and in an environment of cytopenia, hindering chemotherapy. From the tactical standpoint, my predictions of what would follow were unfortunately fairly accurate. I had understood by then that the policy put in place by the Armao-Kean partnership had already taken any means of action out of my hands. Added to that was the bitterness of knowing that the decision to go to the United States was not what H. M. originally wanted (nor doubtless what he really wanted). Finally, when I learned that he was being sent to New York Hospital, I grew even more pessimistic. I still remembered the unpleasant circumstances of my arguments with certain people in that establishment when I was obliged to take Mr. Alam there.

When I was told that the destination was the New York Hospital, we were standing around H. M.'s bed. I whispered to H. M. the Queen what I thought. She immediately spoke up and said, "Dr. Flandrin thinks that...," etc., and repeated what I had told her. Kean and Armao, who were also present, gave all sorts of verbal assurances. They said more precisely that this hospital had been chosen so that maximum discretion could be assured, etc., and that the medical team I wanted would be taking charge of the problem.

There was actually no time for discussion. What we found out later confirms the fact that everything had been well and truly decided in advance. It seems that among the arguments that had helped convince H. M. not to stay in Mexico was the bad opinion some important Mexicans held regarding medicine in their country. Not being informed of any of this, I had naturally understood that my role had come to an end and that all I had to do now was to be ethical and polite and not destroy the patient's confidence in the doctors. I therefore sent a letter of thanks and apology to Dr. Garcia in Mexico City, telling him that circumstances had decided otherwise than expected. I also added an additional report to the dossier of the last six years which I had given to Kean.

I explained to H. M. that I very much doubted whether I could play an active role with him in New York, given what I knew of the medical setup in the United States, but that I would accompany him if he wished. He thanked me, saying, as he was always courteous enough to do on all my preceding visits, that my professional obligations must surely require my presence in Paris and that I had already done a lot for him. He added that, in any case, we would see each other again later. He asked me to express his gratitude to you and also to Professor Milliez, adding that he admired this man who was "so old and so sick" having the heart to come from Paris to help him. H. M. the Queen then saw me in private and on behalf of H. M. and herself gave me a symbolic gift in the form of a goblet made of Mexican silver engraved with the Pahlavi coat of arms, apologizing for not being able to give me something genuinely Persian. She added with her shy smile by way of apology, "You can put it on your desk to keep your pencils tidy!" I gave her a letter for H. M. containing a few personal words and good wishes and expressing my complete confidence in the excellence of American medicine and our colleagues who would now be looking after him. At that moment I felt very much alone.

I arranged to be driven back to the superb Las Quintas Hotel, where I was staying, then I traveled once more the beautiful route from Cuernavaca to Mexico City, going over this long adventure in my mind from your first phone call one Sunday evening...From one visit to the next, and there must have been about fifty, I always thought that for one reason or another it would be the last. This time the end had come. I felt a mixture of something like relief to think that my duty had finished and renewed anxiety because I could not rid myself of the fears I felt for a patient with whom I had become involved and for whom I could no longer do anything.

It is perfectly true that the king and I would have preferred a hospital in Mexico. There was something mortifying about being allowed into the United States for medical reasons when they had refused to receive us as refugees. I personally feared the demonstrations of hostility that our presence would certainly arouse and, more generally, the animosity of the American political establishment toward us. But Armao and Kean were not the only ones pushing us toward the United States: the king's family was bringing all its weight to bear in that direction, especially Princess Ashraf, who thought that her brother would receive better care there than in Mexico City. The debate confronted me with a painful moral dilemma: my personal feeling inclined me to follow Professor Flandrin's advice and stay in Mexico, but on the other hand, I did not want to assume this huge responsibility alone. If something happened to the king, I would never forgive myself. And so I decided not to oppose the move.

By what process did the United States, who feared for the safety of their embassy in Tehran, come to open their border to us? The journalist Pierre Salinger has pieced together the debates that were held at the highest level of the American government at that time. He explains how the decision was made by the White House:

> When the State Department confirmed that the Shah was gravely ill and that the appropriate medical care could not be provided in Mexico City, the Secretary of State recommended that President Carter should allow him into the United States. Cyrus Vance emphasized that it was a medical emergency that could not be interpreted as a residential permit.
>
> The decision was made at the White House on 19 October 1979 at the weekly breakfast meeting that Jimmy Carter set aside for questions of foreign policy. There would certainly be some risk involved, but they owed this to the Shah after treating him so badly for several months when he wanted to settle in the United States and had been informed that he was not welcome.

> Carter himself was in favor of making this gesture to the Shah. His hesitation was only due to the fear of seeing unfortunate events happening to the American Embassy in Tehran. Before making the final decision, he asked the people who were usually there at the breakfast: Vice President Walter Mondale, Cyrus Vance, Zbigniew Brzezinski, Harold Brown, the Secretary for Defense, and Hamilton Jordan, the White House Chief of Staff. The recommendation was unanimous: let the Shah into the United States.
>
> Carter came round to their point of view, then added, "And what will you advise when they occupy our Embassy and take our people hostage?"*

Two weeks later, on 4 November 1979, what President Carter feared took place: fundamentalist and communist students stormed the American embassy. They would keep the sixty-odd diplomats who were there hostage for 444 days.

"We had to choose between an attitude of common decency and humanity and the possible harm that could result for the staff of our embassy in Tehran," Cyrus Vance wrote later. The Islamic Republic refused to believe that my husband was really ill, and it claimed that he was going to the United States to regain power in Tehran with their help.

On 21 October 1979, on the eve of our departure for New York, I wrote in my notebook, "I am very worried about my husband's health. Of course I stay optimistic and I try to impart that to him, but the anxiety is there. He has lost a lot of weight and at times has attacks of unbearable pain. I don't know what to do for him anymore. None of the medicines help him and the doctors can't explain the cause of these attacks. The decision to go to New York

*Pierre Salinger, *Otages, les négotiations secrètes de Téhéran* [*Hostages, the Secret Tehran Negotiations*], Buchet/Chastel, 1981.

has been a very difficult one for me to make. The Americans were on the point of sending one of their doctors to be sure that my husband is really ill and that it is not a hoax to obtain the visa. If they only knew that neither of us wants to go there!"

We left for New York on the night of 22 October on board a small private plane. We had only taken the bare minimum with us, as President Jóse López Portillo had assured us that we could come back to our villa in Cuernavaca once the operation had been performed. We were to make a stop at Fort Lauderdale in Florida to complete the entry formalities, and from that moment everything went wrong. The pilot landed at Fort Lauderdale but at the wrong airfield, so that there was no one waiting for us. It was very hot inside the plane so I got out onto the tarmac to walk around for a moment even though it was forbidden. During that time Robert Armao telephoned, trying to sort out the misunderstanding. An inspector from the Ministry of Agriculture came on board to ask if we were carrying plants and to take any perishables we had.

At last, after an hour's wait, the officials who were waiting at the other airfield arrived and we were able to take off again for New York. We arrived at daybreak. Luckily the media was not there. We asked to be taken to Princess Ashraf's apartment on the East Side, where the children were staying. However, at the entrance to her street one of the Americans who was working with Robert Armao signaled to us not to come any further: a crowd of journalists was waiting outside Princess Ashraf's building. And so the driver turned back and took us directly to New York Hospital.

Two rooms had been booked for us on the seventeenth floor: one for the king and the other as a waiting room for the people with him. They were at the end of a corridor, so that the entrance could be closely watched and part of the corridor could be closed off.

As soon as my husband was in bed and being looked after, I left for Princess Ashraf's apartment. All through the flight from Cuernavaca to New York, I had been thinking of how I would break the news to the children that their father was ill, seriously ill. I intended to talk to them quietly before taking my husband to the hospital, but the crowd of journalists had prevented that. Now it was urgent: the secrecy surrounding the king's illness could be broken at any time by the doctors at New York Hospital. Radio and television stations would immediately broadcast the news, and there was a huge risk that our children could learn of this ordeal from the journalists in the most sudden and painful way imaginable. I managed to warn them in time and, I hope, pass on to them all the hope I had.

The operation was to be performed on the day after our arrival, 24 October. I was allowed to go with my husband to the doors of the operating theater and, just as he went in, probably fearing the worst, he said these few words, firmly squeezing my wrist, "Look after the children, and don't let anyone take advantage of you."

The surgeon removed the gall bladder, but he obviously should also have taken out the spleen. He explained later that he thought two operations at once would be difficult to do, then he said that the incision he had made did not allow him to reach the spleen. At the time, however, he seemed satisfied with his work, before qualifying his optimism. Rereading my notebook for the 25 October, I can see this sudden about-turn: "This morning I had hope, I was confident, full of energy. I tried to build the morale of all the people who telephoned me. But a while ago the doctors told me something that struck at my heart: 50 percent of patients with this disease can survive from twelve to eighteen months; 50 percent can hope to recover. As I bombarded them with questions, they backtracked, saying there were no rules, that it depended completely on the way the patient reacted to the illness.

"I just hope my husband reacts favorably! He felt better a while ago and the doctors seemed confident."

I only discovered much later how clumsily this operation had been carried out. I learned that the fee for the operation had been inordinately high and was told that an anonymous patient was better cared for than someone known. Professor Flandrin, whom I soon had to call back, gave this damning account years later, once again to Professor Jean Bernard:

> As you no doubt remember, I received a call in Paris from the American oncologist, Dr. Morton Coleman, who had been called to the patient. I explained the whole history as best I could, although in theory he should have been familiar with it, since I had given the detailed case history to Kean.
>
> Kean had not kept the promises he made. According to what came out later, Morton Coleman (whom Kean had chosen as oncologist) was amazed to learn that H. M. was being operated on without Coleman's being informed of it and without his being able to make his recommendations. Kean had engaged the head of the Internal Medicine Department, Dr. H. Williams, himself an endocrinologist, to assist. The surgeon had entered the abdomen through a small, oblique, right subcostal incision, having decided a *priori* not to do a splenectomy. There was a much more serious problem still: although the lithiasis was operated on under suitable clinical conditions, he had left an obstructive calculus [stone] in the common bile duct as he had not done the final radiography during the operation. Amazement, disbelief, and even hilarity went through the medical world in the United States and elsewhere. It was not the "best" that American medicine could offer, but the worst, as can be found in any country in the world. It really was appalling. What followed was a string of consequences caused by this bad blunder.

My husband very quickly began to have terrible pain again. He did not complain, but the suffering could be seen in his face. The doctors then realized that not all the stones had been removed. When it was decided to use endoscopy rather than open the incision again, the young doctor who was approached protested that he was going to the opera that evening! I was staggered. My husband was at the end of his tether and this man, whose vocation was to relieve suffering and care for people, was thinking first and foremost about his seats at the theater!

At the same time Dr. Morton Coleman began the fight against the king's cancer. The Memorial Sloan-Kettering Cancer Center is opposite the New York Hospital. The two are linked by basement passages, and we were asked to use these passages, used by the maintenance staff, when we went for radiotherapy treatment. As I feared, as soon as our presence was known, Iranian demonstrators had flocked to the hospital and stood outside every day. Did my husband hear them praying for him to die, screaming "Death to the shah!" at the very time he was battling with death? I don't know and I would like to believe that the Lord spared him that at least. In any event, there was one incident that touched me very much. Some American workers on a construction site next door, appalled by the way the demonstrators were acting, began protesting themselves—but against them. Even if the king noticed nothing of this commotion, he could not ignore the extreme tension all around us. The staff at the anticancer center had shown that they were loath to take us, for fear of becoming victims of vengeance from Tehran. All kinds of security provisions had therefore been imposed, which more or less forced us into hiding. I would be told, "It's set down for 5 A.M." I would get up at four and go to the hospital, only to find that it had been postponed until ten at night, or else the doctor was not there, he had gone to the country. They certainly made me feel how unwelcome we were. And each time we had to go through those gloomy underground passages, littered with bags of dirty linen, with the king in a wheelchair, and myself protecting him against the drafts as best I could. I still had a horrid image of hospitals from the time of my father's death, and the nightmare we were going through then was a sad reminder of it.

Yes, it was a nightmare. I wrote in my notebook at the end of October:

> Dear Lord, if he must go one day, please don't allow him to suffer. Is that the reward for a life of service to others? He never complains; he even finds the strength to smile. Flowers, cards, and telegrams from all over the world. Close friends, kings and heads of state, and also students. I must reply, find the strength to thank them. The world has become so unimportant to me. I feel empty. In Tehran Khalkhali said that he was going to send someone to kill the king in his hospital room. And Khomeini wants to send two doctors to find out if the king is really ill or if he is lying. He claims that the CIA is protecting my husband.
>
> I go to the hospital every morning. Sometimes I go in the front door, but most of the time I have to go through the basement full of baskets of rubbish, broken chairs and tables. I feel sorry for the poor workers in the basement. I stay by my husband's side; that is the only place where I feel good. Outside the people are nervous and worried. I don't want to see their fear, or hear their advice. And yet the small things still have to be attended to, like making phone calls, answering the mail…I can't see the children as often as I'd like. I haven't even had the time to glance at their schoolbooks…
>
> I'm in his room. It's three in the afternoon. He's sleeping and my heart is filled with anxiety, I can't help it. Light is filtering through the blinds. Everything is quiet. All that can be heard is the sound of

the cars below, sometimes the wail of a police or ambulance siren, or the buzz of a helicopter. He should do some walking, but I can't bear to watch. It hurts me so much to see how thin his legs are. I must give him hope, keep his spirits up, smile at him. This man whose hair has turned white in the long years of service to his country...

President Sadat telephoned. He told him, "Brother, my airplane is ready for you. You will be welcome whenever you wish to come." Jehan Sadat has also called several times. "Pay no attention to what the papers say," she says to me several times. And then she adds, "We're here, Farah, we're here."

During these dreadful days the king was cheered by this letter full of love and respect, which he received from our elder son, Reza:

My dearest Father,
I ask Almighty God to restore you to health as soon as possible. I am certain that he will grant my prayer, because the more I think about it, the more I see that you have done no wrong. You have given your whole life to serving the people and doing the will of God. Rest assured that you will never be alone, and the prayers of millions of people are with you. The invaluable service you have done to our dear native land will never be forgotten.

I ask God to keep you forever in his care, you who are my only reason for living.

With all my love,

Reza

My son would tell me much later how shocked he was to discover the way the press suddenly talked about his father after praising his work for so many years. "It's unbelievable. He had become a 'despot,' a 'tyrant' overnight. I really thought that they were not talking about the same man. The one I had known always respected other people so much and was so devoted to his country. Suddenly they were trying to make the world believe that he had reigned like a dictator, but we know that it was a lie."

Yes, the tension around us was terrible, and also the hate, the cries that pursued me. I had the feeling of being hounded by mindless, hostile crowds, which my bodyguards and huge American policemen pushed away from me. I can still remember one of them pulling me toward the elevator with the warning, "Someone could very easily pass by you and bang! Shoot you in the head." As he said it, he pointed two fingers at my forehead. "How tactful!" I thought.

Just a few important people managed to get through to the king and give him their support, despite the security cordon around him. I remember in particular the visit of the former finance minister, Houshang Ansary, and of Dr. Abdol Hossein Samii, former minister of Science and Higher Education. Frank Sinatra, who had sung in Iran, also came and gave my husband a Saint Christopher medal, for the patron saint of travelers, which touched me very much in our state of exile. The king also saw my last chief secretary, Seyyed Hossein Nasr. On his way to the hospital he was stopped for speeding, but when he told the policemen whom he was going to visit, they expressed their sympathy, he said, and let him go.

I managed to get away once or twice to go to the zoo with Leila and Ali-Reza, my poor little ones lost in this storm. At least they were not too unhappy at school: Leila at Marymount and her brother at Saint David's. We had enrolled Farahnaz as a boarder at the Ethel Walker School, to protect her from the terrible atmosphere that surrounded us. It was an excellent school but she was not happy. She felt too far away from us, the change was too sudden for her, and with hindsight I very much regret not having left her with the two young ones—above all when I realized that they didn't spare her, in fact quite the opposite. One day when she was sick, I learned that one of her teachers had remarked, "Is it because you're a princess that you're making all this fuss?" Her father was dying, she had lost everything, but even under those conditions she was not entitled to a little compassion.

Once I agreed to spend an hour or two in a department store with a friend, like any ordinary woman. We had decided to pass ourselves off as French women and called each other Michèle and Jacqueline. At one point we were standing in front of a saleswoman who looked at me intently and said, "Excuse me, Madam, but you look very like someone..."

"Really? Who?"

"The shah's wife!"

I smiled. "So I've been told."

"Well, I'm sorry for you," she added. "It can't be easy looking like that lady at the moment!"

No, it was not easy and the tension increased to the breaking point on the morning of 4 November, when America discovered that, in a reprisal for our entering the United States, its embassy in Tehran was henceforth occupied and its diplomats prisoners of the fundamentalists.

LEARNING OF OUR ARRIVAL IN NEW YORK twelve days earlier, Ayatollah Khomeini had inveighed against "the American plot to bring the shah back to power." A little later he had called on students, especially theological students, to "maximize their attacks against the United States and Israel, to force America to send back the criminal, the deposed emperor." It was therefore clear that this taking of hostages had the backing of the "guide" of the Revolution, and that it was designed to obtain the extradition of the king to Tehran.

It did not, however, have the support of Prime Minister Mehdi Bazargan, who handed in his resignation, as did Minister for Foreign Affairs Ibrahim Yazdi, thus depriving the United States of their only negotiating partners within the new Iranian regime. Without turning a hair, the former president of the Freedom Movement, Mehdi Bazargan, had witnessed the summary executions of hundreds of women and men whose only crime was to have served Iran in my husband's time. As for Ibrahim Yazdi, he had sat with the judges and torturers who had, among other things, given the death sentence to men who were remarkable for their courage, dignity, and their loyalty, among them Generals Mehdi Rahimi* and Nematollah Nassiri. But no doubt they considered that this time the attack on the American embassy went further than their personal "ethics" could accept.

The drama of the embassy quite rightly dismayed the American people, and the press immediately reported their legitimate anger. In my position, it was very difficult to make allowances. Admittedly most of the anger seemed directed against "the medieval fanatic" of Tehran, but here and there comments were made that it was my husband's fault. When that happened, suffering blinded me to anything else. I was there watching his ordeal day after day, and to hear this new rejection, these scarcely veiled appeals to "get rid of him," was sometimes more than I could bear.

The notes I wrote during those frightful days in November 1979 give a good idea of my state of mind at the time:

> 8 November. They have postponed the radiotherapy session, fearing the PLO may attack the hospital. It's terrible because we can't go anywhere else either. I know now that there will be no

*General Rahimi had his right arm cut off before his execution for having saluted when the king's name was spoken.

peace for us anywhere until the end of our days. My husband's illness is perhaps going to cause a third world war. Out in the street some young Americans have gone to our defense and are fighting the Iranian students, who demand our extradition. They shout, 'Take Carter, we'll keep the shah!' Their cries should make me feel better, but knowing that they are hitting Iranians, even followers of Khomeini, I find it very distressing. Without wishing to be, we are the cause of all this misfortune, all this tension.

9 November. He will have his session of radiotherapy tonight at last. I have been asked not to come for security reasons. I have stayed at the apartment, but I can't sleep. At 4 A.M. I telephoned to know what was happening. They told me that "everything is fine," and I think of him being pushed through those dingy basement passages… I couldn't bear it, so I got up and asked for one of the police cars to drive me through the quiet streets of New York. I did call in at the hospital to see him on the way back, and that made me feel better.

11 November. I woke up early to visit Farahnaz's school, which is outside of the city. In one way it's calming, as I can look at the scenery, see the trees, and put on some music of Vivaldi or Mozart. Farahnaz's school gives a good impression, but the poor little girl is not at all happy there. It distresses me to see her all alone. How hard all these problems are for the children.

14 November. I try to stay positive: I don't look at television, I don't listen to the radio, I don't read the newspapers. The tone of the television, in particular, makes me terribly anxious. Carter says that he won't buy any more oil from Iran; the Iranians reply that they will sell it elsewhere and at a higher price. They are now starting to talk about our so-called fortune. They have gone from $23 billion to $30 billion, which is completely false. Khomeini said, "They took with them the equivalent of a year's oil production; they should be extradited and tried." Bani-Sadr declared that there has never been a

worse man in history than my husband. The poor Americans are in a very difficult situation: when you are dealing with madmen, you don't know what to do and it's impossible to predict the future.

15 November. The climate is very difficult but I must keep hoping for the best. I don't want people to be able to say one day, "The poor thing. She couldn't cope with all those problems." I think we should leave here, because they are influencing the American people against us with all their lies about our supposed fortune. They are starting to say that the king should be tried as an international criminal. Khomeini is destroying a whole people, but it's my husband who should be tried. If there is a God, why doesn't he show himself?

16 November. I'm writing in my bedroom. There is a dear little squirrel that regularly comes to my balcony and I give him peanuts. We have become friends. I worked with X on the manuscript of the king's memoirs. This afternoon at the hospital I was very worried. I'm afraid that the United States might extradite my husband or that they support this international tribunal to try him.

20 November. The students have released the African Americans, but one of them quite rightly said, "We are Americans like the others and we don't want our color used in this way." Carter has threatened military intervention if they harm the hostages. It seems that an atomic submarine has left the Philippines.

I haven't a moment's peace. I say to myself, "If we leave the United States and they kill the hostages, people will say that if we had not gone, it would not have happened." But if we stay, perhaps they will set up this international tribunal...I think of my children. I so much want them not to suffer!

I'm quite prepared for them to extradite me, and only me, so that the name and the work of my husband, surely one of the best rulers of Iran, are not sullied; so that no American soldier has to set foot on Iranian soil, so that the world does not descend into chaos because of religious madmen.

> 27 November. It's ten o'clock and the king is to have another operation to remove the stone left by the surgeon. A German doctor has come from Canada. It was planned for tomorrow, but for security reasons, they are doing it at night.
>
> This story of the international tribunal makes my blood run cold. I feel as though I am living on death row. If the king has to appear before a tribunal, what would we hear from all the heads of state who for years praised his work for Iran. Will they also condemn him? If that's the way the world is, I would prefer not to be of this world.
>
> I went into the operating room. My husband was very calm. They had put a tube down his throat, and it was heartbreaking to see him manage a smile for me. At the same time they were saying in Tehran, "We have proof that the Shah is not ill," while I was watching him there with catheters and his sheet stained with blood...My heart aches for him. It's not fair that he should suffer so much, not only bodily but in heart and mind as well.
>
> 28 November. Carter has given an interview. He said, "We are not going to give in to blackmail," which may mean that they are not going to extradite my husband. I thought for the first time that the American president looked brave. "We consider the Iranian government responsible for taking these hostages," he said. "When the Shah came here, no one put pressure on me. It was my own decision and I think I did the right thing. I have no regrets and I ask no one's pardon. When his health permits, the shah can leave."

As early as 8 November, the king had conveyed his consternation to President Carter and had indicated to him that he would leave the United States as soon as possible, to avoid complicating negotiations that gave every sign of being extremely difficult. The idea of setting up an international tribunal to try him was suggested in some quarters, it seems, to mollify Tehran, which was demanding his extradition. It loomed large in my mind, as I can see rereading my notebook, for I think that the press reported it widely. Then no one mentioned it anymore; only the threat of extradition remained. Despite assurances from President Carter, that threat hung over my husband's head until March 1980 when we returned to Egypt, where he would die four months later.

TOWARDS THE END OF NOVEMBER, the doctors thought that the king could soon leave the hospital. They told us that they also needed the bed. We were relieved that we could now begin thinking about our return to Cuernavaca. Robert Armao sent his assistant, Mark Morse, down there to place the villa once more under surveillance and to make sure that everything was in order. Our arrival was set for 2 December. On 30 November we received news that stunned us all: Mexico now refused us asylum.

This sudden change of heart by President José López Portillo was incomprehensible. If the Mexican government feared for its embassies in the Arab countries, as was said at the time, why had he renewed his invitation since the hostages were taken on 4 November? I was later given a different explanation: it seems that Fidel Castro let President López Portillo know that Cuba would vote for his country's entry into the Security Council of the United Nations on condition that he refuse to give us refuge.

When he learned of Mexico's about-face from the consul general of that country in New York, Robert Armao was speechless, according to Pierre Salinger, who pieced the facts of this episode together. "'I don't believe you,' he said. 'We received confirmation from the presidential palace this very morning that everything was OK.' The consul asked him to call the ambassador, Mr. Hugo Margain, who confirmed what he had said in these words, 'The shah is no longer persona grata in Mexico. You must understand—his presence is becoming a threat to our national interests.'"

Pierre Salinger goes on to say, "A disheartened Armao went back to the hospital. He stayed in the room next to the shah's for an hour, wondering how he was going to break the news to him. Then one of the guards came in. 'There's a news bulletin on TV. His set is on. You'd better go and tell him.'

"As the channel the shah was watching had not given the information, it was Armao who had to inform him. For a while the shah just stared at him in disbelief. 'But why?' he said at last."

As soon as it was informed, the White House looked for a temporary solution, then sent Lloyd Cutler, the president's legal advisor, to the king to tell him of the decisions that had been made. All that happened very quickly, and by the time I was told, our new place of exile had already been chosen: Lackland Air Force Base in San Antonio, Texas.

My husband told me about it by phone. "We're leaving for Texas," he said. "The American government asks us to keep our destination strictly secret. Don't tell anyone, not even the children." What? We were going away without telling the children, without saying where we were going? It seemed unbearably cruel and more than I could cope with, but I agreed. Our departure had been arranged for very early the next morning.

I was with Princess Ashraf that evening and, when a friend called inviting me to lunch the next day, I accepted to avoid arousing suspicion. She asked me what Iranian dishes I would like. I lied as best I could.

Unable to sleep that night, I spent hours talking with Kambiz Atabaï. The king was in the hospital and the children were living with me. I thought of them, of how upset Leila would be when she woke up and found I had disappeared without even a few affectionate words for her. It broke my heart; she was only nine. And that is exactly what happened. She asked for me as soon as she woke up—"Where's Mummy?"—and would not believe Kambiz Atabaï when he told her that I had gone. To her little child's mind, it was inconceivable that her mummy would go away without giving her a kiss good-bye. She ran to my bedroom, and even today, I can't talk about this scene without being overcome with grief. Leila's disbelief, her distress when she discovered I was not there…It was enough to drive me mad.

I gathered a few things together very early in the morning and went out into the street. I was immediately blinded by television lights: the whole of the media were there, alerted by a leak from heaven knows where. And there was I, forbidden to kiss my own children good-bye while someone was informing the journalists! I was rushed into a police car and sped off. It was awful and laughable at the same time. There were CIA and FBI men in my own car and laundry vans full of security people surrounding us. The king, who was transported under similar conditions, joined me at the airport. There was a military airplane waiting there for us, guarded by men wearing helmets and bulletproof vests and armed with machine guns. We were told to board. Were the threats against us serious enough to warrant all this? That night I thought to myself that the whole incredible setup was put in place just to drive us mad.

The astounding welcome we got at the Lackland base did nothing to dispel that impression. No sooner had we disembarked than we were bundled into an ambulance without a word of greeting or explanation. The vehicle set off at high speed, turning and breaking so suddenly that we fell against each other several times. Poor Dr. Pirnia, who was with us, banged her head hard against a corner of the roof. The ambulance stopped at last, someone opened the doors, and there was our new refuge: the psychiatric building of a military hospital! The king was put in a room with a walled-up window, and I was taken to an adjoining room where there was no door handle on the inside but a microphone on the ceiling. I was appalled. I couldn't believe my eyes, and the white-coated men, who seemed to be there to watch us, gave us no explanation of what was happening. As my room had a window (with bars), I rushed over to open it. I was literally suffocating, but a male nurse shook his head, indicating that I could not touch the window. Luckily Dr. Pirnia had joined me in the meantime. "Would you please tell him that if he doesn't open it, I'll go crazy!" He then agreed to open it a little, and in the minutes that followed, these ten centimeters of fresh air were a lifesaver for me. To stop losing my mind, I began to describe this room in minute detail in my notebook, and even did a sketch of it.

When Mark Morse, Robert Armao's assistant arrived, I was beside myself and began to shout, "Are we in prison? Has Carter had us thrown in prison? Have we been arrested?" I was allowed to use the telephone, so I called Kambiz Atabaï in New York and a few friends. I said to all of them, "If you don't hear from us, you'll know that we're at Lackland, under house arrest." I was so distressed that I didn't realize that if we had really been under house arrest, they would not have allowed us to use the telephone.

During that time Robert Armao, who was just as outraged, went to talk to the military. It appeared, after a few hours, that they had hastily put us there while they prepared a small apartment for us in one of the buildings used for staff on the base. When we finally found ourselves in these few, acceptably furnished rooms, we felt much relieved.

Our stay at Lackland, which would only last for two weeks, turned out to be much more pleasant than it seemed at first. The base commander, General Acker, very quickly came to see if we were comfortable. Most Iranian pilots had trained in the United States, so the general and his staff had come to know and like Iran through our airmen, and they respected the king. It certainly cheered my husband to find himself in surroundings that were friendly, even close when he swapped aviation experiences with some of the officers.

General Acker did everything he could to make our exile more tolerable. He had us to dinner several times, introduced his officers to us, and when he discovered that I would like to play tennis, found partners for me among his staff. I find tennis and sport in general a form of therapy, a way to keep on my feet physically and mentally. Still today, during the worst ordeals, tennis helps me not to give way. I had to force myself to go, but then I felt the beneficial effects of it. And it was my only free space because the general, who was worried about our safety, had politely forbidden us to go away from our building. At most we were allowed to walk around it, accompanied by our two officers, Colonels Kiomars and Yazdan Nevissi, themselves surrounded by American security men. Our Iranian colonels found it oppressive, and I would tease them, "Well, now you are learning for yourselves how annoying it is to have bodyguards always beside you. I often said it to you in the past, but you didn't look as though you believed me." To show their sympathy with our situation, American officers also brought us cassettes satirizing Khomeini or tee shirts with his caricature on them.

However, on 7 December of that year, 1979, we were shocked by some terrible news: we learned that Princess Ashraf's son, Shahriar Shafigh, had just been assassinated in Paris. As he was entering his sister's house, Villa Dupont, in the sixteenth arrondissement, a man in a motorcycle helmet shot him in the neck, then finished him off before disappearing.

Shahriar was a thirty-four-year-old naval officer. The king was very fond of him and held him in very high regard, as I did. He was still in Iran when the Islamic Revolution broke out but managed to leave the country by crossing the Persian Gulf in a small cutter. As soon as he got out, he started to organize resistance. Liked and admired in the navy for his lack of affectation and his merit as an officer, he had stayed in contact with many of his contemporaries who were still in Iran. My husband had spent some time with him in the Bahamas, and Shahriar had told him that he was going to keep fighting. He was one of the people you could always depend on.

His death sent the king into a mood of silent despair. A grief-stricken Princess Ashraf joined us at Lackland, where we could do little but mourn with her. Good Lord, when would this spiral of death come to an end? All the men and women who had made Iran a great country were disappearing one after the other.

As expected, Sadegh Khalkhali, the bloodthirsty cleric of Tehran, ordered this latest murder, warning that the killing would continue "until we have wiped out all these dirty lackeys of a decadent system." France never found Shahriar Shafigh's killer.

Perhaps grief was a contributing factor in the deterioration of the king's health. There was no longer a doctor looking after him; his spleen began to swell. When I told Professor Flandrin about it by telephone, he seemed surprised that my husband had been prescribed Chlorambucil again. "Another aberration," he would write later.

Our stay at Lackland could not continue, both for the king's health and for the White House, which wanted to see us leave the United States quickly. But where could we go? The State Department informed us that even South Africa, which at some stage had agreed to take us, was now unwilling. It was very hurtful. We had the feeling of being pariahs in the eyes of the whole world, including countries with reactionary regimes such as South Africa, where apartheid was still practiced and where I would not want to go anyway.

Finally, on 12 December, White House Chief of Staff Hamilton Jordan came to tell the king that Panama was prepared to offer us hospitality. Mr. Jordan had just come from there with an invitation from General Omar Torrijos. We really had no other choice but to accept.

That left the medical decision to be made about my husband. Dr. Benjamin Kean, the organizer of the operation in New York, came to examine the king with the doctor assisting him, Dr. Williams, who had been a member of the operating team. This time both of them thought that the spleen should definitely be removed. If it was urgent, the American administration, it seems, was prepared for the operation to be done in the United States, but at the same time, Hamilton Jordan appeared anxious to see us leave the country as quickly as possible. "Let's go," my husband decided. "We'll do the operation later, in Panama."

The house we were given was on the island of Contadora in the Pearl Archipelago, about thirty minutes by plane or helicopter from Panama City. It belonged to the Panamanian ambassador to the United States, Gabriel Lewis Galindo, who was kind enough to make it available to us. The extreme heat surprised us as we got off the plane, especially as we arrived in our winter clothes. The villa had four rooms, one of them being a single large room with a balcony on the first floor, where we settled my husband as well as we could. He needed rest and a little comfort in his weak state, but I never did manage to give him that comfort. If I closed the window, he was too hot, and if I opened it, he was right in a draft, which was not recommended in his condition. I looked at him lovingly, and I was almost out of my mind with worry. What could I do for him in this country, on this tiny island, where we knew no one?

My memory of these first days in Panama is one of deep distress, which comes through in these few anxious lines jotted down in my notebook:

> 16 December. The king never complains but stays calm and pleasant whatever happens. How much more time does he have to live? I don't know. So ill and stuck on this island lost in the Pacific Ocean, with all the damp and heat. My poor husband. Even if they are pretty, even if the people are nice, the islands are stifling. I see the black side of everything tonight; I'm exhausted. Even my sobs sound different. I have no other course but to go on living, for my children, for my husband. All exiled Iranians are unhappy.
>
> 18 December. Young Panamanians have demonstrated in front of the American embassy. General Torrijos has told us not to worry. I hope they won't cause problems here. If they do, where will we go? There is only Egypt, and it's not certain that the Americans will let us go there.
>
> 19 December. The King has not been feeling well for ten days now. They have decided to operate on the spleen, but when? Where? I'm very worried. I alternate between hope and despair; the days go by in a state of confusion. I so admire this man who keeps smiling in spite of his pain. He has lost more weight and his eyes look huge. Occasionally I can see anxiety in his eyes. Dear Lord, let him live.

Happily the children could join us for the Christmas holidays with my mother. They were now living far away from us, but at least they had not had to share this awful, humiliating, soul-destroying wandering from place to place. Here also, the villa was too small to house them, so we rented another villa nearby. These few days were like a short break in the endless ordeal. We all went out together as a family and went swimming as we had in the far-off days on Kish. I took up tennis again and played with a young Uruguayan girl, Mariella, who worked in the nearby hotel. Her kindness made me feel a bit more cheerful. The king, who felt a little better, came and sat on the side of the court to watch us play. He even hit a few balls! These moments stolen from our usual feeling of sad and grim disillusion remain in my mind as memories full of warmth and love. One afternoon I could not resist the desire to put on water skis again; it had been so long since I'd done it. Then I saw people everywhere frantically waving their arms at me: the bay was full of sharks, and we hadn't noticed.

Over a few days the king gave a television interview to the British journalist David Frost. He said that the clerics did not understand the modern world and that they would do a lot of harm to Iran. He wanted to reply sincerely to each question, not hiding any doubts he may have had. Accordingly, when the journalist asked about the reasons for the Islamic Revolution, the king said, "I tell you, Mr. Frost, I still don't understand what happened." Asked about his so-called megalomania, he replied quite rightly, "Is it megalomania to help create stability in the Indian Ocean region?" Finally, on the subject of SAVAK, whose role and image could have harmed the monarchy, the king made this reply, "They could enforce what they thought was good for the country, and they may have been wrong."

THE PANAMANIAN AUTHORITIES CHOSE Dr. Adan Rios to follow the progress of the king's illness. He was a cancer specialist who had trained in the United States, a serious and apparently competent doctor. Dr. Rios came several times during January 1980 to examine my husband and take the blood samples he needed.

I would learn much later that while these visits were taking place, a diplomatic quarrel had begun to decide whether the king would have the operation in Gorgas Hospital, in the old American Canal Zone and still run by the Americans, or in the Paitilla Medical Center, run by the Panamanians. Drs Kean and Williams wanted Gorgas Hospital; Dr. Rios preferred Paitilla, since he had already sent my husband there for a series of preliminary tests in February, when he saw that the removal of the spleen could not be delayed any longer.

That is when the altercation between the American and Panamanian doctors really began, but it was an altercation that would lead to nothing less than the cancellation of the operation at the risk of hastening my husband's end.

Meanwhile, I was naturally very worried. I asked Dr. Flandrin if he would please come to Panama. He therefore had a front-row seat for this war of prerogatives; my husband and I could only see the effects.

Dr. Flandrin's account of the quarrel to Professor Bernard tells a lot about this dramatic episode in our exile:

> I received another call from H.M. the Queen, asking me to come to Panama to make an assessment of the situation. My arrival was no easy matter. I took the Air France Concorde flight to New York and was in transit for a Braniff flight to Panama City. When I left the Concorde at Kennedy Airport, I was surprised to hear a voice announcing, "Mr. Flandrin, would you please contact the information desk." I immediately thought that something serious had happened to the patient. The message to me was something else completely, but it did nothing to lessen my apprehension. I was asked to telephone Robert Armao at his home in New York. I thought he would give me the information when I called him. It was his wife who answered, and she simply said that Bob was telling

me not to continue my trip but to come and see him at home. And so I didn't take the Braniff flight and instead caught a taxi to the address I had been given. All that seemed to confirm the pessimistic assumption that obviously came to my mind. The taxi stopped in front of a building, somewhere near the central part of New York, that rather surprised me. I didn't ask him straight out the question that was on my lips, but it did not take me long to realize that there were no new health problems for H. M. I was amazed and told Armao that we had to inform Panama immediately that I was not coming. He reassured me, saying that it was not a problem. I did, however, take the liberty of asking rather pointedly for some explanation, while trying to stay "cool."

All I could do was to accept the strong drink and the only explanation offered, that we should "all" see each other tomorrow morning to have a "discussion." They had "arrested" my journey; I was waiting to see if they were going to arrest me. My charming host dropped me at a hotel and came back for me the next morning…to take me to Dr. Kean's private office! I was furious. Benjamin Kean was there, jovial, chewing as usual on a cigar. His companion, Dr. Williams, was also there with his white hair, young face, and quiet smile. Besides the engaging Armao, there were three or four people I didn't know. The attention of all was focused on me, and I felt as though I was facing a jury or a tribunal rather than simply having a drink with friends. We quickly came to the point. I asked for an explanation, reminding them quite definitely that H. M. the Queen had expressly asked me to come and that unless I had her instruction to the contrary, I wished to continue my journey. I wanted some justification for this double arrest. They tried to placate me, of course. Kean explained with his usual pride that he was "H. M.'s personal physician" and that he was in charge, etc., etc.…In short, that it wasn't worth my going to Panama! But I was determined to go; I had been naïve and ingenuous, but not anymore. I told them once again that because I had been called by the patient himself, he was the only person who could release me from that request, and that in all probability I would be leaving that afternoon on the Braniff flight that I should have taken the previous day...if no one there had any objections. My determination had the desired effect. I would stay in Panama for a month, without saying anything to my wife; it was up to her to deduce what she could from watching television. I decided not to worry about Dr. Kean and simply do what seemed useful to me.

The episode in New York was only petty small-mindedness; the one in Panama—like the decisions made in Mexico—was the subordination of medical problems to the sordid motives of petty politicking. When I arrived in Panama City, I was put in contact with Dr. Adan Rios. At last I found a doctor who was suited to the task being asked of him. We had no problem understanding each other or drawing up the list of difficulties so that we could make decisions together. There were also no problems with the American doctors at the Gorgas Hospital. After seeing the patient in the residence supplied to him on Contadora Island, my findings were as follows: although the radiotherapy had not gone to full term, the left supraclavicular lymph nodes, which the biopsy had shown to be aggressive, had now disappeared; although having had practically no more chemotherapy, the patient was pancytopenic with, in particular, marked thrombocytopenia and profound neutropenia, in contrast to good clinical tolerance. A few episodes of secondary respiratory infection were, however, beginning to occur, but again not seriously. Above all, the spleen had become enormous, much bigger still than we had seen it in 1974. It seemed that this increase in size was very recent, therefore showing rapid growth, which made me fear a localization in the spleen of the aggressive lymphoma rather than a recurrence of the original lymphoproliferating syndrome. Now that the problem had been clearly set out, we had to know the state of the bone marrow to judge the respective involvement of the hypersplenism or the tumoral invasion of the bone marrow in the workings of the peripheral cytopenias. Adan Rios agreed with my analysis. As Kean and Williams were still in New York, I could then perform my last free act as a doctor on the case by taking a myelogram, undergone by the patient with his usual forbearance.

That took place on the day after my arrival in Panama: I saw no advantage in wasting time. Adan Rios and I took the small propeller-driven airplane back to the isthmus. Stains of the myelogram were done at Gorgas, where I examined the smears. Here I had an almost unexpected, pleasant surprise: the bone marrow had a very good cell count without any lymphoid abnormalities. There was a certain degree of erythroblastic hyperplasia, which made me look for signs of additional immunological hyperhemolysis. Consequently, there was still a chance at that time that the pancytopenia was mainly linked to hypersplenism. [...] After the splenectomy [removal of the spleen], I advised beginning combination chemotherapy of the CHOP type (or a high-dose course of that type). Adan Rios, who was well-experienced in chemotherapy, arrived at the same conclusions.

We told H. M. of our therapeutic proposals and then we began to look at the practical considerations involved in that program. Firstly, the purely surgical requirements did not seem to us to present any particular problems. That was not foremost in our minds. On the other hand, the requirements for hematological intensive care could well present more serious problems. Adan Rios therefore made contact with Dr. Anderson, who phoned Dr. Jane Hester, whose reputation in matters of transfusional resuscitation, more particularly the transfusion of white cells, was beyond doubt. Her experience with IBM blood cell separators seemed a valuable asset that we should not do without. Adan Rios knew her, and she agreed to come, bringing an IBM engineer with her, because they had to bring an IBM blood cell separator with them; as there were none in Panama.

Our plans seemed to be proceeding under reasonably good conditions. Whereupon I telephoned Kean to inform him that the medical situation demanded my continued presence there. And so he made the journey to Panama and arrived at Contadora with Dr. Williams. I explained the situation to them and my wish to see a splenectomy performed as soon as possible. Then ensued a very sharp war of words between Kean and myself. He declared himself opposed to a splenectomy, not for strategic reasons, which could indeed have been debated, but because he thought that splenectomy was very dangerous, usually resulting in death! I quoted the mortality rate to him, which was lower than 1 percent!

As H. M. reaffirmed his confidence in me, Kean had to give in to my decisions. What he obviously feared was losing his control over this affair, and he came back wreathed in smiles to tell H. M. in our presence that he was getting "the greatest living surgeon!" Everyone held their breath, then he announced the name of Michael DeBakey. I had obviously heard the name—he was a great specialist in cardiovascular surgery—but I had no way of judging the suitability of this choice. H. M. had no reaction to this name for the moment: either it meant nothing to him, or he showed nothing. Kean seemed very disappointed, for he clearly thought that the name alone would have a magic effect on the patient's mind. As for Adan Rios and Jane Hester, they showed their astonishment and their opposition. I was present when Jane Hester told H. M. what she thought. She said very firmly and unequivocally that DeBakey had nothing to do with problems of abdominal cancer surgery, and that the whole idea was absurd. I could not make a contribution to this debate, and I had to say that I was in no position to make a choice between American surgeons, none of whom I knew. Kean realized that I had been neutralized on this point and that all he had to do then was to consider Adan Rios's and Jane Hester's opinions of no consequence—which he did.

This strategy would nevertheless meet an obstacle, as the Americans had not taken the Panamanians into account. There was a whole medical hierarchy above Adan Rios which would not hear of all this taking place in Panamanian territory without their consent and participation. The more or less suspicious part played by certain participants, notably Dr. Garcia, a different person from the one in Mexico and a surgeon in the Paitilla Clinic, and the political interference that took place between the American government and General Torrijos have been fairly well clarified, and it is not up to me to comment. I would simply remind you that our medical action took place against a background of negotiations between the Carter administration and Tehran for the return of the hostages, and the reality of that situation was evident, even to me.

Time went by, uselessly wasted. Difficulties had arisen between the Americans and Panamanians on the choice of location for the operation: Gorgas Hospital or the Paitilla Clinic? Relations had soured. DeBakey had arrived in his special plane with an assistant, anesthesiologist, and nurse, the surgeon having been interviewed before his departure from Houston. We had gone from the era of the invisible man, which I had experienced, to one of flashes and live television. The Barnum & Bailey aspect of this arrival did not appear to please the Panamanian doctors, and it seems that an ill-timed comment to an American newspaper by Kean touched off a crisis. It implied that "Panamanian medicine" was not capable of solving the medico-surgical problem, hence the providential American surgeon, etc.

From that moment on, it was open warfare between the Panamanian and American sides. H. M. had been taken to Panama City and hospitalized at Paitilla, as he was showing signs of complications from a respiratory infection. At that time I was the only one spared in this war of words, for I was the only one who did not belong to either camp. Each tried to woo me and play me against the other. DeBakey was completely charming and friendly toward me. The Panamanian surgeon, Dr. Garcia, explained his point of view to me. He even told me one day, "Why do we need this big name DeBakey? A splenectomy is no problem to me. I can do it left-handed with my right hand tied behind my back!" I did point out in response that it was an enlarged spleen in the course of a hematological malignancy, and that situation needed special precautions. H. M. was quite aware of the battle that was going on. The remark he made to me during these days is proof of it: "Dr. Flandrin, you're like the Swiss, neutral between warring sides!"

From being simply tense, the situation deteriorated into conflict. Panamanian soldiers surrounded the Paitilla Clinic, which was very close to the Holiday Inn where we were staying at the time. No one could get in, and that applied to the American doctors as well as to me. The Panamanian police monitored us in our hotel rooms and gave us laminated cards with our photos, which they took on the spot. It was a bit like going through police ID...With these passes we could leave our hotel at last under the eye of television cameras and go to Paitilla on foot. There was a sort of roundtable discussion with the Panamanian and American medical authorities. I didn't get all the gist of their arguments, but it emerged that DeBakey could assist at the operation but apparently could not be the leader. We then went to see the patient. H. M. had dressed and received us wearing a suit. The atmosphere was frosty. He listened to the opinions and, as far as I can remember, the conclusion was that they should not rush things, and the pneumonopathy he then showed led to postponement of the operation for a few days, etc. I kept perfectly quiet, taking no part in this debate. When we were about to leave the room and the other doctors began to go out, I stayed noticeably where I was. H. M. gave me a look of assent, and I remained alone with him. The Panamanians and Americans, watching each other out of the corner of their eyes, did not show any reaction. H. M. asked me frankly, "Dr. Flandrin, do you think I should have the operation here?" I replied, "Certainly not. I have no confidence in what might happen." He said, "That's what I think too." After a few words, I also left the room.

The mistrust I felt then was not about the technique of either of the surgical teams, as I had no experience of any of them. My lack of confidence came from the terrible atmosphere that existed and which seemed to me completely incompatible with what we had to do. It was not a matter of a simple splenectomy, but the first stage of a series of medical decisions that would be long and difficult. A serene atmosphere was essential and it would inevitably be lacking.

I had been in Panama for almost a month and the medical decision taken the very day after my arrival had still not been put into practice. The clinical state of the patient, left without treatment, was definitely declining, and I was thinking of the inevitable anatomical development of the lymphoma which was being given free reign. Leaving Panama and trying to act seemed like the last chance. The American team, whatever its responsibility was for the present situation, must surely come to the same conclusion. We now know the extent to which shameful, hidden political motives influenced everything that happened. I, of course, knew nothing of this, but I had a strong feeling that nonmedical considerations had been taken into account. One day when I was chatting with DeBakey in his room, he received a telephone call from New York. The person speaking to him asked if the decision to operate was really very useful at that time (during the last days in Panama). DeBakey replied that he was only the surgeon and that the recommendation for the splenectomy was mine, but that it did indeed seem necessary to him. He added, "But I'll put Dr. Flandrin on the line. He's here as it happens and can give you his reasons." I think it was Hamilton Jordan on the phone. I gave him my little piece, adding that time was getting short and action should be taken. As far as I understood it, an operation in Panama at that time clearly bothered him.

A relative "peace" was restored after the Paitilla meeting. A false fact, which no one believed: the respiratory secondary infection led to postponing the operation. Everyone went home to wait.

No doubt Hamilton Jordan's difficulty*, discreetly raised by Professor Flandrin, can be explained by the strategy Panama had adopted to try to solve the hostage crisis. This strategy involved my husband's arrest. Did it have the approval of the White House? I don't know.

General Torrijos had wanted to play a part in freeing the hostages from day one, helping get his friend President Carter out of this tragic impasse. The general saw it as an opportunity to thank the American president, who had convinced Congress at the beginning of 1978 to give back the canal to the Panamanian state. The hospitality Omar Torrijos offered us is very likely explained by this original desire to help President Jimmy Carter.

We knew nothing about it at the time but very quickly felt uneasy in Panama. We had the impression that the welcoming

*In his book, *Crisis*, Hamilton Jordan recounts a telephone conversation with Dr. DeBakey. Jordan was worried that allowing the Shah to leave Panama for medical treatment could jeopardize the talks in the hostage crisis. DeBakey made it clear that his patient's health was his first priority and would make no compromises in the matter.

smiles hid less respectable intentions. In a storeroom behind the house, I actually discovered a tape recorder and electrical equipment, which I quickly realized was used to record our telephone conversations. Was the general thinking of extraditing us in exchange for the hostages? Probably not, as the Americans were against it, at least publicly. But he was looking for a subterfuge to mollify Tehran and lead to a resolution.

It was offered to him by Iran itself, which sent two lawyers to Panama instructed to deliver an official request for extradition. It seems that Christian Bourguet, a French national, and Hector Villalon, an Argentinian, arrived during the Christmas holidays we were spending as a family on Contadora. This fact was naturally kept from us, but during the month of January 1980 we were told about it by Aristides Royo, the president of Panama, who very kindly suggested that we choose a local lawyer to defend us against a threat from Tehran. What was it all about? Two lawyers, he told us, were drawing up a dossier on the Shah's alleged "crimes." It seemed hardly wise to choose a Panamanian to defend us against accusations such as these. He could not possibly gauge the work my husband had accomplished or the insanity of these proceedings initiated by the Islamic Republic. This did make us a little more worried about the real intentions of the Panamanian authorities.

General Torrijos never missed an opportunity to reassure us, but what he really wanted was to use this request for extradition to give guarantees to Tehran. How? We found out later. With the response to the extradition request still pending, Panamanian law at that time stipulated that once a request had been received, the authorities were required to place the person under arrest. It seems that the general convinced himself that the king's arrest would have such an impact symbolically that it would be enough to persuade the fundamentalist students to give up their hostages.

Also, according to historians, Sadegh Ghotbzadeh,* who was making a bid for the presidency of the republic at the time and had sent the two lawyers to Panama, also believed that the announcement alone that my husband had been placed under house arrest would be enough to make the students yield.

While the two lawyers were working on the extradition dossier, on the medical front the two teams were engaged in the war described by Professor Flandrin. If we lacked the information to judge the real extent of the threats hanging over our heads, we did at least feel the awful atmosphere surrounding us and the tension all our movements seemed to create. Some journalists we knew fairly well told us, "Leave Panama. Go. It's dangerous." One day Mark Morse, Armao's assistant who was in charge of the everyday problems we met on the island, just simply disappeared, and we discovered that he had been arrested by Panamanian security agents. Armao had to alert the White House to have him set free. Toward the end, we noticed that our telephone was no longer working. I remarked on it and was told that our line had indeed been cut off...because the bill had not been paid! The line was reconnected, but for a few days, strangely enough, it was impossible to reach General Torrijos or his ambassador, Gabriel Lewis, in whose house we were living.

It was in this maddening situation that I called Jehan Sadat, who regularly inquired how we were. I had realized that under the circumstances no doctor would operate on my husband in Panama and that our situation was hopeless. But I knew that I was sure to be overheard, and in my confused state I told her to call my sister-in-law in New York to find out what was going on around

*Sadegh Ghotbzadeh, Minister of Foreign Affairs during the time of the American hostage crisis, was accused of having incited a coup d'état against Khomeini, convicted of treason, and executed in September 1982.

us, without suspecting that Princess Ashraf's telephone would also be tapped. Jehan Sadat understood. "Come," she said to me, "we're waiting for you here in Egypt."

The wife of the Egyptian president later described the incident in her memoirs:

> "Jehan, our situation is desperate," Farah phoned me from Panama in March of 1980. "My husband's cancer has spread to his spleen and if he does not have an operation immediately, he will die. But I cannot trust anyone here."
>
> "Why, Farah, why?" I asked.
>
> She sounded close to tears. "It is difficult to explain over the phone," she said, letting me know that her telephone was bugged. "But we must leave Panama immediately. There are ominous reports."
>
> I knew right away what she was referring to, for I too had heard rumors that Panama might be bargaining with Khomeini to return the Shah to Iran and to certain death.
>
> "But what about the Shah's operation, Farah?" I asked her.
>
> "Oh, Jehan, I don't know what to do. I must get him out of this hospital." I knew exactly what Farah couldn't say, though I didn't want to believe it. Would Khomeini go as far as having the Shah killed on the operating table?
>
> "Can you not get American doctors there to perform the operation?" I asked her.
>
> "The government of Panama has refused them permission," she said, her voice breaking.
>
> "Surely the U.S. government can intercede on your behalf," I said.
>
> "The U.S. government?" Farah said bitterly. "We have had enough of their help to last a lifetime."
>
> Tears came to my own eyes as I listened to her. Her voice, once so strong, was now strained, her former confidence broken. How cruel the last fourteen months had been for the Shah and Farah.

> I contacted Anwar at his office, telling him the gravity of the situation. "I have just told Farah that she and the Shah should come immediately to Egypt," I said "Was I wrong?"
> "There is no question, Jehan," he said. "Tell Farah I will send the presidential plane for them immediately."
> "You are sure? You know there will be trouble," I said to him.
> But he was sure. "It will please God," he said.
> Farah could not believe it when I called her with the good news. "You will allow the American doctors to operate?" she asked disbelievingly. "You are sure?" She had been afraid for so long that she did not know whom to trust.
> "Yes, Farah, yes," I said to her again and again.*

The prospect of our immediate departure worried President Carter, who sent us two emissaries: his legal advisor, Lloyd Cutler, and a man from the State Department who had been posted to Iran, Arnie Raphel. We received them in Contadora and I insisted on staying at my husband's side during the whole conversation. They had refused to have Armao and Colonel Jahanbini present at the meeting. Mr. Raphel began by recalling the five years he spent in Esfahan in very flattering terms for us, saying that he had noticed how much the king cared for his people and how hard I worked for the welfare of the poorest. I disliked his tone from the beginning, for I guessed that by emphasizing our spirit of devotion to the population in this way, he wanted to persuade my husband to sacrifice himself in the present crisis. The more he said, the more I felt a real anger rise up within me. It is right that a king should sacrifice himself for his people, I thought to myself, but it is morally unacceptable for him to sacrifice himself to mollify a criminal state that dares to take foreign diplomats hostage on its own soil.

*Jehan Sadat, *A Woman of Egypt.*

Then Lloyd Cutler described the concern of the United States at the prospect of our departure for Egypt. Our presence in Cairo, he said, risked weakening the already difficult position of President Sadat and would therefore harm the peace efforts in the Middle East. I retorted fairly sharply that the Egyptian president, who had renewed his invitation, did not need anyone to tell him how to act. Mr. Cutler nonetheless repeated the wish to have us stay in Panama where, he told us, the operation could be organized at the Gorgas Hospital.

"I want to die with honor, not on an operating table because someone made a mistake or was bribed," my husband replied calmly.

Then Mr. Cutler, the clever diplomat that he was, pulled out his last card: the United States was ready to open its border to us again so that the king could have the operation in Houston, but in order not to aggravate problems in Tehran, it would seem essential that the king abdicate.

"The people would not understand," I replied solemnly. Then, after a moment's silence I added that if he were to abdicate, the throne would come to our son Reza.

"And if our elder son dies, it will be the second son. And if our younger son is prevented from succeeding, it will be someone else from our family."

"I did not seriously consider the Americans' offer," the king wrote later in the last edition of his memoirs, which he finished in Cairo. "For a year and a half, American promises had been worth very little."

It was 21 March 1980. The following day, Saturday, President Carter rang President Sadat to dissuade him from taking us. He did not succeed, and I later learned that the Egyptian head of state gave him this direct admonition, "Jimmy, I want the shah here, and alive."

That same Saturday my husband told Lloyd Cutler that we were leaving for Egypt as quickly as possible. President Sadat had proposed sending us the Egyptian presidential plane, but the Americans thought it preferable for us to hire a plane on the American continent, which was done during that day. We wondered at the time why they did not want the Egyptian aircraft. We understood in the Azores, when a stopover nearly turned into an attempt to take hostages.

Finally, on Sunday, 23 March, at 2 P.M., three months after our arrival on the island of Contadora, we boarded a DC-8 belonging to Evergreen Airlines. My husband had a high fever but the plane, which was usually used for charter flights, had no comfortable space for him to lie down. I had asked a childhood friend, Elli Antoniades, who had come down from New York to Contadora to see us, if she would kindly come with us to Cairo; I needed moral support. She did not hesitate for a moment. We were sitting next to each other, but I felt so sure that this plane was riddled with microphones that I dared not speak to her.

Immediately after takeoff I wrote, "23 March. Seeing this sick man with his eyes looking so feverish just shatters me. Of course with Jehan we will be among friends, but I'm worried: I just hope that the elements of the Muslim Brotherhood don't cause too many problems...My poor children. My heart aches for them. They were not able to join us for Now Ruz the day before yesterday. I couldn't even explain our situation to them on the telephone nor why, with all these doctors, their father still had not had his operation. They must have known, their voices were more than usually sad. When the pilot announced that we were leaving Panamanian airspace everyone felt relieved. But it is still a long journey to Egypt and I'm afraid my husband might feel ill."

During the night we touched down in the Azores, officially to refuel. We had been told to expect it and I had taken the trouble to look up the Azores on a map before we left. In the beginning, everything went according to plan. While the refueling of the aircraft was taking place, some officials introduced themselves very respectfully to greet the king. Although he was shaky on his feet, my husband found the strength to stand up to receive them with dignity and thank them. I went out shortly afterwards for a breath of air, thinking that we would be leaving at any moment. While walking on the tarmac, I explained the situation in Iran to the steward who was accompanying me. It was cold and he put his own jacket over my shoulders. Another quarter of an hour went by. Why weren't we taking off?

When I went back into the cabin the wind blew in, and I noticed that the temperature had fallen considerably. My husband was getting cold; I asked for a blanket. Then I suddenly began to worry: we had been there for an hour! What was the meaning of this holdup? Was it hiding a final attempt to stop us from reaching Egypt? We were on an American air base in an American plane. Anything was possible. When Robert Armao went to see what was happening, an official at the base explained that the plane had to wait for permission to fly over certain territories, which was hardly a credible reason. More than four hours went by like this, all of us becoming more and more anxious. Finally, expecting the worst, I called a friend in Paris to inform him of our situation. I told him that the king was critically ill and that we were held up in the Azores. If anything happened to us, I was counting on him to let the world know. Meanwhile Armao was trying in vain to contact Hamilton Jordan.

Finally the plane received permission to resume its flight. What had happened? Journalists and historians later gave an explanation for that interminable touchdown. Being almost ready to make an official request for extradition, it seems that Christian Bourguet, the lawyer from Tehran, asked Hamilton Jordan to intercept our plane in the Azores and make it come back to Panama, as Sadegh Ghotbzadeh had said that he was sure to obtain the release of the hostages as soon the king's arrest was announced. Hamilton Jordan had agreed to temporarily stop our aircraft without notifying President Carter who expressed his displeasure when he learned of it. Then, as the hours went by with no encouraging signs from Tehran, he must have lost faith in the propositions of Ghotbzadeh and his emissary Bourguet.

The request for extradition was nonetheless made on Monday 24 March as we were arriving in Cairo. What would General Torrijos have done if it had arrived in time? Everything leads me to believe that he would not have hesitated to put my husband under house arrest.

Many years later the man who had been the Portuguese minister of foreign affairs during this episode in the Azores would tell me that, seeing that our plane was not taking off again, his people had called the Americans. "They were very vague about it," he confided, "and did not give us any reasonable explanation." The Portuguese government took offense and sent its ambassador to the State Department the following day. He received the reply that this was a matter for the United States alone, and consequently no explanation could be given.

FOURTEEN MONTHS OF WANDERING, with much suffering and humiliation, had taken place since our departure from Egypt and, as if to wipe them all away, President Sadat and his wife were waiting for us at the foot of the steps on the traditional red carpet. The Guard of Honor was also there. The king was so touched by it that his eyes clouded with tears. Anwar Sadat embraced him warmly, as he had done fourteen months earlier. My husband was very weak. "As I looked at him," Jehan Sadat wrote later, "I was once again astounded at the harshness of the Americans. The shah had difficulty descending the steps. He was so thin that his clothes looked two sizes too big for him. His face was ashen. If ever a man needed friends, it was he."

Before our arrival a debate in the Parliament had authorized Sadat, by 384 votes to 8, to receive us in Egypt in the name of basic humanity and the hospitality of Islam. The country therefore knew about our arrival, and a happy crowd was milling about at the airport to greet us.

The Egyptian president had prepared for us Kubbeh Palace, situated in lovely grounds away from the noise of the city. As a symbolic gesture he insisted on showing it to the ailing king before taking him to the Maadi military hospital, where a wing had been set aside for him. The conditions were now in place for the removal of the spleen, which had been recommended a year earlier by Professor Flandrin when we were in the Bahamas and constantly put off since.

Conditions were also right to have the children join us. I wanted them to be near their father before this operation, which I knew could be risky. They arrived quickly, and for the first time since the far-off, happy days in Tehran, we were together again as a family without the fear of being sent on our way from one day to the next. All of ten years old, Leila wanted to understand what was wrong with her father. I tried to explain to her that one of his organs did not work well and she, no doubt for reassurance, asked if they were going to give him a new one, a better one.

Five days went by before the operation—five long days that I lived through in a state of great anxiety. Morning and evening I made the long trip between Kubbeh Palace and the Maadi hospital, and I remember that after my sleepless nights, the terrible noise of the Cairo car horns drove me to distraction. I was reduced to using earplugs during these trips to keep from constantly jumping in my seat. But surrounded by caring staff, the king had recovered a certain serenity, and that was the main thing. The Egyptians showed their friendship in a host of ways: some called the hospital to offer their blood, many wrote, and at the gates of the hospital, the merchants and bystanders questioned by journalists from all around the world had nothing but kind words for the king they called "brother." We were far from the demonstrations of hatred that had taken place in front of the New York Hospital.

The medical team was being formed during this time, under the direction of Dr. Taha Abdel Aziz, President Sadat's personal physician, in whom I immediately felt great confidence. Once again I will leave it to Professor Flandrin to relate the conditions under which this team finally performed the long-awaited splenectomy on Friday, 28 March 1980:

> I learned, like everybody else, that H. M. had left Panama for Cairo. The telephone rang at home as I thought it might. H. M. the Queen was asking me to join them in Cairo.
>
> When I left, I did not know exactly what was going to happen. Once in Cairo, I learned that DeBakey and his team had been invited to return. I suppose he knew it when he left Panama. The team arrived, what is more, with reinforcements, still including the self-assured Australian assistant, the anesthesiologist, the nurse, and also a team of biologists replacing Jane Hester, who was definitely put out of contention. Add to all that the Kean-Williams duo, who arrived shortly afterwards. I visited H. M. who had been hospitalized in the Maadi military hospital. From his window you could see the Nile and in the distance the pyramids of Giza, the little town on the outskirts

of Cairo, where my ancestor, Joseph Flandrin, was appointed governor by General Bonaparte during the Egyptian expedition. I thought of all of that while I was at this other monarch's bedside. The scenery had changed since I had looked out from the island of Contadora to the ocean and the flying pelicans, but the medical problem might also have changed. He looked much the same as in Panama, but a month had passed with nothing done and four months of almost no treatment since Mexico.

H. M. seemed relieved to see me. What I said to him was optimistic and encouraging. Both logic and ethics led me to affirm all the hopes I placed in Professor DeBakey. I was beginning to wonder if the logic of my attitude, decided a month earlier, was still valid, but I could not stop the momentum and the best thing I could do in the present state of things was to affirm my solidarity with the team.

The whole hierarchy of the Egyptian Health Department was on deck, headed by a cardiologist, President Sadat's personal physician. The courteousness and calm of this man, Dr. Taha Abdel Aziz, were a great help to me later when there was friction between the French team and the Egyptian doctors. I found an old friend there, Dr. Amin Afifi, a hematologist with the Egyptian team and the son-in-law of President Sadat.

Now nothing stood in the way of the splenectomy, which was done by DeBakey with the help of his Australian assistant and some Egyptian surgeons, among whom was Dr. Nour. The splenectomy was done swiftly and the spleen was large. I insisted on a liver biopsy, which was done. The assessment of spread carried out during the abdominal exploration did not seem to show any apparent lymphoid enlargements. I was in the operating theater, but far from the operating area, which was obviously surrounded by the whole surgical team. I therefore did not see the operation in detail. Nour told me later that when the splenic hilum was being resected, he saw

> that the extremity of the pancreas had been injured. He told DeBakey to drain and not suture, but he did not do so. When the operation was over, the surgeon was applauded as he left the operating block. H. M. the Queen and her elder son followed the operation on a television screen on the floor above.
>
> For the first two days, the results were normal. On the third or fourth day, the patient began to have thoracic pain, low posterior left, with scapular referred pain. That seemed strange to me and I told DeBakey of my fears about what was happening in the splenic space. The Australian assistant sent me packing with a curt reply. DeBakey took him to task immediately, saying more or less, 'Be careful. When Georges says something, there is usually a reason for it!' Shortly afterwards I saw the histological preparations of what had been removed in the operation. The spleen was full of tumerous nodules indicating localizations of the large cell lymphoma. As one might logically have suspected, the liver was the site of periportal nodular lesions of the same kind. More serious than that, a fragment of glandular tissue—pancreatic—was included in the hilum, and I had microscopic proof of it. It was while talking to my friend Afifi that I heard of the incident Nour had observed. I went back to Paris after spending a week in Cairo, leaving DeBakey and his team behind and fearing, like Nour, that a subphrenic abscess was forming.

At the beginning of the operation I was actually too upset, and had turned my head away when the incision was made, but after that my eyes did not leave the television screen. I would have given anything to pass on some of my strength and health to my husband. Reza was indeed sitting beside me. The spleen was enormous: it weighed 1 kilo 900 grams. The king felt a little better, but I was shattered to learn that the doctors had found cancerous cells in the liver. I knew that when the liver is affected, chances of recovery are very slim.

Despite persistent pain, my husband seemed to be slowly improving, and soon the doctors allowed him to leave the hospital. And despite my pessimistic outlook at the time, seeing this man who was so dear to me slowly walking along the paths in the grounds of Kubbeh Palace seemed like a real blessing from heaven. He was alive, he had survived the illness that was consuming him, he had survived the unbearable cruelty of history. We had to make the most of this fire that kept him going. But for how much longer?

Since we were all together again, we decided to stay that way and, as President Sadat and his wife recommended, we enrolled our children in schools in Cairo, on the understanding that the two eldest would finish the year begun in the United States. And so Leila and Ali-Reza went to the Cairo American College from that spring 1980.

It was then that the very painful question of the succession to my husband began to arise. Reza was aware of how seriously ill the king was and conscious of the weighty responsibilities that could shortly fall on his shoulders, but how could I bring up the subject without bluntly talking about his father's death? One day he confided in me about it. He told me that he intended to fully take on his task when the day came, to serve his country as his father had done, to fight and to die if necessary for the welfare of the people who today were under the yoke of fanatical, medieval clerics. I can still remember his words: "I am my father's heir. Life has no other meaning for me than the service of Iran. I am ready to sacrifice myself for my country. If I succeed, so much the better; if not, at least I will have tried. I am not afraid to die." He felt that he needed to hear his father's advice, but how could this conversation be arranged without making my husband feel that we had given up hope for his recovery? It was not humanly possible.

After thinking about it for a few days, I suggested to Reza that he seek the advice of President Sadat, who was then like a brother to me and an uncle to my children. As the president was in Alexandria, we went there together. He listened to us with that genuine concern that is so rare in the great and powerful of this world and very quickly found the solution. "Ask the king," he advised us, "who are the men he would like to have around him today. For Reza, just naming these men will be like a legacy from his father. He will be able to call on them in the future; they will show him the way as his father would have done if his health had permitted."

A few weeks went by in an atmosphere of unreality. Some days I saw my husband smile and I felt that he was a little better and his mind was clear, and I would take heart in spite of everything. To those who called me, I said, "Be confident. The king is slowly recovering. We must have hope for the future." But the next day he would not have the strength to get up, and I was overcome with anxiety. However, the younger children were happy, happy in their new school where the teachers and children were very nice to them, and happy to have us with them when they came home. All the palace staff and the security men showed them great affection. I did not want to spoil these moments that were now so precious, and so I contained myself, praying the Lord to give me the strength not to give in. We did homework together in the evening, like any other family. Sometimes the older ones went out after dinner with friends. I could hear them laughing as they left. That is what it was like from day to day: hope and despair, being acutely aware that every happy moment should be treasured.

During these same weeks, several Iranian personalities met the king. I remember in particular the visit from Mehdi Rouhani, a former air force general. The general passed on certain information about resistance movements to my husband. The king had stayed in contact with General Oveissi, who had set up a resistance network made up principally of soldiers, several of whom were still serving in Iran. The king also received my former chief secretary, Houshang Nahavandi, who was active in the resistance. A little later, after the second operation my husband was to have, General Bahram Aryana, former Chief of Staff, came to his bedside to express his loyalty. General Aryana had also set up a resistance network from Paris and he wanted to inform the king, who had only a few more weeks to live. My memory of that meeting is full of emotion. Lastly, we were greatly touched by the visit of Prince Bernhard of the Netherlands, who came specially to bring comfort and support.

Little by little, the king's strength began to fade and the fever returned, his temperature rising higher and higher. He had been given so many transfusions and antibiotics that there was not one vein intact. He lost his appetite. The children tried unsuccessfully to amuse him; I tried to coax him to eat, but he could no longer swallow a thing. The doctors could not agree on the cause of the fever and the terrible weakness. Dr. Coleman talked of possible salmonellosis. Professor Flandrin maintained that in his opinion the king was developing an abscess. Those close to DeBakey thought it was pneumonia. He had to go to the hospital once more.

I called Dr. Flandrin again, and this is how he describes the final struggle:

> I had no more firsthand news from Cairo, but I was kept informed in Paris by an Iranian friend who was very close to the family. What I heard was rather puzzling, for as time passed, I thought that my hypothesis was not likely to be right: the situation would have deteriorated much sooner. There seemed to be a constant coming and going of American doctors. I had more precise information

later on, directly from H. M. the Queen, and once again everything seemed to fit in with the development of a subphrenic abscess. I told her Dr. DeBakey would have to be called back, because we were heading for disaster. I think I understood that he didn't see any point in coming back and that he simply asked for X-rays of the abdomen to be sent to him. Through my Iranian friend, I continued to express my surprise and my pessimistic outlook, which was all the more understandable as he was describing a continuous deterioration. Kean seems to have left the game very early, and Morton Coleman, the New York oncologist, had come back into play with other American doctors. They were no more inclined than DeBakey to accept the hypothesis of a subphrenic abscess, and a later reading of the file revealed to me that they had gone after the fever with a wild escalation of antibiotics. All to no effect, obviously. For reasons which can no doubt be explained, I was, for all practical purposes, kept out of the game that was in progress. The last news my Iranian friend gave me was quite disastrous. He did not hide the fact that he feared the worst, and I told him that under those conditions all was lost. All that had been going on for nearly three months; I clearly no longer had any part to play in the medical problem. I had taken up my work at Saint Louis Hospital again, and I sent a request to Cairo for permission to go away. I had taken practically no holidays for six years, apart from a short stay with my parents, where I was always within reach of the telephone. I wanted to psychologically cut off. Permission was granted, and I left with my wife to stay with one of my sisters in Nantes. But I did leave her telephone number on an answering machine, as a last gesture of conscience.

We wanted to go to Belle-Île, which I had never seen, but a violent storm kept us in Nantes for two days. It was then I received a call telling me to come to Cairo immediately and to bring an "internist" with me. I arranged this with a colleague, then I had a second call telling me that in fact they wanted a respirologist who could do a fiberoptic bronchoscopy. I was just about to go back to Paris. Once in Paris I was finally joined late at night by Professor Philippe Even, whom I knew, and I explained the situation to him. He said to me, "I have just the man you need, my assistant Dr. Hervé Sors. I'll tell him." Next morning at Roissy airport I noticed a young man carrying a box that looked like a clarinet case. No doubt about it: that must be the fiberscope. And indeed it was. We introduced ourselves and I gave him a quick rundown of the whole story. The request for the fiberoptic endoscopy seemed to fit in with a hypothesis of an abscess on the lung. Before seeing the problem, Sors thought that there had been a pleural reaction above the subphrenic abscess, which proved to be right.

When we reached Cairo, H. M. was not dying, strictly speaking, since he still found the strength to joke with us, Sors and me, about us looking like young men. He said to someone who was in the room, referring to me, "Guess how old he is." I was forty-seven at the time, and he made a great game of seeing people take ten years off my age. But the situation was indeed disastrous. The patient had the facial appearance of someone with a serious infection. There was in fact a pleuro-pulmonary reaction to the subdiaphragmatic infection, which was only too apparent. Sors was positive before he did the fiberoptic endoscopy: the problem was subdiaphragmatic. He did the procedure, which showed nothing abnormal, as predicted. After three months, could something still be done, given this scenario of subdiaphragmatic suppuration? The problem was the surgeon. I did not object to the Egyptians a priori, but not everyone was capable of doing what had to be done. Thanks to Sors, who got in touch with some resuscitators in Paris, a few names were suggested. I had to act quickly, as it was 30 June, and I feared that people would be going away for the French school holidays.

Following advice, I began by contacting Dr. Pierre-Louis Fagniez, who worked at Henri Mondor and who had practiced this difficult "secondhand" surgery. I was told that he advocated an original and effective procedure for tackling such problems of infected pancreatic necrosis. Thanks to the solidarity and kindness of the colleagues consulted, I reached this choice and was able to contact Fagniez at home at the beginning of that Saturday afternoon. He accepted and was able to take the plane for Cairo the next morning. He brought his anesthesiologist with him. I went to meet him at the airport and met this slim, smiling, and relaxed young man on whom we pinned our last hopes.

He quickly saw the solution, confirmed my hypotheses, and explained his position to H. M. He drew him a little anatomical diagram, explaining what he was going to do. H. M. agreed and said, making the appropriate gesture, "Yes. Now we have to take the bull by the horns!" The patient was dehydrated and had to be "topped up" before the anesthetic. Our Egyptian colleagues remained fairly passive, without looking really happy about this new invasion of their territory. As it turned out, they were helpful. In the morning, before going into the operating theater, Fagniez had a conversation with H. M. the Queen to get her formal consent. She had called DeBakey, who was in Belgium at that time, and he had replied that he did not see any objection to the French surgeon stepping in, but he would like to talk to him on the telephone. H. M. the Queen had another call put in to DeBakey, but on that occasion he was not available. H. M. the Queen asked Fagniez to carry on regardless and operate.

There was a crowd in the operating theater: Fagniez, the anesthesiologists, the usual people handling the instruments, the Egyptian surgeons, including Dr. Nour, who were assisting, but many others besides. Fagniez counted thirty-five people! He made a sign to me to do something about it. I gave the example by leaving myself and asking all those who were not involved to leave also. That left about fifteen remaining. I stayed in a small room next door, going in from time to time to see what was happening. Using Fagniez's technique, he had made a limited left subcostal incision to proceed directly to where the pus had collected. After a moment he sent for me; I was gowned and went in. Fagniez and the Egyptian surgeons were all beaming. They were in the process of draining a liter and a half of pus and necrosed pancreas debris. I went out of the operating theater. The news had gone all around the operating block. I went down to the floor below, where H. M. the Queen was waiting in the corridor with Princess Ashraf. I told her what they had found. They spontaneously expressed their joy and relief. H. M. the Queen said to me in her excitement, "Go up and see Dr. Fagniez right away and sing the *Marseillaise* in his ear."

Unfortunately one had to look a lot further. I thought of Mexico again and all the mess-up that was. Could anything still be rescued? Fagniez had only performed a masterly application of Hippocrates' saying: after the Americans' "water," he had applied "iron" to drain the abscess...As for the rest, it should have been possible to apply "fire." The whole cancer problem was still in abeyance, and this fundamental problem had been virtually neglected since Mexico. What followed would be terrible, and it was never possible to resume treatment.

That night and the ones that followed, I slept in the hospital in a room adjoining my husband's. I left the door open all the time, so that I could always be sure that he was breathing, that he was alive. His heartbeats, amplified by the monitor, accompanied my own breath in and out.

All I have left from those sleepless nights—filled with anxiety, the children's distress, and my own—are these semi-comatose lines written in my notebook:

> 5 July. Midnight. I'm afraid tonight. I'm afraid. I don't know if it's lack of sleep or a terrible foreboding. My husband is asleep. I don't know what I'm writing any more, or even in what language. Sometimes I'm swamped by it all, floating between strength and weakness, between acceptance, resignation, and revolt. What day of the week is it? None of us knows. I go from one room to the other. It just kills me to see my husband lying so weak and skeletonlike in his hospital bed. The people in the corridor all look so anxious. Our hearts fill with hope a hundred times a day only to have it dashed immediately afterwards. I haven't the right to give way; I have to find a few words for everyone.

Dr. Fagniez's operation was a success, and my husband was soon able to sit up and then get up. Some Iranians begged to be allowed to see him; after a few days he was able to receive a few people. The former labor secretary came to his bedside to talk about the difficulties of resistance. He said that they needed to explain what Iranian identity was and the essential place the monarchy occupied in history. He would stay in Egypt to teach the crown prince the social geography of Iran.* Staying there, close to my husband, I was overcome by the fervor of the people who came to beg an opinion or advice from this man who was so ill. It occurred to me that he might like me to read to him. He accepted with pleasure and I read him part of the memoirs of General de Gaulle. We had met him together twenty years earlier and he had always remained an example of courage and determination to my husband. He spoke very little now, and in very short sentences.

He was aware of his state, his extreme frailty, and also of what was going on around him. As this month of July was the month of Ramadan, the hospital staff had set up a temporary dining room

*Mr. Shafa took charge of teaching history and another person supervised Persian literature.

with a big table at the end of the corridor so that they could eat in the evening. If he was in the area at that time, he would say to me, "Let's go back to my room. If I stay there they'll feel uncomfortable and won't break their fast in peace." I thought to myself, "There he is, transcending his own state right into the evening of his life, forgetting his own suffering to help others."

Jehan Sadat has kept this memory of those last days, which touches me deeply:

> The Shah was thinner and paler now than I had ever seen him. He breathed only with the greatest difficulty. Yet there was nothing pathetic about him, nothing at all weak. On the contrary, you could tell even by the way he sat against the pillows on his bed that he was still a fighter. The doctors had said that he was in great pain from his cancer. But never did the Shah complain. God must have loved this man to give him the strength to bear hardships so gracefully, I thought as I stood by him in the intensive-care unit.
>
> "Soon you will be better and we will spend a lovely time together in Alexandria," I said to the Shah. I looked at the tears in Farah's eyes. "Be brave. Don't show him your feelings," I said to her. "He is very intelligent and will understand."*

Some nights I would look at the Nile and the pyramids outlined in the distance. I thought to myself, "Kings, governors, and generals in their time have seen this site, this beautiful light, this river. They have lived, they have been happy, they were loved and also betrayed, and then they passed away. Now we are here, and we in our turn will pass away, while the Nile will continue to flow for thousands of years to come." That helped me to accept fate as it unfolded.

*Jehan Sadat, *A Woman of Egypt.*

The king seemed to miraculously regain his strength, so much so that on 26 July I decided to send our three youngest children to Alexandria. I wanted to get them out of the terribly tense hospital atmosphere in which they had lived for a month.

Then that same night my husband suddenly sank into a kind of coma. Professor Flandrin wrote later:

> It was during the fast, and in Egypt, this country of strict observance, there was no question of changing people's habits. We would go back to the Hotel Meridien late in the afternoon and only return to the Maadi Hospital at night, once the fast had been broken and our driver had eaten. And so that evening we were eating at the Meridien, but I had been worried and tense for a few days. As if by some foreboding, I urged Fagniez and our resuscitator not to linger, so that we could go back to Maadi as soon as possible. When we arrived on the floor, there was an unusual silence and a general atmosphere of consternation. The patient's condition had suddenly deteriorated, everyone seemed in a state of paralysis, and we had not been informed of the event, which must have happened scarcely two hours before. The patient had no pulse, no blood pressure, in a context of sudden massive internal hemorrhage. The stunned state of the family and the entourage seemed to have affected the whole medical organization. The marvelous Egyptian nurses who had been our mainstay were now filled with dismay, or in tears and directionless. The Egyptian doctors were not there, doubtless for the same reasons as we; they must have been at home breaking their fast.
>
> This spectacle mobilized our resuscitator into instant action, with Fagniez and myself assisting. A short time after we had recalled the Egyptian anesthesiologist, who had been a great support all along and who got the blood we needed (the resources of the military hospital were working at full capacity),

the patient regained consciousness. I went out into the corridor to join H. M. the Queen and Her Highness Princess Ashraf. Everyone felt indescribably emotional and, even with the passing of time, I can still feel it again myself. Everyone seemed dismayed. Then the incident took place that upset me most in this whole long story, for it concerned not the person who was dying but those who were going to live.

I explained the situation to H. M. the Queen and the Princess. We knew that the end would come that night and I told them so. I asked the Queen to inform the children. It just so happens that they had left that very day for Alexandria. There had been a certain euphoria in the air for a few days, as the king had been able to walk and sit in the improvised dining room at the end of the corridor. The two eldest at least had to be contacted as quickly as possible. H. M. the Queen agreed and asked me to let them know.

I did not understand and said, "But Your Majesty, it's not up to me. Your Majesty should tell them!"

In the grip of so much emotion she replied, "No, it's not possible. I'll never manage it."

I tried again. "But Your Majesty, there must be someone else, someone in the family."

She said to me, "There's no one but you. You must do it."

And so I had to control my own feelings and call Alexandria. I remember especially getting straight on to the elder daughter, Princess Farahnaz, who said to me in her little girl's voice, "Oh, it's you, Doctor. How are things going?" I had to tell her that actually things were not going well at all, and it was not easy. Thanks to our resuscitator, the king was fully conscious for a few hours and could speak at length with his wife, the Queen; Princess Ashraf, his twin sister; the Crown Prince; and his other children.

> I remember in particular the poignant scene of the older girl, Farahnaz, kneeling close to the right side of the bed, holding her father's hand and kissing it, with a kind of ecstatic smile on her face as she repeated in Persian, "*Baba, Baba.*" On the left side of the bed, we continued to watch the arterial blood pressure and to pump blood. We did only what was necessary, and the king passed away peacefully in the morning. While I was there, H. M. the Queen withdrew a little bag of Iranian soil from under the pillow of the deceased—they had brought it with them when they went into exile.
>
> While all that was happening, and in the midst of all that emotion and pain, the sight of Crown Prince Reza during the night and in the morning was quite amazing. This new successor was a very young man, but from the dignity of his bearing and the self-control he showed then, he knew what was involved in his new role. He spoke to me at length, and in the morning I gave him a copy of all the documents in my possession. I remember that he said to me on the subject of my colleagues and myself, "People may say what they like, but I will remember what I have seen."

Yes, Farahnaz was indeed by her father's bedside, Reza was at the foot, and I was standing on the other side, near the doctors. The king breathed quickly twice, then drew in a long breath and stopped. It was over. We all just stood there dazed for a while. Then Princess Ashraf, who was standing at the foot of the bed, whispered to me, "Close his eyes." I did that and then took the little bag of Iranian soil and the prayers we had put under his pillow. For the whole of his life he had carried these prayers on him in a cloth bag. Dr. Lioussa Pirnia then took off the king's wedding ring and gave it to me. I have worn it on the same finger as my own ever since.

We were asked to leave the room then, a moment later. We could go in one by one and kiss the king for the last time. As I put my lips to his forehead, I had a furtive, momentary feeling that he was alive.

The news of his death had plunged the few people standing in the corridor—Iranians for the most part—into a mood of silent dismay. We shared the same grief. "The king is no longer with us," I told them, "but we must not lose heart. We must continue the fight and follow his lead." Then I telephoned my Aunt Louise, who was living in Paris. I did not want her to hear the news on the radio.

Now we had to tell the two youngest, who had spent the night in Kubbeh Palace, that their father had died. When we arrived at the palace, we were very touched to see President Sadat, and his wife and daughter there. The three of them were waiting to be the first to bring us the affection and comfort they had constantly shown us since our first day of exile. The governess told me that as soon as Leila woke up, she went straight in to Ali-Reza as if she had sensed something. She was very close to him. And so they heard the news together from their governess while we were on our way back to the hospital. "Your father is in heaven with the angels," she told them. Leila went out of the room without showing any of her grief, and when her governess went into her bedroom, she found her laying her black clothes out on her bed.

That evening I felt I couldn't get through the night alone and asked the children to join me. Reza, Farahnaz, and Leila came straightaway; Ali-Reza wanted to be alone with his sorrow. We put mattresses on the floor and slept there huddled together.

THE FUNERAL TOOK PLACE on 29 July 1980, two days after the king's death. His body lay in Abdin Palace as they played the imperial anthem. Hearing it made us all extremely emotional, for it was the first time we had heard it since our departure from Iran. The cortege accompanying the body left Abdin Palace in oppressive heat for the El Rifaï Mosque, which would be my husband's provisional resting place. In Muslim countries women traditionally do not walk behind the coffin, but I insisted on being present. President Sadat told his protocol officers, "We will do as Farah wishes."

Lying on a horse-drawn gun carriage, the king's coffin was hailed the length of the journey by a huge crowd chanting, "*La elaha ella Allah*" ("Allah is the only God"). We were at the head of the cortege. On my right were Leila in a white dress, Farahnaz, and Ali-Reza; on my left were Richard Nixon and my elder son, Reza. Then President Sadat of Egypt, Jehan Sadat, and the king's brothers Gholam-Reza, Abdol-Reza, and Ahmad-Reza were around us. Some faithful friends, King Constantine of Greece and Queen Anne-Marie and Prince Victor Emmanuel of Savoy followed us among the ambassadors representing certain countries. King Hassan II had sent one of his closest relations, Moullay Hafid Aloui, who brought a piece of embroidered cloth that had covered the Kaaba stone in Mecca and was to be placed on my husband's shroud.

At the El Rifaï Mosque the king's body was taken down into a special underground vault. Reza accompanied it, then Ali-Reza decided to go too without asking anyone's permission, although it was not scheduled. Doctors told me later how important it was for him to see where his father lay. The women unfortunately were not allowed to go down, so that neither Farahnaz, Leila, nor I saw the king arrive at his final resting place. I have a very moving memory of Air Force Lt. General Rouhani who told me how sad he was to be the only representative of the army to have made the long journey there.

Jehan wrote in her memoirs:

> No state funeral was grander. Anwar organized it all himself, overseeing even the smallest details. Thousands of students from our military academy led the procession, all playing instruments and dressed in uniforms of white, yellow and black according to their rank. Next marched soldiers carrying wreaths of roses, irises, followed by officers mounted on horseback. Then came a squadron of men carrying the Shah's military decorations on black velvet pillows, preceding the coffin itself, which was wrapped in the Iranian flag drawn by eight Arabian horses on a military caisson. We followed behind.
>
> It was very, very hot that summer day in Cairo as we marched the three miles from the 'Abdin Palace to el-Rifa'i Mosque, where the Shah would be buried. The Shah's father too had been buried here before the Shah took his remains home to Iran. At Anwar's direction I marched with Farah, the first and only time I have ever marched in a funeral procession. "Do whatever Farah does," Anwar had told me. "We must help her get through this most sad and difficult day." And so I stayed beside her, marching with my children and her children.
>
> Behind us for as far as we could see stretched the rest of those who honored the Shah's memory. All the ministers of the Egyptian government marched with us, as did former President Nixon of the United States, former King Constantine of Greece, ambassadors from the United States, West Germany, France, Australia and Israel, and countless Egyptian citizens. People lined the streets, the balconies and the rooftops to watch the procession pass. The music was louder than any they had ever heard. There

> were more flowers than anyone had ever imagined. It was the most spectacular funeral that any of us in Egypt had ever seen, and the last chance to show the world that the Shah deserved better than the way he had been treated. Egypt, at least, had not turned her back on a friend.*

I remember coming back to Kubbeh Palace after that very taxing day and thinking how I would tell the king that I had borne myself well, that I had managed to keep my dignity and walk tall despite being blinded by grief from beginning to end. It was strange: I couldn't believe that he was no longer there, that he would never be there anymore. I had to admire the children: they had gone through it all with dignity, holding back their tears or managing to hide them.

*Of all the kings, heads of state, and foreign dignitaries who had known my husband over the thirty years of his reign, none came to Cairo to pay their last respects—none, that is, with the exception of Richard Nixon and Constantine of Greece. The French president Valéry Giscard d'Estaing later wrote these touching words in his memoirs: "I looked at the images of the ceremony in *Paris Match*: President Sadat, with his tall, Nubian silhouette, leading the cortege—and the marked absence of anyone else. I, too, was absent. I never forgave myself that decision. Intellectually, I never doubted that it was justified, but, even if it was necessary, deep inside of me—in the place where one's self-esteem is made or broken—I still cannot forgive myself for it."

PART FIVE

Chapter 19

WE WERE THREE months away from Reza's twentieth birthday, the age when the Constitution allowed him to succeed his father, and during these three months I was regent.* I quickly realized that it was not in name only. The day after the king's

*As I was there and witnessed the king's deepest thoughts during his last days, I considered it my duty to put together the following words the day after he died. I believe they show what my husband was feeling and what he would have liked to say to his fellow countrymen and -women before he passed away:

> At this time when I am living the last moments of my life, far from my native land and in the grip of this horrible illness, I send this message to my people, who are experiencing one of the darkest periods in their history. Remember that our country has gone through highs and lows, but that foreign attacks have never been able to extinguish the torch of Iranian culture and civilization. I am convinced that this torch will banish the gloom that has fallen over Iran, and that a national revival will come. I hope that my son, who is still very young and filled with national pride, like all young Iranians, will raise the sacred flag of Iran and keep it held high with the support of the Iranian people. I trust the young Crown Prince to Almighty God and to the great people of Iran. This is my last wish.

funeral, I had to take on the relations he had kept up with resistance networks in many places of the world. Requests for talks increased. All these men who had chosen exile to carry on the fight—former ministers, political officials, officers, ordinary militants—wanted to suggest plans, seek my advice or my support for various projects. At the time, I was rather annoyed with them for not leaving me in peace during the time of mourning, but on reflection, I think their activism and their enthusiasm saved me from the deep despair that could well have overcome me.

The main resistance groups were in France, Great Britain, and the United States, but there were also some in Germany and Turkey. All those in charge had their own ideas on what should be done to join battle, and they naturally hoped to gain my approval. Some wanted to meet in person and in secret. We also had telephone conversations at all hours of the day and night. Sometimes I had to wait until 2 or 3 A.M. to talk to the United States. These discussions were often difficult, exhausting exchanges in which I had to give my opinion on a plan without being fully informed about how reliable the operation was. We had to fight, even if there were not many of us at the beginning.

With his usual generosity, President Sadat invited me to stay on in Kubbeh Palace for as long as I liked. It was in one of the wings of the palace, at the end of a passage with broken windows, littered with discarded furniture, that we set up our first office. It was absolutely necessary to coordinate and manage the burgeoning activism of Iranians in exile. We were quickly joined by two young women—first Leila Fouladvand, then Lillian Ristak—who looked after the office together. Both of them dropped everything in their lives to come work with us and their unstinting dedication has been invaluable. We were also joined by a French journalist and his assistant Marie-Christiane to coordinate media communications.

To receive people who did not want to be seen in Cairo for security reasons, the Egyptian state gave me permission to use an apartment about forty minutes away from Kubbeh Palace. All these comings and goings in the noise and heat of the capital were exhausting, and I constantly had to make a real effort to stand the strain. I also had to undergo a painful operation at that time and, in spite of everything I was suffering, I can still see myself receiving people, listening, discussing, trying always to show that I am paying attention, and giving hope to those who come to consult me.

I brought my elder son, Reza, into these meetings, knowing that he would soon have the sole responsibility for coordinating the various activities of the Iranian community in exile. We went to President Sadat together for his opinion and advice, and we also met with King Hussein and Queen Noor of Jordan and King Hassan II of Morocco during that time. They all made themselves available to see us and received us very warmly. All through our exile and to this day, Queen Noor would remain a dear friend.

Our greatest achievement in those distracted months was to set up an underground radio where exiles' voices could be heard, allowing us to gather and disseminate information on what was really happening in Iran and to give news of the various opposition groups. The idea for this radio station had come to us while my husband was alive. We had spoken about it together and he had agreed to it. When we asked the Egyptian authorities, they also gave their permission. But it was up to us to get the project off the ground. Given the atmosphere of suspicion that had surrounded us from the first day of our exile, this initiative represented an added danger. We were very conscious of it, and I remember that we avoided talking about the project inside the palace for fear of being overheard. Kambiz Atabaï was now running my office, and if we wanted to talk about it, we went out into the grounds. Secrecy had to be maintained out of respect for the Egyptian government, and besides, we did not want it known that I was behind this project. It was necessary, however, to define the political line and the tone of our future radio station and, of course, to find courageous professionals able to run it at the risk of their lives. For all these questions, we discreetly asked the advice of my cousin Reza Ghotbi, who had organized and managed Iranian television. He was now in exile in Paris, where he had set up a resistance network. The basic principle was to unite all Iranians in exile against the new regime, whatever differences they may have. This radio would be the voice of all, and all could make their voices heard.

Two men and a woman were hired to form the first small editorial staff, because they had worked in Iranian radio and television. We rented an apartment in Cairo under an assumed name, and the trio discreetly moved in. They took European names to avert suspicion, even though their voices were known in Iran, and they went out as little as possible, not wanting to attract attention. Their work consisted of collating and then broadcasting the innumerable documents and testimonies that we received from the whole community in exile, but also from inside Iran. Many cassettes were recorded, especially in Paris, where we had correspondents, and then sent to Cairo. We also had correspondents in the Emirates of the Persian Gulf and an informant in Germany who had a network of correspondents in Iran. We received reports written in invisible ink from our country.

It took nine months of work before we were ready to broadcast. I remember how thrilled I was on the day Mr. Atabaï came and told me that we had made it; our voice could now be heard on the airwaves. I picked up a little radio and ran into my bedroom, shutting myself in to listen. I flung open the window, I was so happy. That voice was like a first step toward freedom, a first victory.

In the meantime we had celebrated Reza's twentieth birthday, and therefore his symbolic accession to the throne, on 31 October 1980 in Kubbeh Palace. The Iran-Iraq war had broken out a month earlier and, all too conscious of the new misfortune that had just befallen our country, we reduced the ceremony to the bare minimum. Before only one TV camera and one journalist from the print media, my elder son said, among other things, these few words of hope:

> My dear countrymen and -women, sisters and brothers, this supreme responsibility has been entrusted to me after the sad passing of my illustrious father, in one of the darkest periods in our history, at the very time when our national and spiritual principles, our historical and cultural values, our civilization, are threatened from within; at the very time when anarchy, economic collapse, and the decline of our international prestige have given rise to the violation of our territorial integrity by foreign aggression, which we condemn.
>
> I am well aware that none of you, whose national pride and patriotic spirit are inborn, that none of you who are deeply attached to your national identity, your faith, the sacred principles of true Islam, your historical values, and your cultural heritage, has wanted such a disaster to come about. That is why, understanding your suffering and sensing your unshed tears, I join in your pain. I know that, like me, you can see the calm dawn of a new day rising through this darkness. I know also that deep in your souls and hearts you have the firm conviction that, as in the past, our history, which is several thousands of years old, will repeat itself and the nightmare will end. Light will follow darkness. Strengthened by our bitter experiences, we will all join together in a great national effort, the reconstruction of our country. With the help of the right reforms and the active participation of all, we will realize our ideals.

> We will rebuild a new Iran, where equality, liberty, and justice prevail. Inspired by the true faith of Islam founded on spirituality, love, and mercy, we will make Iran a proud and prosperous country, having the place it deserves in the concert of nations.

A few weeks earlier Reza had made known to the authorities in Tehran that he was ready to go back to fight against the Iraqi invaders as a fighter pilot. "At this crucial moment in the life of our country," he wrote, "I would like to offer my blood to save the inviolability of our dear native land." We had spent the night sending his message by telex to various ministers in Tehran. Some cut off communication, others accepted the whole text, but none replied. I had made public a communiqué in which I declared: "As an Iranian and mother of the Crown Prince, conscious of the historic responsibilities which now rest on my shoulders, I express the hope that the tragic events we are witnessing today will soon come to an end, and that the foreign forces that think they can invade Iran with impunity will learn once and for all that this land belongs to Iranians. Iranians will never tolerate the presence of foreign forces on their soil."

When my elder son assumed his responsibilities, a confused, difficult period began all around us. When some people learned that the power had changed hands, they immediately turned to Reza and visited him at the palace without even having the courtesy to come and say a word to me. It was hurtful, but so revealing of human nature that I gave a rueful smile. However, there were others who continued to speak only to me, as if nothing had happened, and I remember that in this situation I decided to look down in a fairly obvious way, so that the person would realize that he or she should now talk to my son, who was sitting beside me. I wanted to show quite clearly that henceforth all decisions were made by the young king and that I stayed with him only to help him with my experience and advice.

This was not understood at first. Some leaders came and begged me not to withdraw, pointing out that having reigned for twenty years, I could not abandon them at such a crucial time. That placed me in a difficult situation, as I did not want to give these people, who trusted me and were fighting for the cause in secret, the feeling that I was taking no further interest in it. I constantly had to explain that I was still involved in the resistance, but now under my son's authority. "If you trust me," I would tell them, "trust my decision."

Then came pressure for me to intervene in the composition of my son's cabinet, to introduce someone to him, to please exclude someone else. There again I had to explain how important it was for the success of the young king for him to choose his colleagues himself, calmly and quite independently. I felt that Reza wanted to try his wings, something which naturally should be encouraged. "Give him time to find the people he feels he can trust and work with."

In this difficult climate, where rival ambitions came into play, what I secretly feared came to pass: there were some who tried to make trouble between my son and myself. I kept in touch with the different resistance groups, but I did not want my son's name attached to one group rather than another, and it was this they could not forgive. They all wanted to gain the young king's favor, so that they could obtain the benefits of his patronage. They therefore tried to neutralize my influence by persuading Reza that I bore a large responsibility for the fall of the monarchy because my ideas had been too "liberal" and I had supposedly influenced my husband. These malicious rumors were spread by people I considered corrupt and whose actions had done a great deal of harm to the monarchy. All this play for influence around my son, who was still so young, was very painful for me. He could not see the ambition, the treachery, and the underhanded motives behind it. I thought that one day he would understand, that he needed time to take stock of things, and I told myself once again that I had to bear it. Bear it with dignity. On days when it all seemed too hurtful, too unfair, I would try to cling to what was most important. "We are fighting for the future of Iran," I would say to myself. "Our cause is huge and deserves every sacrifice we have to make. The rest is minor."

After a few months Reza expressed the wish to go and live in Morocco with his entourage. I realized that he wanted to move away to affirm his independence, which was quite legitimate, but it seemed a pity to me to leave Egypt, which offered him so many avenues for action and influence. Morocco would perhaps not be so well disposed toward him. I told him this, and as it did not seem to sway him, I finally gathered our close colleagues around him to announce that I was prepared to leave Cairo myself. "The main thing now," I told them, "is Iran and not me. It is better for the future of our cause that the young king should stay in Egypt. I am therefore willing to go if my departure will make Reza change his mind." That was not the case, and my son left for Morocco as he wished.

I still have painful memories of this whole period when the fight had to be carried out on all fronts at the same time—personal and political. It sometimes became unbearable, but despite all these difficulties, we managed to reestablish a family life that we had not known since we went into exile. We were all living together once again—at least until Reza's departure—in Kubbeh Palace, which President Sadat generously continued to make available. The children had gone back to their studies and were amazed at the kindness that was shown to them everywhere, as I have said, at school, in the street, in the palace itself, where everyone was very attentive toward them. Coming from the United States, where they had frequently been put down, especially by some teachers, they were relieved to be greeted with smiles and goodwill in Egypt. It was like coming back to our own people, our own family and cultural community, and the unfailing kindness we met helped us to smile and enjoy life again, almost in spite of ourselves.

Living together once more had brought back the children's sense of humor, which had livened up daily life in the Niavaran Palace in Tehran. Once again I heard their laughter; I heard them telling stories and jokes. Some evenings I would sit down with the two youngest, like any other mother, to look at their homework and hear their lessons, and I would see Leila's face light up. After all those chaotic months when she had suffered from my absence while she was still so little, now she could enjoy the pleasure of sharing her schoolgirl's joys and cares with me.

SOMETIMES WE ALL WENT TO DINNER IN A RESTAURANT, to a museum or an art show. Sometimes my mother, who was also with us, would make us an Iranian dinner. She had been there through the happy years and she had stayed with us throughout our exile. The children were very fond of her. Widowed at thirty-six, she had never remarried. She was a beautiful woman, very elegant; she was headstrong but never complained. She always had a positive, encouraging word for the children, as she did for me. "Look on the bright side," she used to say, "and the Good Lord will make it happen for you." As a believer, she was a model of tolerance regarding other religions, and everything the Islamic Revolution preached revolted her. As someone who had joined the fight for the recognition of women very early on, she said that Khomeini was doing incalculable harm to Islam and to the very idea of religion. She died in the autumn of 1999, after briefly placing her hand on my shoulder, as if to show me that she knew I was by her side, even though she no longer recognized anyone.

Cousins and close relatives visited us, officers and former political officials too. I have special memories of the friendship of King Baudouin, President Senghor and the King and Queen of Nepal. And so, outside of the immense difficulties we met in coordinating the various resistance networks, listening to them all, giving hope, sorting out intrigues, life was reasserting itself. We were starting to talk about settling permanently in Cairo when, on 6 October 1981, while I was in Paris for a few days, I learned of Anwar el-Sadat's assassination. These are the words I wrote at that time, and even rereading them now sends me into the despair of that autumn night:

> Paris. 2 A.M. President Sadat has died, assassinated during a military parade. I still can't believe it. How difficult it is to write those words. Part of me has died at the same time. Part of us. Dear Sadat, I would like to tell you how wonderful you were—a father to my children, a friend to me. You were as strong as a mountain and calm as the surface of the water. Your eyes were full of love and understanding for people. What a loss for Egypt, for the world, and for us. You have joined your friend, and we are now orphans for the second time.

Fourteen months after my husband's death, grief brought us all together again behind the Egyptian president's coffin. Jehan's strength amazed me. Although her face was haggard with pain, she still managed to find words and gestures to comfort my children.

Egypt had lost its guide, its conscience, and the general anxiety suddenly became palpable. Would the country sink into chaos? You could see the confusion in people's eyes. After the children left, President Hosni Mubarak and his wife, Suzanne, told me that I was still their guest. I was advised, however, not to leave Kubbeh

Palace and even to avoid going out into the grounds: the authorities were no longer sure of the soldiers guarding it. The murderous fanaticism of the Muslim Brotherhood could be hidden anywhere, including under a military tunic. We stayed shut in for several days, wondering if we would be victims of another insurrection. We were expecting the worst, and were prepared to leave hurriedly at any time of the day or night.

In the United States, Ronald Reagan had just been inaugurated before the authorities in Tehran freed the fifty-two remaining hostages on 20 January 1981.* The new American president informed me that I was now welcome in his country. Without that invitation, we would probably not have left Egypt.

Going back to the United States after what we had experienced there was very painful for me. I remember how dreadful I felt passing by New York Hospital. It all suddenly came back to me: my husband's suffering and his courage, while in the street below opponents shouted their hatred; our secret departure for Lackland Air Force Base, and my distress at the thought that my little Leila would not find me there as usual when she woke up.

Williamstown is three hours from New York by road. I went there by car and remember how much I was affected by the sight of the fast-food outlets, that whole way of life so foreign to ours, which took me back to the worst period of my life.

The house my son had bought was a wooden one, ideal for a student on his own, but not very suitable for a family. The wooden walls meant you could hear every noise; the bedrooms

*After the Algiers Accord to free the hostages between the Islamic Republic and the United States had been signed on 19 January 1981, Washington undertook to give back whatever we possessed in the United States to Iran. Now neither the king nor I owned anything at all in the United States. Nonetheless, the Islamic Republic pursued us for fourteen years, obviously without success. It also lost the lawsuits that it brought against us in England and Switzerland.

were small and there were not enough of them. In the beginning I didn't have the heart to arrange anything. I felt as though I were anesthetized.

I think it came to me slowly how beneficial this forced retirement could be for all of us after two years of suffering and distress. Williamstown is a tiny college town of eight thousand inhabitants and only one main shopping street. It seems strangely distant from the upheavals of the world, a charming little rustic town where the autumns in particular are really splendid. Coming from the extraordinary swarming crowds of Cairo, I had the almost painful feeling of being suddenly deprived of my senses: there was not a sound here, apart from powermowers, no longer any sense of danger, but the impression of a sanitized, bucolic world, utterly safe.

Once the first weeks of settling in were over, the children seemed fairly happy with their new life, especially Leila, who quickly found friends. We had found a private school for her, while Ali-Reza went to the public school. In both cases they were welcomed with much kindness and attention to their needs. Leila's school offered to include Persian in her scholastic program, as it obviously was not taught there. As for me, I now had more time to devote to them. I was there for their homework and to listen to them, happy to share their little day-to-day adventures with them.

Farahnaz, who had passed her baccalaureate in Egypt, was accepted into Bennington College in Vermont. She had the misfortune of meeting a professor who had been the ambassador of the Islamic Republic to the United Nations when the American diplomats were taken hostage in Tehran. She did a paper on the oil industry, certainly a very good piece of work, but this man, who never missed an opportunity to condemn the monarchy, refused to accept her work, claiming that she had not done it alone. This injustice was obviously due to her name and was a forerunner of other rejections.

My elder son had taken the responsibility of running the resistance activities from Morocco, relieving me of a large part of the tasks that had absorbed most of my attention during the months following my husband's death. I remained in touch with the movement through letters which required replies and through various important meetings or conversations on the telephone, but my time was no longer completely filled.

On 10 March 1982 the queen mother died. She had been suffering from leukemia, and we had kept the king's death from her to keep her going. For all that time I had to force myself to give her news of her son as if he were still there with us. I simply said that he was too weak to speak on the telephone and she seemed to believe me, being very frail herself. The queen mother is buried temporarily in New York, next to her grandson, Shahriar.

I WAS SLOWLY LEARNING TO LIVE a more normal life again spending part of the year in Paris and part in the United States. I began to play tennis again, always a great help in hard times. There was a greenhouse nearby, and I started growing some plants. I remember how impatient I was every morning to see how my vegetables were progressing. The people around us—neighbors, business people, tennis partners, security personnel—were very warm and most of them called me by my first name. However, some obviously had no idea of the terrible events we had just lived through; often people were unaware even of the dramatic upheavals taking place in Iran, and that ignorance contributed to our feeling of isolation. One day a young woman who was tasting some pistachios from home said to me in all innocence, "Next time you go to Iran, would you be kind enough to bring me some? They're so good!" What could I say to her? Where would I begin? At the same time I had to have some medical tests. The woman filling out my information sheet obviously did not know me. She asked me if I was married. I told her that my husband was dead and she wrote widow. Then she asked if I was working and I replied no. So then she wrote unemployed, which made me smile as I thought to myself, "You couldn't have put it better."

I received some kind invitations to dinner. The people there talked about plays that they had seen in New York or local events, while I smiled vacantly, thinking that I was definitely from another planet. Yes, I made an effort to laugh, trying to put our displacement into perspective. And how could you not laugh sometimes? An Iranian friend in New York, who had a photo of me in his living room, called me one evening to share his mirth, which had a bitter edge. A guest, the managing director of a company had inquired, "Who is the young woman in the photo?"

"It's our queen," my friend replied.

"Khomeini's wife?" said his guest with surprise.

Another time, when I was in an art gallery in New York, a man came up and spoke to me in a friendly way. "I've been told that you are the shah's wife. I'm very pleased to meet you. Would you mind if I took your photo with my wife?"

"Not at all."

He called his wife over. "Darling, come here and have your photo taken with the shah's wife."

Then, when the photo had been taken, "By the way, you're the shah's wife, but the shah of where?"

On the same day, in the same gallery, a woman struck up a conversation with me in Italian.

"I'm sorry," I interrupted her, "but I don't speak Italian."

"What, you're not Soraya?"

"No," I told her, "I'm the one who comes after her."

These misunderstandings apart, I have not forgotten the sympathy many Americans showed me. On every occasion there were some who found the gestures or the right words to express their solidarity. I am thinking of the workmen outside New York Hospital who demonstrated against the Iranians praying for my husband to die. I received numerous letters from anonymous Americans telling me that they knew what the king had accomplished and they were sad to see the state our country was in. I am thinking of Mary and Robert from Arizona, who write to me faithfully every year; of Dane, a forest warden in North Carolina; of David, an American Indian; of Gary, who chose my first name for his daughter, who is now twenty-seven; of so many others. The American people have taught me to look toward the future and never to feel sorry for myself. I like their stubborn refusal to give in to fate, tears, and despair, and their obstinate faith in the future.

In the mid-eighties I decided to end the isolation, which was rather oppressive and could harm the children's wider development. We wanted to be closer to New York without actually living there. I had heard a lot about the Greenwich area in Connecticut, only about an hour from New York. We found a house there that was more comfortable than the one in Williamstown, big enough for us all, and set in a marvelous garden with all the old trees I could wish for, having come from a country where the vegetation suffers so much from drought. Greenwich is indeed a little corner of paradise for those who love nature and the changing seasons. I would never tire of the autumns when the russet and bronze tones reminded me of autumns in Tehran.

Leila was not very happy to leave her circle of friends yet again, but she grew to like her new school. Ali-Reza, who was starting university, was accepted by Princeton, which made me very proud. He began by studying science but branched out into the history of music, which would be a passion of his. Farahnaz was now a psychology student at Columbia, where she had excellent results. She was living in a little apartment I rented for her. As for Reza, he had left Morocco and also settled in Connecticut, so that we once again took up the habit of celebrating our Iranian New Year as a family.

Finally, life seemed suddenly to smile on us once more after being so cruel for so long: one evening Reza called me to say that he intended to become engaged. A wave of happiness swept through me. He had met a young Iranian girl, Yasmine, some time earlier. Her parents, now exiled in the United States, had owned an agricultural property at Zanjan not far from Tehran before the Islamic Revolution. I was delighted that he had decided to set up a family with a young girl from our culture who had also suffered a lot from the events in Iran. She had left the country when she was nine, and her parents had lost everything. The young people would therefore be of like mind from the beginning.

A few weeks later he introduced Yasmine Etemad-Amini to me. Her beauty and intelligence, together with a great naturalness, touched me from the very first. Her reserve made me think of my own shyness when I had been presented to the queen mother a quarter of a century earlier. I did everything that I could to put her at her ease; I told her how happy I was to see her by my son's side. Then, while trying not to frighten her, I described the responsibilities she would have once she was married to the young king. Remembering my own innocence when I had first known the king, I wanted to protect her from anything that could hurt her. She was only seventeen, but she already showed that she had both strength of character and great serenity.

The wedding was set for 12 June 1986. This was the first time since our departure from Tehran that we would all come together for a happy event and one that brought hope for the future. However, we were still in the midst of the Iran-Iraq war and, out of respect for the suffering of the Iranian people, we decided that the marriage would be celebrated quietly within the family circle. Both families wanted to observe tradition despite being in exile. Yasmine wanted to choose her own wedding dress, to be made by an Iranian dressmaker. And I had discovered an artist, also Iranian, who prepared the traditional tray of colored incense. The wife of one of our guards was taking care of the flowers, and Iranian dishes were prepared by friends in the Iranian community.

The ceremony was dignified and moving. There were only about sixty of us around the young couple, and my sole regret is that I had not dared invite Jehan Sadat because of my concern for modesty and discretion. In her case I should have broken the rule we had adopted of inviting only the close family. During the religious ceremony, we did something that had not been done for my own wedding: happily married women—Yasmine's sisters, Ladan and Niloufar; my aunt, Pouran Diba; and Dr. Pirnia—held the traditional veil above the heads of the couple, while two pieces of sugar were rubbed together over it as a promise of sweetness, and a woman sewed some stitches into the material to silence the mother-in-law's tongue, as we say in my country.

REZA GAVE HIS YOUNG WIFE gold coins with his father's face on them and a small Koran. I gave Yasmine a diamond ring.

I was so emotional when the time came to say a few words to them that I can't remember exactly how I expressed my good wishes for their happiness. But I do remember referring to my husband's memory and telling them how sad I felt that he was not there for that wonderful day. In my brief remarks after the ceremony I addressed Yasmine by the title *Shahbanou* to demonstrate that she is now the first lady of Iran and that I wished to stand back a little.

Finally Yasmine released the doves, as I had done exactly twenty-seven years earlier.

Soon after her marriage she began studying political science, with determination and she continued with law after the birth of her daughters. Today she practices as an attorney, with a particular interest in abandoned, mistreated, or abused children. In addition, about ten years ago she set up a foundation to bring very sick Iranian children who cannot be treated at home to the United States. The exile community helps her with this undertaking, donating both money and time, and as she does not want her name to hinder the work of the foundation in any way, Yasmine has entrusted the responsibility for it to one of her cousins.

Yasmine is a modern, intelligent young woman whose knowledge of the world, culture, and quickness of mind are an assured and invaluable support for my son. I feel today that they are a very united, close couple, very aware of world affairs, and I feel sure that if the Iranian people one day turn to them, they will be able to lead the country in the path of progress and development.

When her studies were well advanced, Yasmine added to the happiness of this marriage by giving my son two little girls whose brightness and love are a constant joy. Noor was born on 3 April 1992, and Iman a year and a half later on 12 September 1993. I have now left Connecticut to be closer to them. The Greenwich house had become too large and expensive for Leila and me. I was thinking of looking for something smaller when Reza called me, suggesting I buy a house he had found only four minutes away from them. I was in Paris at the time. He sent me photos of the house and, on an impulse, I said yes. Yasmine called me back immediately. "I know you don't like to be rushed," she said to me very kindly, "especially for something like this, but Reza and the girls are so delighted at your coming to live close to us that, if you are going to change your mind, please do it now. Otherwise they will be too disappointed if you do it later." I was so touched that I confirmed that I was coming.

The decade of the nineties established me in the role that suits me as an ambassador for Iran's interests. My son has fully taken on the political role that he has inherited, as I had hoped, and I have gradually made myself available to represent him for a particular trip or to meet a particular individual I had known in the past.

Since my son succeeded my husband, my political life consists essentially of tirelessly explaining to all those who talk to me—man in the street or VIP—the tragic times that Iran is going through today. I keep abreast of everything that is happening in Tehran and the provinces—a task that takes a good part of my days—but I do it willingly, as I believe that every person I manage to convince is one more ally in the liberation of my country.

Of all the people of note I have met in exile, I have the most clear and touching memory of François Mitterrand. I had wanted a meeting with the French president, and he granted it. To keep the meeting confidential, I was discreetly let in through a gate in the grounds of the Élysée Palace. The president welcomed me and took me to a drawing room. He received me with great warmth and kindness and showed considerable eagerness to hear what I knew about Iran. As we spoke, I realized that he had a wide knowledge of the problems that inflamed that part of the world where my husband had kept the peace for twenty years, despite times of extreme tension.

I also have a very pleasant memory of my meeting with Nancy Reagan. Standing as the presidential candidate against Jimmy Carter, who had wanted a second term, Ronald Reagan had been the only one who dared declare his approval of my husband and the policy he had pursued. I was very touched by this.

Queen Fabiola, King Juan Carlos and Queen Sofia of Spain have remained dear friends. We phone each other, they often invite me to Spain, and when they are in Paris, we are always happy to see each other again. The Spanish monarchy is an example my son Reza likes to quote when talking about the future of Iran.

President Mubarak and his wife, Suzanne, receive me every year with warmth and friendship to commemorate the king's death. Thanks to them, Egypt remains in my heart as a friendly country that has never abandoned us.

I am deeply grateful for the friendship and constant concern for me shown by Madame Chirac. When we meet, the wife of the French president always takes the trouble to support and cheer me with some warm, sincere words about Iran, my children, and myself. I will never forget her visit after Leila's death. She came bringing flowers, with no fuss, to express her affection and how much she felt for me in this tragedy.

One final mention must be made of the valued support shown to us in exile by the ruling families of the Near and Middle East, whose names I unfortunately cannot mention because of our political situation.

WHEN I SETTLED IN THE UNITED STATES, I opened an office in New York and entrusted the running of it to Kambiz Atabaï, who has been one of my most faithful associates through all these years of exile. This office manages the schedule of my international meetings, but it also receives the hundreds of letters and e-mails sent to me every day. Many are messages of fidelity, of affection, but some are requests for aid or help from all over the world, including Iran, and I do everything I can to give them a positive reply. From Iran I receive requests for U.S. visas, and work permits for various European countries, as well as urgent appeals for medicine. Outside of Iran, many messages are sent to me by fellow countrymen in exile who have a sick child or spouse, and who quickly need a small sum of money; there are others who are looking for work and need a hand; or people who are about to be expelled from a country and hope that I can intervene on their behalf. In addition to these appeals, which are not easy to satisfy and often take a lot of work, I receive requests that ask for nothing more than a little affection from me, and in these cases, I am happy to be able to help them very quickly. For example, the daughter of a retired general recently called for help. Living in exile in a small American town, her father had become very depressed.

"You are the only person who can lift his spirits," she told me.

"Right, but what should I do?"

"Please call him."

I telephoned the man and tried to find words that would give him hope. The next day his daughter called me.

"Oh, thank you! Thank you! Your telephone call changed his life."

There was a young Iranian man who begged me to speak to his brother who had dropped out of school, lost interest in everything, and was sinking into depression. I telephoned the boy, listened to him, and we talked. A year after this conversation, I was delighted to hear from his brother that he had finished his studies.

My relations with Iranians inside Iran have increased a great deal thanks to the Internet. Many young people of the generation that has never known the monarchy write to me to find out the story of their parents and to try and understand how Iran, which was so bright, could sink into that darkness. The e-mails they send me are very moving, full of questions and expressions of affection. I make a point of answering them, explaining in simple, heartfelt terms what I know of the tragedy that our country has gone through and that we continue to experience. I make a special point of giving them hope for the future. A young boy of twelve or thirteen recently sent me an e-mail to tell me that he loves me very much and that he must speak to me, but his parents are very worried that the authorities would find out. "I have borrowed a mobile phone for a few days," he wrote to me. "Please call me." Another, a student this time, thought of me when he visited the site of Persepolis. He also asked me to call him. We talked and at the end of the conversation, he told me, "Thank you. You have given me the strength to go on." I could have said the same words back to him: all the Iranians who need me, especially these young people, give me the strength to go on.

One of my great joys in recent times is to have helped a son find his father. They had been separated in all the difficulties of exile, and the son thought of asking me to help.

Yes, all of that takes a huge amount of attention, time, and energy, but the benefits are reciprocal. Whatever I give each day is returned in large measure by the Iranians I try to help. Their phone calls, their letters, and their e-mails give me the strength to look beyond my own suffering in the name of the hope I see in all of them. Could I have done otherwise and refused to take on this role that many of my compatriots have assigned me since our departure from Tehran? "I don't know if it's my choice or my fate," I said to Farahnaz one day when I was exhausted from my work. And Farahnaz replied, "I think it's your fate that leaves you no choice."

WITH LEILA'S DEATH IN LONDON on 10 June 2001, I was suddenly plunged into the deepest, inconsolable despair. One never gets over the death of a child. Leila had just turned thirty-one.

She had been constantly preoccupied with death since losing her father when she was only ten. This worried me in Williamstown, so I arranged a meeting for her with an Iranian college professor in the hope that he could find the words to release her from this anxiety. She had lived through extremely painful times since our departure from Iran—years of mourning and the collapse of everything her life was built on. She began to suffer from chronic fatigue when she went to college. She complained a lot of headaches in particular and could not keep up with her classes. On my advice, she then began to consult doctors, while we worked out a scheme to lighten her workload with her professors at the college. But that did not help at all. She was not happy at the college and, as she was very fond of poetry, literature, and music, I tried to convince her that she should follow her true interests, leave college and do something in the arts. At one time she thought she would do an animated film based on some Ferdowsi stories she liked very much, but this turned out to be too complicated. She could not find her way, and the fatigue that wore her down from morning till night kept coming back.

She was suffering; I tried to help. It was so hard to see her battling alone against an illness that none of the doctors had been able to diagnose! All these ills, all this pain was the burden of childhood unhappiness that she could not shed. I guessed it, but she could not bear anyone to say it or to dare suggest that this mysterious illness could be psychosomatic. It hurt her, as if it were a denial that her ordeal was real.

She was deeply wounded by the malice, the rumors, everything that had been written and continued to be written about the monarchy and about her father in particular. She had an absolute patriotic love for Iran, which in her heart was identified with the love she felt for her father. This led her to reply with a great deal of passion to those who criticized the monarchy in her presence. I can remember how worked up she became during these conversations and how exhausted she was after them. Having left Iran as a little girl and still being so young, it was difficult for her to argue ceaselessly with people who were older and often very bitter or aggressive. She was wholehearted, generous, and touching, which meant that she also gave a lot of herself to her friends. She was the one they called if they needed to hear some encouraging words; she was the one they called when they were low. She always arrived with her arms full of flowers or gifts for her brothers and sister, for me or those in our circle, she who never found consolation herself, knew just how much there was to console in Iranian hearts.

She had checkups, consulted all kinds of doctors, and as the fatigue and pain persisted in spite of their treatment, she began to say that no one could cure her. Then, as always happens in these situations, she came across people, friends, who advised her to take sleeping pills and tranquilizers. She was well aware that they were not good for her, but when her suffering was too much for her, she would take them. Then she could sleep and not feel the pain and fatigue. She took more and more of them, knowing that she was taking chances with her life. All of us around her knew it and we told her, but we could not find a way to reach out to her. She was very close to her brother Ali-Reza, and I heard him say to her with the bluntness of a man who is upset, "Listen, Leila, if you go on like that, you'll die." Like all of us, Ali-Reza was trying to find a way to get her out of this terrible downward spiral. She replied that she loved life, that she didn't want to die, that all these tranquilizers just let her forget the illness that tormented her for just a few hours.

It was Ali-Reza she confided in most. They had helped each other out and supported each other ever since they were small children. She called him and often went to see him in Boston.

He could give her advice and allow himself to be hard with her; she would listen to him. Yet, shortly before she died, she said to her doctor that now she only wanted to listen to her brother Reza and her father. "But your father isn't here anymore," the doctor replied. I repeated what she had said to Reza, and he then told her how dear she was to him and how confident he was that she would get well again. That made Leila very angry. She thought that the young king, for whom she had great respect, should not be worried with her health problems nor told about her weaknesses.

I was in the United States in the days leading up to her death. Leila was in Paris with Miss Golrokh, who had been with her since early childhood and whom she affectionately called Gogol. Leila telephoned me to tell me that she was leaving for London, that she wanted to go there alone, and that she was tired of having someone at her heels all the time. I immediately began to worry, for I knew that she could get tranquilizers much more easily in England than in France. We asked her psychiatrist's advice. He usually advised us not to leave her unsupervised, but this time, as Leila had insisted so much, he said, "Right. She really does need to be alone. We'll let her go."

Leila phoned shortly afterwards from London, from the hotel she usually patronized. She felt very ill, exhausted, her body paralyzed with pain. Her doctor had advised me not to call her too often because Leila had told him that she felt people were continually checking up on her, and that upset her. This time, however, she was the one who had called. We talked and I tried to find the right words to calm her and relieve her anxiety. It was a Thursday. In the end I said to her, "Leila, I'm coming over. I'll be in London on Sunday and we'll go back to Paris together. Don't you want a friend to call in and see you in the meantime?" I named a few, hoping that she would say yes to one of them. But she didn't want anyone to see her in that weak state, and she had lost a lot of weight over the last months. All the same, after hanging up I called an old friend who was very fond of Leila, and I asked her to keep a close eye on her. We agreed that she would not say I had been in touch with her. And so she called Leila the next day, Friday, to hear what she had been doing, and Leila was certainly touched by it, for she agreed to the friend's coming to see her sometime during the day. However, she changed her mind a little later and said to her, "No, come tomorrow instead."

When I phoned this friend again on Saturday, she told me that she hadn't liked to insist for fear of offending Leila, but that she hoped to see her during the day. She added that Leila had said to her, "If Mummy rings, tell her not to call because I'm going to sleep." I always feared waking her, because then she would say, "There you are; I was asleep, and now I'll have to take some pills to get back to sleep again."

I was very worried when I arrived in Paris on Sunday, so the first thing I did was to call our friend in London. She still had not been able to see Leila, who had put off her visit and, in the end, had stopped answering her calls. Feeling extremely anxious, I decided to alert a London doctor whose address and phone number I had kept. "I can find a spot in the afternoon to see her at her hotel," he said.

At the time when he should have been with Leila, I rang the hotel. The doctor was there, but they would not let him into her room because my daughter had hung the "Do not disturb" sign on her door. I begged him to insist and he finally convinced the management to let him in. With a heavy heart I held the line while he went upstairs. While I was waiting, Farahnaz rang from the United States on the other line, wanting news of her sister, and I told her to wait with me as the doctor would be back at any moment.

We waited for about ten minutes.

"They're still up there and we haven't heard anything," the reception desk replied when I expressed my concern.

At last I heard the doctor's voice, faltering with emotion. "I'm dreadfully sorry to have to tell you this, but your daughter is dead."

Scarcely able to speak with shock and grief, I still had to tell Farahnaz then and there. The poor child became hysterical, began to scream and cry, and nothing I said could calm her. I had to leave her like that, make another phone call, and ask Kambiz Atabaï, who was in the country near New York, to go to Farahnaz immediately. It was unthinkable to leave her alone when she was so terribly upset.

I then wanted to inform Reza. It was his aide who answered the phone. Reza was in the middle of a press conference. The colonel went and told him of his sister's death. He mastered his feelings and finished the conference. It was only at the end, his face drawn with sorrow, that he told the journalists he had just learned of Leila's death.

Ali-Reza was in his car when I called him. I told him to park, as I feared the shock might make him swerve and cause an accident. Fortunately he was not alone. His friend Sara was with him. I so much wanted to be with him, as I did with Farahnaz, so that I could share their pain.

I couldn't bring myself to call Gogol. I asked Mrs. Mina Atabaï to do it for me. My younger daughter was more or less her whole life.

Leila's death greatly affected all exiled Iranians and even those within Iran. It was reported to me that as soon as the news began to circulate in the streets of Tehran, people went up to Niavaran to leave candles and flowers in front of the palace gates. Ceremonies were immediately organized wherever Iranians are to be found today. Thousands gathered in Los Angeles, a town that has a large Iranian community. And so Leila, who was tortured by everything that had torn the Iranian people apart, managed to reconcile them on the day she died as they gathered in her name.

In London itself, many Iranians accompanied her coffin to the airport. I wanted Leila to be laid to rest in Paris, where my mother is buried. More than a thousand people were present at her funeral and, in the days that followed, I received nearly seven thousand letters. All of them were filled with emotion and grief. After this terrible bereavement, I still constantly receive expressions of sympathy for Leila, and her grave is visited daily by unknown people who cover it with flowers and little notes full of affection and regret.

No, one does not get over the death of a child, and I have silently mourned for my little Leila since 10 June 2001. I have the power to comfort an old general with a few words, to give hope to young uprooted Iranians; I, it is said, can help a whole community expelled from its homeland, yet I was not able to come to the aid of my own daughter. This helplessness is a daily torment, and every morning I say to myself, "I must find time today to call my children and my granddaughters. The mail and the telephones can wait. I must explain to my countrymen and -women, as Leila told me one day, that after giving them forty years of my life, I now have the right to concern myself with my own family, my children and my grandchildren."

Noor and Iman will soon be leaving childhood behind and entering adolescence. A few months ago, when I was coming to tell them a story and give them a kiss at bedtime, Noor almost became angry.

"Maman Yaya," she declared, sitting up in her bed, "you tell us that we are Iranian. You tell us that we are princesses, but we don't even know our own country. What is the use of showing us all these photos and telling us all these stories, if we can't go back home?"

Perhaps it was this comment that gave me the strength to write this book. I had to tell these two little girls, who are banned from their own country, how it all came about. To try to explain how cruel history was for their aunt Leila and unfair for the grandfather whose serious, silent face they see every day on their father's desk. To tell them that they can be proud to be his granddaughters, and proud also to be the daughters of a man who has been fighting for twenty-three years now to bring back to Iran the prosperity and the prestige she once enjoyed. To say to them, in fact, that they can be proud to be Iranian.

I made the decision not to name certain people solely in order to protect them and their families from the Islamic Republic. I hope that they will understand and not blame me for it.

POSTSCRIPT

FROM 1921 ON, Iran underwent development and modernization during the time of Reza Shah, and this progress was sustained under the reign of my now late husband, aided by qualified and devoted people in various levels of society. Iran continued to work toward the fulfillment of its expectations and potential. Great strides were made in industrial development, agriculture, education, public health, social welfare, and cultural activities. The Iranian oil industry flourished and the National Iranian Oil Company (NIOC) acquired a respectable position among the five major international oil companies in the world. An enlightened and burgeoning middle class became the backbone of the economy. Iran's borders were secure and its foreign policy gained the respect of the international community. Although Iran's national interest dictated an alliance with the West, we had balanced and amicable relations with the Eastern bloc as well as the Third World countries.

During my exile of a quarter of a century, I have not stopped thinking for one minute of Iran, the people and the land that I love above all. With the savage repression that descended on those who had served our country, and the suffering the survivors had to endure, began the decline of Iran.

Brokenhearted, I witnessed the disillusionment of the young generation that had joined the most radical clerics in the streets to overthrow the monarchy. The same young people, encouraged by the Islamic authorities, violated international law and took American diplomats as hostages for 444 days. University and high-school students and those who had witnessed the country's development dreamed of an enlightened democracy, without considering how much progress had already been made in that direction. As soon as the king left, a barbarous and medieval obscurantism swept aside all hope. Today, those who protest for their basic rights face imprisonment, whipping, torture, and in some cases murder.

The country had been strong and well respected. Suddenly all that changed, and the Iraqi regime took advantage of the dismantling of the Iranian armed forces and the brutal mass execution of its senior officers to start a war. The war cost Iran more than a million deaths and casualties, including thousands of child soldiers. Ayatollah Khomeini prolonged the war in order to stoke the waning revolutionary fervor. Coupled with the sheer incompetence if the ruling clerics, this situation bled the economy dry.

The region of the Persian Gulf, which had known peace and stability in the time of the Iranian monarchy, has since descended into chaos, becoming a breeding ground for fanaticism and international terrorism. Since the appalling attack of 11 September 2001 in New York, the whole world now looks upon the region with nothing but fear. We Iranians used to be proud to show our passports when we crossed international borders. Today the suspicious way the authorities all over the world look at us chills our blood.

In the last year of his reign, my husband said, "if the security and the stability of Iran were to be destroyed, the consequences would not be limited only to Iran, or to the sensitive region of the Middle East, they would usher the world into a global crisis."

WHAT HAVE THEY DONE TO IRAN?

Everything we undertook has been sacrificed and wasted. In the realm of education and health, where we enlisted tens of thousands of Iranians to work for the common good, all that effort has come to a standstill.

The ruling clerics have ruined the vibrant economy. Giant state-run institutions have monopolized industry, commerce, and trade to the detriment of the privately run enterprises. Oil, the precious wealth of the country, is now in the hands of a few privileged members of the regime who have amassed fortunes at the expense of the population that has become poorer and poorer. Today a small minority controls most of the country's wealth. Millions of Iranians have fallen below the absolute poverty line. Runaway inflation has forced men and women to seek second, and in some cases third, jobs. Rural areas are left behind in favor of the towns, and the green wooded suburbs of cities are crumbling from neglect. Thousands of villages have been deserted. Unemployment has reached unprecedented levels, while in the three years preceding the Islamic revolution, about one million additional workers from Asia and elsewhere were hired every year.

To provide a vivid example of the deplorable state of the economy, the dollar, which was pegged at 70 rials in 1979, is now pegged at 8,000 rials. There is such destitution that some parents are driven to sell their organs in order to feed their families. Very young girls are reduced to prostitution, and an increasing number of children beg for their daily bread. Malnutrition is widespread. Without hope, without prospects for their future, young Iranians are turning in ever-increasing numbers to drugs. It is well known that the country today has almost 3 million addicts. It is said that a third of the population suffers from chronic depression.

Millions of Iranians have emigrated, many having fled at risk to their lives. This emigration is a tragedy for the country, not just in social and political terms, but also has created a brain drain, which the country can ill afford.

THE MOMENT HAS COME to hold up our heads and look to the future. And I think of the women in particular to lead the way. Under the monarchy women had the same rights as men. The clerics have tried to turn back the clock. They have reinstated the monstrous punishment of stoning and passed humiliating laws making women second-class citizens. But in spite of these inequities, women have not been silenced. Every day we hear of those who are fighting inside and outside of our country against humiliation, fear, and obscurantism. With their intelligence, courage, and daring, they will succeed.

I am thinking of the new generation: the young Iranians who risk their lives within the country to win their right to freedom. Their brothers and sisters who have grown up in exile and do not know Iran will discover it tomorrow, strong with the knowledge they have gained in the countries that have so generously received and nurtured them. Turning their backs on the quarrels that have uselessly torn their parents apart, these young people, I know, will find a way to come together. They will once again open the gates of our ancient country to light, to beauty, and to life.

My son, Reza, is engaged in this struggle. He is fighting so that Iranians will find freedom in a regime of their own choosing, one that will be democratic and open to the rest of the world. I have confidence in Reza. I know that he will succeed, because, in this battle that he is waging with strength and intelligence, his only ambition is to serve the interest of the Iranian people.

The Islamic revolution has deceived those who believed in it; it has lost its legitimacy. Throughout our long history, Iran has sometimes had to endure the burden and the suffering of occupation, but the invaders never succeeded in destroying my country's national identity. Each time, the Iranian people have drawn on resources within themselves, their culture, their history, to find the strength to resist and finally to conquer the oppressor. I have boundless faith in the ability of the Iranian people to throw off their chains and find the path of democracy, freedom, and progress. I know that light will triumph over darkness and Iran will rise from her ashes.

APPENDIX ONE

Women in Iran Under the Monarchy

The Women's Organization of Iran (WOI) was a network of fifty-seven affiliated associations, four hundred branches, and one hundred and twenty centers throughout the country, providing services in child safety, family planning, vocational training, and legal counseling. Its staff of two thousand skilled professionals and seven thousand volunteers assisted roughly one million women each year.

The WOI ran a specialized school for social work in order to train future WOI staff members and a corps of social workers for the public and private sectors. The Organization's main accomplishments in its last decade of activity were:

I. EDUCATION

a. Priority was given to the women's literacy campaign. The use of "women's brigades" for literacy were particularly effective.
b. A concerted effort was made to encourage young girls of primary school age to attend school and to take advantage of mandatory free education at all levels.
c. At the university level, special scholarships were offered to encour-

age young women to enroll in scientific and technical studies. A quota system was established to give preferential treatment to girls who demonstrated the interest and aptitude for technical studies or other sectors traditionally closed to women.

One-third of all university students were female. The year before the Revolution, the majority of students applying to medical school were women.

d. Women's studies programs were prepared by mixed committees composed of WOI members and faculty members from Tehran and other national universities.

II. EMPLOYMENT

a. The WOI and the Ministry of Labor established special joint programs of further training designed to help women obtain better-paid jobs in a variety of skilled and semi-skilled areas.
b. All the laws were revised in an effort to eliminate discrimination on the basis of sex. The "equal pay for equal work" principle was added to all governmental rules and regulations on employment.
c. A new law authorized working mothers to opt to work on a part-time basis until their child's third birthday. These three years would be considered full-time with regard to seniority and retirement benefits.
d. Child safety facilities near factories and/or offices became obligatory under the law. Less than two years after the passage of this law, thanks to the joint efforts of WOI and several ministries, new safety features protected one-third of all children targeted by the law.
e. Full-time paid maternity leave was extended to include all women who were seven or more months pregnant.
f. Laws concerning housing, loans, and work benefits were revised to eliminate discrimation on the basis of sex.

III. THE FAMILY

a. Under the terms of the family protection law, women were given the right to request divorce on the same grounds and under the same conditions as men; child custody and alimony decisions were handled by a special family court; in the event of the father's death, the mother was recognized as the legal guardian; polygamy was virtually eliminated except in instances where the first wife could not have children or was seriously ill, in which case the husband could only take a second wife with his first wife's consent. Although this law was not totally egalitarian, it was and still is more advanced than the majority of legislation passed in other Muslim countries.

b. Abortion was legalized, with the husband's consent. Unmarried women could request an abortion up to to their eighth week of pregancy.

IV. POLITICAL REPRESENTATION

a. Local boards reviewing the qualifications of political appointees were required to include at least one female member.
b. The WOI leader in each province worked closely with the provincial governor.
c. In the last election before the Revolution, an energetic campaign resulted in the election of twenty women to the lower legislative chamber (the Majlis) and three hundred women to local and municipal councils.
d. Women ran for and obtained high-level governmental positions. In 1978, there was one woman in the cabinet of ministers and three in the "sub-cabinet." Outside of the traditional positions at the ministry of education, health and welfare, the ministry of labor, together with the ministries of mining and industry, offered the greatest number of positions for women.

V. THE NATIONAL ACTION PLAN

Approved by the cabinet of ministers in 1978, a national action plan developed a task force in each of the twelve ministries. These task forces would design, organize, set up, and direct nationwide efforts toward women's full integration into all sectors of the economy and society. Each minister was in charge of promoting the program and drafting an annual report to the cabinet of ministers. The chief adjuncts from each of the twelve ministries met on a monthly basis, under the chairmanship of the minister of women's affairs, acting in the name of the prime minister. Women's committees monitored the efforts and progress made within each ministry.

VI. INTERNATIONAL ACTIVITIES

Iran was ranked third worldwide for its commitment to the international women's movement and for its efforts, in collaboration with the United Nations, to address women's issues. This included responsibility for the Asian-Pacific Center for Women and Development, which was founded in Tehran, and the International Research and Training Institute for the Advancement of Women, which was also created in Tehran in 1979. The five-year conference to evaluate progress made since the 1975 U.N. Conference on Women's Rights in Mexico was to take place in Tehran in 1980.

APPENDIX TWO

The Proclamation of Cyrus the Great

I am Cyrus, king of the World, great king, mighty sovereign, king of Babylon, king of the land of Akkad and Sumer, king of the four points of the compass, son of Cambyses, great king of Anshan, grandson of Cyrus, great king, king of Anshan, founder of a royal line whose rule Bel and Nabu cherish, whose rule delights their hearts. When I, well-disposed, entered Babylon, I established my seat of government in the royal palace to the greatest satisfaction of all and amid renewed rejoicing. Marduk, the supreme God, caused the Babylonians to love me. I gave thanks to him daily. My army moved unhindered into the midst of Babylon itself. I did not allow any of my soldiers to terrorize the land of Akkad and Sumer. I kept in mind the needs of Babylon and its numerous places of worship to ensure their well-being. I lifted the unbecoming yoke that weighed upon the Babylonians. I restored their neglected dwellings. I put an end to their misfortunes. Seeing my deeds, Marduk, lord of all, rejoiced, granted his blessing to me and to my son Cambyses, flesh of my flesh, and to my army; and we in turn gave thanks to his glorious divinity. All the settled kings seated on their thrones throughout the world, from the upper to the lower seas, and all the nomadic kings of the west country, all brought me their large tribute money and kissed my feet in my city of Babylon. I brought back and restored to their rightful places everywhere the gods whose worship had been abandoned under the domination of the Tirgris, in the towns of Ashur and Susa, at Agade, Eshnuna, Zamban, Meurnu, Der, and even into the land of Gutium. I gathered the inhabitants together and restored their dwellings. According to the will of Marduk, Mighty Lord, I allowed the gods of Sumer and Akkad, which Nabonidus had brought into Babylon, causing the wrath of the god of gods, to be housed unharmed in their temples. May all the gods whose worship I have reestablished intercede daily in my favor with Bel and Nabu to prolong my days; and may they speak of me with these words: "May Cyrus the worshipful king and his son Cambyses…"

APPENDIX THREE

Message to the People of Iran from Reza Pahlavi

KIBBEH PALACE – CAIRO – 31 OCTOBER 1980

In the name of Almighty God, in accordance with the Iranian Constitution and its amendments, I solemnly declare that from this day, 9 Aban 1359 (31 October 1980), as I enter my twenty-first year, I am ready to assume my responsibilities and obligations as king of Iran. Because of the exceptional circumstances which now exist in Iran, the Constitutional Taking the Oath Ceremony has been deferred to a time when, with God's blessing, the requisite conditions for its performance have been fulfilled.

From today, however, I solemnly swear before the glorious Iranian tricolor flag, and on the Holy Koran, that in my high office I will dedicate my whole life to protecting the independence, national sovereignty and legitimate rights of the Iranian people.

As guarantor of national unity, I shall be the faithful defender of the Constitution.

Our fundamental law guarantees the rights of the individual and of society, and clearly defines the legitimate attributions of the king, and of the powers of the legislature, the executive and the judiciary, therefore, vigilantly observing the respect and application of the various articles of the Constitution, I shall fulfill my mission, conscious of the duties it entails, and thus shall I defend constitutional order.

My Dear Countrymen and Women, brothers and sisters,
This supreme responsibility has been entrusted to me after the sad loss of my revered father in one of the darkest periods of our history, at the very time when our national and spiritual principles, our historical and cultural values, our civilization are threatened from within; at the very time when anarchy, economic collapse and the decline of our international prestige have brought about the rape of our territorial integrity by foreign aggression, which we condemn.

I am well aware that none of you, whose national pride and patriotic spirit are inborn, that none of you who are deeply attached to your national identity, your faith and the sacred principles of true Islam, to your historical values and your cultural heritage, have wanted such a disaster to happen. I am certain that no people, whatever its condition, could wish for such a thing.

I can understand your suffering and imagine your unshed tears. That is why I share your pain; I know that through the darkness you, like me, can see the serene dawn of a new day breaking. I also know that deep in your hearts and minds you have the firm belief that, as in the past, our history which is several thousands of years old will repeat itself and the nightmare will finally end. Light will follow darkness. Strengthened by bitter experience, we will all join together in a great surge of national energy to rebuild our country. With the right reforms and the participation of all, we will reach our goals. We will rebuild a new Iran where equality, freedom and justice will prevail. Inspired by the true faith of Islam based on spirituality, love and mercy, we will make Iran a proud and prosperous country, occupying the place it deserves in the world community.

On this solemn and historic day, I bow before all those, heroes or unheralded, who for centuries, have fallen for the glory of Iran, the independence of their country and the preservation of our national identity. May they rest in peace forever in the sacred soil of their homeland. I also bow before the martyrs of the Iranian Army and all the other patriots who have paid with their lives during the horror of the last twenty months for remaining faithful to the nation's honor. I sincerely share in the pain of their grieving families. I understand them all the more as I myself have lost someone very dear, who died too soon in exile and in unspeakable suffering, struck down more by the ordeals of his country than by his own illness.

I glorify the bravery of the members of the armed forces who, despite insult, injustice and humiliation, have valiantly defended the sacred soil of Iran and the territorial integrity of the homeland. I am proud of the way they have acted.

Throughout the centuries, the Iranian people have inspired amazing epics. Perhaps circumstances are once again favorable for a new epic page to be written; it will reflect the true Iran and its people to the world. Today when, by the will of God, I am beginning a new phase in the fulfillment of my national duty, I send you this message from the bottom of my heart. I already know that your response will be the faithful echo of our glorious history, thousands of years old.

Let us achieve national unity based on fraternity, equality and the love of God. Let us banish hatred, revenge and all other manifestations of Evil.

I salute all Iranian women and men of goodwill wherever they may be. I ask them all to keep their unshakable faith in the future, to defend Iran's independence, their national identity and their faith, without flinching and under all circumstances.

I ask all patriots living in Iran or abroad to close ranks once again to save our homeland.

I entrust to Almighty God the future of the great people of Iran, whose glorious history will, I know, be perpetuated with honor. I humbly ask Almighty God to grant us all his mercy, and to help us accomplish our national duty by accepting our responsibility to all humanity, despite the many obstacles that block our path.

God Save Iran!

INDEX